Caroline Jones is one of Australia's most respected broadcasters and communicators. She has worked in film, television and radio since 1963 as writer, producer, director and reporter. In 1988 she was made an Officer of the Order of Australia.

From 1987 to 1994 Caroline Jones presented *The Search for Meaning* on ABC Radio National. Her previous publications include three volumes of *The Search for Meaning*, as well as *The Search for Meaning* video and audio tapes. Judged by ABC Radio Tapes' sales, *The Search for Meaning* has been, for years, the ABC's most popular radio program. Here's what some of its listeners have said about it:

'These interviews have given me a vocabulary to describe my own experience'.

'As listener and questioner, Caroline Jones honours and encourages the search for meaning of every man and woman.'

'We live in a remote area and these conversations provide connection, hope, inspiration, wisdom and food for thought.'

'Not much in the media carries the same breadth of intellectual interest, personal insight, integrity, and humanity.'

Other books by Caroline Jones

The Search for Meaning Book One
The Search for Meaning Book Two
The Search for Meaning: Conversations with Caroline Jones

CAROLINE JONES

The Search for Meaning

COLLECTION

Acknowledgments

I would like to acknowledge the creative work of *The Search for Meaning* radio series team Stephen Godley, Cecily Doig, Louisa Ring Rolfe, and the technical operators; of the late Ray Bencivenga and his team at ABC Radio Tapes; and of other ABC colleagues who have contributed and encouraged. I am grateful to Dr David Millikan who initiated *The Search for Meaning* on ABC Radio National, and to Christine Morris, Phillip Hinton and Stephen Litherland for research.

I have been enlightened and enriched by the stories and ideas entrusted to me in thousands of letters responding to *The Search for Meaning*.

My thanks also to Stuart Neal of ABC Books, to Dawn Webb for transcription typing, and to designer Deborah Brash.

Editor Glenda Downing has been faithful in translating the intentions of the spoken word into print.

The photographs by Peter Solness deepen the insight of the conversations. Cover photograph by David Haddon. Eleanor Williams lent her study of Kevin Gilbert for inclusion. The photo of Aldo Gennaro was lent by Dimity Figner.

And my appreciation to all those who have agreed to tell their stories in *The Search for Meaning* books, of which this is an omnibus edition containing some of the favourites.Their telling is a generous gift to the reader and an expression of the Australian spirit at the end of the twentieth century.

Published by ABC Books for the
AUSTRALIAN BROADCASTING CORPORATION
GPO Box 9994 Sydney NSW 2001
A Dove publication
An imprint of HarperCollins*Religious*
A member of the HarperCollins*Publishers*
(Australia) Pty Ltd group
(ACN 008 431 730)
22-24 Joseph Street
North Blackburn, Victoria 3130, Australia

First published August, 1995

National Library of Australia
Catalogue-in-Publication entry
Jones, Caroline.
The search for meaning collection.
ISBN 0 7333 0447 8
1. Spiritual life, 2. Interviews—Australia. 3. Radio scripts. 4. Life. I. Australian Broadcasting Corporation.
II. Title. III. Title:
Search for meaning (Radio Program).
128

Designed by Deborah Brash, Brash Design
Set in 10/12 Garamond by
Midland Typesetters, Maryborough, Victoria
Printed and bound in Australia by
Alken Press, Smithfield, NSW

7-1695

5 4 3 2 1

Contents

Introduction

'It is not only the concentration of ownership of the Australian media that is cause for alarm, it is the consequent shortage of journalistic forms. Caroline Jones created a new form, one in which stories of the most personal and intimate kind could be communicated at length, without distortion . . . and virtually without interruption. [But] the lack of interruption grated with her critics and, in the end it would seem, with the management of Radio National.'

MARTIN FLANAGAN, *The Age*, 18 November 1994

Many *Search for Meaning* conversations recount a turning point which altered a person's life in some important way. There was such a moment for me: There were six people around the table. The General Manager of Radio National was telling me that I need to make my interviews 'more intrusive'. 'I don't want to hear so much acceptance. I don't want to hear so much agreement.'

It was a moment of clarity. It was the first time in my professional life that I had taken a high risk stand and said 'No'. It was the point at which I defended the form of interviewing that I had developed on *The Search for Meaning* rather than compromise my approach and present some alternative program.

It was the point at which I lost my job, my long association with the ABC, and the program through which I had made a creative contribution to community life for the previous eight years. There was no animosity, only a failure on my part, supported by my colleagues, to convince the network manager of the legitimacy of my chosen journalistic form, and of my subject matter.

I explained that I had developed *The Search for Meaning* interviews to be revelations of the soul and psyche, that they were produced by deep listening and facilitation, not with a scalpel. I reasoned that if you want to glimpse a sea anemone in full bloom, you do not poke a stick into it. I argued for intellectual tolerance of diversity in broadcasting. Must every interview, no matter what the subject, be conducted in the adversarial style? It may be appropriate for current affairs reporting, for probing community leaders and elected representatives on matters of fact and responsibility in the public interest. But there are other valid interview styles for different subjects. It did not occur to me until later that not everyone sees life as a search for meaning, that not everyone is comfortable hearing revelation of the soul, that indeed this may be considered to be irrelevant. The soul is not politically correct in the 1990s, certainly not in the media.

When my own intellectual reasoning for the survival of *The Search for Meaning* failed to convince, I resorted to concrete evidence of the success of the program with ABC radio listeners. The program attracted the second-highest audience share each week across the network; more audio-cassette tapes were sold of *The Search for Meaning* than of any other program, through the ABC Radio Tape Service. *The Search for Meaning* has always been a big money-earner for the ABC in both trade and educational markets, through its books, tapes and videos.

I was told that managers set directions and make policy decisions, not the listeners. At that stage, I felt like Alice in Wonderland at the Mad Hatter's tea party. As news of the program's demise became public, several hundred listeners wrote in protest but their opinions were given no weight and they received no explanation of the management decision.

I believe passionately that ABC managers must be answerable to the proprietors, that is, to the Australian people. I was astonished that anyone might disagree with me. But disagree they did to the extent that, for the last three *The Search for Meaning* programs, I was placed under censorship, my scripts to be monitored and approved before going to air.

While maintaining composure publicly in the current press coverage about the program's termination, privately I began to feel uncertain, to lose confidence. Since by this time I was a dissenter who had lost both program and livelihood through that dissent, I had to face the possibility that I may be wrong. I needed to re-examine the validity of what I had been doing for the past eight years and the premises on which it was based.

The playwright Dennis Potter suggests that in uncertain times, when there is little public concord on morality and almost everything may be bought and sold, the individual is left with the task of garnering positive clues from life experience to assemble a sense of values which will nourish and secure personal sovereignty which is the most precious of all human capacities. In *The Search for Meaning* we embarked on an earnest inquiry to serve that purpose.

The program has been a telling of people's stories, that is, a telling of their unique experiences of life and the conclusions they have reached based on those experiences. I have sought to avoid the dogmatic because I am never too sure who is talking when I am faced with the well-practised recitation of beliefs. Rather, I've invited the recounting of concrete personal experiences, the formative events and characteristics of childhood, the turning points which have brought fresh insight, the actions emerging out of expanded understanding. And that's what you'll read in the chapters of this book which are transcriptions of some of the favourite conversations from the radio series, 1987 to 1994.

You'll learn from Emma Pierce what it is like to go mad and painstakingly to reclaim a coherent pattern by which to live; Nick Carroll describes the ecstatic timeless moments of surfing; the poet Yvette Christianse will take you inside her experience of writing: '. . . my moment of joy, my moment where my heart is really open, my moment when I'm safest, when I dare to look into the things that I would normally not dare to look into . . . my writing puts me in place.'

Paul Field, lead singer of the pop group The Cockroaches explains what it is to lose a baby in cot death and how family and faith provided the way forward; Barbara Blackman describes the end of her marriage of twenty-eight years: 'I do not see our marriage as failing or breaking down. It finished, was complete. Life had to be different for each of us.'

Aldo Gennaro reveals how producing a dance-drama with intellectually disabled people let him know love for the first time in his life; Judge Marcus Einfeld speaks of the sense of elation which comes from some small victory in the human rights struggle; Kevin Gilbert explains how he maintained a sense of life and freedom even while he was a victim of the institutionalised brutality of Grafton Gaol.

Stockbroker Rene Rivkin amplifies his philosophy of life—'to minimise pain and maximise pleasure'—and what it's like to be very wealthy; Mary Graham gives a brilliant contrast between Aboriginal and western perspectives of life in their attitudes to individuality, to identity, to metaphysics, to communication: 'Aboriginal people aren't all that impressed by democracy. Often it just entrenches conflict.'

Stan Arneil, founder of the credit union movement, describes the unexpected compassion which blossomed in prisoner-of-war death camps. 'No man died alone.' Young composer and singer Trisha Watts is impatient with formal religion and proposes alternative expressions of faith in life; Alice Fitzgerald faces death without fear, extraordinary in a society so terrified of dying. 'When you've got your boarding pass, you don't want anyone to hold you back.'

Pioneering Uniting Church minister, Dorothy McRae McMahon speaks of 'something longing in us as a community. We are people who have a deep sense of oneness with good, love, justice and truth. It is understated. Our spirituality is so delicate and the church has been so heavy.' And Magda Bozic tells her story, unsurpassed in simple eloquence, of coming to Australia from Hungary . . . a telling with the wisdom of maturity, the intelligent scepticism of the agnostic, and the poignancy of migration, so typical of our times, as people are blown across the world great distances by the vagaries of politics, war and circumstance. It is one of my favourites because it plays with the potent image of home on many levels, and because it came about through her challenge as a listener.

Soon after the program began in 1987, Magda wrote to me from Canberra. This is all very well, she said, but you're giving us too many well-known people. Let's hear the stories of people not prominent in public life, the stories of real, ordinary people. I felt that she was right. I wrote back to her with my own challenge: 'What about you?'

So she came on the train one day to Sydney, and we sat together in one of the homely old ABC radio studios in Upper Forbes Street. She was small and intense, with the world-weariness of the central European for whom there are no surprises remaining. Quite surely and sparely she unfolded her story with all the inevitability of a river flowing. All I could do, all that her telling allowed me to do was to listen, at times in tears. I knew then that I was involved in nothing less than the sacred undertaking of gathering the stories of our people.

I discovered also, but not immediately, that the key to doing that effectively would be a deep and attentive listening, rather than the formulation of a set of probing questions. Only gradually it became clear to me that the recounting of personal experience or of story is not a matter for cross-examination or argument. And I say that because I tried it. When I began *The Search for Meaning*, I thought the only tools I had were the current affairs skills I brought from years of *This Day Tonight*, *Four Corners* and *City Extra*. But I soon discovered that they were the wrong tools for this job. When I tried using them to steer, to probe, to challenge, they kept cutting the story short, diverting it from its natural course. Questions seemed to interrupt the natural momentum of the story-telling and the concentration or recall of the teller. I noticed that a supplementary question often led speakers into repetition as though they had said all that was to be said the first time, instinctively as it were, and had nothing more to say. They were making the attempt only through courtesy. The point where I had asked a question frequently became the point at which I later found myself editing out a rambling re-statement of an earlier succinct expression. I had to find another way. And that turned out to be listening, a skill in which I had had some unconscious training.

A good listener is a rare commodity. Most people can listen only for a sentence or two before giving judgment, advice or response. As a shy young person I had discovered that listening was a way of being present and accepted by people without having to brave the challenge of too much self-expression. It came naturally to me, but it was not until later I discovered that this natural talent could be trained and refined for effective professional and personal use.

One day in the spring of 1981, I finished my shift of live morning radio on the ABC (*City Extra*) feeling exhausted, fragmented and lonely. The world at large knew who Caroline Jones was, but I was not at all sure. At the end of twelve years of exciting and intense current affairs reporting, I felt that I needed some help. Rather ashamed at being publicly successful and privately bereft, I asked a colleague for the name of a counsellor. From that first session, the consultation was helpful and clarifying. The most important service the counsellor offered was to listen to me unfold my story, and in so doing enable me to identify for the first time key events and unresolved conflicts which needed attention. The only questions she asked were those which accompanied my narrative, and which took it further, deeper. There was no argument, judgment or prescription. She assisted me to articulate the reality of my situation in a way that I had not been able to achieve through thinking or worrying. It was a great relief.

Later I learned more about listening from Hugh Mackay, and from Elizabeth Campbell when I worked as a trainer of teachers in her fine Peer Support Program, in which thousands of Australian students have been given skills and practice in communication and leadership. Two more valuable personal experiences of listening came with priests during the time when I was preparing to join the community of the Catholic church. I found it freeing to be listened to with full attention, that it enabled me to reach in to retrieve my story with courage to face even the darker aspects. It reclaimed a sense of coherence in my story which had begun to seem disjointed, producing feelings of helplessness, vertigo, and lack of direction and self-worth. It expanded my sense of identity, well-being and integrity.

So these several people, over a period of five years, had given me much personal sustenance with the gift of their generous listening. Without knowing it, they had also given me the tools for the next phase of my broadcasting work so that I could become a facilitator, nationally on ABC Radio, of the stories of a great variety of my countrymen and women. And I could do my listening confident, from my own lived experience, that it was an authentic undertaking.

The discovery put a number of things in place for me. For I had become increasingly dissatisfied with the adversarial method in national public life. It is a method most at home in Anglo-Saxon culture and it now speaks to fewer Australians. It has its strength in that it displays opposing points of view, and allows argument about them. But it also has limitations in that it can entrench conflict and prevent resolution or discovery of motivation. The polarised discussion of issues may sound intellectually rigorous but it is based on a narrow frame of reference that takes little account of the personal. It can objectify and exploit people's experience in order to build its own artifice. Rational argument presumes that the search is over and that its elements can be categorised. It often reflects the concerns of the interviewer rather than those of the subject.

In the later years of my current affairs reporting, I had begun to doubt the effectiveness of always approaching an issue through confrontation, as

I had been taught to do. Argument often seemed to produce more heat than light. The principal product of attack was often defence, rather than information. And to make a national sport in the media of lopping tall poppies may be entertaining but it also keeps capable people out of public life, for fear of frivolous crucifixion.

I know first hand the thrill of pursuit, the exhilaration of the contest but I became uneasy with the power being always with the interviewer. I knew its manipulative potential, the temptation to employ the sanction of 'No time left'; to use quick wits against a more thoughtful adversary; to entice a weak answer with an unexpected question which the interviewee could probably answer strongly given time for more reflection or research. The construction, purpose and effect of three styles of media interview is examined in *The Media Interview* by Philip Bell and Theo van Leeuwen, published by University of NSW Press. The authors suggest that in *The Search for Meaning* I have developed 'a new genre'.

Certainly my listening was rewarded with a deep and varied recounting of experience which indicated that there is a rich subterranean vein of consciousness seldom before discussed in public, most likely hidden for fear of ridicule in a pragmatic society, and yet potent; a powerful if undisclosed influence in the way people live their lives.

This was always one of the points of the program's explorations, to discover how the inner life has shaped the formation of a person and the choices they make. It was not introspection just for the sake of it, but to see what action people had taken as a result of their experience and their inner convictions. I recall the American scholar of myth, Joseph Campbell, saying that what we sought was not just a sense of meaning but an experience of being alive.

When the day came to make our last *Search for Meaning* program, for broadcast on Sunday, 27 November 1994, producer Stephen Godley and I selected excerpts from seven interviews to identify some of the prevailing themes and qualities of the program. It was clear to us that it was the telling of stories which had been central. We came to recognise that a person's experience, their story, is sacred ground, that it's essential to them, that they're lost without it, that it needs to be told, and, importantly, to be heard.

Psychologist Dr Dorothy Rowe claims that old people's reminiscing is a process of making coherent the experience of a lifetime, a vital task of that age, and that we are, at any age, constructing our story, seeking to make sense of all that happens to us. Aboriginal psychology understands this, since the creation and continued existence of their world depends on the telling of stories. So did Greek philosophy, which was told through myths. Perhaps modern people, especially the young, are beginning to feel the loss of a coherent story as they turn away from their traditional religious beliefs and find economics and materialism meagre as stories by which to live.

Patti Miller, author of *Writing Your Life*[1], put it well when she told me, 'If I could be held up to the light, it would shine through me in a dappled pattern, and looking closer it could be seen I was made of densely woven stories which blocked and let through the light in this intricate way. They make a near impenetrable story-fabric of my being.'

The longing to know one's story is not to be denied. Adopted people-want to know where they came from. Migrants return to their birthplace to fill the gaps in their story.

Narrative seems to be crucial to the human condition. The Bible and other great spiritual texts are told in stories. It is the most powerful way we've found to make sense of our existence.

Over the years, we heard how people can derive meaning from all sorts of suffering, illness, impending death, imprisonment, mental illness. One of the most dramatic and moving of all programs was that with Brian Keenan who recounted his cruel experience as a hostage in Lebanon[2]. It was a revelation of endurance, of self-discovery and of meaning won out of terror, boredom and despair. He invited us into the claustrophobic world in which he spent four-and-a-half years, sometimes ill and chained to a wall in filthy, cramped spaces. In the worst of moments he sometimes found beauty, even ecstasy. Sometimes the human spirit reclaims hope and life from a destructive circumstance.

One of the most challenging aspects of making the program was the opportunity to encounter many Aboriginal people. It was the story-telling which provided common ground. We were dealing in the same currency and that opened the door for communication free of a political context. I was often very moved and shamed by what I heard, but excited too, to make a connection, to begin to 'grow peace', as Mary Graham puts it later in this book.

A good deal of preparation went into *The Search for Meaning* interviews. Each guest was invited to reflect on his or her experience through a questionnaire so that by the time we met, a train of thought had commenced, and could begin to be articulated.

I found that it was helpful to begin with a vivid early memory. Sometimes this would provide the key to an image recurring throughout a lifetime. Clare Dunne sees her delayed birth repeated as a pattern through her creative life. In childhood, Rupert Sheldrake saw rusty wires looped between willow trees. Wooden willow stakes, cut for fence posts had sprouted into trees. Much of Sheldrake's scientific work has been devoted to replacing

1 *Writing Your Life. A Journey of Discovery*, Patti Miller, Allen & Unwin, 1994.
2 *An Evil Cradling*, Brian Keenan, Vintage, 1993.

the utilitarian perception of Nature with a vision of Nature alive.

The recounting of early memories allowed a 'once-upon-a-time' atmosphere to be established in which the story could best be told. It seems that reflective conversation occurs at a different level of consciousness, below that of factual, practical intellectual discussion. The pace slows, the expression is somewhat inward-looking, the speaker is relaxed rather than guarded. On those occasions when I introduced a question about a person's work, for example, the mood would be broken, the expression changed. The person would be forced to come back 'on duty', as it were, to step out of the expansive 'story' space into a narrower, more demanding exercise of the mind alone. The sudden switch also seemed to cause discomfort and I learned not to provoke it.

Observing the depth to which a person will respond with an experienced attentive listener, I usually invited speakers, at the end of our talk, to reflect on what had been discussed and to contact me if they felt later that a certain revelation may be for private rather than public consumption. It happened once or twice, when a relative had been mentioned without their permission. But generally, people told what they were ready to disclose at that time and remained content with it. Often when we stopped after an hour and a half, they were unable to remember much of what had transpired, and listened to the broadcast later with some apprehension. I don't recall anyone complaining that they had felt betrayed by the process, and that was reassuring to me.

I know from first-hand experience what it is to be plundered by a journalist writing a personal 'profile'. It can be an entrapment in which the journalist, like an old dog with a smelly bone, keeps presenting you with the comments of a series of your critics against which you are required to defend yourself. He or she never seeks to analyse the motivation of your critics (some of whom have an axe to grind) and you are stuck in an aspic of unpleasant claim and counter-claim devoid of intellectual enlightenment, but titillating perhaps for those who are privately satisfied by the punishment of others.

The last time this happened to me I wrote the journalist a letter of professional challenge, suggesting that his method—the prevailing conventional method—was threadbare and perhaps even immoral and unethical. I suggested to him that he should make his own appraisal of my work, ask me his own questions from his own genuine interest. He did not reply. He has been promoted now to editor of one of the major newspapers.

As listener, I was always privileged. I felt the trust of those who spoke and was grateful for the generosity of their telling, because I knew they were offering rare spiritual, psychological and emotional sustenance to the listener. It took us some time to understand that what is most personal is indeed most universal, that when people tell their own stories with depth and honesty, they speak to the human condition.

I remember Michael Leunig claiming that it is at our deepest level that we find our common ground, and that the best news is truth. 'It seems that I have this search to find my people, my culture, to find a place where there is some common agreement . . . the great secrecy that evolves as we grow older, these hidden aspects of life, hidden sadnesses and hidden fears and hidden desires, they disturb me, they separate us . . . I guess I'm trying to confess publicly by saying "Look, I have this really strange, rather pathetic feeling—do you? Surely you do! If you don't then I'm greatly mistaken and my life is just a foolish kind of joke." '[3]

There was nothing practised about his description of his search. He was trying out words to express normally secret thoughts and wonderings. We heard him think aloud, sifting through ideas in an unguarded way. It was intimate. It resonated with the inner musing which other people have. He was pecking around like a bower bird, looking for blue bits which might be gathered to furnish the nest, to make it beautiful, to make it home.

He said that at our most sophisticated and clever, we are most separated from each other. But the inner search leads us home to somewhere that is comforting, familiar, connected.

Our listeners' letters have often said, '. . . to hear people speak on *The Search for Meaning* makes me know that I am not alone'. Leunig is doubly courageous because he has to exist in the smart world of the media where cynicism rules and people are fodder for headlines, and where the journalist seldom exposes his or her own soft underbelly, nor the disarray of his or her personal life. But Leunig does it, and countless guests on *The Search for Meaning* have done it, and in so doing, have connected powerfully with listeners. Because what they say has the authenticity of lived experience.

The response of listeners has been essential to *The Search for Meaning* process. People have written in their many thousands to tell something of their experience of life. The program seemed to liberate them to this disclosure. People have chosen passionate language to describe their reaction to a certain program, or even to a single thought which resonated with their own, or contradicted their assumptions in a creative way. They have described where and how they listened, as if to capture the essence of a moment of consequence.

In thirty years of broadcasting, on some of the ABC's top programs, I have never seen a correspondence so voluminous, nor so socially significant. It was my colleague Cecily Doig who responded with grace and sensitivity to mail and telephone enquiries, a vital component of making a program which respected both its guests and its listeners.

3 *The Search for Meaning Conversations* with Caroline Jones, ABC Collins Dove, 1992.

It is worth noting that *The Search for Meaning* was initiated by Dr David Millikan. As head of the religious programs department of the ABC, he was open to exploring meaning on pathways beyond the boundaries of formal religion and saw the personal spiritual quest as one vital strand of program output. That is also true of his successor, Ronald Nichols. The personal spiritual quest occurs in all the great religious, mythological and psychological traditions. It has been too little acknowledged in public in this society. I hope that our program on ABC Radio, this book and those which precede it, have helped to change that.

I concluded the series as I began it in 1987, convinced that 'it is better to light one small candle than to curse the darkness'. One of Australia's foremost thinkers, Emeritus Professor Charles Birch, described *The Search for Meaning* as 'a great adventure on radio which had spread understanding far and wide'. He was one of our greatest encouragers, especially at those times when we felt we were swimming against the conventional tide.

I listened to the final recorded edition of *The Search for Meaning* on a hot Sunday evening with dirt under my fingernails from the afternoon's gardening. As the program settled into its characteristic reflective mood, I was touched as always by the generosity of the story-telling and I cried for what we had lost.

I cannot say that I was either right or wrong, but at least I had demonstrated another broadcasting form, and provoked some discussion about its legitimacy. No doubt you will come to your own conclusion as you read this book.

I hope that it will provide you with good company and food for thought; and that it makes another small contribution to the search for meaning which goes on, in a million creative ways, across this country, in the telling and the treasuring of the stories of its people; and in the sanctity of each individual's inner landscape.

CAROLINE JONES 1995

Nick Carroll

If the racing sailboat is a powerful symbol of Australia, what of the surfer, black wet-suited and watchful, on the heaving swell, soon after dawn, off wild and lonely beaches round our coastline. At midday the little boys, zinc-nosed and towy-haired in Hawaiian board shorts patterned with pink hibiscus, mimic the manoeuvres of their heroes.

At dusk, the endless postmortems of the day in an extravagant private language designed to exclude the non-surfer.

Next day the search is on again for the perfect wave, up and down the coastline and through their dreams, as the weeks of glorious summer extend into autumn.

This is a rebellious tribe, enjoying its outsider status, conforming to its own code while making a cult of non-conformity.

Australian surfing champion Nick Carroll writes about the risks and the marvellous skill of board surfing and its devotees in a way that unlocks some of the allure of this mystical sport.

Like many surfers Nick Carroll has the calm gaze of one who has experienced something out of the ordinary and has never lost the wonder of it.

The ocean has been for him teacher, comforter, and playground since he was a child.

Here's how his story goes:

NICK CARROLL: Because my father had been a journalist all his life in one way or another, he had a lot of books. Even when I was six or seven I was trying to read all his books. Reading was encouraged because both my parents were intelligent people who enjoyed reading and liked the idea that I'd do the same. I don't think we had a TV until I was about eight and so I didn't have that other media to draw on. Then probably the biggest thing that happened in my young life was that my mother died when I was about nine and that was pretty intense. When that happens you know, like it or not, you are robbed of a direct source of love. To get over that I think you turn within yourself to try and look for something else in your life.

In what form do you remember that turning-in took when you were only nine?

First of all I can remember my father as a really powerful person, who had a lot to give us, but at the time I think it was an incredibly painful thing for him to go through, and he turned to his work. Over the next eight or ten years he became very important in his organisation. We didn't really sense that, we didn't realise how important he was growing and how much he was learning. I think he became a little bit hesitant and afraid of expressing love towards us. So, let's see, what did we do? I think I started reading a lot more. My little brother was searching for something that he could be good at. I think my sister was doing the same thing. I think we decided to express ourselves through latching on to something. For me and Tom, my younger brother, I think that did become the sea and surfing. Before my mother died we were normal beach kids. Like any family group, we'd go down to the beach and as we were living next to the beach it was a natural thing to do. At that point it felt like just a frolic and a fun thing to do. In the years after my mother died, the ocean began to seem like something more. It was more a focus for solitude. You'd go out into the sea and you could be alone, you could relax, and you could throw yourself into an activity that was all-encompassing. You could think about things that were well away from human relationships, which seemed to be so painful.

And if part of that was a search for love, did you find any love in that experience, or were you finding a substitute for it?

No. That's a good one. There's a lot of camaraderie in the ocean. One thing was I felt, when I was younger, reading and so on made me do quite well at school and so I was the teacher's pet. Everyone hates a teacher's pet so you tend to be out on your own a little bit. By surfing, by riding a surfboard in the ocean I got to meet a lot of people who weren't at school, a really unusual assortment of people from all sorts of areas in life, who also went for a surf. In that sense I made a lot of close friends in a short time, which was very exciting. I thought it was inspirational actually.

And apart from the camaraderie with people you were meeting who also surfed, what about your relationship with the sea?

The very nature of the sea makes it an all-encompassing activity. You have to learn so much about what the ocean can do, about your equipment, your surfboard and what that does, and you have to learn a lot about yourself, your own physical capabilities, how you can expand them. Then you have to learn about what kinds of waves do what and which ones you want to catch, and what is actually happening under the wave, why they're actually there. There is so much to learn that it becomes incredibly involving. Your mind is focused a lot on the ocean. I don't think that the sea is a metaphor for life, if your life is restricted to surfing magazines. The sea has been used for hundred of years in all forms of literature. It's as true there as it is for a surfer who experiences the sea as a thing that is absolutely essential and unchanging, but at the same time changes continually and you have to be on top of that. That becomes an incredible really intense sort of relationship with the ocean. Many would call it 'she', but I don't think that's necessarily right.

Do you?

No, I didn't think of it like that. What you do (and this is what a lot of surfers would do, I know I did), was to think of the surf and the sea as unchanging, the way human relationships aren't, or the way we perceive human relationship as not being. If you've ever had someone betray you, you then stop trusting people. Tom and I and my sister stopped trusting human relationships when my mother died and so I turned to the ocean and I thought, 'Well this never changes, this isn't going to betray me, this isn't going to disappear. This can absorb all my fears and concerns and worries and insecurities as a person.'

Have you had moments, Nick, when everything seemed to change? Moments when the whole of life seemed to be refocused or altered and you suddenly saw a new truth or saw things in a fresh way?

I think that something a surfer learns about faster than most people is about fear. A lot of people do themselves a disservice by keeping their lives really safe. They don't do a lot of things because they perceive them as being dangerous, which is terrific if you want to be safe. At the same time you miss out on learning a little bit more out there on the edge, especially learning about fear. I think a really good turning point for me, in learning about the ocean has been a number of occasions when I've been in the surf and the surf's been very challenging, very big, and I've definitely been afraid of it. I've come to a point somewhere in there, which is difficult to explain but I've reached a crisis point with the fear, that it's grown so strong that I am almost ready to panic and basically throw everything to the wind and just get out of there as fast as I can.

I can remember something that happened recently in Hawaii at a place called Sunset Beach. There is a very big wave and it's a very challenging place. You're very aware much of the time that humans are not really meant to be out there. I've experienced moments out there where I'm in a situation in which, if I make a mistake it is really life and death. I'll do something in the midst of my fear like suddenly catch a big wave and ride it and see that I do have control over this situation. Then it's not necessary for me to panic, and it'll change. But I find it easier to write about these things than to talk about them.

Still, you talk about them very expressively, thank you. Is there something about the moment when you're absolutely concentrated there on what's happening, that is, as well as being frightening, a moment of a great peace or joy or something very extraordinary?

Yes, surely. I guess, if you want to put it into a religious framework, Eastern religions deal with moments like that better than what we consider are usual forms of religion because they do deal with cathartic moments. The Zen Buddhists deal with them very well. You get moments like that where your whole body, soul, and mind are just concentrated on doing something in the surf. When it's very big and you catch a wave and you take off and there's usually, on a big wave in Hawaii, several seconds during that wave where you really throw yourself over the brink, you really have to forget about everything, totally, to make it. You have to forget about trying to do something, you have to just get up, trust your instinct and just fall into the wave. It's during seconds like that that you seem to just totally disappear, you as a being don't really exist at that moment. It's hard to express, you throw yourself into the moment so heavily that you're actually inside everything that's happening, you're inside the wave, you're inside the surfboard and what it's doing. You're inside all the landscape around you and the ocean as it's surging, you get totally inside the moment and it's so intense that time disappears, everything disappears. You disappear, you're not thinking of you Nick Carroll or whoever. It's way beyond that.

If you're going to make a very big wave you have to be totally unified with everything that's happening. You have to know absolutely everything about what the board's doing, what's happening with the wave, where the water is on the wave, how fast the water's moving up the face of the wave, what's happening with the wind, where there might be a couple of people in the way, and I don't think you can know about that if you choose to take the form of thinking that we do in our everyday lives, when I'm very aware of me, Nick Carroll. Your brain just can't handle it, it has to throw stuff away to fit it all in. And so a lot of what it throws away is the useless stuff, the ego, the 'I'm Nick Carroll, I've got fears, worries, doubts etc., etc.'—all very useless stuff. To take all that information in about what's happening, to get right inside it, you have to ignore a lot, and discard it.

So in one moment you're talking about all that you have to know, in one moment here you're describing a mental activity, all that you have to know, the calculations, the wind, the water, what's happening underneath, and then something different happens, doesn't it?

The mind is stilled and there's a moment of no mind. Of just you and being and . . .

Absolutely. Maybe the two are intertwined. Maybe in the moment of having to know everything all at once you burst through the barriers of trying to put things in order.

In quite a bit of your writing about surfing I think I hear a feeling of gratitude. Would that be right?

Yes, surely.

. . . 'God we're a lucky bunch, we surfers.'

Yes, we are. People are lucky all over the world and surfers are just one bunch of people who are particularly lucky. They've got an amazing playground to play around in and it's a fulfilling activity.

And whose playground is that? You say here (I'm just reading from one of your articles), 'God we're a lucky bunch, we surfers.' Is it God's playground? Is there a God for you?

I don't know. There's definitely a religious aspect although I don't know whether 'religion' is the right word—it's probably more spiritual. There's definitely a spiritual aspect involved there and I would also hesitate to put a particular name on it like 'God' or 'Buddha', or 'Mohammed' for that matter, I think it's more an awareness of the pulse of life on Earth. That kind of awareness is something that you don't normally get in life where you're too concerned with what the boss is going to say when you show up late for work. That's what surfers learn about, the pulse of life on Earth and if God's inherent in that then they learn about God too.

Do you think that your experience with the sea has given you a relationship with the sea and the land that helps you better to understand Aborigines when they speak of land?

You see things in the country which are just amazing. For a country which is obviously very old and beaten down it is intense. The land just throbs with power. You can really see why Aborigines have come to value the land the way they have and you can really see where the Dreamtime's come from.

Do you have a feeling about the land, that you belong to it, more than it could belong to you, in the sense of buying and selling and owning?

Land ownership's hilarious isn't it?

Is it?

People come along and they say, 'Right, this is mine'. For instance, when white people landed in Australia 200 years ago they claimed the land in the name of the king and then thirty or forty years later they sold it for money, and then another thirty or forty years later someone else sold it for money. But who gave them the title to that piece of land? Where did they really get it? Is it the Government that gave it to them? Does that give them the right to do anything they want to it? Because the Government said 'Okay this is your piece of land'?

But you probably own some piece of land, don't you?

No, not yet. I will, I'll have to.

When you own it you'll have a different feeling about ownership, will you?

I don't know. I just find the whole idea of the fact that people will hold out for land and buy it and then do what they want to it is weird. But that's fine.

Do you think you borrow it or it's a gift for a time or something? What is your idea of ownership?

It's a real trust. You get it, you can't just use it. You've got to leave it the same way or better than you came to it.

A number of the letters that people write to surfing magazines describe times of real crisis or tragedy or illness or hardship or heartbreak, and they've gone to the sea in those times and have found a great deal.

When I was editor of *Tracks* I must have seen about 5,000 letters. Of those letters I'd say maybe 20 per cent would have dealt with people having faced loss and recovery in some way. They turn to the sea, I guess, because that is permanent and they know a lot about it and they can retreat to the ocean and use it as a kind of medication to get themselves back on top. It's terrific that they have that possibility in their lives because a lot of people can't turn to something like this cleanliness, the sea and surfing, they have to turn to things like drink and drugs which aren't good for you.

So the sea really can be a healing experience?

Yes. It's healing

Where do you find the most beauty in your life now?

That's hard. Probably being married. I find a lot of beauty in that. Beauty is everywhere, isn't it? You can look at anything and see beauty in it. The ocean's incredibly beautiful.

Is there any relationship between those two sources of beauty, marriage and the sea?

I would really like there to be. I try to take my wife surfing, I try to show her that side of it and she's really eager to learn about the ocean. I think we're dealing with different things. The ocean for me is really a thing which I deal with in a solitary way whereas being married is an enormous step in human relations and there I'm dealing with things that aren't just me, I've got to give a lot of myself. It's more of a sharing thing than an individual improvement scheme.

Well, having felt as a little boy that you were lacking love when you lost your mother, have you got any observations on the need we have for love in our lives? And I don't mean just the one-to-one relationship but the need to feel cared for and to feel important to a significant number of people.

It's vital, isn't it? It's probably the only really significant area of our lives in a way.

Is it?

The need to have and give love. People, in shutting themselves off from it, think they're gaining a lot of the time. They think because they've experienced something like the loss of their mum, or a divorce, they think 'Well right, well, that's not the go, I'm not going to go through that anymore, I'll just shut myself off and then I'll shut the gates.' But then they wonder, they spend the rest of their lives wondering why things aren't really happening. Why they don't feel good and complete. Probably the answer to that is that they've robbed themselves of what makes life worth living.

And that is love?

Yes, I don't know whether this is true as I've got no way of telling. I suspect that maybe there are more pressures on people in relationships now than there ever has been. In that sense then a lot of people do run away from love and to reject love is even considered wise by some people. A contempt of love is common and maybe that's because so many people are robbing themselves of it.

And a cult of the individual too. Do you feel that at the moment?

Yes.

What's that all about? Self-containment, I'm hearing a lot of that now.

I think it is because of the way society is—the overt goals are put up as being valuable in society, to be the best at what you do, and to reach factor

X in what you do. The champions are lauded in our society.

Well, you've been one.

Yes. I've watched my brother become a champion, being lauded and watched. People attach themselves like leeches to him and try to use him in all sorts of ways. I've watched the media gibber about people whose media value is that he or she is a champion or the best in that field.

This is the great surfer Tom Carroll we're speaking of.

Yes, Tom is one of them. You see it in other ways. The media just latched onto McEnroe for years and they'd do anything to him because he was a champion. You see it with business people. When they're number one in their field they're lauded. To be a champion is a really solitary pursuit. It's perceived as a thing where you can't allow other people to affect you. You've got to be able to shut everything off and just concentrate on that goal of success. That's all very fine, they become successes but then, at the other end, where do they go? What do they do? Do they just stay shut off and go and find another goal? Do they go on doing that for the rest of their lives? Do they spend the whole of their lives pursuing something someone's told them is a good idea to pursue?

I guess some people do. What is your own idea of success, of being a success?

Well right now I actually think that success for me would be to have children and to bring them up well.

And that's the main contribution you see yourself as having to make now?

That'd be a pretty big one. Having children and bringing them up well I think makes running BHP look silly. It requires immense ability to give rather than to keep thinking of your own goals. You've got to just give all the time and I haven't tried that yet. It's probably going to be a rather challenging experience. Very much one to look forward to.

Rev Dorothy McRae McMahon

The Reverend Dr Dorothy McRae McMahon is Director for Mission for the National Assembly of the Uniting Church in Australia. Until 1993 she was minister at Sydney's Pitt Street Uniting Church for ten sometimes dramatic years. Her progressive and compassionate ministry with people on the fringes of society attracted the violent bullying of several right-wing groups. But, nothing daunted, Pitt Street Uniting Church continued to champion human rights, to support the peace and environment movements, to respect Aboriginal spirituality and to keep open house to the divorced, to the victims of rape, to gay men and women, to the lonely, the alienated; and to identify sin freshly in today's language as being greed and the oppression of debt, and whatever public policy lacks compassion.

In Dorothy McRae McMahon's church, God is as female as God is male. It's a church that encourages questions rather than handing down judgments.

One of the features of Pitt Street Uniting Church is the creating of imaginative rituals to encourage and affirm people in trouble. For example, when women in a country town were being terrified by a rapist a patchwork quilt was made, carrying the stories of many women, to make a centrepiece of solidarity. And a ritual was conducted in a way that offered a Christian context but respected the various spiritualities of those involved. A similar service was designed for child incest victims.

Dorothy is convinced of the potency of ritual and symbol. Two of the images that give meaning to her own life are the common cup of Holy Communion, or the Eucharist, and secondly the crucifixion and resurrection of Jesus Christ, an image which some find grim and frightening, but which says to Dorothy that to enter death experiences with faith, courage and company is to open up the possibility of new life.

REVEREND DOROTHY MCRAE MCMAHON: Yes, I think one of the most formative moments, or times, of my life came when our son Christopher was brain-damaged by his polio vaccination, and we were faced with a situation where our innocent and beautiful and intelligent child was forever . . . well, damaged, severely damaged. He never spoke again and he was forever intellectually disabled and a dependent person, and a miserable person, too. So it wasn't as though he was even a happy retarded child: he was actually miserable and confused, and, in many ways, I longed for him to die because it seemed to me that his life had little meaning, and I think that probably is true. It seems to me still that his life does not have a great deal of meaning and purpose, so how was I to understand that in the light of a God of love, and how was I to handle it myself?

The way that I first tried to handle it was to pray very deeply with a group of friends for his healing. That didn't happen, and so I then had to ask myself what prayer means . . . But to proceed on with the image of crucifixion and resurrection, I went into a period of denial, by saying, 'Well, there must be some purpose in this and I will find it, and I don't have to enter the pain of it because, really, there must be some very important meaning in this event in itself'. So I lived like that for some time, and it was some years later that I went into the sense of real grief that this had happened to our child and that he would never, apparently, recover from that damage. I had to face what that would mean for my faith. And in the end, my faith was stripped right back to seeing that, while God is in ultimate control of the universe, I believe, God has set it free in a way which means that many unjust things are going to happen and innocent people are going to suffer, and that there is a deep brokenness that lies at the centre of the Creation. But that God is there, loving us, in all of that and can really only offer us the fact that God is with us—the incarnation itself, and also the witness of the death and resurrection of Jesus—that Jesus entered the death with us and came out safely, a risen Christ, and that that is a revealing act. It reveals the centre of all truth and all reality, and when I was prepared then to go deeply into that grief and anger and pain, I could be angry against God for life having delivered that to us and to our son, and I could simply go into that safely and be honest about how I felt about it and come out at the end finding that the witness of God was enough to sustain us all, particularly as I was able to do that with other people. I think that the saving grace of God is corporately given; it's not necessarily given to us individually. We're meant to, in fact, be a community of people with the resources for healing and energising and saving.

I'm still understanding more about crucifixion in that event you're describing than I am about resurrection. Where is the new life in it?

For me, the new life was that having gone through that deathly experience of grief and pain I came out stronger at the end of it, and freer, and less afraid of life rather than more afraid. Because I'd looked it in the face: I had felt it, experienced it, named it truly and honestly, and there I was, still strong, at the other end of it. So I was able then to believe that there were many things in life that I could handle like that.

Dorothy, what led you to ordination?

As a Protestant, I could do anything else but preside at the Eucharist as a lay person, so that the only way I could preside at the Eucharist was to be ordained. I felt there were other reasons for wanting to be an ordained minister, but really that was central; that was the thing I wanted to do, that was the thing I felt called to do. And I must say every time I celebrate the Eucharist, every time I preside and lift the cup and break the bread, I have a most amazing experience of my being and my doing being totally whole and integrated.

So that's the time in which you are most you—most Dorothy?

Yes. It's again one of those paradoxes where on the one hand I'm most me and on the other hand I have an enormous and powerful sense of simply being a vehicle for something that has a life of its own. I remember at the time of my ordination, when the hands of the church went down on my head, I felt the weight of that. And then when I approached the moment of breaking the bread I had this extraordinary feeling of taboo as a woman, as though my hands might somehow destroy the thing I loved most, which was the Eucharist, the elements of the body and blood of Jesus Christ. As I approached it in faith and fear I found that I was given this gift of enormous freedom which said, 'But your hands have nothing to do with this—they are simply the vehicles for this presence of God. And if you are faithful they will be a true vehicle for that. But they do not have any power to destroy the presence of Christ. That's free of you, so don't worry.' And I was able to come out the other side of that feeling absolutely free. So it's a strange mixture of being more there than usual and less there than usual.

Is there an artistic depiction of Jesus Christ which speaks to you?

Yes, when I went to the Sistine Chapel, somewhat against my intentions—I was persuaded to go there and I thought, oh, it'd be pretty boring and, although I'm fond of art, I felt somehow I didn't particularly want to go through all the processes of arriving at the Sistine Chapel. But a friend encouraged me to go, and I arrived at the time when they were cleaning the ceiling and when the vivid colours were coming through. I know some people don't like them, but I loved them. As I looked at the Christ leaping off the wall, with muscles and just a wisp of material covering him, which almost seemed useless—this passionate, energetic, muscled figure—it was an experience of transformation for me . . . a transfiguration, even, I'd go as far as that, where the Christ stood there in life, so full and so human and so enfleshed. So many of the pictures of Jesus are draped with things and look like a wimpy person who's very unmuscled and unenfleshed. Even though we say he took our flesh, we cover it all up.

That's too ethereal, is it, for you?

Very ethereal, very meek and mild, sometimes with powerful eyes that look almost accusingly at you. But this was a real live person. It was wonderful.

You've talked about the ritual, the power of the ritual of the Eucharist. I know that in your church you and your community have designed some other creative rituals for special occasions.

One of them is a service for restoration at the ending of a marriage. We did this because, most particularly in this day and age, if you are divorced you go into a court—and some people don't even go into a court, they don't appear at all and it just happens with a bit of paper being sent to them. At the very most, most people have two or three minutes where a judge simply says, 'You are now divorced'. And people come out of one of the most significant moments in their life—or significant traumas in their life—without any sense of having gone through anything. It's as though this whole thing has happened in a matter of seconds and has not been acknowledged in a way which lifts up the significance of the moment. Also, of course, many people carry with them a huge burden of guilt and grief, but guilt in particular, especially if they have been the people who ended the marriage. The church has asked of them solemn vows when they were married and now all that's gone and what did it mean, and how can they be in any sense released from that moment and restored to a sense of oneness with God again and oneness with themselves? So we have developed a ritual where we go through a moment of real confession, of naming the things that have happened for that person. We always gather around them a small group of people so that again we are doing it corporately, and we are saying that we all confess that there are many things in our life where we don't know whether they're wrong at our beginnings or they're wrong at our endings.

So it's a form of service where what has happened is described and agreed to or supported by the community.

Yes. It's an honest moment where we say, 'This is what's happened to us, and we can only stand before You, the holy God, and confess that this is who we now are and we were not able to do anything else with our life experience'. Then we ask the person or people concerned to kneel, and we lay hands on their head and we anoint them, which is the sign of oneness with Christ, and we announce that, even though they cannot be saved from the consequences of the situation, they are not condemned and that God frees them to a new day. Then we share the Eucharist together and we share the common cup. We always have a particular chalice which we buy for them and at the end of the sharing of the common cup and the bread we present the cup to them and say, 'Take this cup and when you are tempted to feel more human or less human than the rest of us, remember that we have shared this common cup of humanness and this common cup of hope, and take hold of your new life again', and they take that away with them. So we try to create for them something which is a memory for their reference and also a powerful affirming act which reinforces what we believe is the gracious forgiveness of God.

And what results have you seen from that—what effects, what responses?

I've seen many people rise to their feet from kneeling with just a whole new life on their face, and they're ready then to put behind them the things that have been binding them. It doesn't mean that we don't carry with us the powerful and painful learning experiences of such a failure and a tragedy in our life, they are embedded within us forever. But they become creative learning things for our life rather than dreadful dead guilts.

I do think guilt is probably the only negative pain that has no possibility of redemption within it if you stay with it. It has nothing creative in it, because if you stay guilty what you are basically saying is that you will not allow God close to you and you will not allow yourself to be close to you either, that you are not ever worthy of forgiveness. It's a paralysing thing; you can't live out of that, you can't move out of that. You have to lay it down and say, 'Well, yes, I have failed, but I'm not condemned. There is no condemnation; there is a free and gracious amazingly generous gift that is given to us to start again.'

And the power of the ritual is that all these other people here around me in the community in the church are saying, 'Yes, that's the way we see it, too'.

That's right. They're saying, 'We, too, failed and we want to say that we know. Listen to our faith. If you have none, if God seems to be absent from you—and often God feels to be absent, especially with guilt—rest on our faith. Be carried by our faith at this moment and our common humanness with you.' And people rise and take up their life and go on.

May I talk about you as minister? It strikes me as being an enormously difficult role. On the one hand people want you to be something of a heroine, expecting that you will stand up for issues of social justice, knowing that you'll be in a demonstration if you believe in it. On the other hand there are media images of wimpy ministers, crass or foolish or moralistically unpleasant. It's such a difficult role to take on. How much can you be you—Dorothy—as a minister of the church?

It's a struggle, because being an ordained person, a priest or a minister, is a very, very dangerous occupation (laughs). I'm quite sure of that. I always knew it was, watching my own father as a minister and other people, too. It's dangerous because there is a grave seduction in it. People will invite you to believe you are God and feed that in you, and there's also a danger in that, because so many people bring to you the tragedies of their life and the struggles of their life that you can, without realising it, become so bowed down with the pain of other people that you have to begin defending yourself against it. There are ways of doing that; there are ways of stepping back from it so that you build a shell around yourself so that you no longer feel your feelings or theirs, and if you don't feel theirs you're not feeling your own, either. Because of the sort of role that you are expected to fill, you often block off your own feelings very solidly because you're not meant to be human and grieving and confused and failing and in pain, so you can become a cypher of a person very easily.

Have you ever felt that danger for yourself?

Oh, yes, I have. Oh, yes, quite often when I've gone on a retreat I've thought that I've been going there to unload the pain of other people so that I could be more useful as a minister, and when I've arrived there and moved into the silence I find that I'm up to the neck with my own pain, every time, and that it's my own unresolved pain that I'm really dealing with and therefore I can't bear other people's pain any more because it's loading on to my own and triggering off my own. In terms of thinking I'm God, well, yes. I mean, you're up front and people say how terrific you are and how important you are to them and how dependent they are on you, and unless you have honest friends and an honest congregation who will challenge that in you, it's very easy to be seduced into that and to become a dehumanised person, well removed from seeing that you're just, before God and everybody else, a very ordinary human being.

But to what extent is it safe enough to show that? Say something's going with great difficulty in your own family life, can a minister like yourself afford to reveal that to people?

I think it's a matter of degree.

Have you done that?

I have done that. The big crisis moment for me was when I felt, or my husband and I felt, we should end our marriage, which was a few years into my ministry, and that was the toughest thing, I think, that I've ever done in my whole life. For me, it was a total shattering of the person who I thought I was. I was faced with recognising that I had made vows that I could no longer keep and that I would have to shift my image, which was important to me, of being a respectable married woman and one who could sustain a marriage. I knew I was about to enter into hurting somebody else and, well, everything just meant that after many years of agonising, I came to a point where I just stood before God, and I felt as though I was going to step off a cliff, really. It felt like a moment of total danger and jeopardy. In the end all I could do was to say, on my knees, 'God, I can do no other', and to take that step and to tell the Elders Council that I was about to end my marriage; which I did, and I think I'm enormously fortunate in the people of Pitt Street. But first of all, I found the gracious arms of God underneath me in a way that I have never experienced before. I just said, 'God, I am totally dependent on your grace; I have nothing else to depend upon', and there was the grace of God for me in a way that I have lived out of ever after. My life is full of thanksgiving for that experience of grace when I had nothing.

What do you mean by that experience of grace?

It was an experience where I simply felt surrounded by a cloud of understanding and love and forgiveness.

From people?

From people and from God, both. It was really a powerful experience of the God who is other than myself, and I had that experience of nearness. I've often experienced God most close at the point of death, or when I'm in the most deathly experience of my life God has become so close to me that I really think God hovers round death very, very closely. And that, for me, was a death experience, the death of a relationship. I experienced that on my own with God very profoundly.

Do you mean the presence of some benevolent other? Isn't it hard to find the words when you say . . . ?

It is, it is; it's very hard to find the words. I don't know whether you've ever read books by an American surgeon, whose name eludes me, who's written a book about near-death experiences called *Life After Life*.

Is it Raymond Moody?

I think that's right, yes. He listened to the stories of people who had been clinically dead and who'd come back to life from that near-death experience, and they described this experience of . . . well, something which appeared to be after death. For me, it's like that. I experience a sense of absolute awareness of who I am before this holy and warm presence, and I know with stark truth who I am. That's very hard to bear, but as soon as I experience that moment of absolute truth it's simultaneously a moment of warm light encompassing me with absolute unconditional love, and I can only respond with tears of gratitude and the warmth in my very being, which will forever give thanksgiving to God and share that with other people.

Is there cause and effect in that? Are you saying, 'I have experienced that grace when I have been able to expose myself in all my frailty'?

Yes, I am.

That that was the cause of it? You're saying 'That's how I have to be: I have to be absolutely human and honest—rigorous'.

Yes, it's that entry into death again, you see. It's that crucifixion experience which you enter into voluntarily. You say, 'I will now experience the death of my life as I have known it by saying honestly before God who I am; by holding my arms wide', if you like, 'and being transparent, naked, before God'. And being prepared to trust that God can cope with that and is not destroyed by it and will not remove God's presence from one; that God Herself, or God Himself, however we name God, will not go from the awful person that you believe yourself to be.

And in this case, not only that God wouldn't go away but that the congregation, the community, wouldn't. I mean, did they wear it and bear it?

They did. They supported both my husband and myself in that, and trusted that relationships are complex, that no one can know what happens to people in a relationship and what is right and what is wrong. All they could say was, 'Well, God loves you, we love you, and we, too, are failing, and we will be with you in that'. I thought that my ministry would be severely diminished by that dreadful failure. In fact, it was not. More people trusted me with their life because they said, 'Well, you're human, too. You know what failure is like and you can stand with us and accompany us towards forgiveness and new life and you will not judge us, because you yourself have given evidence of your need of grace.'

Have you got a story apart from the Christian story, another story from literature that guides you, or helps you in your determination to be human and to show the frailty of you as well as the strength?

Yes, I am very fond of an old British story called *The Velveteen Rabbit*, which was written in 1922 by an Englishwoman. It's the story of a toy rabbit who wants to be real. To paraphrase just a little extract from it, the rabbit has an old friend, the Skin Horse, and the rabbit says to the Skin Horse, 'Well, how can you be real? What does it mean to be real? I want to be real.' The Skin Horse says, 'Oh, that takes a long time, you know, and it's very uncomfortable. First of all you have to have someone who loves you, who loves you for a long, long time. And your eyes drop out and your hair is rubbed off and you become loose in the joints, and then one day you find you are real.' The rabbit feels very sad that it has to be so uncomfortable and takes such a long time, but then the story goes on. A little boy loves him and one day the little boy says, 'Don't take my rabbit from me. My rabbit's real, it's real!' and the rabbit lies there and his little boot-button eyes are shining and he takes on a look of wisdom and beauty. That's a very inadequate rendering of the beautiful words of the story, but for me that's what being real is about. It's about going through many things which rub all sorts of things from you. Often you become less beautiful in the traditional sense but more beautiful in wisdom. You become knocked around by life a good deal, because you're honestly and rigorously going through it. So it's a hard time; it's a very passionate way to live, but it is the only way through. It's that crucifixion pattern again, and you rise with many scars and wounds and blood that comes from your side, if you like, and nails in your hands and feet, but you come out the other end as a person of wisdom.

How are you nourished? You've suggested some very powerful ways, but what about having a massage, or going for a swim or . . . do you let yourself do any of those?

Oh, yes. Oh yes. I love having Shiatsu massages when I can afford them. I find it a wonderful gift from . . . I think the Japanese invented it. It's terrific. I love the sense of having my body cared for. It's taken me a long time to do that; in fact, it's only really in the last few years that I've stopped a stoic approach to my body. Probably as it gets older I'm aware of it much more, but I guess I came out of Christian tradition which said, basically, 'Override your body. Put up with it, pull yourself together and press on'. I think bodies are to be respected as much as any other part of oneself now, so, yes, I'm swimming now and again, and riding my bicycle. But the thing I learnt to do recently, which was a wonderful breakthrough for me was . . . I went through a hard time in my life and I didn't feel very loved in some ways, and I broke through that with a lot of care from other people and I went to a sort of disco place and I danced. It was wonderful—I just danced. I'd done a bit of ballroom dancing a long time ago, but I danced, and I danced by myself, and I danced my own steps, and it was wonderful, absolutely wonderful.

Freeing?

Yes. I just thought, 'Well, who cares if my body's now middle-aged; who cares if anyone would be embarrassed about looking at this; I'm just going to dance.' And I did, and it was a wonderful sense of personal freedom: that I was okay and I could do it. Actually, that reminds me—I don't know whether everyone has seen *Strictly Ballroom* . . .

It would seem just about everybody has. It's been very popular. Why?

Yes, it has been, and actually I'm proud to say that the senior cameraman was a young man in our congregation and so we're very proud of it. And I've talked with Stephen Mason about that film. Clearly, the people who made it thought that the key theme in it was that to live with fear is to be half alive. Now, that is a powerful theme that runs through it, but I think it's very special for Australian audiences because, without realising it, those people made something that hits deep into our understanding of our life and our longings here, and even of the meaning of life. You see, when you look at a film like *Crocodile Dundee*, there we are, larrikins. Okay, we like to think of ourselves as larrikins and it's our being unpretentious and fun and really just laughing at the world and ourselves. But *Strictly Ballroom* takes us one step deeper into our psyche, and there's a central moment in the film for me and it's about my understanding of what I'm doing in ministry and what the church needs to do and what we're trying to do in this country. The young man, you see, wants to dance his own ballroom steps, and you have the president of the Ballroom Association saying very firmly and issuing press releases saying 'There are no new steps', which the church sometimes does within itself and to people. The central image for me is the old grandmother. The young man meets and takes as a partner a young migrant woman of a Spanish-speaking family, and he goes into her family and he dances his own steps and they laugh at him and he feels angry about that. Then the old Spanish-speaking grandmother comes up to him, she opens up his shirt, and she says, 'Beautiful body'. Now, that's very important, that we always say to people how beautiful they are first. And then she puts her hands on his chest, one on top of the other, and she says, 'Now, listen to the beat'. And she beats out a flamenco rhythm and says, 'Feel the beat, feel it'. She keeps beating out this beat inside him and then she virtually says, 'Now dance your own steps'.

For me, when you set free a work of art into a community, people do with it what they will. And what I do with that is, I say, 'We are a society which longs to dance our own new steps but we're afraid of that, because we go all over the place with them, and we end up as larrikins and so on and we laugh at ourselves, and that's nice. But the task of the church and the task of anybody who cares about the meaning of life for this community is to help us strip our life back and find out what the essential rhythm of life is about; the things from which we must not move if we are to sustain our life here with the values that we want; the central themes that are absolutely important for life here together. If we will find that central beat, then we will know what our new steps must be.'

There is longing in us as a community, something weeping in us as a community. I think we are a very weeping, grieving community.

The other bit of literature that I love is Les Murray's poem, 'An Absolutely Ordinary Rainbow'. It's a poem about a man simply sitting in George Street, weeping, and people gather around him and they stand in respect and awe and long for tears as children long for a rainbow. I believe in my ministry that I have felt, over and over again, the tears, the weeping, the unnamed and unshed tears of this community of people, the weeping of the Australian community. I don't know what underpins it: maybe we are grieving for the fact that so many of us were people who came from somewhere else and left where we belonged. I hope we are weeping for the fact that we took somebody else's country and we have never, in fact, done justice to them; we feel guilt and we don't know what to do with that.

I think there are many things that we grieve about, and we have never established rituals of grieving or celebration. We bomb ourselves out with drinking and race around the place being larrikins, but underneath our larrikinism is a deep sense of grief and a longing to know what is at the centre of life. And whoever is able to release that weeping will be able to get at the heart of this community and will gain its confidence in taking its own new steps and, perhaps, daring to be a bit more confident about saying that we are people who have a deep sense of our oneness with good and love and justice and truth.

It's understated, it's delicate: our spirituality is so delicate, and the church has been so heavy. We are very understated people; we are not Europeans, we are not Americans in our way of naming the 'otherness' of life. We are people who sort of feel embarrassed about all that, self-conscious about it, and yet I have no doubt at all that we are not a secular society, we are people who have some quite deep connection with things, that's why we are so often indignant about injustice. We're fragile people: we kick at authority because we haven't got much confidence. We're brash, we're unpretentious. We don't like people who are pompous and pretentious, and I'm glad we're like that; it's a relief to come back to us being like that, and that's why we don't like people parading around. On the other hand, we love the drama and the colour of ritual, but we just don't know quite how to be unselfconscious about getting into that.

Back again to keeping in touch with your own self and body and being. Have you got time for any sort of hand work, or anything else which is revealing of yourself to you?

Yes. I must say, before I indicate my more noble craftwork, I also read detective stories endlessly. I'm a bit of an addict of detective stories. I always have been.

What's the appeal?

I like the puzzle of it, somehow. It's a bit odd, actually (laughs), but it's just a complete escape.

The craft thing that I've enjoyed is sculpture, and apart from this year when I've been writing more, for the last three years I've been working as a student with Tom Bass, who is a well-known older sculptor, a marvellous man who's done quite a lot of public sculpting. And just to get my hands in the clay and to work and work and try to express something about my life, I've found is even more profound for me than retreat work, really. You work away quietly in a group of people. You are accountable to yourself to try to keep working until you have worked as far as you can work, which is a salutary experience for me because I'm the sort of person who normally whips something off and then says to myself and everybody else, 'Well, of course I could have done it a lot better had I had more time' (laughs), which is a nice way of not being truly accountable. Whereas Tom Bass, just as I'm thinking that, oh, this is really pretty good, will say, 'Oh, dear, we do have problems there, don't we, Dorothy' (laughs), and make me work further with it. So it's a mixture of things, working in the clay.

You like your hands in the mud?

I do, I do. I love the feeling of the clay on my hands, there's an earth quality about that. And simply not to be clean all the time and to mould something and to work physically with something as earthy as clay is a wonderful experience.

What do you find that you're producing? What are the subjects or the themes that are emerging out of the clay?

Well, the first thing that I did was a weeping woman, and that was myself, I think, but it also represented the weeping of the world. But I'd have to say I very much did that for myself. The next thing I did was a militant madonna (laughs).

What did she look like?

Well, the inspiration came from a controversial sculpture in the grounds of Salisbury Cathedral in England. This woman had done a sculpture that is controversial becasue it's a quite ugly madonna figure who's striding along. I think it's called 'The Walking Madonna' or 'The Striding Madonna'. Anyway, it's a life-size figure, and she's a scrawny old woman and she's walking really fast—you know, you can see her skirt stretched out—and I love that sense of movement. When you think about it, most madonnas are very still, so I thought that I would do a walking one, a striding one, and then I decided she was militant. She's carrying the child and she's protecting the child but she's got her fist raised, too (laughs). She's the *Magnificat*: she's the madonna strong and free who said that Christ had come to free the oppressed.

Then I did a figure of two people in unity, which was the unity of relationship. The last one I did was after I had quite a few experiences of connection with women who had been raped—and I've done a study on rape—which is a figure of a woman kneeling with her hands over her face, trying to protect herself and leaning backwards, and she's all hollowed out as her body is trying to withdraw from the attack, as though she's withdrawing her whole being from the rape. Of course, it also expresses the terrible ravaging of rape for a woman's body, and interconnected with her is the shell of a woman lying around her knees. The two women are integrated, really: one has energy and the determination to withdraw from the attack, and the other is the death of the attacked woman. I did that to debrief from the endless pain, really, of dealing with abused and shattered and ravaged women from child abuse and sexual assault and rape and bashing, which is very common in my experience.

To debrief yourself from it?

Yes, to express it and, in expressing it in that clay, to debrief myself from my own outrage and pain as I stand beside women who go through that.

Dorothy, time must be a challenge for you. That's the other thing I want to ask you about being a minister, being a mother, being a woman, being so busy, how do you now think about time, because I don't think you'd ever have quite enough, would you?

No, you never do, and one of the things you have to come to terms with is the sort of spirituality which sustains you and energises you but also releases you to see who you really are in the scheme of things. It's a job that is never ended, of course; how can you ever end a job like that? So the way I perceive myself is as one tiny, unique and important speck in a great continuum of human existence, and it is God who is bringing in the reign of God, not me. I'm participating in some of it with God, in terms of any moment that I participate in which is more true, more hopeful, more loving, more just, but I'm freed from thinking that I am the Messiah. I am not God, I am not bringing it in, so I'm this special person, in the sense of everybody being special in playing their part in this great continuum of endeavour and hope. I'm meant to be a person who plays, laughs, relaxes, and abundant life is mine, too. I'm not to live a driven life because that's not a very good modelling of the life that we're called to, anyway; that's a terrible modelling and it's a dehumanising thing. Also, to burn oneself out is no help to anybody. I work very hard but I also play and relax and enjoy myself.

So it sounds as though you don't think so much about the length of time as about the quality of it.

Yes, if you see time as eternal then every moment has a potential to be an eternal moment, and that's the way I see it, which I find very freeing when I'm dealing with people who are dying. Death is something that I feel comfortable with, really. I'm afraid of pain but I feel very comfortable around death, particularly because I work often with people with AIDS, people in the prime of life dying. I see people who can live as vividly in a matter of months as many people live in a lifetime, and if you see life as about eternal moments rather than length then, in fact, it comes into another sort of perspective, so you don't feel so anxious. Again, you come back to that corporateness, too, you see. If we're living corporately it isn't dependent on me, I'm only one part of it, and it's enormously freeing to move into that and to live more graciously with oneself. I don't always do it; I have a tendency to try to take on too many things, but that's usually when I'm feeling superhuman and it's time I remembered that I am not.

Rene Rivkin

I met Rene Rivkin in his own high-rise glass office tower surrounded by the sophisticated communication paraphernalia of a financier who must be instantly in touch with everywhere, round the clock. Everything was beautiful—the furniture, the young men and women he employs, the works of art, the food served for a boardroom lunch with two other high fliers.

Rene Rivkin was born into a white Russian Jewish family who fled to China as refugees from the Bolshevik Revolution. They lived in some style in Shanghai, the Paris of the East. The little boy saw the huddled masses on the streets outside his home and vowed to avoid poverty at all costs. He achieved his aim by gambling successfully on the mass psychology of the stock market.

Today he's a very wealthy man given to bouts of depression. He has survived a nervous breakdown, a brain tumour and the market crash of 1987. He sees no particular meaning in life. His philosophy is to minimise pain and maximise pleasure, but he has no illusions that money can buy happiness. Beauty is the doorway to an elusive serenity which Rene pursues through a passion for art.

Rene, I was hoping that you might reflect on your childhood firstly, to think about the influence of your mother and your father and what your environment was when you were quite young and as you were growing up.

RENE RIVKIN: In China, certainly, I had a rather happy childhood.

We lived, in those days, in the lap of luxury. In Australia it might not be considered so. We lived in an apartment which was a nice apartment, quite large but not as large as the house that my children live in today for example, but we did have a rather large staff of perhaps ten or eleven. We had amahs—wash amahs, cooks, drivers, the whole shebang, of course. And my parents used to indulge me with toys. I certainly never came across a child with better toys than I had. In fact, not that I've ever reflected upon it, but maybe my predilection for toys today stems from my predilection for toys in those days. Then we came to Australia in 1951 and things got tougher because my father struggled for the first few years. And, of course, there were no staff and all that sort of thing. But life was very good.

My only recollection as a child of being unhappy was when I could see myself getting fatter and fatter, and that, I think, had an enormous influence on my life in adulthood.

What did your father do in Shanghai?

I think he did what a lot of people of our style did, he dealt in whatever was going. He was a trader, which I think was also quite interesting, probably because I am really a trader, except I trade in stocks and shares, bullion and other things financial, and he traded in other things; he traded in goods. I recall he used to trade in nylon stockings, there was a shortage during the postwar period in nylon stockings, and he traded in that. He traded in rubber tyres, I know that. Sequin beads were something else he traded in. But basically, trading in anything that was going, anything that you could buy cheap and sell high.

What do you think has been your father's influence on you?

I think there's been a great deal of influence. I think his trading background in China would have influenced the way I grew up. I'm not sure that's what he wanted to achieve, because very clearly he wanted to achieve someone who was different from the way I am. He wanted to achieve either a doctor or a lawyer for a son. Every Jewish father's dream is for a lawyer or a doctor. And he went part of the way by, I wouldn't say forcing me to go to law school, but certainly strong encouragement to go to law school, which I did, and I got my law degree. But I never went into the law. I was always going to be a stockbroker.

But apart from that we lead very separate lives. We see each other once a week, precisely. I go to his place and my mother's place every Saturday for lunch and we take the kids, of which I have five, and that's very pleasant. But we don't do business together and we don't discuss business.

And, Rene, the influence of your mother as you were growing up and now?

I'm not sure there was much influence by my mother. She's a most loving and wonderful mother. I always used to say to her you couldn't wish for a better mother than I had, and I stick to that today.

You've spoken of the difficulty of being fat as a youngster. Would you say some more about that?

Well, I think this is another Jewish syndrome which drives me around the bend, quite frankly, because I'm actually going through similar problems with my wife now. That is to say that I have five children, beautiful children, who are all nice and slim, and my wife walks around after them with a spoon full of food, around the house feeding them because she thinks they're too thin. And, of course, because of my traumas as a child being fat, it actually drives me around the twist. Now getting back to my childhood, my mother was, I think, lucky enough, to put it sarcastically, to find some dopey doctor in China who diagnosed a disease akin to tuberculosis of the lung. She claimed I was very thin and the doctor, to her great joy, agreed that I was thin. The doctor confined me to bed for a period of six months—I was about three or four, I think—and fed me cream. That was the diet, cream in any form—whipped, sour, running, drinking, any cream—and I got to like it, and I got to like food, and in six months' lying still, basically—I wasn't allowed to get up other than for vital purposes—I grew fat. I guess my stomach expanded, because that's what happens, and I've had difficulty with my weight all my life, really. I was a very fat twelve, thirteen-year-old boy, even ten-year-old boy, and I remember being bullied by the school bully at Rose Bay Public School because I was fat. And I think that most children need and want to be the same as every other child, and being fat removed that ability to be the same as every other child.

Did it make you feel wretched?

Yes, it did. I was miserable about it. But, of course, like all fat people who are miserable about being fat, the thought of not having food is even worse than the thought of being fat. I mean, I clearly have the problem today. I'm 99 kilos and think I ought to be about 88 kilos. That's not obese though, that's just overweight. Most of my life I've been obese.

Are you working on it?

I'm working on it in so far as I could get much fatter.

I have an enormous capacity to gain weight. I could gain a stone in three days if I let myself. I can go to the fridge and pig out, as they call it. I can have a stick of salami and I'd love it. And then, of course, in the classical pig-out, I'd sit there suffering afterwards, hating myself, just like I used to hate myself when I used to smoke cigarettes because it was obviously such a dumb habit, a dumb dirty habit, and I couldn't give it up.

I gave up cigarettes in 1973, but until then I smoked seventy cigarettes a day feeling awfully dumb.

What about exercise?

Oh, I hate exercise. It's boring and it's smelly . . . it's so unintellectual. I mean, there are some people who actually say they get to think very well when they are doing their exercise, but in my case all I could think about on the one or two times I've every tried it, is how quickly this torture is going to end. It's hopeless.

Besides which, Caroline, there's really, in my case, not much point, because I'm fit enough to do what I do, and I do quite a lot; I'm activating twenty hours a day. There's nothing I can't do by virtue of being unfit, other than perhaps live longer, but of course my views on old age are that it's not something you want to prolong anyway.

Rene, how Jewish do you feel?

Oh this is very simple in my case. I feel very Jewish, but that doesn't mean I don't feel very Australian, because I don't know what Jewish means. My wife is an Anglican and I wouldn't have dreamt of asking her to convert to Judaism—I didn't, and I'm happy to say she didn't convert to Judaism, so that's fine. Most of my friends are non-Jewish, although I have some Jewish friends, and I've integrated perfectly into Australia.

So is Judaism your religion or . . . ?

If it's anything it's my religion, except I'm not religious, I'm an atheist. So you ask an interesting question that I'm incapable of answering in any rational way other than the way I feel. I feel that I have Jewishness in me.

What does it feel like to have Jewishness in you?

Happy. I'm happy that I'm Jewish. I guess the test of whether you're happy whether you're Jewish or not is if you had your time all over again would you choose to be Jewish or would you choose the easy way out and be non-Jewish, and I'd choose Jewish every day of the week. Why would I choose to be Jewish? It's a membership of a club of some kind that I like.

I like the Jewish feeling, which is again hard to express—it's something that you know you have in you. I think Jewish people are basically colourful people, that's not to say that non-Jewish aren't colourful, but I think Jewish people, on balance . . . there's more Jewish colourful people as a percentage of Jews than there are of non-Jews, if you like.

How do you feel about Jewish jokes, of which there are many of course?

Oh if they're good ones that's fine. I'm not one of these people who walks around seeing anti-Semitism under every door. In fact, as I was looking for the photographs of my childhood last night I saw a letter I wrote to the *Sydney Jewish Times* defending Sydney Boys' High School. I was eighteen at the time. A letter to the editor defending the fact that I had not experienced anti-Semitism once at Sydney Boys' High School. I was there for five years and there were accusations in those days that there had been. And I defended the position that clearly there wasn't any anti-Semitism.

So no religion . . . ?

No religion. I mean, the religion that I have if I have religion is that I think that if I were a Christian they would say about me that I was a good Christian, whatever that means, but I guess it means being good. I regard myself as being a good human being and a good member of society. That's the religion that I have. And you can do that very successfully without believing in a God or without going to organised religious instruction.

So is the purpose of your life clear to you?

Oh no. The purpose of my life is perfectly unclear to me. But for that matter, it's unclear as to your purpose in life, or anyone else's purpose in life, because I don't know what we're here for; I don't know particularly what one of us can achieve, whether you'd be better or worse during a very short period here relative to Eternity.

So how could you sum up a philosophy of life?

Well, that's very difficult. I think I have been searching for the meaning to life for many years because I don't regard myself as one of those people who thinks life's wonderful and all I ever want to do is stay here having a wonderful time. I think the world's a mess and I don't know what we're here for, and I don't actually know why half the world's population wants to be here. Now clearly that's not the Australian side of life I'm talking about. I'm talking about, if you like, Bangladesh or the starving Ethiopians and so on and so forth, that form some vast percentage of this world's population who, it seems to me, ought to want to die as quickly as possible, particularly as a lot of them believe in an afterlife that's good. I mean, I cannot understand, for example, why—even for that matter the Christian religion—why if Heaven is as wonderful as it is taught to the population, why is there a struggle to stay on this Earth?

So for you there's no destination after this life?

Absolutely not.

Then what is the meaning of every day, how do you put meaning into every day?

I think the meaning that you have to accept is that we have to maximise pleasure and minimise pain during the period that we, by some fluke or quirk of fate, happen to be on this Earth, because I can't see any other meaning to life.

Principally, how do you do that?

Well, in my case, I guess, I happen to have fallen in love with things artistic, things beautiful, and not only does that require a lot of money, but also it enables me to relax in the brief moments that I can relax. So therefore that explains to you my motivation in working hard, because my life would be incomplete if I couldn't be involved in art and buy art. I think some would criticise me for saying 'Well, you can be involved in art by going to the National Art Gallery or to the Gallery of New South Wales and yes you can; but in my case I also happen to like it around me where I am. I like beautiful things, and I think the world actually is a very beautiful place, and where it is not beautiful it is only because man has damaged its beauty.

And with the lovely art works that you surround yourself with, is it only to look at them, is it also to touch them?

Oh, it's to touch. I think I'm a tactile person, and some of the things I collect are Japanese miniature sculptures in ivory. They are very tactile. And I also collect jade, which I think is a very tactile material. And even these worry beads, for example, are very tactile—gold, warm. Gold is very tactile.

Would you tell me something about those? Why do you have those?

Well, in about 1972 I was in Greece and I saw a lot of Greek men with these things. I perceived that Greek men also smoked very little. And so when I gave up smoking in 1973 I took up worry beads. In fact, subsequently, I think six months ago, I read somewhere that Greece has the highest per capita smoking of any European country. So I gave up for the wrong reason. But I play with them all day every day since about 1972.

How many beads are there?

I've no idea. There's no significance to the beads because they're well worn by now, and this is probably in fact one and a half sets of worry beads because from time to time the string breaks and I've lost a couple of beads, so this is an amalgam of beads.

Is it like a comforter?

It is a comforter, yes. A lot of people doodle, a lot of people twist their hair, and a lot of people do other things. This is just my outlet for nervousness.

Nervousness?

Oh, I'm a very nervous person. I mean, I actually wake up with butterflies in my stomach . . . three or four days ago I had a real attack of the jitters, butterflies. You actually feel it and you say to yourself 'What's happening, what's going wrong?' And, of course, my wife panics: 'What is going wrong?' It's not normal to have butterflies, I think, for no reason. I don't know what's going wrong. Nothing's going . . . I've just got a general malaise of nervousness.

Unease.

Unease—something's going to happen, something bad.

So it's like a fear?

It's a fear of something bad without my being able to put my finger on what it is.

Do you often have that feeling?

Quite often I wake up with butterflies, yes. I've had it twice this week.

So when you're happy and things are going well is that almost a fearful feeling because you're thinking 'Oh my goodness this is going well; when will it go wrong?'

No, because I'm a self-analyst.

I psychoanalyse myself ad nauseam. I'm probably sick of myself, quite frankly. I think I know myself very well and by virtue of the sort of person that I am, which I would describe as minor manic depressive, I have very high peaks and very low troughs. So I can be in a top mood now but I can't be in a normally high mood, so I have a very ebullient state and I have a very low state.

What's the ebullient state feel like?

Well, it's not the way I feel it, I think it's the perception of others who are around me. In fact, in this office they call me the Exocet missile. My repartee, for example, is not unlike Paul Keating's—I can destroy people verbally. I don't mean to hurt them because most of the people I have in the office I like, but I'm just very quick at repartee when I'm ebullient.

What else happens when you are up?

Well, of course, when things are at their best they seem so good as not to be true. This condition inevitably ends in a downer sooner than later. Over the last few months I've had fewer downers than I've had over the last few years. But typically, they used to appear three days up and one day down, three days up and one day down. Apart from just feeling terrific, there's not really much else to report to you on that.

I had a nervous breakdown in 1983 where I was down solid for, say, a year, or a year and a quarter. That manifested itself in basically being in tears all day, lying in bed, hiding under the bed covers and crying. Of course that's most demeaning for a man who . . . well I was forty at the time, or something like that, and I'd been successful, and it's an awfully weird and unpleasant feeling where you feel so helpless. I recall a story which most people don't understand. One day I was walking with my wife in London. I saw a magazine for £2, and I said to my wife, 'We can't afford it'. She said 'What do you mean?' And I said to her that I'd forgotten where all my money was. And people think I'm exaggerating, but that's exactly what happened—I could not remember where any of my money was. What was in my pocket was clear, what wasn't in my pocket I had no idea where it was. Scary.

But you came out of that breakdown. How did you come out of that?

I went into business with Wardley Australia, which is a Hong Kong bank affiliate, and I slowly started to get out of it when I could see I wasn't hopeless, because one of the things about having a nervous breakdown is one is convinced one is utterly hopeless and incompetent. But as that business with Wardley went better and better and better, I gained more and more confidence, and I think success defeated the nervous breakdown. My father had a nervous breakdown in 1961 and I think he got over it as a result of his next successful business venture.

So feeling better about yourself depended upon achieving something in business, doing it well again?

I think so, because I am certain that part of my psyche is that I have a rather large insecurity complex. I may appear to the world at large as an extrovert, I'm in fact, according to my assessment, an introvert. The test I always use of whether someone is extroverted or introverted is when one walks into a room of a hundred people—and one doesn't know a single person in the room—there are some who walk in and cope with it beautifully and they look forward to meeting the next hundred people, and there are some, like myself, who feel like going through the floor and disappearing. And I feel like going through the floor, and I think that is ultimate and positive proof of being an introvert.

So a lot of what you do, because you appear to be at ease with people, you have to put on a brave front, do you?

Undoubtedly, undoubtedly. And sometimes I'm capable of it, when I'm on my highs, and sometimes I'm actually incapable, when I'm at my lows. In fact, even with my best friends very often, when we're going out to dinner or something, I say to my wife that I don't feel like going out because I know I'm going to perform badly because I'm just not confident. And she says 'What about?' And I say 'About being interesting enough to maintain the evening at the level at which they expect me to be on the days when I am good.' Now that's the ultimate proof of total insecurity.

So you think that you have to prove that you—Rene Rivkin—are worthwhile through performing?

Yes! Yes!

Through being entertaining and . . .

Yes! Yes! The person they think I am, and the person they have grown to know and like, and the other person they don't really know. I'm the only one who knows him that well.

Are you frightened that if people really saw who was inside they may not like you any more?

Not that so much, but if I continued to be the person that I don't like, being that introverted person, then I think they'd find me less interesting.

So really you cannot often be yourself?

No. But there are two me's. There's definitely this schizoid situation where there's the me on the high and there's the me on the low, and, therefore, there are two different me's.

And you prefer one to the other?

Yes. I don't like the one who's down. He's a miserable person. He's not vicious, fortunately. All he wants to do is go to bed, put the sheet over his head and leave the rest of the world alone. And I think that if you've got to be a depressed person, then I think that's the best choice isn't it, because there are some who manifest themselves by beating their wives up, beating their kids up. That's not me. I just want to be left alone. My wife's not so good at that because she immediately gets depressed because she doesn't like when I'm depressed, so she goes depressed and instead of staying away from me, which is what I'd rather, she actually tries to be with me. So what you get is a depressive club rather than what I'd like, which is just to be left alone. It irritates me that I can't have the control over myself not to get depressed, which of course has something to do with God or the perception of God, I have no doubt in my mind. For example, one of the reasons that I am an atheist is I don't want to be controlled by anyone else, whether it's actual control or the feeling of being controlled. I want to be my own boss. I think one of the greatest pleasures that I have in life is by virtue of my financial position being independent. I can actually say what I like about things, people. I'm regarded as being outspoken, which I think I am, and that's a great pleasure, and if I were subject to organised religion and concepts of God then I don't feel that I'm the boss, as it were.

So when you were ill with the brain tumour, which was successfully removed, you weren't in control then, were you? Were you tempted to pray then?

Well, yes, of course I was. I have fixed standards for myself and my morals, and I don't want to be regarded as a hypocrite. So, yes, I was lying in hospital the day before surgery and I contemplated that I should start praying to God, then I realised that if I would do that I couldn't do it hypocritically, and if the tumour were not a malignant one and I was to survive, as I have, I would then have to go to synagogue regularly; I would have to go to the high holy days and be a properly religious Jew. And I was not prepared for that for two reasons: one is that it would make life according to my understanding of life unbearable, and secondly, I would have been a hypocrite if I had turned to it at that minute. And this was a process of several hours on that Friday. And I decided, 'damn it I will not, I will stick to my views and take a punt'. And having won the punt I'm very pleased, because in a sense, to myself, I have confirmed that my stance on God or otherwise is correct.

But what will happen if you lose control, which you would lose if you lost all this?

Well, I wouldn't cope very well with it, quite frankly. In fact, I'd be a hopeless coper. I am sure that I would have a nervous breakdown because if minor matters created a nervous breakdown in 1983, this would be regarded as a major matter by me, and I'm sure I'd have a nervous breakdown. Now once I were in that position I think it'd be very hard to recover quickly financially, but I'd imagine that you would recover from a nervous breakdown, and then by virtue of the trading skills that I have, I guess I would do it all over again. But Caroline, one of the things that I respect myself for in life is that in business I'm actually conservative. The perceptions are, in stock market circles anyway, that I'm quite a gambler. The reality is I'm a very conservative person. My having come through the 1987 stock market collapse very well proves it, to those who are interested, and confirms to me that that stance is a correct stance.

Do you know, Rene, how much you own?

I don't . . . not really I don't. People here who look after my affairs are amazed that I'm not good at that. I regard myself as an income producer and I leave it to others to look after matters relating to the revenues I produce.

It would be a matter of millions of dollars.

Oh yes.

And it would be different this morning than it is tonight?

Yes it would. Yes it would.

Is there some wonderful opportunity in that to make a difference in the world, to help where help is enormously needed?

That's, of course, a good question. The answer is that on a world scale my wealth is peanutty, and certainly I could make some people happy, whether it's ten or a hundred I don't know, whether it's a thousand. On a world scale though, it would be totally insignificant. I am active in charity work. I am, I think, a good donor. Certainly those who get money from me regard me as the softest touch they know. I like donating money to good causes. But then of course I find, oddly enough, that it produces all sorts of begging letters ad nauseam, and maybe they are good causes but my wealth is not the sort of wealth that can just keep sending money out to whoever has a worthy cause. I think some causes are worthier than others anyway.

So you have to make a judgment.

I have to make a judgment. Basically, however, this is probably unusual, because in my office we have a rule that we donate to every worthwhile charity that walks through the front door. What we do though is give more to the better causes, the causes that I'm closer to, and less to the worse causes. I know that's an unusual attitude for an organisation because usually what other organisations do is pick one or two favourite charities and the rest can get knotted, as it were. And I find that hard because they can all pull on my heart strings. I'm a real softy, Caroline.

Is there any guilt in having a lot of money when you see that others are poor and you know that people in this town live on the street?

There are brief moments, not brief moments actually, long moments, where I have pangs of conscience about it and that's the day, funnily enough, when I usually make my best donations to charity, presumably to salve my conscience.

Does it feel better after you've done that?

Well I don't know whether it feels better by virtue of it, or it would have happened anyway. I think that my wealth just isn't enough to save society. It's just not. So maybe if I had twenty billion dollars lying around, the guilt would be very strong. I don't know. But at my level I can't say that I have guilt every day, no. When I see some sort of poor case somewhere I'm—I'm a crier for a start—so whether it be a sad thing on television about some thalidomide child, some child with cancer or something, yes, I feel guilty that we're happier than others. I think that the world is an awful place, an unfair place, which gets me back to this atheist concept because

I can't believe that there is an all-powerful, benevolent God, because the evidence points precisely, if anything, to the opposite; that is, to an all powerful and malevolent God, because the world's such an unfair place.

So you take all the negative evidence you see and take it to prove that there is no God. But what of all your gifts and all the beautiful things that have come to you? You could as soon use . . .

But I'm prepared to accept a concept called luck. I think there is such a thing as luck. I think I've been very lucky, but there's no evidence to prove that God gave me the luck. The only answer that I have some difficulty with in this atheist or non-atheist debate is how did the Earth get here, how did the world get here? And I guess my answer to that, which those who are religious may find ridiculous, is that I just have to accept the concept that it always was here. The world was always here, ad infinitum going backwards, somehow or other, and it doesn't have to be by a God who is all-powerful and benevolent. I mean, it could be . . . why can't anyone accept the concept maybe there is a God, maybe he is malevolent, and maybe he's not all-powerful? That's a concept that I can understand because the evidence points that if there is a God, that is the God. If that is the God then I can't be devoted to him.

To what extent do you enjoy some peace of mind?

I don't think I have any peace of mind. I think you can only achieve peace of mind when you're totally relaxed, and totally happy. I certainly don't regard myself as totally happy because I think one can only be totally happy if one has found the reason for living, and I haven't, other than the search for minimising pain and maximising pleasure, which I think is a fairly shallow reason for the billions of people who live on Earth.

Do you keep yearning for a more satisfying reason?

Yes, I do.

Do you read, do you study? Where do you look?

No, I don't, because my entire life is devoted to stock markets and affiliated situations; that is, making money, art, and my family, and the fourth is being a good member of society. And I must say that, if I say so myself, if all members of society could be . . . not as good as I am because that sounds awfully self-patting on the back, but I just think that if all members of society were as caring as I am about fellow society, it would be a better world to live in.

Do you find then that you're thinking all the time?

Oh, all the time. It is annoyingly the case that I am thinking, all the time.

Is it like a torment?

It is a torment, oh yes, because I just cannot rid myself of thoughts that get into my mind and are not willing to leave until they're ready to leave as opposed to my wanting to eject them.

What about when you lie down to rest?

If I'm asleep then, clearly, I'm asleep.

Can you sleep?

I sleep very poorly. I sleep with the help of sleeping pills, and it's very interrupted sleep. During the week it's in the nature of four hours roughly. It can be a broken four hours, which I think can be worse than an ongoing four hours. I wake up very often bodily tired; the brain's always working, to its credit, the brain is always okay, even if I've slept one hour a night—and that's happened—the brain's just fine for the next day.

Your memory's still good?

My memory's superb. This was one of the reasons that the brain tumour was discovered, because my memory started deteriorating to the point where I kept forgetting people's names, kept switching words, and that's what I mentioned to the doctor, who then discovered the brain tumour. But fortunately, the memory's come back with 100 per cent efficiency.

You are unusually frank.

I think that if I have a charm at all, if I do, that's it: I just tell the truth.

Does it feel risky sometimes?

No, no. I don't care. No. I mean, I think I've satisfied myself that it's an acceptable way of being because I've been frank for many many years now and I can't see the down side in having been frank. I don't see that it's cost me financially, or it's cost me in health or in my family. I like it, I like telling the truth.

And, Rene, when you allow another interview, another photograph to be taken, another film to be made about yourself, when you see the results of that, does it help you better to see yourself?

No, Caroline, because I think I know myself very well. No, it doesn't help me better to see myself at all. Most of the interviews are unlike yours because they are more connected with how I make money, relating to that rather than what I think is the fairly complex human being which I know myself to be.

Is that sensitive boy who was overweight as a teenager still in there somewhere?

Sensitive certainly, undoubtedly, and undoubtedly I keep attempting to prove to myself that I am clever, successful, and all that sort of thing. I'm always trying to prove to myself that I'm good. That's undoubtedly the result of that uncertain fat little boy, yes, absolutely.

And the maximisation of pleasure, how do you do that? I mean, you're famous for beautiful parties. Do you have close friends, do you find . . . ?

I have some very close friends, yes I do. I like a variety of people. I find people in the art/journalist world—not journalist but the higher levels, not just a journalist if you like, but people who run magazines and what have you. I have a couple of very good school friends still. But I wouldn't say I had a hundred good friends. I mean, I don't think anyone does. And I think anyone who thinks they do is basically quite stupid.

What about all the people who come to the parties on which you spend very generously?

Well, yes. Firstly, I'm not the extravagant party giver that everyone thinks. That is to say that I have had one hugely extravagant party for 300 people at Hamilton Island. That was a business party, because most of the people who attended were clients of mine. I like people, but I'm often disappointed by people.

You love beautiful things very much—how do you feel about ugliness when you encounter it?

I'm often accused of employing people around me who are good looking rather than bad looking, by the way.

Do you do that?

I think either consciously or unconsciously, the answer's yes. I don't know if you noticed my secretary, she's very attractive; and if you notice the people here generally, I think they're quite good-looking people. But I'm prepared to accept ugliness in the world—I have no choice really—but I think that the world, as I have said to you, is a very beautiful place, subject to the negative influence that human beings have had upon it. I once went to Rio de Janeiro, which I think is the most stunningly located, topographical situation. It's one of the ugliest cities I've ever been to. I hate it. And, of course, human beings spoilt it. Prior to the human being it was sensational. So I think the world is a beautiful place.

Do you ever find yourself envying people who live perhaps more ordinary lives?

Yes, indeed I do—and it sounds ridiculous. I think it always happens on a downer rather than an upper. It's often happened to me when I drive to the office at 6.00 or 6.30 in the morning, as I often do, and I see a garbage truck, of all the illogical situations. I see a garbo with his truck and think how lucky he is. I think to myself how lucky he is because he doesn't have a care in the world, he doesn't aspire to art or to Rolls Royces or to overseas trips. Their expectations are far less, their work is not mentally demanding; they just go and do it and then they pursue the simpler pleasures than I have, and they're obviously at peace with the world, I think. Maybe I'm totally wrong. But I think that provided the average man in the street has enough to keep himself in a decent style of accommodation with decent food and a decent holiday once a year, I'm sure that that person is happier than I am.

You could choose to be more like that person?

Well no, you couldn't, because one of the things about getting to where I've got is it's always easier to be on an incline than to go down from where you've been. Once you've had those things it's much harder not to have them than if you've never had them. About that I'm not in any doubt. So the person who's never seen or been, if you like, in a Rolls Royce or a Mercedes Benz, he doesn't aspire to one. Once you've had them you actually want them very badly and you'd hate to then not have them.

Do you ever catch a bus?

I haven't been on a bus for thirty years, no.

A train?

No, no. But, I mean, that's not evidence of anything other than the fact that I live five minutes' or seven minutes' drive from the city. I have parking here and there's no need for me to do it. If it satisfies your question at all, my kids often go on the train.

Do you clean your own shoes?

No, I don't. I don't clean my own shoes, I have a butler who does that. No, I mean, I don't deny that the perception of my lifestyle by others would be that this guy is intensely lucky and ought to be intensely happy. But, of course, that's the point—what others think should be the case has no relevance. It is what one thinks of one's self. So that if I think that I'm blissfully happy, that's fine. If I think that I'm quite unhappy for vast sections of my life, then that is the case, and what others perceive is irrelevant.

I think the world's actually got it all wrong in terms of attempting to increase people's wealth, if you like. Redistribution of wealth is always the argument. What you have to seek to do is to redistribute happiness, but not wealth, because I have a firm conviction that wealth doesn't make you happy, it makes you unhappy if you had wealth and lost it. But for those who've never had it, who've had a happy life until that point, if you add wealth into the equation it often makes them unhappy.

So what now do you most hope for in life?

There's only one thing I could possibly hope for and that is to minimise the displeasure of growing old and the infirmity that it seems inevitably to bring in old people. I mean, all I want to do is to die as healthy as possible. I don't want to linger until I'm seventy or eighty or ninety, with arthritis or with one leg or with some condition, some vile condition. If I died tomorrow it wouldn't worry me one bit. Now my wife always complains that that's dreadfully selfish because I'm needed for my five children and so on and so forth, but if you take aside that consideration, whether I'm scared of death—not at all. If I died tomorrow that would be fine by me because I've experienced in my forty-four years all there is to experience really, apart from having grandchildren and growing old. The experience of having grandchildren is probably a good one, though it's very hard to argue that growing old and infirm is a good experience to wait for.

What else do you hope for?

There's nothing else left. I mean, you only have to take the experience of life, there's nothing else to hope for.

You say you haven't experienced peace.

I don't believe I will. I have no false belief that I will experience peace. I think you are either capable of doing it or not capable of doing it. I think that one might take up yoga or all sorts of attempts to do so, but I guess I'm dogmatic enough in my views and, if you like, my respect for my intellect, which I do have—I believe I know the answers in advance. Now I believe that if I took up yoga it wouldn't create the peace that people think yoga might create. Certainly, I think it would create one hour of peace a day, that hour that you do yoga in, but it doesn't affect the problems and ills of the world.

Maybe you don't really want peace?

Oh, I think that you're part of the way there. I think that I am a masochist, and I think that I'm happy being unhappy, a little bit. I went not so long ago to a funeral, a Catholic funeral, and really, since my brother died in 1979, I was very bad at funerals for the first four or five years. I either couldn't go or I was hopelessly in tears; embarrassingly so, loud, and so on and so forth. After those four or five years I was then able to cope. Anyway, I recently went to a Catholic funeral, and the priest was an Irish priest, and he walked in with a smile and it was all happy and beautiful and wonderful, and I couldn't believe I was at a funeral—it was like having fun. And the bereaved daughter of the woman who died didn't look bereaved—she wasn't happy; but the rest of the people were basically happy. I thought, 'How beautiful'. Drove out and thought to myself, 'God, I couldn't cope with that'. I think there are times to be unhappy, and a time to be unhappy is when there is a death of someone you love. And I thought to myself, 'Well, if my wife dies or my mother dies, I would almost feel an indebtedness to her to be unhappy'. It's almost like being unfaithful. Now whether that's the Jewish psyche or the psyche of someone somewhat demented, I don't know.

When you look at this beautiful Buddha you have in the boardroom here, what comes to you?

Nothing, other than beauty. The enormous beauty and serenity in it, because oddly enough, whether it be Buddha or Christ or the cross itself—if I were permitted I'd collect crucifixes, I find it a very peaceful thing and I've often wanted to buy my wife a beautiful crucifix to wear, but my parents would think that I'd gone around the bend. So peace and serenity and beauty. Nothing else though particularly, just pleasure that I have it.

Could you say any more about the serenity of the cross?

Not really. It just seems to me that for some reason the Christ on the cross is a most inspiring thing. I can't put into words why. I think it's terribly sad that someone was crucified—he was quite good looking—it was all in the cause of nothing, didn't achieve anything for any purpose because I think that the world would be better without Christianity versus Judaism versus Islam.

But the symbol of Christ on the Cross?

It's just a beautiful serene thing. I like serenity. Incidentally, I don't know if you realise that that is the test of a good-quality madonna, or the good-quality Buddha, or the good-quality crucifix—the serenity in the face of Christ, or His mother, or Buddha. The more serenity you see, the more in the art world it is regarded as a better version of that particular subject. It is the test.

Paul Field

This conversation is about family. It's about how parents imprint their children with ideas about what matters. It's about love, music, fun and faith. It's about how to help ourselves and other people at a time of loss for which there is no explanation, only mystery and suffering. It's about how we need to register in our bodies as well as in our minds the vital experiences of our lives.

Paul Field is lead singer of a band called The Cockroaches *They've enjoyed quite a following across Australia.*

Paul was born in 1961. He's married to Pauline. He's also a teacher; Pauline has an economics degree. They've had three children: Luke, Bernadette and Clare. The pattern of travelling for a popular band has allowed Paul good long stretches at home to know and help care for his young family. One of the children they were not to know for very long: for no apparent reason, this healthy, unusually contented little girl died in her cot in 1988 and for a while the world fell apart for all the people in her orbit.

How Paul and Pauline went through the experience lies at the heart of this conversation.

To begin, Paul Field remembers his own childhood.

PAUL FIELD: My fondest memories of growing up as a kid are often things like Christmasses and birthdays, which were great, purely because of the numbers—I mean in a family as big as mine you've got an instant party. And things like Midnight Mass at Christmas . . . well, it's obviously an exciting time with that many kids. But also, Mum would play the organ at Midnight Mass and, even as a young bloke, Midnight Mass would be very moving—they'd have violins playing and the girls singing and so on . . . to tears, really—you'd be that moved . . .

So, thinking of things that have helped form what I did later on, I'd say music was a really big part of my upbringing. And it's a big part, actually, of the church too—it's always been singing and so on; it's seen as a good thing and something enjoyable.

Any strong expectations on the part of your mother and father that you would follow this or that profession?

Not in professions, no. They certainly wanted us to learn an instrument, for a start. All of us were taught an instrument . . . I was taught piano, a couple of my brothers learnt violin and so on. That was the only real thing that they said had to be done really. They wanted us at least to have the chance of learning and after a few years a couple of us weren't so good at it and they were let off, they didn't have to continue. But those who did well at it, were certainly . . . well, encouraged to keep it up. Apart from that, it was really whatever you would like to do and whatever you enjoyed doing—go for it!

Even when you and your brothers said, 'Well, for us it's going to be a rock band'?

Yeah, well, we were still at school when we started playing. Thinking back on it now—I'm putting myself in their position—I'd have given them a bit of a worry, I suppose. But they thought it was great, they were very proud of us playing in a band.

Even when they could see that maybe that was going to be your work, your principal work, as well?

Yes, they always have—they think it's great to be able to make a living out of music. As I said, Mum loves music, she really lives for it. And so do a lot of us—most of the family. It's great to be able to make a living out of doing it.

My father was a chemist in the outer suburbs of Sydney, in an area that is basically working class. When we first moved in there, it was certainly just houses plonked on dirt, there were no services and so on. The area was full of babies and so, being a chemist in an area like that, he really grew up knowing all the kids and getting to know them very well. And as they got older, he started to treat them for—not nappy rash and things like that—but for things like drug problems and he became involved in that. He dispensed methadone, he treated addicts, and counselled addicts as well. And there are a lot of people now . . . I've moved back into the area—and it's a great feeling, people come and say, 'I've got a lot of time for your father . . . ', and so on. It's a really warm feeling hearing that.

Did you and the others get drawn into the drug culture at any stage?

No. Being in a band you do certainly come across it at a very early age, and we were certainly offered a lot of stuff. I mean, anything you wanted really, you'd come across, but because of the experience with my father and growing up in an area where you see people 'OD' and things like that, there was . . . it offered no attraction, there was no romanticism to drugs at all. It was very black and white to us. And so, once you let people know that, they're fine, they then stop offering, which is great.

Will you say something about what it meant to you to meet Pauline . . . and to enter into married life?

Yes. It was a very physical thing when I met Pauline . . . you hear of literally having your breath taken away from you, and it really was like that: every time I saw her, I had a 'stomach feeling' about it. I met her through friends. When you fall in love it's like that—when she came into a place, even if I hadn't spoken to her I'd be lifted—and it was just a great exciting feeling anytime I saw her. She tells me it was much the same, which is good. It was fairly easy to do, I didn't really have to work that hard in the sense that we got on very well, you know what I mean? We got on incredibly well from the moment we spoke to each other and it was great.

It was a fairly reckless kind of life, my first couple of years out of school. I'd finish work and go into town to see a band or so, and in those days (this is before random breath testing) you'd certainly drink a bit in a hotel and drive home—there were no worries about that. And quite a few times I . . . because I lived a long way out from town, I'd be dozing at the wheel—and I've said it on a number of occasions, that 'I was looked after'—I really was. They say falling asleep at the wheel is not the best thing to do and that happened to me on a number of occasions. After meeting Pauline, I took a bit of care of myself really, there was someone to do that for. You wanted to do things for her and certainly, as a teenager, wanting to do things for other people really doesn't enter into your mind, I don't think.

And then when you have a baby, whoa! That's even more so like that. I really did want to have children. I loved being in a big family and my mother, she has a great love of babies and so on and it must be in my blood, I think. I know my father wasn't allowed to attend any of our births and Mum often said that that was wrong, that he wasn't.

We wanted a baby as soon as we were married and it was . . . we announced it to everyone as soon as we became pregnant and it was big news. And so, being at the birth . . . there was no question for me that I had to go along. And it's quite an amazing experience. Anyone who's having a baby should, for a number of reasons, firstly to see what your wife goes through. I don't think there's anything that could compare to that—you know, the pain, physically, . . . and so on. In Luke's case, our first baby, it was a thirty-hour labour, which is incredible.

And you also witness the miracle of life when you see a baby being born. I know that's said a lot, but it's very true . . . as soon as they're out and they breathe and so on. And also, as far as I'm concerned, the first person or people that should welcome the baby to the world should be the parents, not someone you don't know. And that's what you should be there for—number one: 'Welcome to the world, our baby.'

And then, Bernadette was to come next . . .

Yes.

You were there for her birth too, no doubt.

And Bernadette's birth was equally as happy. Between Luke and Bernadette, Pauline miscarried and . . . miscarriage is also more a personal thing than the loss of a baby. You grieve still, but not a lot of people understand about a miscarriage, particularly if you look forward to . . . I mean, you look forward, you anticipate the birth of a baby, and if you believe that's a life inside—which we do—a miscarriage is incredibly traumatic. And so, we had one in between Luke and Bernadette. So her birth was another great lift for us.

And she was to be with you . . . not for very long.

No, no. She only lived seven and a half months.

Pauline's Mum and Dad hadn't seen the babies as much as, say, my relatives, who live close to us. And they spent that week with them and they were just revelling in the happiness. And it was September 2nd, which is the National Cot Death Day—it was the Red-Nose Day. Pauline's Mum and Dad had been to Mass and they'd come back and Pauline and Luke had woken up and they were having breakfast and they were watching the 'Today Show' and the people on the show were wearing red noses. And they were just discussing with each other the pros and cons of that—you know whether it was a good idea and Pauline was just saying, 'Oh yeah, I think no matter what they do, as long as they can raise money and awareness and so on, I think it's great.' And she literally went from there in to get Bernadette. Her head was under the blanket, she was turned the wrong way round, but all babies do that—Luke did it all the time. But she said, from the moment she walked in she knew something was wrong, it was just too still. And, anyway, she found her dead and just screamed out and she carried her into the kitchen and tried to do mouth-to-mouth and couldn't and they were saying, 'No, she's alive, she's alive!'

Anyway, they were beeping the horn when they got to the hospital and the people raced out and just wheeled her away. And a few minutes later a guy just came out and told her that she was dead. And then they cleaned her up and brought her out to Pauline and she was able to nurse her for hours and hours and hours, which was great for her to be able to do.

In my case, I was on tour . . . one of these fortunate things again: my father, who had just retired, had come on tour with us, which was just an impulsive thing that he wanted to do, and we were having a great time with him—he was really enjoying it.

And he was sharing the room with me as well . . . I went in to have a shower and he came in and . . . I just had the towel around me and he put his hand on my shoulder and said, 'Come out.' And it was kind of like, at first I thought, 'Strike, what have I done?' It was something very serious, I knew. And he just sat me down and . . . Pauline has a sister named Bernadette as well and he said, 'Bernadette's dead,' and I said 'Which one?', and he said, 'Your Bernadette, your baby.' And I can just . . . I think I just yelled or let out some yell of some description and . . . I spoke of the stomach feeling that you get say, when you fall in love, well, this was a very physical feeling as well—it was like the wind being knocked out of me. And I just kept saying 'The poor little thing, the poor little thing . . . ' And then I just went back into the bathroom and cried and cried and then packed and—I was quite stupefied really—they drove me to the airport and I really didn't know what to do, what I could do . . . that's the feeling of helplessness at that stage. And you'd see babies at the airport and so on and it was like twisting the knife almost, it was quite unbearable. And I rang a mate of mine who I used to teach with—to touch base with, I think; I don't know why. They'd been informed, which was good. And it was just good to be able to cry and talk to him over the phone, which was important at that stage.

And then I arrived back home many many hours later, in the early evening, and I said to Dad, 'Oh, look, I've got to go home to get some gear.' (This was before we went up to Pauline's parents' place.) I didn't have to get some gear: what I wanted to do was to just go into Bernadette's room, which I did. And the same thing again—just to touch base, or something—I went into her bedroom and . . . picked up her blanket and things and smelled them and . . . that was really good to be able to do because . . . she wasn't there, but you could smell her, it was almost like she'd just been there, though they'd been gone nearly a week. And then I drove up and met Pauline, and as I walked through, I don't think I said anything to the rest of them, it was just, 'Where's Pauline?' And we just hugged each other and cried and cried and she then explained what happened and so on. Luke slept with us that night, in the bed with us. And she just basically went over everything that happened and we talked all night really, which is good to be able to do.

The next day a few friends drove up to meet us. It was hard for a lot of people to know what to say to us.

In the days and the weeks that followed, what was helpful and what wasn't helpful?

One thing I've learnt is, certainly, just to say what you really feel, and the simplest thing is 'I'm sorry that Bernadette's dead,' or 'I'm sorry for what's happened . . . ' When people say things like that, it really is like—just temporarily but nonetheless for that moment—they're in touch with you. It's like a weight lifting and you think 'Thank you'—that's what you really feel like and that's all they need to say.

People really do mean well and they want to say the right thing. They want desperately for you to stop grieving—which is the problem, I think. And this is something we've learnt: that people don't like to see you crying and wailing and weeping, but our baby—and whoever you lose, whether it's your mother or your sister or brother or your own baby—deserves a million tears, and they deserve to be mourned. And a lot of societies do that really well: you know, they let you go for it, and you need to, you physically need to do it; if on no other level, you need to be able to do that. And it was strange, a couple of times I was told . . . no, on a number of times I was told to be strong for Pauline. But that wasn't true because Pauline needed me to be myself and it's illogical to stop crying about the death of your daughter. I think there'd be something wrong if, for example, Pauline didn't cry; and I feel it no less. And that was the strange thing, anyway: a lot of people assume that perhaps the father has less of a mourning.

It's certainly different to a mother's, it *is* different—I didn't carry her in my womb for nine months and so, obviously, there is a difference. But nonetheless, that was my baby. So, while at least between Pauline and myself we were able to cry and talk non-stop (which was great for us), with a lot of other people I wasn't able to: it was Pauline's problem almost, or something she needs help for. So if there's one thing you learn there, it is to firstly say you're sorry but, also, let people grieve because they need to and they deserve to.

I went on tour because we were recording an album, well, the album was out shortly after she died and I had to go on the road. I was given the option, 'Do you want to?' but this is my livelihood and we had to, really.

So we toured. And whilst we were back in Queensland, it was very warm and sunny and the rest of it, but I hadn't really been able to pour it all out and being away from Pauline also was . . . it was a terrible time to be away from her . . . and I became very angry and frustrated within myself. I've read a number of things actually, about how you can develop sicknesses or symptoms that are related to your loved ones' death, and cot death, we thought—at least at that stage—had something to do with breathing . . . But anyway, when I was up there I developed pneumonia—incredible pains in the lungs and I found it very hard to breathe and so on . . .

. . . and coldness . . .

Yes, I was knocked flat by it. It was like my body was physically grieving.

While I was up there, I kept in contact a lot with Pauline, obviously, on the phone but there was one point in time where I think I reached the lowest I've ever felt, the most alone I've ever felt, the most depressed I've ever felt. The sadness of her loss just hit me and I can remember walking round whatever town it was at night and just crying and there was no one to cry to and I couldn't speak to anyone about it. I mean, who could understand anyway? That's the feeling you get. And so I then rang Pauline and at first I was almost not communicating really with her, I was just talking about things. But she could tell I was upset and eventually it came out: I said how bad I felt and that was a good release anyway, but I said, 'Look, I need . . . . ' (Pauline had been going to a counsellor) and I said 'I need to do this, too,' and I did.

So you went together?

Yes, and that's very important. I know a number of people who've . . . you know, perhaps the husband hasn't gone or the wife hasn't gone. I think it's very important that you both go.

Why is that?

Because you get to hear some things that . . . even as much as we had talked to each other, you hear things that you weren't aware of and you get to understand what they're going through. Because although we're as close as anyone could be, her grieving is different from mine. And there are days when she feels fine about it and I don't, and there are days when I feel fine about it and she doesn't.

So are there things that you'll say in the presence of a third party that make the situation even clearer than your own dialogue.

Yes . . . I was told so many times 'Be strong for Pauline' kind of thing and eventually you do things like that. You might feel incredibly sad one day or you might have a thought that seems . . . I would often go up to the shop with Luke and, in the supermarket I got quite angry a number of times. Kids behave terribly sometimes in the shops—scream, and the rest of it—but also sometimes parents are very short with them, and that used to really bug me. I felt like going up to them and saying—this sounds terrible—'You don't deserve to have a child!' That sounds terrible, as I said, but that's the thought you have. And what really bugged us as well was that it seemed so unfair that we who wanted babies so much . . . and Bernadette was so well loved and so well looked after and there are so many babies who are not wanted and not well cared for and not looked after . . . why us? I mean, if there is a plan that God has or whatever, he got it wrong—that's what you feel.

I certainly still believed in God—I believe that God is love, and so I believed in that. That's what kept us going—that was the only thing that kept us going—the love for one another and the love we felt for Bernadette. That's what hurt so much. But we were also very angry with God for that very reason: so many babies aren't wanted, but ours was; so why? And it's not as if I've got a direct answer to that, as such, but we spoke with a number of people. The counselling was one thing, but on the spiritual level . . . the first priest, actually, that I spoke to the day after Bernadette died didn't even mention Bernadette's death. He just kind of dropped in to say g'day, and I think he thought I was just a young bloke and the rest of it—I don't know what he thought—but he didn't even mention her death, and that infuriated me.

I'm glad he wasn't the only priest that spoke to us, but a bloke who I came to know through teaching, Father Paul Glynn, a Marist Father, who had spent most of his life after the Second World War in Japan, in Nagasaki—and you talk of grieving and loss: well, there's a large amount of it there, obviously! He spoke to me on the phone a number of times and he spoke to myself and Pauline together a number of times. He was just talking through her death on a number of levels and just as he spoke to us—I mentioned before sometimes it was like a physical thing—it was like a release, and that's a real gift. You speak of the power of the Holy Spirit, or whatever: I think he certainly had it. He spoke about Our Lady going through the same thing, not only the loss, but witnessing it like she did, and so on. He mentioned the whole idea of sacrifice and, really, in our faith, that's a big part of it: Christ himself had to be sacrificed. It's a terrible idea, really, the whole idea of sacrificing, but out of things that are terrible, completely terrible, sometimes good can come. And, particularly shortly after your baby's died, you can see nothing good coming out of it—there's nothing good about death—but over the time good *has* come of it: we're certainly better people from it; our love is deeper for each other; and, certainly, we have a lot more compassion for people who have gone through traumas, whether it's death or whatever. You really can feel for them on a real level, and there have been a couple of times when that's really helped some people.

On our behalf, it makes you very aware that death is a part of life. I suppose, in some ways, before Bernadette's death we were quite naive to ignore that. Life is very precarious: any one of us could die for whatever reason, and we don't live in a perfect world—that's the reality.

Does it make you value life more, do you think?

Yes. Yes, I mentioned before about our society saying 'Be strong' and things like that; well, it shuts things off and that's bad. For example, just the whole thing of: 'if you get a pain, take a pill'; 'if you've got a problem, have a Bex and a good lie-down'—that whole idea, rather than talk rather than, 'Well, okay, this is really bad, but that's part of life.' The whole emphasis is on escaping from it and that's perhaps why so many people can't respond to death because there's no escape from it. Everything else is like, you know, there's a very simple answer to it—as I say, take a pill or have a drink or go out on the town or something, and forget about it. But with death you can't: it's always there. It's like an eclipse: if there was an eclipse of the sun, life would continue but everything's different. When it happened, and for many, many months after Bernadette died, I really didn't think I could be happy again, truly. I mean, I could laugh at various times and that's funny, because sometimes you feel, 'Oh, I shouldn't be laughing,' but, see, we had Luke, who's three years old, and he got us through that. He continued to give us great enjoyment.

You see, for many people an experience like that is the cruncher, isn't it? You hear many people say, 'That was the end of meaning: we could not make sense of that, so don't talk to me about God, or faith, or meaning, or purpose, or anything else.' And yet here you are, saying, I think, that you can't entirely make sense of it; it's desperately painful, but death is part of life; there is a mystery in that, yet somehow life goes on; and, yes, somehow one can be happy again.

Yes, well, being the age I am, I'm very lucky; because Pauline was pregnant within two weeks of Bernadette dying. That was our response to it, that we wanted another baby—not as a replacement at all, but on a lot of levels. Just to give us that happiness again, perhaps. And, on another level, Pauline was robbed of the experience of raising her daughter and so it was a natural feeling to want that back. But the pregnancy was very hard, particularly for her, because she was torn between . . . not torn, actually—this is important: you have both feelings, but both feelings can exist, that you grieve all the time for Bernadette and also you look forward to this baby. And we both felt so, perhaps, guilty, because as the pregnancy developed it made Bernadette's death even sadder. It was like we were saying goodbye, almost, you know? And it was a very hard time emotionally, for Pauline more so, carrying this new baby. You'd think, 'This poor baby, it's not getting the feelings we should be giving it.' But once she was born it was changed: we did honestly feel that happy again. Up to that point . . . as I say, I really do get a great feeling with babies, but I couldn't . . . it was like twisting the knife every time you'd pick up a baby, and it really was, it was unbearable. And that changed with the birth of Clare, our new daughter, and we felt great again. We still mourn the loss of Bernadette and we feel happy about the birth of Clare.

That's such a deep and important point that you've made, to me, anyway: that contradictory emotions don't have to cancel each other out. That's not the aim one has to seek. Somehow we can let those contradictory feelings exist together.

It is, because particularly . . .

That's hard, too!

Wel, if you're doing it by yourself that's where you become overwhelmed by it all, because that's the thing with grief: it's not as if, okay, Monday I'll feel like this, Tuesday it's less, Wednesday it's less, and Thursday . . . it doesn't work that way. That's an important notion, too. Because other people think, all right, it's been so many years, or so many months, since whoever died, and people who haven't experienced it would say, 'Oh, she's over that now', or 'He's over that now'—well, that's rubbish. You don't get over something like that; it's always there. The perspective can change: like now, with the birth of Clare, Bernadette's death has a different perspective. Whereas before it was quite bleak, there was no light, well, Clare has let light in on that death. I mean, you can feel good twenty years later about winning the lottery or something great that happened to you—you know, getting married, or whatever—why can't you feel bad about something so many years later? And you do.

And the worst thing is—speaking about what can other people do—is that after a certain time the subject's kind of closed and they feel it should be with you, too. Particularly during the pregnancy with Clare, with some of my friends it was my only topic of conversation. And I started to get a bit worried about it, I thought, 'Strike, people will walk across the other side of the street eventually, because every time I speak to them, no matter what we start off speaking about, Bernadette's death comes into it.' But it was so necessary for me to do that and they understood. But you get a bit worried about that.

Particularly touring around like I do, I meet a lot of people and it's funny how someone meets you and they see a wedding ring on your finger (I'm the only married guy in the band) and they say, 'Oh, you're married, are you? Got any kids? How many?' And I'm never going to see this person again, but for a while there it was disloyal to Bernadette to say 'Just one'—I had to give them the full story, 'Oh, well, we had two but my daughter died.' And it feels terrible to have to do that—I mean, people's reaction is shock, and in a lot of cases they didn't want to hear that—they were just making conversation. Then for a while there I could *not* mention that. After a while, though, you get the choice—you don't have to tell everyone; you can choose who you tell that to, people you feel at ease with and so on, and that's another weight off your shoulders after a while. But certainly until that time, if you catch a bus or something, you feel like telling the guy sitting next to you what has happened to you. That's the biggest thing—you really do feel like telling people, and you *need* to. And if people don't let you, then you get very twisted inside. That's very important, and I suppose you could, but it's very hard to do that alone . . . even your wife and yourself or your friend and yourself, or whoever, you need to be able to talk with someone about that. We found with the counselling that that was the avenue, and with a number of other people, too.

Guilt's a big thing. You certainly go through everything, and Pauline was very concerned about the autopsy report. They said it was cot death, but she wanted to see if there was anything she could have done and so on, whereas in my case it didn't concern me that much. She was dead. So that was a different reaction.

And was there any explanation that was satisfying?

Oh, not medically, anyway. No, there was a healthy baby that died, full stop. It is a mystery but then again, there are now breakthroughs with cot death. They're talking now of being able to do a blood test at birth determining whether a baby is likely to, perhaps, die of it, or not. It would be amazing if they could do that, and that's Australian research that's going on.

Yes. And through your music you work, I think, to support that research.

Yes, it's important to mark important days for yourself when grieving the loss of someone. Bernadette's birthday is only a few months after she died—she was born in January, you see—and we happened to be in Melbourne together so we went to Mass. My brothers came along with me, which was great, and we just wept throughout Mass. But that was really important to do, to mark it. I organised a concert to raise money for research into cot death. It was on a small scale when I first started—I thought just ourselves and perhaps another band or two—and I sent letters around to various people and the response was fantastic. It still surprises me to hear of the number of people who have had some contact with it—the death of a child, or cot death itself. It touched a chord with everyone, and it was great. The music industry, for all the clichés and the sordid tales about what it's like (which are true as well), responds well to a lot of things, whether it's the environment or this issue, and that's a really good thing about it

And when you sing, is Bernadette sometimes in the singing?

Yes; not all the time, but yes, in every show I do she is, I suppose. Not every song—it's just not appropriate—but often in love songs and so on I do think of her. It's interesting: when we went back on the road shortly after her death a young girl was up the front at the stage and I was midway through a song . . . Some people occasionally tug on your leg or want to say something or request a song, or something like that, but she was quite persistent. And it might have been in an instrumental break, or something, but I ducked my head down and she said, 'I was sorry about Bernadette's death.' At the time I really didn't know how to handle it. I thought, 'Oh, thanks, that's really nice of her,' but on the other hand it was very strange. But obviously she'd read about it and wanted to say something and that was the only way she could communicate with me and, looking back on it now, I think it's lovely.

But she is, she certainly is there. We recorded a song shortly after she died, and we did a filmclip for a song called 'You and Me', which is basically a love song, and my mother can't watch the clip nowadays because it was a week or two after the funeral, and although it is supposedly a love song I look at it now and I can see it, too, in a number of the live appearances we did on TV and also the clip: it's like a mourning song, really, when I'm singing it—you can see it on my face.

To be a person like yourself who takes part in worship, who takes part in religious ritual, requires the embrace of a mystery. Does the contemplation, or just the acceptance, or the being there in that situation, speak in any helpful way to you about what's happened with Bernadette's death?

Well, there are a number of things there about going to Mass: for example, I speak about the warmth and the embrace of being in a big family; well, going to Mass is like that for me. It's quite hard to explain, but after you've been to Communion and you've been to Mass you feel good: there's something about a lot of people being there and praying and so on. There are some times when you do get a lot out of what is said in explaining the mystery, and so on. That's why we go every week, because you get a bit out of it every time. Oh, there are some times when you don't, but there are some times when you do, and you keep going back because the times that you do, through the words that are spoken or just the singing of a hymn or the good feeling that you get out of it, it's worth it in itself to go. The mystery—how do you explain it? It's like . . . you know, until you've witnessed a birth you can't realise . . . they can tell you what happens but it's very hard to explain the mystery of why a baby's suddenly breathing when minutes before it was inside the womb, and then suddenly everything switches and it's into living mode. I couldn't explain that. Doctors can't really explain it: they can tell you what happened but . . .

You can't explain it but you experience it.

You experience it, that's exactly right. And you do when you go to Mass, and not only just in Mass . . . I pray a lot. There's a few of the formal prayers that I say a lot, probably to Our Lady. I went to a Marist school which, I suppose, emphasised the importance of Our Lady and praying to her. And I pray a lot to Bernadette now, too. Father Glynn spoke of doing that; his younger brother died before he was born and he was told to pray to him. It takes a while before you can grasp the idea of that but it's a comfort sometimes, too. We ask her now to look after us and help us through the loss of her, and that's good to be able to do.

So, you've got a lot to give the world and the community, haven't you? You're a teacher, you're a musician, you're a husband, father, a man of the community, a man who's suffered. How do you see your gifts and what you have to contribute now to life?

I think firstly, what I've got to give—whatever that is, the few things that you mentioned—you certainly give that to your family first, and if you do that well, then it reaches the community. It's through Bernadette's death that we're reaching the wider community now. My father has always said that the best thing you can do for your kids is to love your wife and show it, which he has done, and that's a great thing to go by.

As though that radiates out?

Yes, that whole idea. It really does, you know, so whatever gifts you have, that's the way you do it. It's the same with Pauline: she's got an economics degree and all sorts of things on a formal level, but the way she reaches others is on a completely different level and that's in the love of her children, the love of me, and so on, and that's what touches other people. And that's what is important in life—it really is. In times of desperation, like we were in, it doesn't matter what job you do or what your income is, or anything like that. It's said a lot, but that is the truth. It doesn't matter: none of those things matter. It's if you can give love and be loved, really, that's the biggest thing in life. I mentioned believing that this is not a perfect world; well, I think these things can happen and it's how we respond to them as to what we become, and it's very important to be true to yourself as far as that goes. And the thing about my parents encouraging what we wanted to do . . . well, that's the way it should be. Music is one of the great things in my life. It's not everyone's cup of tea and the music we make's not everyone's cup of tea, either, but it's very important to my life, and if they'd said, 'Hey, you won't be able to make a living,' or, 'It's a bit iffy, as far as a life goes; we want you to do this,' that would have been disastrous. And that happens a lot with people, doesn't it?

Is it all of a piece—your religion, your family life, your fatherhood, your marriage, your music—is it somehow all part of the same fabric, or are they in different compartments?

No, it is part of the same fabric. I suppose you don't necessarily think of that all the time, but I do now. For me, anyway, the Catholic Church is certainly a family thing. People often joke that if you come from a big family it must be Catholic—as if you're handed orders, or something like that, and you're doing this because you're a Catholic. Well, that's not true: it's only that the family's seen as something great to belong to. And it's the same in my case: I enjoy so much being a part of that, and the faith, as well, and the rest of it. And, as I mentioned before, music is a part of our faith, too. It's been a great thing throughout the ages. It can pick you up, it can put you in touch with feelings that you didn't think you had. There are pieces of music now that I really think of Bernadette when I hear. For example, we have some Irish friends; well, at the funeral these two friends were just here from Northern Ireland and they have great voices, and they knew this song—actually, I think it's a Scottish song—'Will Ye Go, Lassie, Go?' which the Clancy Brothers used to sing; it's actually about the loss of a relationship. The first verse is so beautiful. (The last verse, though, is a typically Irish thing: if she won't be with me, then I'll find another—so we changed that.) Anyway, they sang that at the funeral and it was beautiful; it was great. The whole church was able to mourn through that song. The funeral, as far as the Catholic faith goes, is something that is very different from what I've seen elsewhere.

How different?

Well, it's a celebration of the life that was and, also, not only the life that was—because she only lived seven months—but the love that that brought and the love that still exists. That's the thing—the love that we had for Bernadette came from within us, and that's important to know; that hasn't died. So it's a celebration of a lot of those things. And it's also important because all the prayers that you go through in the funeral are also part of the grieving, and it's important to do that: it's a marking of their death and their life. I didn't see Bernadette after she died—and I've since read and talked to a lot of people—and it would have been good if I did. It was kind of like her body had been taken to a different place. I was just asked over the phone 'Would you like to see the body?' and the natural response to that is 'I wouldn't *like* to!' Someone, perhaps, should have advised me that it's good in your grieving to see the body. Well, I didn't, so my way of working through the grief was being very involved in the funeral, and I spoke at the funeral for a long time about her death. It was very hard to do but I wanted to do it and I felt release after I had spoken. I also carried her coffin from the car to the graveside—it was very small, obviously—and I don't think I'll ever do anything as hard as that again in my life. I knew what I was going to do, but as soon as I touched it . . . it's the same thing again, a very primitive reaction I suppose—a noise came out of me:

I groaned, that's what I did, I groaned. But I'm glad I did that, because if you don't, you'll miss out on this grieving: you won't get in touch with a lot of things within yourself and it will just bank up on you—if you don't do these things. That was great advice and the funeral was a real way of getting involved in that. It was full of music. It was full of beauty, full of love, which is what Bernadette was, and it should be that way. It was strange, too. It was a big funeral, as you know. We had musicians, we had my friends singing, we had lots of things like that. And people's reactions were different, too—some friends didn't go to the funeral; people we'd known for a long time didn't go to the funeral. I think, on their behalf, they wouldn't have known what to say or they didn't think it was right to go, or something, but it is certainly part of the Catholic faith that everyone's in it: if it's death, you're all in there, and that's the great thing about it. But it's a pity; there's a few friendships that have been changed because of that—you don't feel as close to them any more, which is sad.

And a few others you've gained, I suppose, that you didn't have before.

Oh, of course! People who respond to the situation you feel very close to, you know. And mentioning how you've changed—well, there you go—there are people we're now in contact with that we weren't beforehand, and they tell us that their lives have been enriched through this experience, too.

There's the whole idea that, as far as we are concerned, where Bernadette is, we're being asked to go there, and we will be reunited.

Mary Graham

Mary Graham is an elder of the Kombumerri people of south-east Queensland, lecturer at Queensland University, consultant on Aboriginal Affairs and member of the Aboriginal Reconciliation Council established by the Prime Minister. She's had years of involvement in Aboriginal concerns in the areas of human rights, welfare, health and legal services.

Mary is a chess player, a devotee of Russian films, the mother of a son in his twenties, a freelance editor for Queensland University Press, and currently writing with Lilla Watson a book on Aboriginal perspectives.

As a young woman, puzzled and alarmed by western culture and behaviour, Mary took to the books for answers: to the classics of western literature, poetry and philosophy. One of her favourites was Voltaire; he advised her to doubt everything.

In the years since, Mary Graham has been on a long journey through the history of thought, to arrive home to a reconfirmation of the validity of her own Aboriginal way. But that journey in education equips her brilliantly to draw insightful contrasts between the western way, which she finds seductive, and the Aboriginal way, in their attitudes to democracy, to individuality, to silence, to identity, to metaphysics. She talks about the need for a collective spiritual identity in Australia. She speaks of the Aboriginal understanding of what it is to be human and the necessity continually to practise that humanity.

MARY GRAHAM: When Aboriginal people say they became human in this country, that's exactly what they mean. They disagree totally with, well, they don't lose any sleep over, what anthropologists say about coming from some other country over a landbridge, or coming from the north—they don't agree with that at all. But nobody argues too much because they just let anthropologists say whatever they want, you know. But most Aboriginal people say 'we became human in this country'. So what that means is that the spirit ancestors—and that is taken for granted, too, because in Aboriginal metaphysics it's not just energy and matter as in western metaphysics, it's energy, matter and spirit; that's simply taken for granted, there's no argument or speculation about that at all—so spirit is just accepted as a real thing.

So when Aboriginal people say the spirits—creator beings, spirit beings—made humans, made everything in nature, they perhaps became almost, human, and they made land itself. Then they made the people to look after land. So everybody's got their own stories. Every Aboriginal group is an autonomous group so, of course, there's no impulse towards centralising or hierarchy or anything like that: everybody is equal in an autonomous group, which is why, also, there aren't any leaders in Aboriginal society. So every group has their own story about genesis, about how they came to be there, and also the rules for living there, and basically what it all means is that land has created us—it's thrown us up, it's invented us. Land has invented us, it looks after us, we look after it, it looks after us, and we look after it, and so on, and so on, and so on.

Then after a while the meaning comes that—and this is basically the meaning of life, I suppose, for Aboriginal people and there are variations with all of those different autonomous groups—but basically it means that the land is the law, as in natural law, not the positive law like western law, so the land is the law and you're not alone in the world: the two great axioms of Aboriginal thinking. So land is the thing that has invented us, has actually given us meaning.

I think another way of looking at it is that you can very well get meaning out of ideas but you can't see ideas, you can't touch them, and if you put a hundred people in a room you can get a hundred different ideas and they might all be absolutely brilliant, have all the answers to everything, and quite often they are. You look at the whole history of western thought, wonderful ideas, brilliant ideas: some of them are similar, some of them are totally opposed to each other. So you can't actually see ideas; you can see the results of them.

The other thing is that you can't get meaning from ideals, either, because again you can't see the ideals like love, or courage, or virtue, or any of those things. You can see an *act* of courage or love. The other thing, too, is that you can't get a meaning of life from a great personage, a great figure like a great teacher, because in the end they're just human beings, too, with all the vulnerability of humans. They're brave sometimes and they're cowardly some other times, they're smart and not so smart, sometimes all at the same time, but really you can't get meaning of life from personages, from people. Just about all they can ever be is to be great examples.

The only solid thing you can get meaning out of is land itself, because it's the only thing that exists, besides us.

So how did you first begin to find your place? Does that happen in early childhood?

Yes, it happens the same way for all Aboriginal people. Now, I'm not talking about the unfortunate history of Aboriginal children who've been taken away from their people and been adopted by white people or put into institutions. Very sadly, a lot of those people look for their original identity again and that's an ongoing process and very traumatic for them. But for most Aboriginal people from everywhere in the whole country you get this meaning from early childhood. You're told and you're taught, sometimes in formal ways but mostly in informal ways, about the history of your group. The history of your group is basically the history of your mother's group and the history of your father's group, because the whole idea is to keep humanising your existence, which is why—and I know it's the same for other cultures, too—it's more important who you are than what you do.

So you keep saying, and this is what Aboriginal people do to each other when they meet, 'My mother is so-and-so, my father is so-and-so, and they come from such-and-such a country'. And when it's done very formally you say what their languages are, what my name is—and I mightn't tell you a private name, a personal name, but only my own family name.

So basically you are given all this information as you're socialised into an Aboriginal society: your father's story—his people and their story—and your mother's people and their story. What that actually does, then, is answer the question of 'Why?', because your identity is located in land: you are a locus of being, whereas westerners are a focus of being because the individual is so important. This is also why westerners are always looking for meaning, because they have to, because their discrete identity is searching for it: they're not placed anywhere. But when you're placed somewhere—and it has to be both sides, mother and father—when you're placed then the answer of 'Why?' is already given to you. It's given to you through birth and all those stories, and so I learnt that exactly the same way as every other Aboriginal person learns that.

And you are a member of a big family. What pictures come to you from childhood?

Oh, big groups of people (laughs), lots and lots of Aboriginal people, lots of cousins, relatives everywhere. In fact, your first friends are usually your relatives, so you're surrounded by people who are connected with you. Also, it's such a great array of different personalities so you learn about that sort of personal development yourself from all of that and learning things from your own parents. Again, like most Murris, most Aboriginal people, you're learning that when you're born into a mob of people, what it actually means is that you're born into a world full of obligations and responsibilities—in fact, hardly any rights (laughs), but all responsibilities and complications. Because in a kinship system, like most kinship systems around the world, you are obliged to different people in it, and as you grow older you're obliged here and there in different ways.

Is that difficult? You're suggesting it's difficult, I think, and yet one accepts it. Is that what you're saying?

No, it's not difficult, it's . . . sometimes it's difficult just in the sense of personal relations, that's all, because not everybody gets on with everybody else. But it's part of Aboriginal perspective, I think, or view of life, that you're not meant to be perfect; there is no great ideal to live up to, so to be as human as possible, that's pretty good.

I think perhaps an old religious ideal for westerners is to try to perfect one's life. For Murris there's not that great need, it's not necessary, because the question of 'Why?' is always answered. You have relations with other people, and all humans are given a great repertoire of human emotion which you are supposed to feel.

You're not supposed to think that conflict is bad: conflict is just perfectly normal, because Aboriginal people have different logic. It's not Aristotelian logic about 'if not p then q, and either p or q'; it really is a logic that's based on the premise that all perspectives are valid and reasonable. So there's not one absolute right way or wrong way of looking at things. There are bad things in the world and bad actions but there's no realm of evil—a realm of hell or heaven, or anything like that—because humans are just human and you're not expected to be good and you're not seen as bad. But there is a saying, or a phrase, that Aboriginal people everywhere quite often use, and that is to say that someone is a 'poor fella'. So Aboriginal people . . . in a sense, we are all—Aboriginal and non-Aboriginal—alike: we're all 'poor fellas'.

Meaning fallible, human, vulnerable . . . ?

Yes, very vulnerable, weak and frightened—more frightened than not (laughs)—and snatching bits of happiness and laughing, but quite often wondering what's going on. So you're allowed to be as weak as anything, and there's no great emphasis or need for you to love all of humanity because it's too damned hard to love everybody (laughs)—some people are mongrels! You know, you don't like this one, you're going to flog that one (laughs), and that's perfectly all right. So conflict is seen as a perfectly normal thing: you're supposed to have conflict; you're not supposed to look at conflict as bad and absence of conflict as good.

And you're not supposed to work towards resolving it, necessarily?

You don't resolve it so much, but you manage it, you manage it.

Are you taught ways to manage it as you grow up?

Oh, yes, there's lots and lots of different mechanisms whereby you can manage. If you resolve it, again you have some kind of ideal ahead of you. Do you know what I mean? You have an ideal. Again, that puts far too much weight on people's shoulders. Aboriginal people have been watching Europeans for the last two hundred years, we've just been observing things all the time about them—and we've seen that Europeans put enormous loads on their shoulders about how to be good, how to find out things, how to make things more neat and comfortable, and always pursuing something: their discrete entity is always pursuing things because they don't have any meaning inside, because they're not tied to something.

Let me stay with something you brought up a minute ago. If in your cultural beliefs there's no great realm of evil, is there also no particular realm of good?

No, that's right.

There's no need for God, or gods?

That's right. No, there's no God, there's no voice inside one's head telling you, 'Now, be a good person', because you're not a good person, you could never be a good person, but by the same argument you could never be a bad person. You can do good things but nobody pats you on the back for doing a good thing—you ask most Aboriginal people! (laughs) Also, by the same token, you can do bad things but you're not bad forever, you're not shunted away. Sometimes there is a form of exile if you've gone too far beyond, but if you're exiled from your group you are expected to go away and learn. Usually it's because of something to do with some spiritual law: you've broken law somehow, and it's extremely important then—it's very important. You're expected to learn it.

Mary, given the strength of Aboriginal collective identity, do you ever experience loneliness?

Yes, sometimes. Sometimes in a group, in a crowd of Europeans (laughs), because in a way you are expected to be an individual. Do you know what I mean? When an Aboriginal person is with other Aboriginal people you're inextricably tied to them, not because of racial bonds but to do with meaning, I suppose. For example, you don't have to talk, actually, in a group with Aboriginal people; in fact, silence is quite often seen as a way of learning things. If you're silent it's quite okay, you don't have to fill the silence with chatter or anything like that. You are allowed to be silent, so you are truly together with people whether they're talking or not, whether you're discussing something or not, whether you know them, actually, or not.

But with Europeans, whether it's in some kind of formal or informal gathering, social or whatever, sometimes it's very lonely because you're expected to almost perform; to put on another mask. For Europeans, I think, when they're navigating through society, going through society, their role, what they do, is most important. Do you know what I mean?

For example, say I'm a doctor and I'm giving a talk to some nurses, the relationship is very, very clear from the beginning, absolutely clear; but for Murris, in that protocol when we introduce ourselves to each other, the whole idea is to say who we are and who our parents are. What you're actually doing is re-humanising all the time, because one thing that Murris have learned over a really long period of time is that it's the easiest thing in the world to forget that you're human. You can forget it in about five seconds. So it sounds crazy, but the idea is that you have to keep practising it all the time.

What's the alternative to being human? When you say it's easy not to be human, what is it that you can easily slip into?

Well, roles. You can fall into roles where what you do is far more important than who you are, of being human. Being human is far more important than acting it all the time. Because what would one say about the Nazi who kills thousands of people in a weekend in a gas chamber and then comes home and is a very good family man and good to his children? So what does it mean to be actually human?

Murris have learned over a long period of time that you have to practise it all the time, and what it basically is is emphasising those human attributes: my mother is so-and-so, my father is so-and-so.

Telling the story over and over again.

Telling the story over and over again. For example, take the story of Arthur and the Round Table. From an Aboriginal perspective it's not important to find scientific evidence or physical evidence of where that castle was, or where Arthur lived and how he lived. It is far more important to simply tell the story, because the story is the thing. Telling stories all the time is the process of re-humanising all the time.

So there's a great power in the story.

Oh, great power.

Now another thing that I find really interesting, Mary, is that when I'm talking to you or to other Aboriginal friends I ask a question in terms of 'you'—what was it like for you when you did so and so, and frequently the answer will come back not in terms of 'I', but we, or Murris, or Aboriginal people. Now explain that to me. I ask you as an individual and you answer me as a member of a group. Why is that?

You see, learning that the meaning of life comes out of land also taught Aboriginal people that in order to look after land, in order to keep re-creating humanness all the time, what you end up with is a custodial ethic rather than a controlling ethic that turns into agriculture and so on. But in order to keep the custodial ethic going, and given that humans are what they are with this great repertoire of human feelings and emotions like jealousy and hatred—because it's normal to be jealous and hate somebody—they've found that you have to do something with the ego. So what they did was work out ways and means, all sorts of mechanisms by which the ego is allowed full display, but at the same time there's all kinds of pressures on you to keep your ego back, to be modest, don't brag, don't big-note yourself, don't show off too much.

But if you lose your temper, and you have to do something with your temper because again that's the human part of you and you have to allow that out—you can't sort of sit on it and say that conflict is bad, so you're allowed to express all of that jealousy and hatred—but one of the main mechanisms there was that you always had minders around to make sure that you didn't go too far.

So, to put it in a brief sort of way, with the idea of Helen of Troy, in Aboriginal perspective it would have been perfectly all right for two men to have a fight over somebody called Helen of Troy, have a duel. But the very idea of ideologising that conflict and being far more organised about it and ending up with a huge war over somebody called Helen of Troy, a Hellenistic war, and millions of people dying, that is absolutely inconceivable for Aboriginal people. But it's perfectly normal to have a fight, to have a duel.

The impetus is there for you to learn about things, yet it's not that you know things in an artificial or formal way, but you display your knowledge of things by your behaviour. So you have to behave in a modest way and don't show off. It's built in, you see, so that's why the idea of hierarchy is unknown. The nearest thing to hierarchy in Aboriginal society would be a hierarchy in knowledge, and again you're not given a label or a medal, there's no system of chieftains or anything like that, because if you had something like that where the ego could have that kind of free rein you'd end up very quickly with a hierarchy, and a hierarchy always mitigates against the custodial ethic.

All human societies have elites. Aboriginal people understood that, too, because we're all different. Where some people are slow and somebody's fast and some people are good at some things and not others, you have elites, but there are mechanisms there by which those elites must not turn into a class or a caste system, because you'll end up with a hierarchy straight away, and as soon as you have a hierarchy . . .

Another way of looking at it is to look at, from an Aboriginal perspective, the old Greek myth of Narcissus: of a beautiful boy falling in love with his own image in the water. From our point of view that is like the individual, the ego, discovering itself, and upon discovering itself it falls in love with itself: in other words, it becomes obsessed with self, it becomes obsessed with only its own concerns. Now, again, Aboriginal people understand that sort of thing very well. A lot of the dreaming stories are actually about psychology, about how to understand why we do the things we do, and all possible contingencies, all possible behaviour of humans has been taken into account in those stories, including that kind of thing about being egotistical—almost like morality plays, I suppose. You know, if you do this, this will happen; if you don't share then something else bad will happen; so don't put yourself forward all the time.

You've spoken of the danger of over-egotism. Is there also a feeling of protection of one's self at the core?

It's a part of Aboriginal protocol that you don't look directly at people, don't stare at people directly, don't ask direct questions, don't ask very intimate questions directly—quite often Aboriginal people think that's acting like police. Always allow the other person their space and their dignity: for example, not putting people on the spot so that they might have to say no, because nobody likes to say no, it's highly embarrassing. The idea of shame is extremely important for Aboriginal people, shameful behaviour. Everywhere in the whole country . . . if you put another individual Aboriginal person on the spot, in a sense it tears that person open inside and they are exposed, so to speak; the very core of their whole being is exposed and that's really taking away their dignity, so that if you're discussing, say, some crisis, quite often you'll talk in a roundabout way, in a very subtle way. You don't come straight to the point about things, because in that sort of protocol you're actually testing the waters or testing the atmosphere, and when people do come together to talk about things establishing an agreeable atmosphere is the most important part of it. The meeting won't start until, for example, gossip will have taken place—people talking about mundane things, everyday things. The meeting doesn't start when the issue is brought up, the meeting has already started when people are gossiping, because you are establishing a really agreeable atmosphere and what it really means is that you grow peace. You don't make peace, you actually have to grow peace over a long period of time. You can't make it, because again it comes back to the idea of sides.

In a cross cultural workshop I was conducting the participants—police and Aboriginal people—were asked to write down what they would like to happen in the next workshop. The police—hundreds of them—said they wanted to learn more about Aboriginal problems of alcoholism, bad health, unemployment and housing, and so on, and about last on the list they put getting to know them, becoming friends. All the Aboriginal people, without checking with each other, all put that first of the priorities, and they put all the problems down the bottom, because it's just a totally different view of becoming friends and establishing good relations.

So, Mary, what is the Aboriginal perspective on democracy?

Well, as much as it might be disappointing for government and bureaucracy, the idea of democracy doesn't hold much water for Aboriginal people, either. Democracy is seen as not the greatest thing in the world. Consensus decision-making is seen as far more important, because everybody in an Aboriginal world is their own law-bearer. Nobody tells you what to do or orders you to do things. I mean, an older person has got great authority, that's for sure, but they don't have the kind of authority in that they can order you to do things every day of your life; they have the authority over you to do with their knowledge about things.

The very idea of democracy is seen as a bit immature for Aboriginal people. It's seen as concretised conflict; it's saying that actually conflict is good and that you have to have two sides there to sort it out. But what actually happens is that two sides to a conflict or a crisis actually sets it, it's there forever, whereas in a consensus-style decision-making the whole aim of it, from an Aboriginal perspective, is to grow that agreeable atmosphere and always aim for that harmonious sort of relationship. On the way to that harmonious relationship, though, you might have arguments because, again, everybody's allowed to do that, it's okay to do that, it's okay to burst into tears. Sometimes it's a bit like Italian opera without the music—it's quite amazing! (both laugh) But the aim of it is harmony, so that it's all means and very little ends, because relations are far more important than the issue or the topic or the problem.

Yes, the process is respected or seen to be important.

Yes, very much, and that usually infuriates state and Canberra bureaucrats, because when they want a decision made by Friday at five o'clock quite often it's never made by Friday at five o'clock, it's two or three weeks late.

Well, Mary, what you're describing so clearly is a collision of two different systems of thought, two different ways of seeing and understanding what it is to be human in the world. Yes?

Yes, Aboriginal metaphysics is a totally different metaphysics from western metaphysics. And, you see, it still operates, regardless of what some people want to say, in every corner of the whole country. It really does, because culture is a two-sided thing. The externals are dress and customs and what you eat and so on, but the other part of culture, the most important part, is how you feel and think and act, and that hasn't changed very much at all, regardless of how urbanised people in some parts have become.

So the crucial western theory of Charles Darwin would pass you by altogether, I imagine.

Oh heavens, yes!

Yes? You are not, in fact, descended from the apes?

Oh, God, that theory, from our perspective, I think, would be seen as the expression of a really immature culture basically trying to justify colonialism, and they're finding it really hard, because they have to stay being Christian to think well of themselves at the same time as they're doing dreadful things to millions of people around the world. Do you know what I mean? So basically it's seen as immature, because Aboriginal society is a very, very mature society: they've worked out a whole lot of things to do with human relations above all, and meaning in life. Where there are records of people talking to Aboriginal people and trying to give them things, the Aboriginal people just didn't want anything. I think Captain Cook said, 'Well, they don't seem to want anything we've got'.

And that was puzzling . . .

Yes, that was puzzling for the Europeans, because there is still this fond myth that Aboriginal people, or indigenous people in general, all are dying to become western. They certainly might want certain things of the west but they don't necessarily all want to become western. They're quite happy being Aboriginal, Indian, Chinese, or whatever. You see, it's unheard of, it's inconceivable why someone would leave the home of their ancestors as Europeans did and come to somebody else's country. And it's still strange to Aboriginal people today (laughs)—you know, the very idea that somehow colonialism is normal. It's still not normal, for Aboriginal people, for people to do things like that.

So, if I say to you, 'success'—now, what meaning does that have for you?

I think success for me is to do with having good human relations, having good relations with people, proper relations, and doing the correct thing for my mob, basically. Success isn't measured in terms of material gain—though winning the Lotto tomorrow would be very nice (laughs).

Why?

Well, it would help, but it's not seen as being successful because all of a sudden you have money to be able to buy things. If that did happen and I bought things I'd probably do exactly what most other Aboriginals would do—start sharing it out. Your car is other people's car and your clothes are other people's clothes . . . food and everything—your house is my house. So those sorts of things are just taken for granted, and the idea of going somewhere in the world—from an Aboriginal point of view we are all not going anywhere at all; we are all just staying right here because there's nowhere to go.

Where does that leave death?

Well, yes, we're going to die.

Yes, and afterwards? Do you have a sense of afterwards, or doesn't the question have meaning?

Then you're with your ancestors, because you're in this great grid with other people and they're waiting for you. But the emphasis is not very much on death: it really is on life itself and living it to the full. Life is . . . I don't know . . . it's a one-shot thing.

Mary, you're a chess player.

Yes (laughs)

What's the pleasure in chess?

Oh, well, probably it's the duel, the idea of the duel. Somebody wrote a book once about the finite game and the infinite game. There are only two different kinds of games in the world and that's those two—the finite and the infinite. Finite games are things like chess games, and they're wonderful. They're like duels and you can shine in them, you can show your prowess. Of course a real duel with pistols and swords (laughs), that's a finite game, too, and some would even say—I don't know if you could take it that far—the never-ending duel between men and women is a finite game (laughs). And a war, or a courtroom drama, a trial, is a finite game. A finite game is one where there are only two people or two sides, there has always got to be a winner or a loser and you've got to either win or lose, and there is a definite finish—the game finishes when one has lost and the other has won.

An infinite game is a game where there are any number of players and the whole point is not about winning or losing. You can just simply play to your heart's content, and it goes on for ever and ever and ever. You can have a finite game within a infinite game but you can't have it the other way around.

The problem with a lot of societies, especially westerners, is that they take the finite game as the real thing: they think of it as the most important thing and they take it too seriously. They should see it as just a great drama, as part of the infinite game, because really that's what Aboriginal people are on about—the infinite game. So white Australians will be waiting for another two or five hundred years for Aboriginal people to become part of one Australia. They'll be waiting for a long time because Aboriginal people are on about other things, far more important things than the finite game.

The thing that annoys a lot of Aboriginal people ... they think it's wonderful that the conservation movement is gathering pace and everybody's a 'greenie' and so on but, really, as their God is dead and Marxism is bankrupt now, people are looking for someone else to come along and tell them what everything means. They're waiting for another chance to have an 'ism', and what they've done is simply tag 'ism' to the end of 'environment' and now they have another thing to ideologise about, with a whole great array of goodies and baddies—developers are baddies, greenies are good and people that want to be green are good—so they're back to square one.

It's as if they can't accept the idea of the custodial ethic, and especially in something to do with the environment that's the most important thing: not the controlling ethic, because that idea of a duel, of a battle, leads directly to a controlling ethic. It's something to be controlled and tamed and bought and sold. So Aboriginal people can see that westerners see land as property or real estate and, of course, Aboriginal people go out and buy land themselves. If you want a house you have to get money, loans to buy a house, but people know that you can never really own land. You can't, really. Even in the western system you can't really own it: the bank owns it, or the local council owns it—rates, and all that.

So you don't really own land, but the most important thing is the idea of the sacredness of land. The idea of the sacredness, that's the most important part, and it comes back to the idea of Aboriginal logic. A geologist might say to an Aboriginal group that Ayers Rock, Uluru, is made up of sandstone—which I think it is, I'm not quite sure—and the Aboriginal people would say, 'Well, that's very interesting, tell us more.' Another scientist might come along and say something else about the place and they wouldn't disagree with that, either, so that particular object can be described in various ways. But for Aboriginal people it would be what is significant about that place, and the significant thing is always the sacred thing, it's always the spiritual thing, the fact that that place is somebody's dreaming, because really that's what dreaming is—it's to do with mind, but it's more to do with the sacredness of everything.

Land itself is sacred and anything that land has thrown up is sacred, including other people, so humans are sacred beings and you can't, you mustn't ideologise conflict because, as we've seen, it would mean millions of people dying and no conflicts are worth that.

But by all means . . . if there's anything Aboriginal people have learned in thousands of years of existence it's how to keep boredom at bay, and there's nothing like having a good fight (laughs).

Do you go to the movies?

Oh, yes.

What do you choose to go to see?

Well, I like European movies very much. I don't care much for American movies; they seem, again, to be a bit immature, but Americans have made little movies about different things and they allow their humanness to come through. But in those big block-buster things there's something quite monstrous about them, and I suppose that's why I like Russian movies particularly, because they seem to show this . . . I don't know, they have a very good way about showing this humanness and emotions and feelings—sometimes it's right over the top. A lot of Aboriginal people I know who are into movies and movie-making say the same thing about Russian films, too. They like this particular thing that comes through, that humanness.

It's satisfying.

Very satisfying, yes. When I was younger, about fifteen, one of the first things I ever read was Voltaire, because I wanted to find out why things are the way they are, especially to do with westerners: who are these people? And when I was young I thought one of the best ways of finding out why people are the way they are is to read poetry and plays, maybe, or novels. I like Russian novels, too, all the classics. But that was one of the first things that really opened a whole other world to me of philosophy. I got into reading a great deal about all the different western philosophies, and the one I started off with was Voltaire, which was really good, because one of the things I picked up from him was that you have to start doubting everything—doubt. So I thought that was a pretty good lesson to be taught by a westerner about westerners: to doubt everything (laughs), and I went on from there.

So has it been exciting as you've studied the different philosophies? Exciting, or sometimes does it transfix you in a feeling of conflict, so that you think well, where do I go next?

Well, I went through all of those sort of periods. That's what's seductive about western society: you can lose yourself in your head; you can live life thinking that ideas are real things. But then you see the results of ideas, whether it's Marxism or anything else. It's like going through a field of wonderful flowers, but there's something artificial about them; you suddenly discover they're all artificial.

But it's a worthwhile journey to make, isn't it?

Oh, it's a worthwhile journey, and the trick is not to get hung up on one particular one, because in the end it's relations that matter.

And it seems that you've gone on that long journey of education and come to recognise that what you have in your own Aboriginal metaphysical understanding has been reinforced—you're very happy with it.

Oh, yes! I had an idea of it, but a vague, unformed idea when I was younger, that this is it. I instinctively went away from any anthropological version of Aboriginal society because I always thought that anthropologists could not come near it—not at all, not at all. They study it like a scientist would study the car—'Oh, yes, this is the colour and this is the paintwork and this is what that's for, and this is how it works', and yet they wouldn't know how to get in and drive the car.

How, now, do you put your education and all your understanding about what it is to be human—all these tracks that you've followed—how do you put that to work now?

I suppose by writing—or having a go, at least—with my very good friend and sister Lilla Watson, who I've learned a great deal from, too. I've learned from my own family and a lot of other Aboriginal people but especially with Lilla, so we decided to co-write a book on Aboriginal perspectives and we're eventually going to finish it, I'm sure (laughs). I suppose the worthwhileness of it is to try to get, again, as my friend Lilla says, to get Europeans to explore this challenge of looking at things in a totally different way—a totally different metaphysics.

Now, by saying that I'm not saying that we would want, or anybody would want, westerners to stop being western, because sometimes I think that when young westerners become Buddhists and go after other religions . . . I'm not saying it's a bad thing, but sometimes I think they're never more western than when they don't want to be. So they have to find something in their own metaphysics that is proper, that is life-enhancing, not looking for something elsewhere, but at the same time the biggest change would be to recognise that spirit is a real thing and there's not a duality between physical and spiritual. As Aboriginal people say, the physical thing is evidence of spirit but somehow coming to terms with spirit. In other words, trying to get to the point of a collective spiritual identity, and then we'll have something to talk about between Aboriginal people and westerners, because a really mature society is one that has a collective spiritual identity. Australia hasn't got that yet because, again in our terms, white Australians are only two hundred minutes old: they're two hundred years old, and in our terms, it's only two hundred minutes old. They haven't learned how to deal with a whole lot of things, how to come to terms with things—they're still living life through rose-coloured glasses, looking at colonialism as if it's a romantic career and that sort of thing.

There's a great German writer called Gunter Grass who wrote a book called *The Tin Drum*. I don't think it pleased some Germans very much, but most of them liked it; he is a great writer. He was talking about German people and who they are, where they come from in spiritual terms, in psychological terms. Some people have said that maybe Patrick White tried to do that. I don't know if he did, or not, but that's what's got to happen in this country: a white Australian writer has got to write a novel like *The Tin Drum*, not exactly the same but something in that vein.

To do the same job, as it were.

Somebody has got to write a book like *The Tin Drum* about the whole period of colonialism, and I couldn't imagine an English writer, or Spanish or Portugese or Dutch, writing a book like that because it would mean demystifying the whole thing of colonialism . . . What it would mean is literally admitting that you're wrong—do you know what I mean?—that they're wrong about something.

Somebody said that's what makes Gorbachev so great: if he wasn't great for anything else except saying that 'we were wrong'—that is, the whole Stalinist era of treating their own people badly. He said that and that's an enormously large thing to say, that 'we were wrong'. What it would mean is . . . who would it be? . . . who would it be?—the prime minister, or all the prime ministers, contemporary royalty, whatever—but someone in a very high-profile position saying that colonialism was wrong. Nobody's asking Australians to all of a sudden turn the land over to Aboriginal people and go back to wherever they came from. They're saying that a mature society is also one which owns its own history—exactly the same thing that Australian returned servicemen are saying to the Japanese. Well, they've got to do that themselves. If they really want to belong in this country they've got to own their own history, and it doesn't mean heaping ashes on their head and wallowing in guilt because, again, from an Aboriginal point of view, that is a waste of time. All it really means is saying 'we were wrong'.

There have been some church leaders who've made that move. You're saying that's a valuable thing to do.

Oh, very, very valuable.

I need to ask you something else. You're not saying, are you, that the only valid spirituality is your Aboriginal understanding?

Oh, no!

No, I didn't think you were saying that. You're saying there are the spiritual traditions of Judaism and Christianity and so on: they have their validity, but somehow in Australia we haven't found our . . .

Well, it's such a young society, white Australian society. Most old societies have already worked out . . . everybody has got these old stories and legends and myths about how they came to be—you know, Greek gods, Chinese myths—and really they're all like action guides to understanding human nature and psychology. Australians haven't got that yet because they're so young. They've made attempts to do that through Anzac and so on, but you can't do it out of things like that because you've got to tackle the big questions of life, death, birth, and they haven't lived long enough to do that, you see (laughs). But also they are still getting their stories from some other country.

And that's perilous, you're saying?

Yes, yes. People want to stay in this country—when I say stay, of course they're going to stay physically, but if they want to really stay in all those other meanings that's what they've got to start doing. I can't reiterate that too much—a collective spiritual identity.

Dr Ron Farmer

Dr Ron Farmer is a man who's known the extreme panic and terror of a catastrophic nervous breakdown, and this story of how he's come to make sense of his life will touch and strengthen every man and woman.

Ron Farmer is fifty. He's a clinical psychologist but, as one of his long-standing professional colleagues says, it's difficult to separate Ron's clinical work from his everyday living. The two seem to merge.

Ron is a husband, a father, a man deeply interested and involved in the best possible education for our teachers and for our children. He's been to the top in his own profession. Indeed he has taught or influenced many of the Australian psychologists in senior positions today.

With Professor Lovibond and the late Dr Robin Winkler, Ron Farmer founded the Master of Psychology degree program at the University of New South Wales.

During his six years there, he supervised the clinical training of almost 100 postgraduate students, the first psychologists in Australia to be given specific training in counselling and therapeutic techniques.

He's also taught many hundreds of students at all undergraduate levels in the faculties of Arts, Science, and Medicine and supervised many Honours and Masters theses in practical clinical research. Yet during these years he experienced fears and phobias which sometimes paralysed him and for which he could find no ready cure in conventional psychology, even at his own advanced level of knowledge. His desperate need led him on a search for healing and for meaning. This story is told in the gentle, simple way of a person who has been broken apart and who puts the pieces together again with a changed sense of priorities, and with an unmistakable authenticity.

Today Dr Ron Farmer works in private practice and with

people who are developmentally disabled. From his deep theoretical knowledge of human behaviour, and his own gruelling experience, he has made a series of self-help cassettes on depression, insomnia, stress, relaxation, self-esteem, weight control and nervous breakdown (which he has profoundly redesignated nervous breakthrough).

Dr Ron Farmer's generously unguarded telling of his own journey may well intersect at certain points with your own. And for Ron, as with all of us, many of the patterns and pervading influences of life were laid down in childhood.

RON FARMER: I suppose the thing that stands out in my mind is that when I was eleven . . . no, before that, when I was nine . . . I was electrocuted to the extent that I was in hospital for six weeks. And what occurs to me is that after that I didn't seem to know what was going on (how people connected or what the rules were, if you like), so I spent most of my childhood sitting up in a tree, out of school hours. I would avoid going to school until everyone else was in school, lunchtime I'd go off by myself; and it seemed to me that I was avoiding contact with people out of some sort of fear.

I think I covered that fear fairly successfully with people until I had my breakdown and then it just couldn't be contained any more and it just exploded. So I'd say—going back to that experience with the electric shock—that somehow that did bring about quite a striking change in direction for me.

With all the knowledge that you now have about the mind and the way human beings are, and about psychotherapy, what do you make of that experience of electrocution?

Well, somehow, I know through the use of ECT [electroconvulsive therapy] in psychiatry, that what happens is that the established connections are wiped out temporarily so that the person can get a new start. And it seemed to me that that happened to me, that what I'd learnt about how you go up to another kid and say, 'Hey, can I play this game with you?' I seemed to have forgotten how to do. And the other aspect of it is that . . . I've read that sometimes if someone is hit by lightning or is electrocuted, then it can be a psychic awakening. I feel just intuitively—I have no evidence for this—that somehow that's connected with my abilities in psychotherapy and to see and to talk about new directions in therapy and in how to look at life.

You've been so much at the forefront of advances in psychotherapy, I suppose many of the major people in practice today, you would've *taught . . . and yet in the midst of that is your own breakdown or break-*through, *as I think you're inclined to call it. Would you speak to us about the nature of that breakdown or breakthrough, how you experienced it, how you now think of it and what you learned through that?*

Well, although there were many warning signs I didn't recognise them at the time. So it came as a great shock to me when I had my first panic attack. I thought I was going to die. I was just sitting having breakfast with my wife and a couple of children and a friend of hers and I just suddenly felt weak all over, as if I couldn't breathe, and I just had to lie down. And so I lay down for about half an hour and then I was alright and in that strange state that I was in, of denial, I just said, 'Oh, it must be a passing phenomenon,' so I didn't even think that I should go and see a doctor. So I just went off to university and while I was preparing for a lecture I had another one; it took me twenty minutes to recover from that. And then I had another one in front of the Psychology I class of 400 or 500 young people and I just said, 'Excuse me, I've got to go,' and I went out to the secretary and said, 'I think I'm having a heart attack, call an ambulance.' And then I couldn't move for about an hour and a half; I couldn't even lift a finger, I could barely speak. So they did all these tests on me . . . which didn't show anything. And then after a while I felt alright again—and again in that strange state of denial I just said, 'Oh, well, back to work.' So it wasn't until I started to get a few more, until eventually I was having maybe ten or fifteen a day, that I really began to become frightened of being frightened. And then, of course, it snowballed and I ended up not being able to get out of bed for ten days; I just couldn't move.

For fear?

Out of fear, yes, fear . . . fear of the unknown. I didn't know what would happen but something dreadful, I thought. I couldn't face any of my friends and within a space of about two or three weeks I developed about fifty debilitating phobias, some of them very strange things; like, I couldn't look in a mirror, because on one occasion when I'd staggered out of bed, I went into the bathroom to have a shave, I looked in the mirror and I didn't recognise the person I saw in there and so I had a panic attack—so I couldn't look in a mirror then for about six months. And so, in a whole range of ordinary life situations, whenever a panic attack occurred, I would then have a full-blown phobia of that situation.

What I didn't realise at the time was the nature of the fear. All I knew was that I was terrified, in that there was nothing in all of my training and all that I was teaching, to explain what was happening to me.

So what happened?

What happened was that I did have the benefit of having at my fingertips everything that was available in the world on behaviour therapy. So I applied everything I knew in terms of systematic desensitisation, assertive training, guided imagination, thought-stopping—all the standard techniques that I was teaching—and these did make life possible so that within two or three months I was back with my full complement of work—except that I could never see anybody face-to-face alone in therapy again while I was at university. I don't think anybody realised that. I could interview clients in front of a class as a demonstration; that was quite okay, but face-to-face . . . I just couldn't handle their emotions as well as my own. So, I struggled through and, knowing that orthodox psychology and psychiatry had nothing to offer me meant I had to keep looking, because I knew I didn't want to go the road of just using drugs to cover up the fear (because they don't work anyway) . . . I also knew that if I didn't explore, then I'd be stuck in this wasteland of timidity and avoidance.

So you kept searching?

Yes, I kept searching and . . . I think there's a divine guiding principle in everyone's life, which arranges the universe in the exquisite majesty and beauty that it has. And it doesn't appear sensible to me to even consider that that same magnificent principle would not be having an influence on us. So I feel that I was led and in being led, like everyone, every step of the way, so I was led to hear Baba Ram Das on tape, not long after he'd come back from India. He was Richard Alpert. He was a professor of psychology at Harvard and he got involved with psychedelics, with Timothy Leary and so forth, but it wasn't enough and so he went to India and changed direction and took on a totally spiritual life. His tape of the talk he gave at the Menninger Foundation in Topeka, Kansas, moved me tremendously, because he was talking a language which sounded challenging and delightful, but one which I'd never heard before . . . like the 'oneness' of everything and 'layers' of understanding and that 'all there is is love'—what's he talking about, all there is is love, what about that chair? That's love too.

It was just so mysterious but fascinating and so that was of great value to me. My friend Chris Clarke (he was a lecturer at the University of New South Wales), introduced that to me and I then went on to John Lilly's *Eye of the Cyclone* and . . . with his sensory deprivation work . . . and then, of course, the wonderful Carlos Castaneda books, on his adventures with Don Juan, the Mexican sorcerer. That led me more and more to feel that there were mysteries in the universe that couldn't be put down in textbooks, couldn't be taught as a scientific discipline in the way that we know it. But, of course, it's always never enough, so I kept looking and then I discovered Gurdjieff whose best line that he ever said was, 'Remember to remember that you're asleep.'

What do you make of that?

I think it means that who we really are is like the passenger in a coach. The horses are out front: they're the emotions racing along. The driver sitting up top is the mind trying to control these emotions with the reins. The carriage is the body and inside is the passenger fast asleep. And I think when Gurdjieff says 'Remember to remember you're asleep', it's like the passenger waking up and . . . 'Hey, hey! Where am I going? I want to be in charge here!', and telling the mind what to do, telling the driver, 'Don't go there, go there,' saying to the mind, 'Look, get control of those horses!', saying to the mind, 'Don't let the emotions dominate your life. You determine where you want to go. Use the emotions as power, but you decide on the direction.'

So, in all this new understanding that you were gaining, what sense were you able to make of nervous breakdown?

Well, I became increasingly gratified that it had happened to me because it's like I was living in a prison—as perhaps everybody is to some degree . . . And I think we have to live in a prison, it's like, this is what keeps us protected from energies which we don't understand. But there comes a time when perhaps the wise person inside ourselves says, 'Look, enough of this mucking around!' and it blows the prison up so that we then step outside—well, we're forced to step outside and to begin an adventure in this new landscape.

The breakthrough for me was to recognise that this fear which was dominating my life was really a special energy which was there to chart my course, to define my path in life such that if the fear remained, then I was going in the wrong direction. If the fear diminished or changed into something more welcome, then I was going in the right direction. And so it was my direction-finder—the fear. It drove me. It gave me a light that illuminated my way so that now when fear comes I welcome it, because fear to me is the door to the unknown. It says, 'Here is a door. Beyond this door is something which you have not yet been aware of, so step through the door,' so I step through the door and fall apart and become a new person again.

That must be a very provocative idea to someone who's just learning that for the first time. And you've now made a wonderful series of tapes along these lines for people who are suffering in many ways, but I also feel, listening to the tapes, that they're for all of us. They're really a plan for life, a plan for dealing with the challenges and the setbacks and the distresses and the small and large fears and the small and large deaths of every day.

Yes, they are like that. What's on the tapes is really age-old wisdom, it's not . . . they're not my creation. We live in an age where we have the benefits of wisdom of centuries of all cultures and all religions and all philosophies and we have access to this. All that I've done, really, is to immerse myself in it and see what makes sense to me and what works for me, and then to put that into a language which might suit some people.

What a beautiful paradox, that through the breakdown or breakthrough comes this great body of teaching that you now pass on—and not as a lecturer, but as someone saying 'Well, look, this is how it's been for me, this where I went searching, this is what I've found.'

Yes, in some ways that gives it validity for many people. And it also gives a lot of hope to people, because they see me as an example who's had a catastrophic breakdown—and it really was catastrophic, one of the worst and most severe that I've read about—and yet out of it comes this man who talks about it as being an extraordinarily enriching experience. So that does give hope to a lot of people, I know.

Yes. So where are you now? What do you most treasure in your life? Where are the real sources of, I suppose, satisfaction for you now, and purpose?

I think the main satisfaction in life is a life of devotion, a feeling that this divine principle of which we are all a part is something, such that the more we recognise it and give allegiance to it, the more we experience our true nature. Devotion is something out of which we ourselves get the most benefit. So, the life of devotion is more important to me than anything else: where we devote ourselves to endeavouring to become that divine principle—through service to other people, through being honest, through seeking that state of peace and truth and love within ourselves which is our true nature.

So that's really what I live for mainly: to become who I really am, in the same way as the flower is naturally who it really is and the horse is naturally who it really is. I want to be naturally human.

Do you find that you need some sort of ritual to keep you tuned in to that aim?

I do. I need to have a number of rituals: I have affirmations, I have mantras, I have techniques of simple meditation.

Would you speak about any of those three?

Yes. Well, for instance, one of the mantras that I use is very, very simple. When I was standing outside waiting for you, I was looking at all the colours and I just started saying, 'When I see colour I see harmony, when I see colour I see harmony, when I see colour I see harmony . . . ' and that automatically allows that state of harmony in me to be recognised and to expand and grow until I feel, 'Yes, the whole universe is harmony and I am harmony and . . . '

Do you say that over silently to yourself or sometimes out loud?

Yes, silently. Some things I say out loud like, if I'm alone and I walk under a tree and the tree just happens to touch me, I experience that as God or my spiritual teacher touching me, and I automatically say, 'Oh, thank you, thank you'—it's like I've just been touched.

And affirmations, what form do they take and how do you practise affirmations, Ron?

Affirmations for me are like affirming who we sense that we truly are, and they're usually words taken from an advanced teacher, whether it be Jesus or Mohammed or Sathya Sai Baba (who is my teacher) and whichever one feels appropriate at the time. Then we say those words to ourselves. It's like, for instance, one that I used a few months ago when I was feeling down: I was saying, 'I am not weak and helpless, all power and strength lie within me. I am not weak and helpless, all power and strength lie within me'—a very powerful statement.

And you might say that over several times during the day?

Hundreds, yes. It's like . . . now it's automatic, I automatically think that . . . it's reconditioning the mind according to what our sense of discrimination or wisdom tells us is the appropriate way to think, so that we no longer think as our parents or our society have taught us to think but how we ourselves have chosen to think.

So you're giving great power to the thoughts, the power of thought, here.

Yes, I think that thought is the creative instrument, that it creates who we are and it creates the world.

So, you're saying, the thing is not to give it the power to be a cage but to use it as a powerful liberation and devotion.

Yes.

And the meditation . . . ?

Well, a very simple meditation I like doing is where I look at a candle flame burning and then I imagine that flame coming towards me and entering my head, illuminating my mind so that no dark thoughts are left. And then the flame travels down into my heart and grows brighter, so that there are no dark feelings left. And then the flame goes down in to my feet and I say to myself, 'May this flame illuminate my pathways so that I always travel in my right direction.' Then the flame comes up into my hands and I say, 'May this flame purify my actions so that what I do is for the good of others and humanity.' Then the flame goes into my heart again and up into my throat and I say to myself, 'May this flame purify my speech, so my words are soft and always speak the truth.' And then into my eyes, so I say, 'May this flame illuminate and cleanse my sight, so that I see the oneness in everything and that good is really the basis underlying everything.' And then into my ears 'So I listen to what's good.' And then out of the top of my head. I then see the flame going into people until it's in everybody all over the world. Then I see it going into a tree and then into all trees all over the world; and then into a grain of sand, and all grains of sand; a drop of water, all water; a planet, all planets—until everything's light.

So I begin to feel connected then, through this light, which is love. And then I imagine to myself, 'I am in the light' and then I recognise the light is in me and it's an expansion. And finally I say, 'I am the light.' And that for me is my connecting tool, if you like, that's how I get connected with people and the universe and with life itself.

Ron, how do you describe yourself now? You've been a great teacher of psychotherapy in the formal university setting—how do you describe what you do now?

I suppose officially I'm called a clinical psychologist, but really, I guess, I experience myself as a seeker. I feel that's what life's about: that we've come back to live in a body because we're still seeking. We're seeking who we really are: we're seeking that feeling of all-rightness, that feeling of understanding, that knowledge that all that we're seeking lies within us, not out there.

Again and again in the marvellous range of tapes that you've made come many images from nature, I think, but particularly the seed. How do you use that idea?

I love the image of the seed. When I had the breakdown it came at the peak of my academic career. I was giving lectures all over the country and appearing in the media, and many, many changes were taking place in psychology and psychiatry and therapy itself. And suddenly I collapsed. I wasn't sure of anything ever again after that. I was like a ripe apple on a tree and I dropped, and then I rotted—I just fell apart. But then, inside that rotting apple was a seed, and given the right conditions the actual compost of the rotting apple nurtured that seed so that it began to grow.

So I'm growing into a new tree and, I guess, producing different sorts of apples.

I was very influenced by . . . when I went up north, up towards Nimbin, a friend introduced me to the I Ching, and she said to me, 'Your very first throw will describe the central pivot of your life, the main lesson for you to learn.' So I meditated and I threw the coins, and the line that stands out for me, which describes what I had to learn, was 'The tree on a mountain is seen from afar, whereas the tree down on the plain is only seen when you're close up to it. The one on the plain puts its roots down quickly and is easily blown over; the tree on the mountain, on the other hand, puts its roots down deeply and carefully because strong winds blow.' And so that's what I was doing while I was living up in Nimbin, finding my roots and putting them down.

This idea of our suffering holding within it a seed for new enlightenment is a challenging one, isn't it? Do you find that people with whom you work take to it fairly readily, or is there sometimes a long period when they just can't see that—a sort of waiting time, an enduring time?

Yes, there is an enduring time. I feel that, like the rest of nature, everything has its own perfect timing. Even though you *know* the tide's going to come in, there is a time when the tide will turn. It always will turn, but it can't turn before that time. I think when I do therapy with people I'm reminding them of something which they know is very familiar but they can't quite recognise. But the seed is there, so when the timing is right then they'll go *with* the tide instead of against it.

And one of the tapes that you've made is about depression, which surely everybody has experienced in some degree, at some time or another. And there's a lovely image in there of the dark sky and the way in which you use the stars. Could you explain something of that?

Yes, that's a lovely one. There are many ways in which the teaching is given from many different sources, but in effect it says: the darker the night, the brighter the star. And we know this just from experience: if we have a torchlight, you really can't see that light in the daytime; it's only at night that you can see the light from the torch. And in a similar way I think depression comes, to provide that background, that darkness, so we can discover our own inner light, or our own delight.

So, that's how I see depression, and on the tape *Overcoming Depression* we use a lot of guided imagination where we provide this sort of background of darkness with an image of light gradually developing—and the one with the sky is exquisite, isn't it? It's where the person imagines they're out in a desert or on a mountain and everything's black, so black, and they're waiting for the first star. There it is! The first, faint tiny star. And there's another, and there's another. And more and more stars come until the whole sky is ablaze with light.

It always takes people on a journey of transformation: from a feeling of overwhelming heaviness and blackness to one of liberation and hope. It's as if the dark does have a purpose. The dark is there so that we can see our light, because usually we can't see the light. We're so busy running around, watching a bit of telly, talking to friends, getting a promotion in our job, someone giving praise, or dealing with money issues, that we don't really have that contrast that we can use to discover that the happiness and peace we're seeking lies within. And so depression comes—this blackness. So that we at least have a . . . like a blackboard, you can then write chalk on it. That depression is there so we can dive in and dive deep and find our delight.

You know, Ron, I'm tending to find out some of these things in the middle of my life. I wish that some of this had been part of my education. Is there any way that we can do that for children now?

I think so. I'm involved in the worldwide organisation of the Sathya Sai Baba Education in Human Values program. The aim of that in every country in the world is to give children the opportunity to discover that their real nature is love, their real nature is peace and right action and non-violence and truth, and that these qualities lie within them, that they don't have to seek outside themselves in order to discover this richness and happiness and strength. Children respond very, very well to this, and the teaching methods we use are through story-telling and role-playing and singing. Children love to be recognised for the wise beings that they really are, because they haven't left their wisdom very far behind, whereas we're a long way away from it. We've grown away from it, whereas everyone knows that you look into the eyes of a baby and you know you're looking at the universe in there; you're looking at love in its purest form.

The children that we work with between ages six and twelve are not far away from that. So when we say 'Inside you is a diamond,' they always nod their heads. And they love the image of a sculptor working with stone: that the form is already within the stone and all the sculptor does is chip away the bits that get in the way. Children love that. They know that all of the . . . 'Tidy your bed. Do this. Speak the truth,' . . . these are all just ways of chipping away the bits that get in the way of their own exquisiteness. So it's not as if we're teaching them values: we're teaching them how to allow their own wonderful nature to emerge and to be dawning in their life. And it's in the children that I think the hope for the world lies. Adults . . . are so hard to change.

Okay—how would you bring those ideas into an arithmetic lesson?

Well, into an arithmetic lesson . . . if a teacher wants to introduce Education in Human Values into every aspect of the teaching . . . then, say, at a primary school level, let's say that the teacher is getting across the idea of division. Normally a teacher might say 'Johnny's got twelve apples and he's going to divide them amongst two other boys and himself. How many do each of the three boys get?' Well, now, introducing Education in Human Values into it, you'd saturate that, maybe, with love—with the sub-value of sharing—and the question would be put: 'Johnny has twelve apples. Now, he always liked to share what he had with others, and so he asked his three friends if they'd like some, too. He felt it would be best if they all got the same number. How many did each of the children get?' You see, it changes totally, and if we can imagine these young people growing up into scientists, so that *everything* they've learned is saturated with their inner goodness, then these people would be the ones who'd be deciding the direction of science; these people would be the ones who are running the country.

And what signs do you see in the world today, of a greater saturation with these human values?

I think it's coming more and more . . . Again, the darker the night, the brighter the light. I feel in many ways the darkness is increasing. We can see that in so many areas, with the new drug 'crack' and the young people falling apart with drugs, and the violence and disobedience in schools, with parents . . . the breakdown of marriages and so forth. The darkness is definitely increasing.

But the light, the light, is getting so bright, isn't it? We just see it in the developments of science. Fritjof Capra in *The Tao of Physics*—a wonderful book—demonstrates that the language of the most advanced physicists is the same as the language of the esoteric spiritual people from Christianity and Buddhism and Hinduism; that it's the same language; that there is no difference between you and me, or between that building and that lake: it's just an appearance of form. There really is only one energy, and that energy is love.

So, you're saying the empirical sciences have brought us, in all their advancement and forward-thrust, back to—or up to—ancient wisdoms?

Yes. And these ancient wisdoms were discovered through intuition. We all know these truths intuitively. And there were people who sat in stillness in such a good way that these truths came to them.

I've got a friend in Thailand, Dr Art-ong Jumsai, who is one of the leading scientists in the world. And I don't know whether you remember that when they were trying to develop the Viking spacecraft to land on Mars they were having great trouble with the landing gear, they just couldn't get one that worked. So a number of scientists were asked, including Art-ong, and the first thing he did: he went away and he meditated and he meditated. He didn't think about the problem, he just sat still until his mind became absolutely motionless, and then, he said, suddenly, after . . . I don't know how long . . . it might have been a few weeks . . . suddenly there appeared in him the whole blueprint and it didn't go away. He wrote down all the details, sent it off, and it worked: the thing landed on Mars. So he is a living example of . . . and he teaches Education in Human Values in Thailand. And, do you know, just recently the Governmnt of Thailand has said that every school in Thailand now will be teaching Education in Human Values, because Dr Art-ong designed it and he's just been elected to Parliament. So every young child in Thailand will be learning that truth lies within: we just need to become still.

In what other countries are they taking up Education in Human Values, and to what extent in Australia?

It's very slow in Australia, and perhaps it's appropriate, because I think Australia one day will be like a tree on a mountain: our roots will be put down very, very carefully. We don't have the same spiritual background as a place like Thailand, which is saturated with Buddhism. But a place like Ghana, Nigeria . . . these people have taken Education in Human Values on totally. The Teachers' Federation of Nigeria has made it official policy that every teacher in every school in Nigeria will be learning about Education in Human Values and how to integrate it into every aspect of the curriculum. So it's more in places like Africa and Asia that EHV is racing ahead. There are significant advances being made in England, America, all countries really. Malaysia is moving very fast.

Ron, what do you mean about Australia becoming a tree on the mountain?

It's just an intuitive sense I have. Some of it comes from the Reverend Ted Noffs who, as you know, doesn't speak publicly any more, but when he did he described Australia as being a very, very rich place spiritually. And there are so many indications of how Australia does seem to have a sense of new directions that I just feel, in line with Ted Noffs, that Australia is a spiritual giant which will awaken, and when it does I think it will set a very good example to the rest of the world. We see the beginnings of it with all our national, all our federal parties, agreeing that rather than opt for the mining treaty in the Antarctic they'll go for a national park. Now that, to me, is a spiritual step, and I think there'll be more of that coming from Australia.

Ron, when you listen to the news and you hear about the economy, how do you process that?

I figure they don't know what they're doing! I don't know what they're doing, either . . . .

That appears to dominate the news.

There's no mention of human values in it. There's no mention of love, there's no mention of peace, no mention of right action, no mention of non-violence. There's no mention of truth—truth isn't even practised. And so to me they won't be able to go in the right direction until some recognition is given to these basic human values which we all share. I feel that just from the teachings of Sathya Sai Baba, the little bit that he's said about economic principles is that the only thing that has any real value is the heart of man, or the heart of mankind. And so until that is given prime value, more than the value of wheat or a car, then I think we're going to keep going around in circles and making mistakes.

What would bring that change? I mean, if you were to go into the Stock Exchange today, or maybe to the Futures Commodities Market, where they're actually buying and selling an idea, and said 'Well, the answer is in the heart of man,' what would be . . . I suppose they wouldn't hear you . . . ?

I think maybe one in a hundred would think, 'Oh, I agree with that,' but they wouldn't say anything.

So, what will bring the change then in that area, which appears to dominate at the moment? A crash, a darkness . . . ?

It could be a darkness. Hopefully, it won't be. I have great hope for the children. It doesn't take long for children to grow: I mean, we've got people even at the age of twenty-six, as we were saying before, who have such wisdom—just at the age of twenty-six. It's not a long time from the age of ten to twenty-six; it's only sixteen years. So we can, I think, know that great changes are coming, through our children.

Is humour important in your life—laughter?

Yes, very much. In fact, I had a little friend, Lucy, with whom I shared a house for a number of years, and I noticed that she would come up and say, 'Tickle me, tickle me!' And I used to marvel at how she would just lie there and shriek and I determined that I would learn how to do this, and now I can. I ask people to tickle me sometimes and it is just exquisite! First of all, it's painful, just like a breakdown, and then there's the trust and the letting go and the falling apart and the dissolving into everything, and then it's just a joy. I love laughter, but more than laughter I love bliss. I love what it is that triggers off laughter; I love that feeling of the honey that everything's saturated with.

But sometimes you encounter anger, rage, fear around you, don't you?

Yes, I do. I feel that when that happens it's an opportunity for me to realise tha none of that can hurt me, really. It can hurt my ego—it can destroy my ego. Well, that's good. Who wants my ego? I want to be me, I don't want to be my ego. And so, within that anger, within that rage, can be something productive for me. But also, within that anger, there's a tremendous force waiting to be harnessed for good.

I mean, look at Mahatma Gandhi: in his youth he was a very angry young man, very angry, who treated his wife and his children abominably, and through studying the *Bhagavadgita*, reading it every day, and making his life a totally spiritual journey, he learned to harness that energy. And it became so powerful that he, with the people of India behind him, threw the English out of India. You see, he learned to harness that power so that it wasn't used for destruction, but it was used for good. I feel that's what all this anger's about: it's just out of ignorance that people are misusing that anger.

So, we've got to find the way to harness that energy. You talk in the tapes about the danger of the anger turning upon oneself. Now, what does that do?

Yes, when we turn that destructive energy towards ourselves it's like denying who we really are. I think if we're going to hate anything we should hate the habits that bind us. Like, if I watch TV too much, then if I feel any anger coming up in me towards someone, I'll immediately think, 'Right, television—yeah, I hate that habit of watching television—I hate it, I hate it.' And that gradually reduces that habit, you see. So the energy can be harnessed, but it takes a bit of practice.

But directing it against ourselves, I think, is one of the greatest mistakes, because it's a denial of the truth. Our nature is exquisiteness, and how can you hate exquisiteness? It's just a total distortion of the truth. It's something that we've been taught by some adult when we were little. It's just not right. People who go so far as to commit suicide . . . as soon as they've tried to do it, from what I've read, they find out they've made an incredible mistake: they took a wrong direction. To hate oneself—that is, one's own exquisite nature—is like using gunpowder to blow up your own house: you just don't use it for that.

Now, what will we find on the many tapes that you've made? What's the range of subjects discussed there? What are the ideas we'll encounter?

Well, there's the *Nervous Breakthrough* tape, and that's of value to every body who is looking for a meaning to life; but it's of particular value to those who are going through difficulties. The *Self-esteem* tape reminds people that all of the mistakes and apparent failures we make are stepping stones towards success. The tape to do with overcoming depression is to help people recognise that the darkness is so we can discover our inner light. The tape we've made on *Weight Reduction for Beauty and the Ideal Form*, helps us understand how we can develop control over what goes into our mouth and develop a respect and liking for our true nature. Another one, called *Mastering Fear*, teaches the nature of fear: that, like the *Course in Miracles* says, there are two emotions—love and fear—and fear is but the shadow of love. It doesn't really exist: it's there, pointing the way back towards love. The *Relaxation* tape has been in use for a long time; it's a general all-rounder for reducing tension. And the *Insomnia* tape, too. And the *Anti-stress* tape is a bagful of little, wise techniques, if you like, for reducing stress.

Ron, what are some of your thoughts on being a parent.

Parenting, I think, is the art of doing work on oneself so that the child has a model to follow. Parenting, I don't feel, is so much about setting rules and saying 'Do this and don't do that.' But, rather, endeavouring to refine one's own personality, so that it makes it easier for the child to retain their own godliness, so that we don't take them away from that. We want to do as little as we can to distort their true goodness. And in order to do that we have to dive deep and find the goodness within ourselves.

So children learn more from us as models than from us as lecturers?

I feel so, yes. I remember my eldest daughter saying to me when she was about twelve and I started to talk to her again, 'Dad, now don't get offended, but don't give me another lecture.' It shook me; it really shook me. And I pondered on it for about four or five years, until eventually I began to realise that if I did want to influence my children it wasn't through giving them lectures, it was through setting an example. And so that's why I don't drink and I'll never ever drink again in my life: it's not that I want to say to them, 'Don't drink,' it's just that if they are to be assisted in any way to not get involved in drinking as much as other Australians do, then perhaps my example will help.

How do you know that it does, or will?

I think it's just trust. You trust that if you dive deep and discover your own strengths and goodness, then in some way which we can't predict, this light will shine on whatever it's meant to shine on. It might not be on your own children; it might be on the next-door neighbour's children.

You asked me before what's the last thing I would like to say, and I suppose it's a quote from Sathya Sai Baba and it says something like: 'When you're seeking this happiness and strength and goodness within yourself, you have to dive deep.' We can't be like someone who is told, 'Look, there are pearls in the ocean.' We can't just go and put our feet in the water and walk in up to the knees and say, 'Well, I can't see any pearls.' We have to go to where the person who knows about the pearls says they are, and then we have to dive deep, again and again, and then we will find the pearls.

Self Help Therapy Tapes
P.O. Box 118
Rozelle NSW 2039

Yvette Christianse

This conversation with South African-born Australian poet and writer, Yvette Christianse, is about the experience of otherness, of being an outsider, of being hurt by feeling different and of finding a creative way to express the turmoil. Anyone who's known this feeling of exclusion, whatever the circumstances, may well relate to her story, demonstrating once again that what is most personal is also most universal.

And that clearly is the intention of Yvette Christianse, who gives us a poignant impression of growing up in what she calls the 'pigmentocracy' of South Africa, where shades of skin colour are precisely measured and used to classify people and assess their worth, what they may do, where they may live, and what rights they may be denied.

Although Yvette's maternal grandfather was English and white, her grandmother, from the Island of St Helena, was of mixed race and dark, like Yvette and her mother. Yet her sister is fair.

This mixed-race status designated the family for a suburb in no-man's-land on the uncertain edge of Johannesburg. Life outside the security of home was deeply confusing and precarious.

So what you'll read is something of the detail of prejudice which oppresses in a subtle, relentless way, producing self-doubt and a repressed anger which, for the child, turned into puzzled sad feelings of dirtiness . . . for the adult into a life-threatening illness. After that, each day now seems a treasure.

With the eye and spirit of a poet, Yvette responds to all that has happened to her. She is able to transform the pain into beauty. She offers her poems as community singing which calls to every man and woman, regardless of colour, creed or nationality.

Yvette came to live in Australia in the early Whitlam years and felt immediately at home. She was eighteen. She graduated as a teacher. Australia played a vital role in freeing her thoughts.

Today she lives by faith and trust: faith that she will breathe the next breath, that she will be loved; trust that she will put pen to paper and write something of value.

Aboriginal Australian readers will feel a special kinship with Yvette, as will those with a disability, and perhaps many migrants. But this story is for everyone who cares for justice and wants a more loving human community.

Yvette Christianse strives to outgrow the apartheid of her childhood, rejecting the Freudian idea that we are pinned by the heels to our infancy no matter how hard, how far, or how valiantly we aspire and run. But she knows the early memories are powerful and formative and she begins her story with one of her first shocking experiences of real difference and apartness through skin colour. It came at school when she was still very young . . .

YVETTE CHRISTIANSE: I was very fond of a friend I had there, and I remember coming out of the classroom one day—I'd been held back for some reason—and I came out of the classroom and she was waiting there and I was so pleased, I was deeply moved by this. And she came along and walked beside me. And then another young girl came (this was my first year of school, so we were quite young—I started school early—I was about five), and they sort of walked really very close to me, and I remember the sound of our suitcases clucking against each other and I had this wonderful feeling of warmth, and they walked me right round the back of the schoolyard and then beat me up—because I was a different colour. And it was quite appalling and I knew, I knew, that if I hit them back I would really hurt them. But that, and then getting put off the bus . . . I think it was my second year of school (I did miss a year of school because I was very ill—I had rheumatic fever) I was put off the bus by a white bus conductor, because he said, 'Oh, what are you doing on this bus?' And so, I was put off in the middle of nowhere; I was quite lost. Maybe that's why everything being in place and knowing where I am is very important . . . yes.

What about going to the pictures or going to the post office or . . . ?

I remember (I would've been about nine or ten) standing in a queue to see something at the pictures with some of the other children from our neighbourhood, and the manager coming out and saying 'What are you doing in this queue? You know you shouldn't be in this queue!' And I can't describe the anger and the loathing of this man; I couldn't understand why he was so personally angry with me. It was humiliating, it was the most appalling thing. And the thing that you feel is that . . . you don't understand exactly what it is, even though you realise, well, it's something to do with your skin, it's something to do with your colour. It's the reason why Mamma doesn't ever come and fetch you from school. It's the reason why, when you are in hospital, Mum doesn't come and see you. It's the reason why, when you're in hospital at Christmas and Santa Claus comes and some visiting dignitary comes to give out teddy bears, or whatever it is, to all the children, she stands at the foot of your bed and she looks at you and she's so *angry* with you. And she looks particularly at your legs because you're laying on the bed-covers (which was hospital rules in those days—I don't know if it still is—but you didn't sleep under the covers during the day, you were on the top), and she's looking at your legs against this white bedspread, and you're suddenly aware, so potently, of the colour of your legs, the brownness of them against the bedspread. And you don't know why, but you want to put them away, you want to hide this. And she goes away and she has these agitated words with the matron and with this Santa Claus who is supposed to be this wonderful person, and she goes away and all the other children in the ward have got something and you have not, and that there's something . . . why? Now, you think, 'Can they see something really wicked in me? Is there something terrible in me? Because these people are good, these people come around and they do good things, like giving children presents.' So if the good people think there's something in you, you must be bad, you must have something that is wicked, that is unclean.

So, yes, I think when you stand in a queue and that happens, you apologise, in a way. And yet, inside you, there's a part that is the most exquisite holy part of yourself, that knows 'No. No, this is not so because at home I am loved. At home I have in Papa's back room my hammer and my nails and he teaches me how to put things together, he teaches me how to love the smell of varnish, how to love the way he brings the grain out in wood when he varnishes something. And at night when I go to sleep, I have Mamma, whom I can sleep with and she . . . '

'Mamma' is grandma, yes?

My grandmother—that's right. And she will tell me wonderful stories. And in summer they will open the curtains and there will just be the lace curtains, and the apricot tree will come surging in as shadows from the moon, and the whole bedroom will be a kaleidoscope, and in the leaves moving on the wall Mamma will find stories to tell me, and Papa will listen, and Mum will come home from work and will bring me a book, and Martha will be there. I have these things; but in the heat of being told to go away, when you're standing in a queue, those things have very small voices, very small voices—and what you have mostly is very bright blood in your head, that is so blinding, because you are afraid: what will they do to you? And why? Why?

Were there ever times when you disowned your family or a member of your family?

Yes, I think that's my greatest shame—and one that I understand now. Because my grandmother was so dark, she never came to school to fetch me or anything like that. And I sort of understood that there was a thing where your friends didn't come to your home. Now, I went to a white school, a Catholic school—and so I didn't have that kind of thing after school: playing (except with the children in the neighbourhood, the children who were like me). And I remember being ashamed of my grandmother's skin when a school-friend had come one day and it was . . . I describe it as . . . I think, one of the most appalling moments of my life, because I knew what I was doing . . . this fabulous woman, this marvellous, marvellous woman; so generous of spirit, so human. I remember that moment, dreadful moment, and for me it would be the same as, say, victims, survivors of an air-crash who survive only because they eat the bodies of the people who have not survived—the self-revulsion. But it doesn't defeat me anymore. That is my victory, because I understand why people do those things, and I feel immense compassion for people who are in situations like that. I understand. But it's hard. I don't know whether I've ever forgiven myself deep down; part of me has.

So many women in your childhood?

Yes. Yes . . . I think in South Africa, one of the things that maintains some degree of humanity (it's a word I keep coming back to, but I really . . . I celebrate that word; I don't think people really use it rightly, properly; it's a marvellous thing) . . . In South Africa, one of the things that really does maintain that, which reminds people that they are human, that they must, that they can't help but feel love is the whole nanny system. That's terrible, it sounds like I'm supporting that system—which is not good, because nannies (black women) who have their own children can't nurture their own children, because those children must live somewhere else in a township. (They don't even have suburbs; a suburb is a thing which is very located, which is permanent—if you think about the word. But black people live in townships—and if you think about the word 'township', it really doesn't have the same permanence. It is something which can be blown away by a wind.) But for the lucky, lucky children who do have the love of those nannies, of those black women who give this involuntary love, who give this wonderful warmth to everybody because they are just being human, they—the lucky children—have something which the system doesn't know they're getting. It's subversive in its strange way, that nanny system.

And when I was in South Africa in 1985 and coping with being there, which emotionally . . . and physically it was just bad to be back there, but in another way it was good because I could release all the old things: open the doors, look at the devils . . . poof! and away they'd go. But when I was walking down the street on a midday, a weekday, I just knew that in every house that I was going past, there was a woman there who was putting everything in place. There was a woman there who was nurturing and sustaining the good things that we get when we are children, that sustain us through our lives and make us genuine people, that make us . . . that give us the roundness, that give us the space we take when we take a breath, that allows the world to come into us—it was a most potent feeling, it was really something to rejoice in.

And I think the women truly are what hold that country together. Because there are women who are mountains in nearly each household. And so, in my family when I was at childhood, that kind of humanity, that kind of respect, that old-fashioned respect is what I remember so strongly from my childhood: the respect you had for your neighbours, for the coalman, for the bottleman (the man who used to come round collecting bottles in a sack; I'm sure you had them in Australia, too . . .

Yes.

. . . a marvellous sound the bottles make.)

Yes . . . and the iceman . . .

Oh no, I didn't have an iceman, we had a refrigerator . . . a fridge. No, we didn't have an iceman—and we didn't have a night-cart man, which is what . . . something in Australia they had.

But you respected everybody, the manhole-cover man (did you have those? They came and checked the drain out) . . . Oh yes, you respected them. My grandmother would make a pot of tea for them. They'd be out there on the corner checking out the . . . I suppose it was the sewers they were really checking out . . . well, at morning teatime, if they were there, they were sent a pot of tea and a pile of sandwiches. And my grandmother wasn't unique, it was just the wonderful oldfashionedness that women did for each other and for other people . . . .

And, Yvette, who are some of the male influences in those first eighteen years of life in South Africa?

Yes, well, my grandfather, of course, who was just a lovely man. I never understood that men didn't cry. I remember coming to Australia and hearing about this—men crying and this big fuss they were all making about . . . 'Oh, yes, men can cry,' and I never understood that this wasn't supposed to be 'normal', because he was a marvellous man. I suppose everybody's grandfather is a marvellous man, so I join the ranks of having a marvellous grandfather. He worked with wood, he was a cabinet-maker, a master cabinet-maker, and so he brought home every evening the sawdust; and so he reminded me of a tree. He was a tender man. If he hurt another creature . . . I remember one day being in a car with him on a Sunday drive, a dog ran in front of the car and we went over it and the dog died. Well, the two of us were sitting on the pavement crying our eyes out and, I think, crying more than the dog's family were crying. So, yes, my grandfather was a very strong influence, because he was very patient with me, he took a lot of time and he played with me.

And there was, around the corner from us, a school where they had a Sunday school, a Methodist Sunday school, and there was a man called Brother Hack and he was fabulous, because he could tell Bible stories as if . . . oh, he was better than the movies! And he would come out and play in the playground with us, too, in his absolutely immaculate suit. And he was like something out of a Bible story in a modern period, because he would come out there, he was immaculate—the immaculate conception. And, for me, the influence (if I have to say what kind of influence he was) was storytelling. Even though I had storytelling from my family, it was a different storytelling. And, I think, to have the outside storytelling for a writer, for a poet, brings a new sharp edge.

Washdays

I

On washdays, our backyard steamed.
The women—my grandmother and Martha,
nanny who vanished into Soweto
one evening train.

The wet sheets are warm,
they plaster against you
like a clasp of love.

Moisture leaves the small yard,
farewelled by handkerchiefs,
bruised dungaree knees—

all the private coverings
of hearts and fevers,
antimacassar courtships.

II

Our lives rise in clouds above our yard.
I don't know what shapes they take,
what shapes their rains take,

or if they reach other places,
if needles of rain unpick
for America, England
our dreams and fears,
our illusions and griefs.

III

The backyard is a lake at dawn,
taking its light from a hot mist
and I am a tiny boat,
a brown duckling, forgetting,
lifting too, paddling clouds,
heartsinging as Brother Hack taught me:
'I know I am, I know I am,
I am H-A-P-P-Y.'

I leave that walked-smooth ground,
leave the hiccuping lane,
the coal bin that clucked
against the shovel;
leave the feet that play 'Catch'
between walls of steaming sheets;

leave behind folding time,
being swung in crisp whiteness,
laughter, laughter in the hammock;
two brown women staunch as trees.

Sleeves hold out after me,
handkerchiefs tremble—
I leave you behind
to the Victoria Sponge,
the split-pea soup, Sunday School,
my grandmother's arm that is a bough
of my apricot tree

I leave behind Martha's vanishing,
her leaving of tears and relics
that come out on holy days,
leave these mothers of unbearable farewells.

Speak to us about your writing and how you experience your writing, how that helps you find out more about you, about life . . .

Yes, my writing. My moment of deepest self-love, my moment of joy, my moment where my heart is really open, my moment when I'm safest, my moment when I dare to look into the things that I would normally not dare to look into. I hold my pen like a lightning rod sometimes. Oh, my writing . . . my writing puts me in place; it says, 'This is my worth, this is me.' I can say, 'I can name you—whatever you are that is hurting me.' I can name all those faces in my childhood that ever put me off a bus, that ever looked through a counter. I can name the faces of the policemen who beat a black man. I can name the dreadful things that entered my inner world and entered all my nights, my sleep—when I should have been dreaming of wonderful things—the things that became the demons, real-world demons, so terrifying. I can name them when I'm writing because I stop the world and I am taking a deep breath and I am absolutely in place. I am in the square and I draw this marvellous circle around me—and that's where I reclaim words. I reclaim the word as simple as 'colour'. I don't flinch anymore when I use the word 'colour' because it's a small 'c' —when I'm writing. And when I'm writing, I am honouring the whole tradition that my grandmother and my grandfather and my grandmother and my mother gave me: the tradition of courage. And I'm honouring the wonderful sustaining friendships that I have in this country now, which is . . . as soon as I arrived in Australia in 1973, I felt as if I had come into my front door, and I'm sure you've heard many people who've migrated here, say this . . . that they feel they've arrived home. The first day I got off the plane I sighed—I'll never forget that, I felt this . . . well, when I'm writing, I honour that feeling. I honour the friends that I have here, my friends. I tell them like my living rosary, I say their names to myself sometimes. And it's a kind of tithing, when you write. When you write, you're acknowledging everything, because when you think further back, everything that's been given you—the love, even the food, the clothing, the teaching, all the good teachers that you've ever had . . . well, what on earth are you going to do with this, that they've given you? Well, surely you must say thank you in some way. Well, I don't think this consciously when I'm writing—that doesn't exist. But sometimes, if I dedicate the poem, or sometimes I have a special person in mind when I'm writing the poem, then that's it.

So there's feeling of homecoming in Australia . . .

Yes.

. . . and yet, you've also been very ill, since you were here.

Yes, maybe you feel safe enough to be ill in your own home.

Do you think so?

Well, yes. It was quite a few years after I'd been in Australia, I was confronted with a life-threatening illness and I wasn't surprised when I got the illness because I know it was . . . it had been caused by all my anger and my wanting to put myself away, my wanting to put my body away, apologising for my existence and how best to apologise to somebody who is 'a good person'—remember, who brings presents to children in hospitals—how best to apologise to those people. You take yourself away, you say, 'I will do the right thing for you, I will cease to exist, so that only "good people" can live.' And the anger of knowing that is not so, and the inner conflict . . . you know, I'm not the only person; think about all the people who are there now, who have these daily inner conflicts of knowing 'No, I am as good as . . . and often better. I am—really; and I'm not being allowed.' But you must deal with the conflict of being not good enough and knowing that you are good enough and, yet, at the same time behaving as if you know you are not good enough. No, no no no—it's not very good, so it can make you very ill. I think I was lucky that I got ill because then I could release it all, I could say, 'Well, poof! Off it goes!'

Did you?

I think so. It came back—I cleared it and then it came back. And that was the worst, the time which was really bad, but it also . . . Oh, this is a terrible cliché: it was, I think, the best thing . . . No, it wasn't the best thing but it was a good thing, a good thing that it came back, because then I could put it in perspective. I could say, 'Well, I'm sick, let's say that it's like a cold and I have to get it out of my system.' Don't make it any bigger, just put it in perspective that it is something that is in your body, and trust . . . oh, trust that you can get well. In the same way that I trust that when I pick up my pen and I am moved—moved like, say, in Genesis: if you are like the water, and the wind moves over you—I am moved like that to pick up a pen and I trust that something is going to come onto that page, this fabulous magic is going to happen. Well, I trust that I'm going to get better. I trust that every footstep I take takes me towards a moment without pain. I trust that every footstep I take takes me to light, takes me deeper into the love of all the friends who came and supported me, deeper into myself—oh, into myself, where none of all that business from childhood exists, where it has no place, to the *sanctum sanctorum* of the self, which always simply *is*, which always simply exists. That is what I can touch, that is what I touched when I was ill, and that is what gave me my life, and that is what gives me my life now. That is what gives me my writing. Yes. Yes.

What else can you say about that sense of what is*? That's like your faith, really, isn't it?*

Yes, yes. I don't know how to describe this sense I have of 'is-ness'. I suppose it comes from trying to call this notion, this concept of God something other than 'God' because I have trouble using that word, because it's associated with a lot of things . . . I suppose, again, with my childhood, because the God that they taught me in school—I went to a Catholic school, I was Anglican and I went to a Methodist Sunday school (which my grandfather said was very good for me) . . . .

And presumably the Afrikaner leaders are men of the Church . . .

Absolutely! Absolutely!

. . . was that confusing?

Yes it was, it was deeply confusing for me. I couldn't understand why this God . . . I don't think I thought, 'God, why are you doing this?' but I couldn't understand. I would go to Sunday school, and Catechism every morning and they would be telling me these wonderful stories about the rightness of God and, you know, if you go to a funeral . . . There was a lady down the road, she was like Maude (you know in the film *Harold and Maude*), she used to go to funerals all the time, but she didn't just do it herself, she always took me and her grandson, so I was always going to funerals. My grandmother thought she was taking us to the park, for years. I thought this was a normal thing for children to do: to go to funerals, and even funeral parlours and kiss corpses—I didn't know . . .

But I couldn't understand this God, especially when you go to a funeral and it is all so reassuring, 'You are in Me', and 'I am the Way,' and 'If you believe in Me, then all . . . ' I couldn't understand this: why, when I walked down the street, did this thing I live in actually bite? Why? Why? And why did really sad things happen to people? Why did the people . . . the evangelists who used to come round to our suburb once every fortnight or something, and dump their pulpit in the middle of the crossroad where we lived, and preach to us from these Bibles (with their wives in these lime and rose crimplene suits), preached to us about . . . '*Hera!* You will be saved! And God so loved his son,' and all of these things . . . why did they look at me as if I was something that just crawled out from a rock? I couldn't understand this business, these funny people—goodness me! So, I don't think that this God spoke to me: this God was sitting like a very heavy weight on the back of my head.

So, for you, it's almost the coursing of your blood in your hands which is more a testament to life, to faith, than some external dogma that someone wants to teach you.

Yes. You see, I've been raised to think that we are all—for instance, if I go the orthodox way—we've all been created by God; but at the same time I was also raised (I don't know if this had something to do with the orthodoxy or not) that we are all in God and everything is God, right? So if everything is God, my grandparents are God, and my mother is God, and I am God—all the family, all the friends. So if I celebrate them, and if I celebrate the life, the physical life that I've been given, and my blood with all its mysteries, all its mysteries about colour that I don't even know about—because where I lived you didn't ask too far back in case you really came, well, right up against the 'Big Black', you know . . . So, yes, I celebrate these things, they take me every single day of my life a step deeper into God, into what *is*. Yes, then every day of my life is a celebration. It isn't always—I forget it sometimes. Then somebody reminds me, somebody reminds me.

Speaking in Tongues

We have learnt their names:
half-caste, play-white, upstart;
and we have their history
trekking through the rivers
of our blood;
and in these rivers, with their Colonial bridges,
fish sing
with the voices of our mothers
telling us of our fathers.

I went to school with Jan van Riebeek,
in the hull of a Dutch East India barque,
wished for my own Rosetta stone
while the declension of pronouns
stumbled in Latin farmyards.

I prayed and hallelujahed
Anglican and Catholic,
Baptist and Methodist,
shared Ramadan feasts
and circled a Buddha.

When I bled
it was the same colour as everyone.
When I stood in a queue,
their bodies went silent
and were like ships too careful
to come close in a storm.

And I have never known
what names are buried
in the banks of my body.
I do not know what languages
coined them, what trials.

I am lost. I am lost
my mothers, my fathers.
Lost in the lateness,
lost in the detonations
of the present
and futures like gulls
pecking at sea-spray,
lost in my own happiness too

because I carry you
and you speak in tongues
that surpass brutality.
And when you dance in my cells
my body moves, bright with life;
moves through the sunlight of books
you never read—
I read them for you
if you ever were a slave,
I read them for you
if you ever looked up
and were moved to tears
for something other than your pain,
I read them for you
if you ever loved,
if you cheated with a single atom of joy.

God, in his cassock and clouds of incense
has risen and dissolved
and left me in peace.
I take my blessings from you now
and my skin sings for you,
my hair curls for you,
my teeth, my eyes, they are the offerings
you give back to me.
I hear your heavy work songs die
and I hear the shout of your new songs
in the vast sunrise
of a country you never knew.

How do your dreams inform your writing and your living and your understanding?

Well, the background of my family has always put importance in dreams, we used to talk about our dreams every morning. In the morning you talked about your dreams and at night you had stories—there was a lot of togetherness. But the dreams? Well, sometimes my dreams are telling me either I'm clearing stuff, or otherwise a new way to go. Maybe I can tell you an important dream that I had?

Yes.

Well, the house that I lived in in Curry Street in Johannesburg—I love the name 'Curry Street' . . . I loved that house because for seven years of my life—an important number—it was the stability. And that was where I had my first conscious being in the world. But, because some terrible things that happened to me in that house (I had been molested as a child by two people who were friends of the family), because that'd happened in the house, the house then became very painful—although, the house was a good house because it was the house of love.

So, in my dreams the house was for many years in darkness, it was always a night-time dreaming that I had of the house, and there were things that I couldn't see in it, and dreadful things which lurked in the house. And then something very important happened to me about a year ago. I dreamt that I was coming to the house and I needed to go in, but the house was full of demons. It was like a chook-house—you know, the activity that there is in a hen house—but these were not friendly little hens, they were very demonic and everybody was avoiding the house, but a friend was with me. She didn't come into the house; I knew I had to go in. And I went up the stairs, and I went into the front door and knew that I had to go. And I opened the door, and I was dying with fear inside. And all the demons ran into the bedrooms, ran into the house, into all the small rooms off the passage-way. I went further in and I opened the bedroom doors and the demons disappeared, they just did not exist in there. And I was terrified—I cannot describe it . . . it's almost—you know when you're so afraid you cannot move, paralysed with fear. But I knew that I had to go. And it wasn't me that was moving myself, it was my heart that was moving me because my heart knew 'This is it. You have to do this because otherwise . . . ' Well, I didn't know what otherwise. And then all the little demons disappeared; there was only the big one and this was the devil (which comes from my religious training), and the devil just retreated as I moved up the passage-way (you know those old-fashioned houses with the long passage-ways?). As I moved up the passage-way this devil just retreated, just retreated, until we got to the back door. And then he went out the back door and slammed the back door really hard, and I knew now I must do something and I was terrified but I opened the back door and I put my face out—and all ahead was light, it was just into light, it was the most holy, the most exquisite light; and this devil did not exist. The backyard was mine again—because it had been in the backyard where a man—'Mr L', I call him, who was German (it's funny, these pure-race people)—he had molested me in the backyard and that was the place where I used to play with Papa. But now the backyard is my own and if I do dream about that house now it's in the daytime and I'll play in the backyard again.

So what that dream, I think, told me is that I must have the courage to look my demons in the face—and it's not just easy mouthing of things, it's not just thinking it, it's not intellectualising it, it's to trust, to really trust. That's the marvellous thing that I learn every day: to trust, to trust. You see, my body knows, my blood knows—my body doesn't even have to trust my blood, it's moving in my body right now. My heart is moving. Whew, my heart moved when I was put off the bus, my body moved when I was beaten up after school, my blood did not waver—it didn't run away somewhere. Well, it came out of my nose a bit, but that's as far as it went!

So that dream was a milestone for me. I rejoiced for weeks after that dream. I'm still rejoicing. I think I'll still be rejoicing in fifty years. Yes, dreams . . . I'm lucky in that I can have important dreams like that.

So these wonderful times of illumination come; and then, as you say, 'Sometimes I forget' . . .

Yes.

And it's good to know what it is that one can do to get back into the faith, into the trust—for you, is it principally writing?

I think it's more the preparation, because writing isn't just what happens on the page: You know, it's putting the thing in the pressure cooker and it happens in there. How do I do it? Well, sometimes . . . if you've got things, like daily living, there are all sorts of pressures, things that I'm sure everybody can identify with: paying your bills, going up to the grocer, making an appointment, being late, having too many things that you're doing, you've got to be at three places at once, 'How am I going to do all this without letting somebody down?', 'Am I doing this right?' 'Is it good enough?', and all these things. Well, for me, I know when that's all getting too bad because then my head is like a frying pan—you know the sound that a frying pan makes, all sizzling away? Well, what I just do is: I just lie down on my bed. If it's that bad, then I lie down and I trust I'm not going to fall further than the bed because the mattress will hold me; so that means I can just let all of my muscles go, and even if my body is saying, 'Oh, no. I'm not going to let go in case . . . ', I'll just say, 'Alright I'll just trust that it will happen.' Then I pretend that at the back of my head there are two big doors, and the doors fall open and everything goes shooting out the back and it's like a whole lot of pots and pans. Clang! clang! clang! clang! It all goes out and then it's all nice and empty—no more devils inside.

'Washdays' and 'Speaking in Tongues' are published in the anthology, *The International Terminal*, ed. Christopher Pollnitz, The University of Newcastle, 1988.

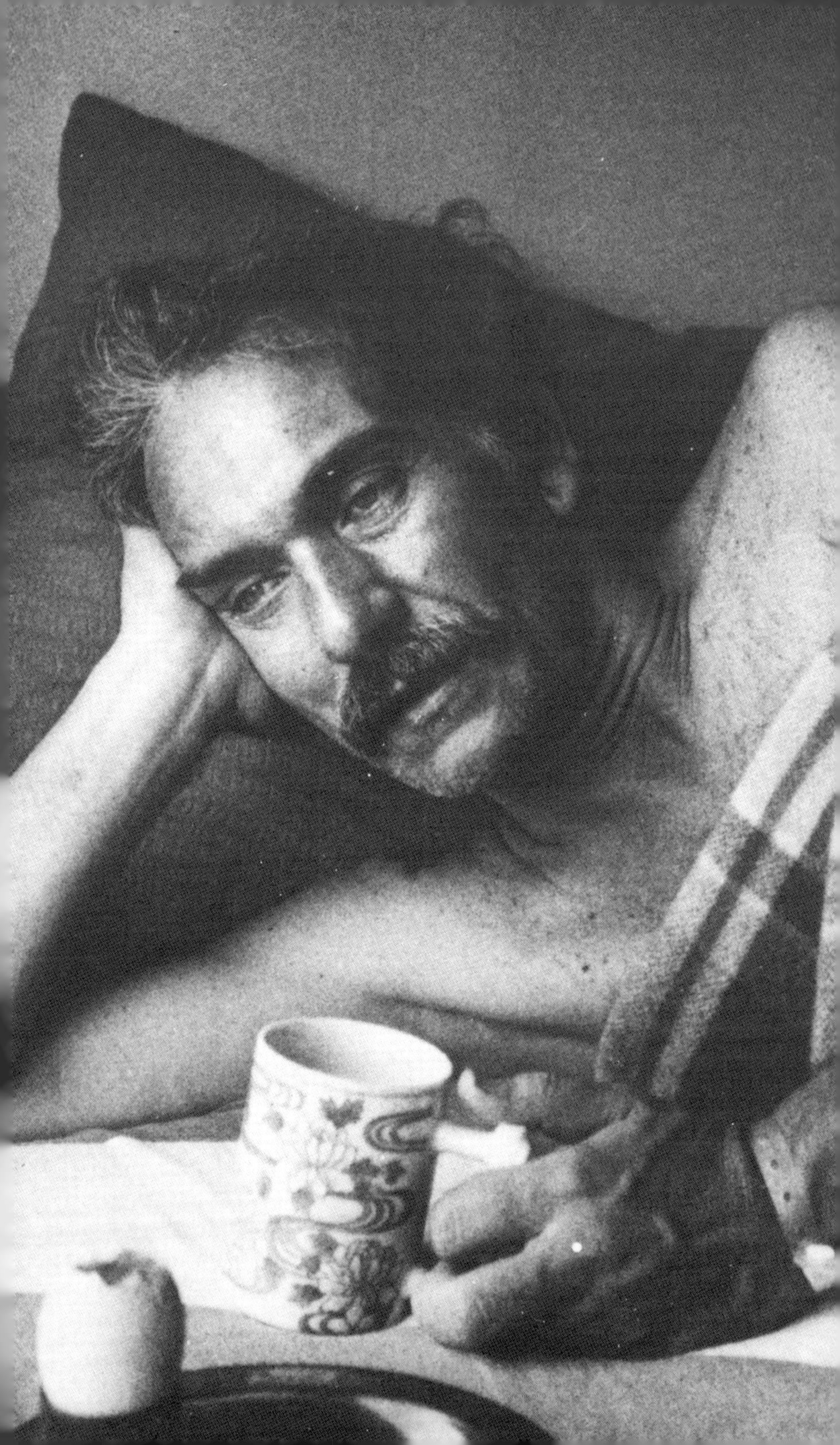

Aldo Gennaro

Aldo Gennaro della Francesca was one who sought to heal through art. His special gift was to encourage people, often those with disability, intellectually different, or mentally distressed, to find their own creativity.

You may remember a wonderful documentary on television a few years ago called Stepping Out. *It showed Aldo preparing, over the weeks, with a group of intellectually disabled people, a glorious performance full of colour, music, light, and energy, at Sydney Opera House . . . one of the most joyful events ever seen on Australian television.* Stepping Out *by Chris Noonan is a magical film that has taken off round the world, winning awards, a film that suddenly shows us a new way to see, that opens our eyes to something not understood before. And that was the talent of Aldo Gennaro.*

Aldo was born in Chile. He thought he may have been autistic as a child. He trained as a priest in the austere, contemplative Augustinian tradition, spending much time in silence.

Leaving the priesthood, he studied psychology, drama, education, and fine arts in Chile and in the USA, *where he worked for a time in the black, Puerto-Rican Harlem of New York with youth.*

In his extraordinarily productive years in Australia, through the 1970s and 1980s, he was in demand in every State, working with communities, and often for and with groups on the fringe, those disadvantaged, intellectually disabled, unemployed, psychiatric patients, re-located Aboriginal families, and prisoners.

He produced plays and events, and ran workshops, always drawing people into a circle in which they could discover more of themselves and of their creativity. Around this country Aldo taught and inspired. Wherever he went there was fun, and something new and joyful began to grow.

Where Aldo was, there was kindness and healing. He touched and enriched the lives of very many Australians.

Suddenly, in the midst of all this activity, Aldo was diagnosed as having the AIDS virus. His life changed dramatically.

The fiery energy was muted; the dancing no longer possible; a new reflective mood came as Aldo sought out the richness of life in making typically creative, practical and spiritual preparation for death.

Aldo Gennaro died on 27 February 1988, at St John of God Hospice in Sydney, among friends.

ALDO GENNARO: In the very early stage, when AIDS was diagnosed, I decided not to follow the medical language and the medical terminology. Somebody asked me what stage AIDS I have, I always answer, 'one step to heaven'. I think I am floating between the second stage at the moment. I'm probably moving into the first one but I don't know. I haven't had any immune system for quite a long time. I don't know how I have kept some sort of protective little aura around which doesn't allow some of the infection coming in. One of the problems with people with AIDS, is not so much that we can infect others but that others infect us. We are very vulnerable to any type of disease around the community or from friends.

What is your state of mind?

It is very good. I feel a little bit vague.

Dreamy?

Dreamy, yes. I spend a lot of time doing some sort of daydreaming. Little visions I suppose, I don't know what to call them. But that has always been very much part of my mind. Visualising things around, creating little stories from the things happening around me. And now I feel I have more time to indulge to myself in this type of dreaming and have written some material recently. I spent a lot of time doing drawing and painting. I love it and I now have more time to do it.

I would like very much to hear of some of the events of your life and your interpretation of them.

Very recently I have been in touch with the very early stage of my life. By reflecting and meditating about the process of death, the process of dying, I got in touch with my pre-born stage. When I was conceived my mother was mourning the death of a daughter (my sister), and of course she was in a lot of pain.

So it sounds as though you were born almost with some special understanding of dying or grief or sadness because of the feelings you had from your mother when she was carrying you?

Yes, yes I think so.

Do you?

I think it has had a lot of influence. We've never openly discussed that with my mother because it still hurts. For years I have been enormously influenced, by more than anything in the emotional structure, in my emotional body probably more than my intellectual.

Yes. Your life has been so much one to do with sound, with dance, with movement, with creativity. I wonder what you were like when you were a little boy growing up?

As a matter of fact I was very different. I was always removed from everything around me. My father used to call me *giraffo*, it means 'giraffe'. He felt my head was always somewhere else.

In the clouds?

In the clouds, probably. I was never present. I used to be an observer and I think that I've had the role all my life. I think I've been an observer, a witness of some sort of process around me—a reflection, and sometimes I see the society and world around me as a reflection. It's to be on the fringe, it's to be part and at the same time removed. It was very difficult for me to deal with that early experience later on, because I really wanted to be part of it. I want to feel human, I want to be human. I was probably in my late twenties when, for the first time, I started loving my body. I have memory of the time. Poetry I wrote when I was fourteen in some parts says, 'We are angels of broken wing in a dream of a god who went to sleep and forgot us'.

A very lonely feeling, Aldo?

Yes, a lonely feeling, but at the same time there was some sort of connection which now I understand a little bit more about. But I've always felt connected with something deeper than the social structure.

Would you say something about your experience in the monastery, because you decided that you would be a priest, an Augustinian priest, and this was still when you were living in Chile?

Yes. Following that state of mind between the ages of seven to fourteen which was removed and quiet and silent, I felt I got in touch with a lot of spiritual energy. I felt at the time the only way I could source that spiritual energy was in the church, the traditional church. In South America we are Roman Catholic and we have very little connection with any other religions, so there are no alternatives like we have here in Australia. I went there when I was fourteen with some sort of spiritual experience but not with spiritual knowledge. Probably looking for that, looking for an understanding of mysticism or spirituality, acknowledgement. And the things I learned in the four years were more to do with the structure of church, with the history of the church, with the bureaucracy of the church, but very little of the deep meaning I was looking for. I was a little disappointed at the same time. When I look back now I think it was a very interesting experience.

Did you spend a lot of time in silence?

Yes, the Augustinians in Chile have the Spanish tradition and they are hermits of St Augustine. We spent a lot of time in silence and we used to pray in Latin, which was a very foreign language to me. For three-and-a-half years I never had a conversation or communication. In another level was the study or reading or discussing mysticism but there was no communication on any humanistic level at all.

So in a sense, more loneliness?

Very lonely. But an extraordinary thing was the feeling of collective consciousness. When you can experience the silence of yourself, you can experience all that unity, all that collective consciousness. Probably the collective around me was very faulty, we never felt together and it was very competitive too, intellectually and academically. But it was an inner self, an inner consciousness, I know of that, it gave a very strong feeling of unity and collectivity.

One of your great gifts has been, somehow by your presence, and your particular ability to make contact with people who are intellectually different, people who have been emotionally hurt or feel mentally distracted, people who are in hospital or institutions for that reason. Now do you understand why that is so, why you have that special gift somehow to reach through, beyond words, beyond the accepted intelligence tests, because much of your work has been of that nature? What insight have you into that?

I think it's a process which involves probably like a Red Indian or an Aborigine would say, 'talking with the heart'. I think also it's the 'body language', which is very subtle and very open to us. I'm lucky to have been involved in drama and dance and having become very much aware of our body as an instrument of communication. Also, it's a gesture language, which appeals very easily, especially in minority groups which for one reason or other have been cut off from the rest of society, like intellectually disabled people who have a very rich communication through gesture, whereas we have very little. Then there's another one, probably more subtle, probably to do with a spiritual awareness which I call 'the elf'. This elf is a little energy inside of everybody, which communicates sometimes very differently to the impression of the person, when it comes around. Sometimes you can see the elf is in contradiction to what the person is saying in relation to who the person really is. Little elf is very naughty. So through that element I have become aware of my own communication and also in the communication with other people.

Do you think that your own experiences, at various times of your life, of finding it hard to communicate in words somehow have helped to bring out of you the other ways of communicating?

Caroline, this is why sometimes I feel all our lives are a constant process. When I was four years old I lost my speech for nearly eighteen months and later on I went to the convent where I spent four years without speaking. When I went to the USA I couldn't speak the English language: because I spent three years of silence when I just listened, and I used to be very involved with dynamic groups there. I was doing a lot of work in the community and I still didn't have any communication skills, verbally. You see, I rely on a lot of little signals and it's a type of energy of which we know very little and such an important part of any creative process. The receptive energy is what we use all the time in our active energy. The moment of silence and the space of silence between music is as important as the music itself. Probably it has been very helpful to me, and later on when I started using other means of communication with people and also with art.

Many people, I think, will remember, especially, your wonderfully dramatic and beautiful production at the Sydney Opera House with some residents of the Sunshine . . .

Yes, the Lorna Hodgkinson Sunshine Home.

Because a lovely film was made of that as well. So we saw the residents of this home, whom many people would think of as just people with Downs Syndrome, in this marvellous, colourful, creative, vibrant performance. Would you tell us something about that experience from your point of view?

Yes. I have always been interested in drama. I felt that drama could assist, especially in the learning processes. When I went to the Sunshine Home I wanted to establish the activity therapy centre for the residents who could no longer perform any functions in the institution by themselves and were more intellectually disabled than the rest of their community. First we asked, 'who wants to be a clown to entertain the rest of the residents of the home?' Here they were, the 'rejected', but suddenly, that group functioned to provide some sort of entertainment activity and that was very much welcomed by the rest of the residents. They understood the language, it was to do with dance and songs, and the bloke called on to be a clown was claiming, 'Yes, I can be a clown. There is nothing to be ashamed of in being a clown, not because I am Downs Syndrome; or when I go in the street and look funny and talk funny, I can be a clown, I can laugh from inside and invite you to laugh with us.'

Of course it was somewhat controversial at the time. Some people were accusing me of making fun of them, but later when I looked at it, we were having fun all together. Nobody was making fun of anyone. It was very powerful. The ones who understood immediately were the rest of the residents, who approached me later on and asked me to start a drama workshop in the evenings. Then we established this group which ended up performing at the Opera House.

I do remember when that was being rehearsed. Then seeing the performance and seeing the residents you'd been working with, with you, was revelation to me. The presence of love and joy between you and them was tangible and they couldn't keep away from you. You had brought them so much life and joy and love. It was a most wonderful thing to see and that is what I remember most. And I always wondered how you were feeling about that.

That was the first time that I experienced love in my life.

Was it?

Yes. A lot of feeling. That was the first time that I experienced real love in my life, unconditional love. Those people have the ability. They don't love you because you are special, they love you because the only thing they do is love. It doesn't matter if you are young or old or skinny or plump they give their hearts to you and that comes from very deep within themselves. Every time an intellectually disabled person touched me, I felt something very special. I felt a sense of release and I realised some sort of healing was happening inside of me. For that reason I relate very strongly mostly with intellectually disabled people, for they are very wounded people and they have the ability, they are the healers. They are the only real healers that I have become involved with in my life.

I remember that between dances when there was a few moments of rest they would come and sit around you. It was like seeing a great decorated Christmas tree, because they would come and sit by you and everybody had to reach out and touch. Everybody had to have just a few fingers on Aldo's arm. It was such a beautiful thing to see.

That was one experience that was just 'Ahhhhhhhh'. We were working in circles, that was very new for me. The circle has a quality of making the energy equal, but also, I took the responsibility—I don't like the word 'responsibility'—I took the function in that group to facilitate some of the process and it was centred in the energy, this beautiful diffuse energy. Intellectually disabled people have the ability of diffuse thinking, they do not lean on focusing, like other people who use their intellect in that way. They have a sequential, lineal structure in their thoughts and some of them can conceive five or six thoughts at the same time. So sometimes you need to have somebody focusing and my function was focusing. In the time of chaos, when everything was between rehearsal there was a need to come in and make contact with this focusing point.

To see that perfomance and to see the preparations and the aftermath was to actually see joy alive and love happening. It was a wonderfully *exciting time, wasn't it?*

It was wonderful, probably one of the most wonderful experiences in my life. The performance at the Opera House where there was glitter and it was very exciting, but it was the process to the Opera House that was very exciting. I think that the film *Stepping Out* got a lot of that image across, which is very pleasing to see. I get very emotional when I see *Stepping Out*.

Of course. And the film has gone around the world?

Yes, and did very, very well.

And where is God now for you?

I don't believe in God anymore. I experience God, I don't believe in God. Belief is intellectual . . . which I indulge myself, dreaming about different shapes and forms, but God is an experience.

So this is much closer and much more real, much more part of you?

Yes, it is and more constant, and more permanent. It is very creative. When I recognise and I acknowledge to myself that energy we share, it is a very nourishing energy. But how little we do things and share collective experiences together.

So ritual is important, is it?

I think ritual is very, very important. I think we live in a society of rituals.

And we have a lot of rituals. I think that ritual is very important to our worship, to the celebration of our life.

Do you think that it's especially important in relation to our ideas about death?

Yes. The process of dying and death by itself is a ritual which has been removed from us, completely. I am very lucky. I have started to put together the music that I want at my funeral. It was a wonderful thing to do. How little we participate in arranging our own funeral but we participate in arranging our weddings, we can choose the guests, the people, the party.

I think that in a lot of life's events we have an active participation in that ritual. But very little do we participate in the ritual of our death. Probably because we are not present altogether. But it doesn't mean we cannot go to the creative process of preparing it.

And you are doing that?

Yes, I did.

Are you afraid of death, as a fearful event that looms before you, or do you think of it differently?

I am frightened of some aspects of dying. I am frightened that I'll not be able to move or be able to get up in the morning and have a shower by myself and I know there will be the time when I can no longer do these very simple domestic activities. That frightens me a little. At the same time I feel it will feel like I'll be in a cocoon, hanging there. I know there will be people around who will probably want to assist me in very domestic things. I am frightened of that. I am frightened of losing my sight. I am frightened that the virus will go to my brain. I have always had little fears, they're minimal, they disappear very quickly. I do not have constant fear. I do not have any fear about the process of dying, when we are becoming a very refined energy, that refined moment of energy—the transition of that energy to another quality, another dimension. I am really looking forward to that moment. Sometimes I compare it to when I was coming to Australia, a continent somewhere. I had some images but very few. I didn't know what sort of people would be here, I didn't know the way they did things. It was another dimension, but it was very exciting. The same thing happens with the movement to the afterdeath dimension. It's like going to another country. I have a feeling there will be a lot of people I know there. Already I know a lot who are there, so it will probably be a time for reunion and celebration.

What do you think that we must understand about so many people having this disease of AIDS? What is it that we really need to see and respond to?

I think the first thing that comes into my mind is love. Homosexual people have been rejected for a long time. We have made fun of them. We have ridiculed them. Homosexual people are not aggressive people. They are gentle people and we have received so much aggression from many different levels. I think we need love, we need compasssion, we need understanding not so much compassion . . . love . . . we need love.

And love to be shown how?

Love shown in the way we talk about gay people, in the way we support gay people in this trouble. In going to our gay friends we should recognise what value they add to our lives. Assist them in what they are dealing with at the moment. Be there, just be a friend. I am sure a lot of gay people will be very happy to embrace new friends, with no difficulty.

Do you think there are some people now who are ill with AIDS or who are dying, who do not have the friendship and the support and the love that they need?

I think so. I think a lot of gay people at the moment are going through a very difficult time. They are dealing with the deaths of friends, of lovers. They are dealing with their own process of dying. Some of them are feeling very lonely and very confused. At the same time I would like to say here that it's extraordinary how brave gay men are, how much courage they have. They have been creating support groups, and they are looking after one another. (For the first time they have been in a community house.) We are creating a very close nuclear family. I think we have a lot to learn from that process. I think the gay people at the moment are presenting a beautiful model of support and caring and nourishment for one another. But it's much more. It's also good to see a lot of non-gay people participating in that process, especially women in the care profession.

Is there anything else that you would like to say to us about what is happening with you now?

Letting go. It's like the things that you let go are giving birth to new energy, more refined energy, more subtle energy; but the process of letting go is a very loving process, it's not a processing of rejection. I can't socialise in the way I socialised before. I could not dance any longer and to me to move my body around was so important. I got in touch with my body in that way, with so many centres of energy. I am losing concentration about things. My mind comes and goes very freely now. I think the social aspect starts, little by little, cutting yourself from people and things probably has been one of the more difficult, in the sense that part of yourself is very rapidly changing.

But you say that in a way it's leaving room for something more happening with the spirit?

Yes, I think it gives birth to new friends, to a new relationship with myself, to a new relationship with whatever is to happen in the future. Letting go also is living day by day. Something I always wanted to do and never knew how to do it. I knew there was so much truth and knowledge in living day by day but I never knew I was planning a little bit ahead. Now I'm living day by day and I think it's liberating. I think letting go is to do with freedom, it's finding enormous freedom within ourselves.

What about Dolores?

Ah, Dolores is a very exciting companion, Dolores.

How did you come to have Dolores?

I was working in Bathurst at the time, and a lot of Aboriginal families had moved from Bourke to Bathurst and I was doing a project in the Bathurst Gaol. After, I got in touch with Aboriginal children, who used to live behind a community centre I was restoring. They used to come in and do paintings and play with pottery. It was very lovely—we had a lot of close contact. One day their dog had puppies. A puppy would have been a small problem to me. I said, 'No, no, no, I don't want a dog, a dog will tie me down too much, I don't need a dog.' A few days later they came with one and said, 'You must have it.' It was the most beautiful present I have ever had, an excellent companion.

She's very tiny.

She's very tiny, she's a mixture. I think she has a little bit of Australian terrier or something. I can put her in my backpack with no problem at all. She comes with me wherever I go. We have a funny relationship, an independent relationship but also a very close relationship.

Trisha Watts

Do you recall the lively, slim, dark-haired young woman who led the singing at the Pope's Youth Peace Rally in 1986—a striking performer with a strong delivery and a vibrant jazz rock style? I have a vivid image of the Pope dancing hand in hand with happy teenagers

Through her troubadoring Trisha Watts is well known around the country, especially to youth, with her ability to communicate in their language which is her language, and to introduce spiritual ideas in a secular setting. She composes with lyricist Monica O'Brien and works through a cooperative called 'Willow Connection', which links music, spirituality and the creative arts through workshops, retreats and concerts, and the development of creative ritual and liturgy.

Like many other young people today, Trisha is shaken by the uncertainty of values and employment, and finds the established structures confining. She also has creative ideas about how to make a difference in the world. In this conversation we identify some of the elements which have formed a talented young Australian.

TRISHA WATTS: Probably, growing up on a farm, my long-lasting memory has been of waking up in the morning to sunrises and walking outside to frost and feeling the seasons, the weather—really being in touch with the sensual things that living on a farm brings. I think walking out and looking over the vast paddocks, just like a never-ending land, has really affected me, has got me in touch with solitude. And just growing up with a family who loved to play and to sing and to do creative things. Living on a farm you have to create your own fun, so we used to do that all the time.

And where did you sing?

Oh, everywhere! (laughs) We used to sing out in the paddocks or inside around the piano. We grew up in a big family, so everyone learnt the piano, and we sat around and sang there, around the fireplace, and we'd always yell out across the paddocks, you see. I think we developed these big voices because we had to yell to the animals and to each other. So it was just a common-day language: it was the first language really I learned—music.

And did you ever sing in a community setting?

Well, my family was my first community and I learnt harmony that way, but I think mainly through the church. My father was a choir conductor and at the age of seven I joined a choir and sang until I was eighteen. So every Sunday we'd all hop in the car and go in . . . the thing I always remember was just sitting in those choir seats and really singing full-on hymns, hymns which I grew up on. I never really understood the words or anything, but the sound of the music really has had a deep impression on me.

I grew up in a Christian background where it was often said 'You must have an answer', and certainly in a Christian upbringing you're told that Jesus is the answer, and that, for me, has always been a huge riddle. Because whenever I look at life, or look at the lifestyle of great people such as Jesus, I can see questions. I don't have an answer: a question comes to my mind. That saying of Rilke's, 'Live the questions; one day you might grow into the answer', to me was a huge encouragement, an affirmation, because I thought my questions were okay. Keep questioning; that's when you really discover the depths of what life is about.

And does writing songs help you to live out the questions?

Oh, absolutely!

And the voice is very important?

The voice, to me, holds a lot of power. From a very young age I was extremely shy and too scared to share what I really thought, and so voicing came through the music. As I fell in love with music I found a way of sharing my voice and being able to hear it through other people. Somehow I think in a lot of our culture we've been cut off at the neck! (laughs) We live in this 'head' society that's very mental: we use a lot of mental energy, and that leaves the whole other part of the body behind, where it's not heard. So, for me, the challenge is watching singers who really communicate to me. The ones who touch me at depth with some guts and soul are those who sing from there, not just from their heads—they sing with their hearts, with their bodies. I've always been fascinated by African singers, for instance, and some of the different countries, especially Third World countries, where the music comes from the earth and people who struggle with being grounded, so their music emerges from a deep place, a place of lived experience. I think that's what I'm trying to find. The voice is the thing that connects it because it sits right in the middle—you know, it runs right through your whole body—so my challenge is to try to link the head and the heart and the body and the spirit, integrate all those things but do it through the voice. If you can do that with other people, if you can allow their voice out and encourage it, then healing takes place: enormous healing and enormous reconciliation, letting go. Society says 'hold it together' and singing's about letting it go! It's a paradox.

So I feel that there's a lot of treasure hidden within voice that I'm only just touching on and I want to know more about that. I think it's a very spiritual thing.

You've mentioned also the importance of listening. Have you discovered from Aboriginal musical friends anything about listening?

Yes. I think it's mainly their ability to stay with one song for a long time. They don't do a song for two minutes and then move on to the next one, they stay with it . . . it's like a mantra, almost hypnotic. The music's like a process and they journey with it, they play with it, and they let it affect them, let it shift their consciousness into another place. So they really do listen. I think they listen at a deeper level. They can kind of let go of the music and let their whole bodies be surrounded by it, and it brings them to a place of real solitude, I think, because after you've experienced it it's just a matter of sitting with it and being drawn to this place they call 'dadirri', which is the place of deep inner listening where you can sit by a river and let it heal you. It's that whole concept of sacred space and sitting in it and allowing the sounds to heal you.

Can you relate to that idea?

Yes. There's a song, actually, that emerged from experiencing this. I was listening to a talk by an Aboriginal woman, Miriam-Rose Ungunmerr-Baumann, and she speaks about the place of dadirri and the need to tap into the deep water that runs under everything, that connects every living thing. And if we stay in touch with that we're always in touch with the healing. It's called 'Deep Waters'.

> Deep waters flowing, calling all to follow
> Watching, listening, waiting, silence finds a home.

This song brings up so many memories for me of truths, because it really taps into the seasons. The land teaches us that if we stay in touch with the really earthy things, the whole concept of living and breathing, really basic elements, we forget to deep-breathe, we get so caught up, choked up, in our living that we forget to take time to breathe deeply and drink in life. I think we are people who love to live in the summers of our lives—the sunshine, happiness, the beaches, being Australian people . . .

Activities . . .

Lots of activity, always on the go. And living in the city it's hard to let go of that and to enter into your own season of winter, our place of dying and letting go and nurturing so that budding can happen naturally in spring-time—let the rising happen. The voice does that, you see: it accommodates all those things. Whether we like it or not it's very truthful: it will tell you what season you're in.

Quite a number of your songs are, I think, simple in structure and repetitive. Why is that?

It's quite a departure for me to be writing repetitive material. Most of my material in the last ten years has been contemporary songs. But I felt a real need, or a calling forth, to offer something that would change people's consciousness. A repetitive mantra does that: it's hypnotic, it has a sense of lifting you into another space, another time. And that need to surround people with a sense of beauty and simplicity is an intuitive thing; it's hard for me to put it into words: it's just a sense that I feel that this is what I need and maybe others might appreciate it, too. You know, I need to slow down and I need material that helps me do that; and mantras do that, they're meditative, and they call you to a silence.

> Listen and see with your heart
> Come, rest, and wait in the wilderness
> Listen and see with your heart.

Trisha, there's a wonderful evolution in your music. If we go back a few years you're singing jazz and you're singing rock, and now something new . . . It's a sort of development, growing . . . ?

Mmmm. I think a lot of it is trying to find my own style that really suits me as a person, and also during those years I was experimenting, trying to see where I fit, where is my identity as an artist and as a performer, and what style is really me. And I guess in singing all those styles I still don't really know (laughs). They're all parts of me. What's so exciting is that when you're working on the edge of your art form you never really know what you're going to fall into, and that's where I feel I am at the moment, trying to trust that inner voice and trust how to be a mediator. The things that I experience in the outer world I then take in and process within myself and then it comes out in another form, and at the moment I'm exploring the very gentle, quiet, atmospheric music, which I think is more the mystic in me that wants to bring up the question of mystery in life.

Life to me is not black and white, it's very mysterious, and there's that part of me that lives very much in that world, so I try to give it a voice. It's almost the unconscious voice of our world; to be able to take in what's happening outside and then sit down and be confronted with your own solitude, your own dark places. I find that I have to go often to my dark places to let the music come, because it's in my confronting of the fear that the song rises and says 'It's okay, I'm with you, and this song will help heal that part of your life'. It's a very creative thing.

What are some of your dark places?

Mmmm—my dark places! I guess a lot of those are the wounds that you have from childhood, which every person carries. No matter how wonderful your parents are, the wounding can come from anywhere: that place where you may have felt rejected, or where something has cut across the true child in you and that part of you hasn't been affirmed, or it's been criticised, ridiculed, or something. So you carry that all the time, that woundedness: it constantly resurfaces and you have to address it, and it comes up in all different places at different times. It's a constant healing. I don't know if I can be really specific, except that there are times when I know there have been wounds and they come up in all relationships that I'm in.

It's marvellous that you can think of those as points of creativity rather than just being fearful, or burying them, or running away.

Well, I think that's what happens. The creative process takes over, because when I get stuck—I get to a stage where I get stuck and I can't move, I'm just completely blocked and paralysed—I know that I have to do something about it, otherwise drown. So it's in the choice to do something about it that the creative happens. It's that choice to respond to it and draw it, or write about it in my journal, or walk, or sing, or dance, or talk with a friend, go for a swim—they're all creative things that involve the body so the healing can happen. So sometimes I write from that contracted place.

The other place I write from is that sense of expansion where it's like you fly—it's this flying experience where you're just lifted up and suspended and this song comes forth out of it, this feeling of being elevated and being liberated. I really am following my bliss. I'm very fortunate to be able to do this and create the work that I want to do and just dare to do it (laughs) and hope that something happens. And in doing that I find that I fly a lot in my work.

When you're performing?

Definitely when I'm performing. It constantly happens when I'm performing. It's somehow a sense of being a channel. It's a communion that happens for me when I perform.

A communion with those who are there, too?

Yes, it's with the audience and with this Greater Being, with the Creator, and allowing a voice to come through. I just become the body for the voice. It's like this other sense takes over and comes through, so it is a very flying experience. I also experience it when I'm in silence sometimes, that sense of letting go and abandonment to the Other. I experience it with community often, with dancing or playful things: being able to play or smell a rose—very sensual things. I'm very tactile and love the senses. I can get carried away with something visual or something I hear: it's just being able to be captured or to gaze upon. It's the contemplative element.

I think all of life and humanity is sacred. I guess I still have a very strong sense of the incarnate, God being enfleshed in people, and that when we are talking about humankind it's an enfleshment of the likeness of our Creator. It says something very sacred about humanity, that 'we are not human beings who are searching a spiritual way—we are spiritual beings who are searching for a human expression', which to me is kind of like the angel in all of us (laughs) that is seeking to find expression through the human.

Have you another model of meaning, or a metaphor, I suppose, that helps you to make sense of life?

Yes, probably the nightingale is the one that I really identify with—the little bird, the singing bird. She's someone who flies, who loves flight, who dares to fly, who dares to jump out of the nest and trust that the wind will hold her up—'the wind beneath her wings' sort of thing. But she's also a bird that sings: she is the cream of the birds and birds are the greatest singers ever. I actually had an experience recently when I went to see the movie *Bodyguard* with Whitney Houston. Everyone loves her voice, it's beautiful. And there was a phrase in there when someone said 'If she doesn't sing, she'll die', and oh! that cut through to me. I thought, it's the same for me: having been given the gift of voice, of singing, if I don't sing, I die. It's my great purpose, to use this. That's what I am. And so to stop the nightingale from singing, to capture her and stop her voice, is like . . . she just dies. And so that's one of my fears . . . claustrophobia: you know, that I'll be held in, that I won't be free to fly and to sing. So, yes, that's a strong one for me, the nightingale.

When I was about twenty-three I ran into a Native American Franciscan nun and she really influenced me, because when she came to Sydney—she was speaking at a youth gathering I was involved in—she arrived with just one little bag for four weeks and I thought, this woman is very strange, she only carries one dress, and she said to me, 'Honey, you've just got to live simply and just embrace life as a lover'. I thought, did she say lover? (laughs) My gosh, this is really unusual. But that's really had a big impact on me. She said, 'When you touch people, touch them into life. When you sing for them, sing them into life. Don't pull them away from what their call is; encourage them and nurture them with the gifts you have.' She was the first person, I think, that for me pulled together a religious way of life that's appealing. I think I'd been brought up with this sort of 'goody-goody' thing—you know, you've got to do the right thing to be into religion—and while I have always known since I was a little girl that I had spirituality, I wanted a contemporary spirituality, one that crosses across all beings and that's not stifling, narrow—that 'I'm right and you're wrong', that's so pretentious—but one that gives life to everything and allows everyone to have a voice and have an attitude and a way of living.

So is your singing and songwriting and work with the voice and work with people, in a sense, a vocation or a ministry?

Yes, yes it is.

I don't know why I want to label it like that, but the question came to me.

Well, I guess it is. In the past I've worked very much in ministry worlds but I see it as much wider than that. I find that word often a limiting word, because we often only use that word in a Christian context, and I suppose I see the voice and the power of the voice as much wider than that. It takes in all of humanity and all faiths. So, yes, I do see it as a vocation. I see myself as a healer, I suppose, deep down, and a catalyst, a change agent.

I remember you with young people, masses of them, when the Pope was here. That must have been a tremendously powerful event to take part in.

It was extraordinary. It's something that I'll never forget. I think what was the most exciting thing was seeing all these young people, twenty or thirty thousand young people, from all over Australia. I'd been working with a lot of them in my travels throughout Australia. At that time I'd been travelling a lot and there were all these little youth groups out bush that had been saving to come to this occasion. And just that sense of the power of a united voice that was saying, 'Look, we are young, and we're vital, and we're the dreamers, and it's not about tomorrow and we're going to make a difference; we make a difference today'. And so to have the Pope here, and joining in the dancing and the singing, it was like wow! (laughs) I thought that was pretty radical.

Yes, you had him dancing with you.

Yes, and to me it was saying a lot more than words say.

Trisha, as a sensitive person, a young person, an artist, how much at home do you feel in today's society?

I find that I'm in the middle of such extreme changes. The things that I've grown up with, my foundations that were strong anchors for me, are really shifting, and I suppose a lot of that anchoring is because so much of my upbringing was within the church structure, which is a very strong thing. But now that I'm finding my own voice, my own authentic voice, I'm coming up against a lot of the structure and it's rubbing really badly (laughs), and I don't feel comfortable within the structure. I suppose it's that, coming from a mental, thinking, way which is very patriarchal—there's always someone up the top, there's someone underneath. That I find really difficult now.

It's the wrong shape for you, is it?

It's the wrong shape! I want something that's more circular, that's more a shared level where people are equal and where people do have a voice. That includes the voiceless; that there's space for the voiceless to be heard. Now, that really goes against everything in society, but if we are to give voice to the spirituality, the rising consciousness that's there, this changing myth that's happening, then somehow we have to change the structure and I'm not sure how that's going to happen. At times I feel really displaced in that because I don't fit; the things that used to work for me don't work any more and I'm finding I'm in very new territory and the ground is really shaking. And yet I feel I'm part of the shake-up, I'm part of the drum that's shaking (laughs) and saying, 'I don't like this; this isn't just, it's not just, and so we've got to shake the place up a little bit and let the new life come through the concrete'. But that's pretty scary, I find, if I don't have people around me who are speaking a similar language, who are frustrated and are impatient with the slowness of change. If I don't have people around me who are thinking expansion-wise, then I get overwhelmed and I can't function, so for me it's important to have people around me who challenge me and who can say, 'Continue the work you're doing, continue . . . '

But I see the change coming through from the indigenous. A lot of the time I've met with people who often seem voiceless. When I take the time to listen to the stories of the poor amongst us, our stories, then there's a lot of power in there. And it's coming, I think, through ritual. I think we're going to see a lot happen through sacred ritual over the next few years. I think that's the only hope we have.

But do we have satisfactory sacred ritual?

Well, I don't think we have enough. No. No, I don't.

Are you part of developing that?

I hope to be, yes. I think a lot of the sacred rituals that have worked in the past within our churches have been wonderful but they're not speaking the language of the people now. I mean, we're talking about a world that's very literate, that's very educated, that's multi-media, visual, auditory, every level. We're very sensate today, so that the spoken word isn't enough. To be preached at, that's not enough. I want to experience the truth all over (laughs). I want to be moved, I want to really be challenged, and I don't always receive that, but I do receive it through the Arts. When I'm in a situation where ritual is happening where the Arts are given a voice, whether it be through painting or through dance or through drama or role-playing or puppetry, mime—whatever it's going to be—music, it's working at all these other levels of our being and it communicates. And I think it's also creating the sacred spaces; it's creating places of silence, places of the dance where the rage can be released as well. When I say the rage, that comes to my mind when I think of the corroboree, or the Native Americans when they dance; they do these circular dances for days, and it's like a huge expression of—I don't know, I don't even know how to explain it—I haven't really experienced it that much. I just feel that we need to do it because it's healing. We hear of the people wailing over in Ireland or at the Wailing Wall. We, as Australians, don't know what that sound is, to wail as a people. We don't even wail at our funerals, we're told to shut up, hide our emotions; and I feel there's just so much there. That's just one example, but there are lots of rituals that allow us a passage forth, a rite of passage into the next place.

Trisha, you've spoken of yourself as being an introvert. Do you sometimes experience loneliness?

Yes. I think it's part of the human condition and I think it's there for a reason. I've just started living on my own, so that's getting me even more in touch with it. But somehow it's in the aloneness, or in my loneliness that, if I can stay with it long enough and not run away from it, not be frightened of it but see it as part of the big picture . . . when I'm able to do that I'm able to get in touch with the giftedness of my friends, the people that are there for me, and my family, and also the giftedness of compassion. It gives me the place to spring from when I go out and I'm with others. I can identify with their loneliness. When I hear it in another person, when I hear that heartache or that grief, I know it in myself; I can say, 'Yes, I know that', and I can be with them rather than run away.

May we see Christ's loving face
May we be an icon of His grace.
May we see Christ's loving face
May we be an icon of His grace.

This song 'Icon of Grace' really does touch on what we were just speaking about: the loneliness. It's something in that loneliness, that lonely dark hour which the mystics often talk about: they write about that dark hour of the night, of the soul. It's in that place that somehow the grace, the compassion of our God reaches out to us and says, 'I love you unconditionally. You are accepted, you are everything to me. Trust it.' And grace to me is just one of those breathtaking things. When you experience grace, a real, deep . . . it's almost like a forgiveness, or acceptance—more than forgiveness, it's acceptance, acceptance of where you are. It's very powerful.

And do you have a sense of pattern in your life?

Constant patterns . . . I'm a pattern-maker. I really think that in another life I must have been a tapestry weaver or something, but I just see things interweaving so much. Whether it's science or environment or politics or learning how to bring up a family, it's all interconnected laterally. You're thinking sideways, thinking up and down: heaven-earth sort of thing; thinking forward, backwards. It's all this interweaving that is just so fascinating to me. And I love working with other people from all different backgrounds because they stimulate something in me. It sort of keeps you awake when you get these patterns crossing across; and yes, that's what life is, really, I think.

And when you think about this new album, this new CD, Deep Waters, *going out into the world, what do you imagine that it will do and be for people?*

Mmmm. I have a very visual thing that happens when I think about it, and it is of deep water, the spilling out of this life-giving water; that people, I hope, will be able to sit in or drink from or be cleansed by. This is a metaphor, you know—that it be something they can sit by and let it speak to them, rush by them or flow by them. It's something to do with giving voice to the sacred presence and I hope that that touches into their experience of the sacred presence.

You mentioned earlier being idealistic, or sounding idealistic. Do you feel sometimes as though you're carried away into the air or flying?

Oh, it's a constant problem (laughs).

Is it?

Well, it's just this sense of . . . because I do get so caught up in the ideas or the spirituality behind things, I'm just constantly aware that I must try to base myself on the ground, because I'm aware that there are so many things going on in my life and in others' at this changing time of our world. There's a lot of mess, there's a lot of displacement, there's a lot of confusion, there's a lot of losing identity, and I think there's that real struggle, that creative tension, between having to pay the bills every day and having to make a living and trying to be authentic in that and do something that's meaningful.

Do you experience that?

Oh, every day!

That challenge of the practicalities of life and having to earn a living and get the washing done and . . .

Oh, yes (laughs). And yet, somehow in the midst of all of that I get this . . . One of the verses that I love, that I grew up on, was that God creates out of chaos, and that gives me a lot of hope (laughs), because my life is so often chaotic. You've got to laugh at yourself, and in the midst of all of that there is the presence of this 'sacred'. Somehow I think we're called to keep our feet on the ground and fly at the same time, and that, for me, is the challenge.

Stan Arneil

While he was a prisoner of war, Stan Arneil wrote in his diary, published in 1981 as One Man's War,[1] *that if he lived he would give his life to work for his community.*

And so he did. With his wife Dorothy he has raised six children. He has been active in marriage counselling, welfare and drug rehabilitation work. In the early sixties he started a nationwide crusade—to establish and promote the Credit Union movement which would benefit hundreds of thousands of Australian families.

In his early twenties Stan Arneil volunteered to join the newly formed 2/30 Battalion AIF under the command of Sir Frederick 'Black Jack' Galleghan. In the Malayan campaign the young sergeant led his platoon into savage hand-to-hand fighting in rubber plantation and jungle.

When Singapore fell to the Japanese in 1942, Stan and his men were among the 130 000 taken prisoner. They endured together years of appalling illness, pain and hardship. They were starved and beaten and sent to work and to die on the terrible Burma-Thailand railway. Stan Arneil kept his secret diary to chronicle their suffering. For him it was an ordeal in which his sense of values was forged, and which he would see in retrospect as being a privilege.

STAN ARNEIL: The average person is really quite unfortunate in as much as they're caught up with day-do-day living: keeping the shoes cleaned—we didn't have any boots so we didn't have to have them mended; having their clothes pressed and ironed—we didn't have that; finding food for their families—we didn't have those problems, everything was there, and the hardship brought out qualities in people that were latent, that probably would never have been brought out.

There was no theft, there was no calumny, there was no doing wrong

[1] *One Man's War*, Stan Arneil, Alternative Publishing Co-operative Ltd.

things. Every single person on that railway was ready to step into the shoes of somebody else; ready to lift somebody and take them back home, back to the camp; ready to help carry a dead man back. Nobody held back, and this was only because of the circumstances which were forced upon us, the privilege which was forced upon us, to suddenly realise that we were as nothing—without God's help we were nothing.

When you began to see that happening, Stan, did it come as any sort of surprise to you?

Well, it seemed to be always with us, from Sonkurai, No. 3 Camp in the monsoon period. We were cut off from the north and the south; it rained twenty-four hours a day; we were in the mountains; the clouds were just hanging over the camp so that it was a twilight; we had very little food, barely enough to sustain ourselves; we worked from twelve to eighteen hours each day, barefooted—ulcers, cholera—you name it, we had it. And there we realised that we were nothing in ourselves, we couldn't even help ourselves, so everybody turned to God, and we prayed most of the day, all day. You woke up at night, you said a prayer, 'Please, God, help me and get me out of this. Help Stinny Reinhard, help somebody else.' And we were so fortunate because in that camp we had a Catholic priest, a little fellow from Queensland. And he used to stand at the entrance to the camp—there were no fences, of course—as we walked out, some of the men near-naked, just G-strings, barefooted, nothing, in the rain, with their picks and shovels over their shoulders, and the troops would break out irrespective of their religion—Catholic, Protestant or Jew—and either go to confession or talk to him to gain some encouragement, and then we'd go out to work.

It was is if we were, in that camp, in the presence of God. It was as if He was all around us, and we put our hand in the hand of God, and that is the only thing which got us through.

Do you believe that this was a common experience for everybody, because if you'd asked, I suppose, some of those—what were they, nineteen, twenty, twenty-one-year-olds who went over in the 2nd/30th—if you had asked them on embarkation, 'Are you a person of faith, do you believe in God?' you would have got quite a variety of answers, wouldn't you?

Most of them would have not been, but there's nothing like the imminence of death to bring you back to basics. Death is something which most people don't even talk about, but when you rush back to camp at night-time to know if Yappy Gardiner's died during the day, and then you see his body put on a funeral pyre, knowing that in the next few days it might be your own, this becomes a situation where people understand the real truths of God.

We didn't have any worry, I suppose, about committing sin. In my day everybody had so many venial sins and so many shortcomings. I don't think we had very many shortcomings, really. That seems silly to say, but I don't think we did, because we were all outgoing—I'm talking about everybody—outgoing: selfishness had gone, there was no such thing as individual selfishness. Everybody had their little ration in their turn and everybody tried to help somebody else.

The lack of religious services was a problem at times. In one camp where we were later on, in the tunnels, we had no priest in the camp at all and we were in a very bad way in that particular camp and very debilitated and not very happy. So a group of the Catholic young men there, getting older—this was some years after the war started—said the rosary every night in one part of the camp. It was an effort to get to God, and we said the rosary and asked the Blessed Virgin would she pray to Our Lord that we be helped or relieved. Strangely enough, it was as if she threw a cloak over us and we were enveloped for a little while in some comfort.

Later on in that camp a Dutch priest did come, but the Eucharist was so scarce that we actually had to draw lots to see who would go to communion and then go back to the end of the line. That's where people learned how important it was to prepare for death, because death could come any day, and there when we had the opportunity to attend religious services, Mass, of course nobody every missed.

It conjures quite a picture. You know, you mentioned 'when we were working in the tunnels'—that's Johore isn't it?

Johore, yes.

You said 'We were getting older then'. I thought, my goodness, what were you then—twenty-two, twenty-three?

I started at twenty-two. I was away for four and a quarter years. Three and a half years is a long time when at Christmas we thought we'd all be out in six weeks, and we'd be out for Christmas, and we'd be out for the next Christmas and the next Christmas, and in the finish it didn't seem to matter much. We were there, and home was so remote. We had no news of the outside world, no contact with home. I don't think we received the first letter until eighteen months after we were taken prisoners of war. We became a monastic community with the incredible privilege of being able to talk. People don't talk now. We talked together on every known subject. Sometimes we might take a subject and take a week to talk about it.

Like what, for example?

Anything, from interior decorating to racehorses—any subject at all. We'd call in opinions from other platoons, other huts' opinions on certain things which had happened. But conversation was part of our life and that's a great blessing, too.

You made the extraordinary statement a few minutes ago that selfishness had gone. It sounds like the perfect experience of what they call, I think, 'unconditional love'. That sort of mateship, that sort of friendship.

Well, it was unconditional love. It was not just mateship, it was an actual love of one another, and that's very difficult to obtain. A few weeks ago I had a week away on a little fishing holiday with two of my friends, Curly and Doug, who are mentioned in the book. We have been friends for fifty years: I love those two men, they're part of my family. In our own battalion we meet regularly, we write to one another, we have our own little magazine. We are part of one family, loving one another and accepting any of the disabilities that people have.

Why do we have to go through such extraordinary suffering—I mean, you hear them say of Britain, don't you, 'the war brought out the best in us'—why do we have to wait until something like that happens before we can love one another in the way that you describe?

People are so busy and so concerned with material things that mean nothing. There are no pockets in shrouds: you can't take one single cent with you, and yet we have the extraordinary situation of people seeking the power and the material things which will be gone.

When you were a prisoner of war in Singapore and in Thailand, you came to the understanding that this sort of deprivation—hunger, homesickness—was a privilege. When a problem or a setback or a crisis comes up in your life these days, are you still able to contemplate it in a similar way?

Oh, of course, and I've had many serious problems, including stillborn children and sadness like that, sadness in my family, but it's all part of the plan. I've got to accept these things and work towards my own destiny, not blaming anybody at all.

Is that how you thought about the Japanese when you were going to war?

Oh, I hated them!

Were you taught to hate them?

I was taught to hate them—I hated them.

How did they teach you? What did they tell you?

Well, that they were animals. Sir Thomas Blamey said a dreadful thing for a man in his position—that they came out of the trees like apes, they couldn't read, they were all myopic, they could do nothing. Their bullets couldn't hurt us—we were told that by a Major Dawkins, who was killed by a Japanese bullet later on. We were taught to hate: all young men in war are taught to hate the other side, that's part of war. It's so stupid. How could I kill anybody now? How could I actually take the life of a person? And yet we were there, eager to kill, and they were just as eager to kill us, and we did. There were 5000 Japanese casualties on the island of Singapore. In the Malayan campaign, which few people know anything about, we lost just under 2000 Australians killed in one month from six battalions. That is a far higher rate than anywhere among the Australians in the First World War or the Second World War, including Gallipoli. That's a lot of young men to be thrown away.

My own friend, who I grew up with in school, sat bedside in school, who was exactly my own age, was killed alongside of me on the first day of the fighting in the war. He was a magnificent young man; his death was just a waste.

I guess there was also some fun and some humour when you got the chance during those years as a POW, wasn't there? Changi, apparently, had its moments.

Oh, there was great fun. We had lots of fun and lots of wonderful experiences. For example, in Changi a dear man, George McNeilly, a Salvation Army man, had charge of the records which had been left in the Changi barracks by the British. Of course, they were beautiful records of operas and so forth, and he actually broadcast in conjunction with David Griffin, Sir David Griffin, who was later the Lord Mayor of Sydney. We used to lie under the stars at night—as clean as clean, squeaky clean, because there was plenty of water and we all had two pairs of shorts then which we'd wash out every day—on these beautiful tropical nights with the palm trees and the bright stars in the sky. We'd lie down on our backs and listen to George McNeilly first of all explain the record that was to come, then play it, then follow with the next. You couldn't get that at the Opera House!

Those must have been experiences that many of you hadn't had at home.

We were only kids, we had no idea of life at all—most of us were in the army since we'd left school—and here was this lovely, gentle Salvation Army man explaining Verdi's operas and the whole lot. It was great.

I'd like to talk to you about the influence that your experiences as a prisoner of war had on you in your life after that from several different points of view, and the first is this: I can imagine that when you first came home you must have been quite intensely grateful for the electric light switch, for the running water, for the ability to have a bath, for a cup of tea and, no doubt, for a piece of toast and Vegemite, and so on and so on. Does that sort of gratitude last?

It holds me now. I'm just having a cup of cold water, a little drink of water. I'm very lucky, in as much as I've never lost sight of the fact that at one stage I didn't have it and so I appreciate it. I actually appreciate the electric light. I appreciate being able to have a drink of water which I don't have to boil because of the cholera germs. So that's another great thing that the prisoner of war life gave to me and to most others—values. You can't really value anything until you've lost it. That's where our great privilege was: we'd lost everything and suddenly everything comes back in its right perspective—a glass of water, that's really something.

The other thing that you and many of your comrades learned, I am sure, because it seems to be in every page of that book of yours, One Man's War, *is compassion.*

Well, we couldn't judge anybody, and we were sorry to see people die. We knew of the trauma that would happen at home when they died, and every man there in Thailand—that is every man—did his best to look after them, to collect some grass and boil it up if somebody was sick, to go out and collect the banana fronds, anything at all to try and help. Compassion was bred into us, I think, by the circumstances, and we had that sense of closeness to such a degree that we didn't even have to talk: if we were with somebody there we drew comfort from their nearness.

Now, I was in hospital once in Sonkurai, very ill with ulcers—I'd clipped the toenail right off my toe and that's where they started—and my friend was lying alongside of me. Now, just being there was really something; you didn't have to say anything, and you didn't have to ask anybody then to do something for you, they would see what had to be done. Douglas, my friend, used to wash a dreadful case—I won't mention his name—of beri-beri. He was an enormous person, like a rhinoceros—no neck, no nothing—with beri-beri, and his legs split open one night. He was so huge, lying like a rhinoceros, and Douglas used to lovingly wash him all over with a wet rag. We'd lift him up and turn him over like that and no hospital orderly could have been more gentle or more compassionate. It really wasn't a very pretty sight at all but Doug was never asked to do that, he just did it because it had to be done.

Will you tell us about the influence that your experience as a soldier and as a prisoner of war had on the work that you chose to do when you came back to Australia?

Well, it was again the waste of time and feeling for people who couldn't help themselves. There were a lot of prisoners of war, as there are everywhere, people who are not leaders and they can't help themselves, so I began work after a little while at the Australian Broadcasting Commission where there were some tragic cases of people who gave the total of their skills for a remuneration which was rock bottom. Cleaning staff were my favourites, the old ladies of the cleaning staff; the lift drivers and this type of people. So I joined the union, or association, as it was called then, not to bring power to anybody, not to gain some stupid work practice which had no value, but to try to get a better deal for the people who needed it, to try to obtain justice. And I think we were fairly successful in a very hard school.

Many people know you, I'm sure, for the work you did in initiating and then promoting the Credit Union movement throughout Australia. Did this arise out of the same sort of feelings?

Well, it was. Sadly, the Credit Union philosophy as I tried to teach it is no more, but I was sickened to see decent people—middle class and lower income earners—unable to manage or handle their affairs and to be treated like animals by the people with the money.

When I began there was no such thing as a personal loan from a bank. It wasn't possible because the people had no collateral, and I preached the story that the best collateral one could have is honesty and that an honest man will pay his debts. It doesn't really matter if he gets out of work, he will still pay his debts when he goes back. That was the philosophy, which I still believe, and we began the Credit Union movement and I developed it throughout Australia on a cooperative, sharing basis, where everybody helped one another. We did counselling sessions to try to teach people to look after themselves.

In those days everybody did share a reasonable interest on savings and the lowest possible rate of interest on loans, but now, with big business, the absence of the volunteer, it's gone the other way. The Credit Union movement relies for its money on saying how high they can pay interest on savings or deposits. Some people now have $100 000. God help us, in my day there wouldn't be $100 000 in some Credit Unions, but a lot of people would still be gaining a lot of help from them.

I worked hard in the Credit Union movement and I'm sorry it's gone the way it has. That's only my opinion, but the little man . . . there was a symbol for the Credit Union movement of a little man under the umbrella as against hard times and sickness, and that's gone.

Didn't St Francis have something to do with the Credit Union movement?

Yes, St Francis was really a great cooperator, you know. He loved rats, he loved everything, even the wind and the sun. He was a cooperator, and his prayer, the prayer of St Francis, was adopted in the United States Credit Union movement by a man called Tom Doig, a magnificent man. It intrigued me because I've always had a great affection for St Francis and I introduced it into the Australian Credit Union movement as part of our meaning, and it is a meaning, not something said as a gibberish. Today, I suppose, still, at every general meeting of every Credit Union in Australia, they begin by reciting the prayer of St Francis.

Which goes . . . ?

I'm not very good at reading, but it goes like this: 'Lord make me an instrument of your peace. Where there is hatred, let me sow love; where there is injury, pardon; where is doubt, faith; where there is despair, hope; where there is darkness, light; where there is sadness, joy. Oh, divine Master, grant that I may not so much seek to be consoled as to console; to be understood, as to understand; to be loved, as to love; for it is in giving that we receive, it is in pardoning that we are pardoned, it is in dying that we are born to eternal life.' It's a very good prayer.

I'd like to talk to you about the need you think there is to make peace with old enemies. Have you done that, for example, with the Japanese, with the Koreans, in whose 'care' you were during the Second World War? Do you hate anyone now? Do you resent anyone still?

I resent what some people do. I very much resent what some people do at the expense of others. We don't have a great example in some of our politicians in this country, so I resent that. I don't hate anybody; I haven't got time to hate anybody, it would be a useless exercise which would get me nowhere at all. I may not love somebody, but I certainly have no place in my heart for hatred.

You have forgiven those who hurt you, who beat you, who maltreated you?

Oh, yes. I'm sorry for them, really. I really feel sorry for the people who've hurt me, and I've had a lot of hurt. That's their problem, It's not mine any more—I'm over it all. I feel sorry for anybody who still hates the Japanese: it only hurts them. I don't know how they can still do it after all these years, when they've met these nice Japanese people. We live on the Japanese with our products. The Japanese have demonstrated that they will accept conditions. Remember that there was not one single case of brutality or killing of an American serviceman after the Second World War in Japan. Hirohito said, 'The war is finished; we will accept the Americans', and that was it: they all obeyed him. Had it happened in Australia it would have been different. But for poor people who hate anybody, I feel sorry for them. There's no real point in it.

I remember a story a lady from Ireland told me years ago, which is true, about two sisters who lived at opposite ends of the stret and they didn't speak to one another. My wife asked this lady what was the reason originally. She said, 'They don't know; they've forgotten what the reason was!'

That's a good story.

It's true!

You always seem to me such a happy man. I'm not wrong about that, am I?

No, I'm grateful for every day. I really am a happy man. Thank God I'm here today. I've got a day coming up tomorrow, I hope, that I'll enjoy with my wife and family and try to help somebody else.

Every day to me is a bonus. I'm sorry that hundreds of my friends never made it, never saw the sunrise—they never made it. They died and they didn't even know why they died, but they died without a whimper, and they died because they believed that their death was worth it.

So I'm a happy man. I'm here, and please God, if God wills it, I'll live a little longer.

Is your faith ever shaken?

Oh, no! Oh, no, I know I'm going to meet God one day, in the next few years, too, probably, because this is my age now. I understand that. One problem that worries me, and so far it hasn't come off too much, is what I call waste of time. We were put on this earth and the air we breathe belongs to God—that's the air we breathe: we could be snuffed out like that. And we were given time—it's a fantastic thing, time. So I feel I don't want to be judged on having wasted the time that Our Lord gave me and I don't have an opportunity to rest much.

Yes. I'm laughing, you know, because I don't really think you've wasted much time!

I do what I can.

I would love to ask you what is your definition of love after forty years of marriage.

Well, I've been married on Saturday for forty years. A definition of love? Dorothy, my wife, is a part of me and I'm actually a part of her. The one thing that I find very difficult—I don't know how I'd take it if she were not there. But we are no longer two people; we're one person. She has her own thoughts and I have mine, but we don't disagree; we've never had an argument—I suppose there's still time—but she gives in and I give in. It's not a storybook love: she is just part of me.

She didn't even want to see me when I first saw her. She thought I was a damned nuisance because she was engaged to some other fellow. I shouldn't tell those things, but he wasn't worthy of her in my opinion, anyway (Caroline laughs). But that was an exciting period. And then we had the tremendous period of having the children. My God, it was great fun! We used to look after these little kids and just live for the children, and it was an experience which, perhaps, matured us away from the excitement of youth. No, I wasn't a youth then was I? I felt like a youth after I got back from the war because I lost my youth in the war. But we just grew together and there is nothing like married love: there is just nothing like married love with a family around you and knowing that the family love you.

So I say that I'd be one of the luckiest persons in the world. As a matter of fact, Caroline, I don't know of anybody as lucky as I am.

Somehow you make it sound easy, and it can't have been all that easy. There are always times of pain, disappointment, difficulty . . .

Well, there's pain: I lost my job once on a political basis. I lost everything—superannuation, everything I had, everything—and Dorothy said, 'Well, I didn't marry you for your money'. Well, she didn't, because I didn't have any when we were married anyway!

We've had lots of ups and downs. We've had various attacks against me, particularly in the Credit Union movement because feelings run high in people's movements, but we've handled them all and I wouldn't change my life. I wouldn't change the downs, even, because the downs seemed to have made us stronger.

We do have a lot of fun and sometimes we just sit there. We don't have a very exciting life—we don't go to parties, we don't eat out much, very occasionally—but on Saturday night I'm meeting my daughter, her husband and two grandchildren from Newcastle, and my son and his fiancée, and we're going to have this lovely dinner after we all go to Mass. Now, you can't beat that for a fortieth anniversary present!

Margot Cairnes

In this conversation we explore questions like, 'How possible is it to tell each other the truth and still remain friends?', 'What do people who get angry with us have to teach us?', 'Why do we attract certain people?', 'If there's a split between the real self inside, and the self I show to the outside world, what's the consequence of that?', 'How safe is it to show people who I really am?', 'Why are some Australian managers killing themselves by leaving the real person at home and putting on a highly controlled mask at work?', 'How good are we at seeing things as they really are?'.

Margot Cairnes is one of an emerging breed in the Australian business world, a developing profession of 'corporate wizards' or 'company doctors' who come into an organisation to facilitate some real and concrete change, and often improve the communication climate at the same time.

There have been distinguished pioneers in this field. Margot Cairnes, in her mid-thirties, is among the younger ones proving to be very effective. Her degrees are in education and management. She has worked as an executive and today is the high-paid, high-powered principal of her own company.

Margot always aims to take her real self to her work and as she ranges over a spectrum of issues, we see an integration of the adult aware of the imprint of her childhood, the corporate whiz-kid, the single mother, the beautiful woman speculating on the passing of physical attraction, the playgirl and the career woman, spiritual being and hedonist.

Here is someone who enjoys her body, who also prays continually; a woman whose life has been touched by very real setbacks, who describes her way of life as making strength out of weakness; a woman who can say 'I enjoy failure', and who has devoted herself to becoming all that she can be.

As we read Margot Cairnes's story, bear in mind that this

young woman has been called in to work alongside some of the top management people in this country as an agent of change, and that she is highly successful at what she does.

So she's speaking from a position of rich experience with often demanding executives (mostly men) and with her own growing children.

Margot's openness is engaging and her honesty challenging.

MARGOT CAIRNES: My childhood was a very rich mixture of horror and creativity. Our family was not a happy home, my parents were not happy in their marriage, and we had a lot of problems around alcohol and aggression.

But my parents were both very amazing people. My father was a successful businessman. His great love was music and, as a child, I have a lot of memories of being around my father sitting at the piano—playing, singing, dancing. It was a bit like . . . I always thought it was like being on the set of a musical comedy: a little bit unreal, but very exciting. And Dad, in fact, produced a lot of musical comedies and made a lot of money for charity.

My mother was a very successful journalist. She had been a war correspondent during the War—she had been attached to General MacArthur's headquarters—and when the men came back, there weren't so many good jobs for the women, and she became the Social Editor of the local paper. But her real love, again, was theatre and art and music—and she also wrote the music, drama and art column. So, our home was full of a lot of music, a lot of art, a lot of very interesting people.

And we did have amazing parties; my parents had incredible parties. As a child it was a bit confusing because the adults were behaving a lot like children. But they were all amazing people—they were intellectuals, academics, painters, artists, poets. But at the same time the richness of that, the richness of poetry and of the discussion . . . I remember once coming out of my bedroom early in the morning and falling over the entire cast of *Boys from the Band* who had been to the party the night before and couldn't quite make it home.

So, I guess it was a mixture of confusion (because it was very confusing—you know, what was happening and why did adults behave this way?) and, again, excitement because this was a whole other world. And, certainly, my friends at school didn't have this kind of world going on in their homes. It was . . . their homes, I understood, were a lot drier and more stable—but also a lot less exciting, a lot less interesting.

So what sort of ideas were you forming about creativity, I wonder, and creative people?

Well, it seemed to me that there was a lot of fun and excitement in that creative world but also a lot of pain. So when I married, I actually went into a . . . almost a creative void for about fourteen years: I turned my back on all of that. I went off and studied science, initially simply to get away from the creativity, because my feeling was that all these creative people were all kind of crazy and I really didn't want to spend the rest of my life around that craziness.

And how did that work, that moving over to the other side—the scientific, the calmer, the quieter, the drier, I think you were saying?

Yes, well . . . it was a bit boring really—and it was no less painful. So what I found out was that creativity isn't painful and that a lot of creative people . . . and if you look back through history (I mean, I've read a lot of the biographies of the very creative people), a lot of them do have a lot of drama in their lives, but they're not necessarily . . . they don't have to go together. So you can have the creativity and the fun and the excitement without having the drama and the pain.

Well, I'd like to explore more with you how you've come to those conclusions, maybe through some of the events of your life which you feel have been points of new insight. What would you choose to tell us about?

Well, I guess, when I left home I'd been so 'there' for my parents in my home—I was very much the homemaker—so when I left there was a kind of a freedom and a liberation around that. But I married very young, so I very quickly put myself back into that role.

But, I guess, getting married—I was nineteen when that happened—was very much about growing up very early and taking that responsibility. But within a few years of my marriage, I decided that I did want to go back and I wanted to go into a more creative atmosphere, and I went to university and studied education. And it was a real revelation to me because I'd turned my back on the intellectual world for such a long time, and going back and studying again was like a new world: all these ideas and thoughts and people. I did a lot of economics and a lot of politics. And I was particularly interested in childcare: how we as a society rear our children, and how we provide for them on an economic and a political basis, and where they fit into society, and how society operates on where we're going.

Any insight into why that was your concern?

Well, I think, because of my own childhood being so confusing, I just had a fascination for that.

I think that's quite an interesting story: I was the first person in . . . I don't know, twenty or thirty years . . . to win the university medal and the Department of Education gave me a prize for being the best practical and theoretical teacher to graduate that year—but I couldn't get a job. I was put on a list and I was told it was seven years before the Department (who had put me through university) would employ me.

So, at that time I went off to Darwin and I ran an organisation up there which was actually made up of, I think, eleven different companies. I had a staff of about sixty-four, and we had a turnover in the millions of dollars each year, and I was involved in managing all these companies, which were non-profit organisations so we got some funding, but we also had to make ends meet (I think we were funded thirty per cent), so I ran both a business and a government organisation simultaneously. And doing that, I learnt a lot about getting on with people and a lot about politics. I used to fly to Canberra all the time to negotiate our funding and negotiate with the State ministers. I helped rewrite the Act and I reorganised the organisation. And so, I began to—through experience—discover a lot about how the world worked, which was also very confusing. That led me to go and do some more study, which again helped to clarify and then sent me out doing the work I do. So there was all that sort of positive experience happening.

On the other side—in the personal arena—my marriage failed, which was a very traumatic experience for me. I found that very painful. And for the first time in my life, I guess, I had to turn around and admit to the world that I had failed at something. And I found that very hard to do: for me, being a good student and a good child and a good wife were very important, so turning round and saying to the world, 'I'm sorry, I've messed this one up' was hard.

And I guess the most recent event that's really been a life-turning event for me was the near-death of my daughter, which happened two years ago. At 11.30 in the evening, when I'd just moved into a new home, my daughter stopped breathing for thirty minutes. I was alone at home and the telephone wasn't yet connected, so it was very traumatic . . . basically, I had to respirate her until the ambulance arrived. A friend luckily was there when she . . . just before she collapsed, and I asked him to race and ring the ambulance, and when she did collapse and the breath stopped, I respirated her until . . . until the ambulance came and put her on oxygen and gave her adrenalin. But that was a very . . . oh! . . . It was an exciting experience, because I felt very much how important the relationship was and how important love was and how important life was. And every second of that experience was so valuable to me and to her, and it's been a turning point for all of us.

Have you seen the world a little differently since that night?

Very much, very much. I now see the flowers and I see the boats and I see the water and I see the trees and I hear the music. When you come that close to death, life becomes very important and every second takes on a value beyond that which it had before.

What do you think now about apparent failure or weakness or vulnerability? You said that when you had the first experience of that after many successes, it knocked you.

Well, I actually relish it. I enjoy failure. That probably sounds a bit perverse, but what I find is that when I have a success, I tend to grab it and run away. When I have a failure, I sit and I sit with it and I learn from it. And that brings strength and it brings joy and it brings advancement.

When my daughter became very ill, again that felt to me like a failure: I wasn't the perfect mother, my child was very ill and needed a lot of help. What that meant for me and my two children was that we went on a voyage of self-discovery together. We went on a voyage of learning about each other and about the problems that we had in relating to each other and the problems that particularly my children had in expressing negativity. Because until that time I'd been so positive that they felt that to be anything but positive was not acceptable. And so, when they had a problem, they didn't know how to talk to me about it. So we had to learn that.

How?

Oh, by sitting down and telling each other the truth—which was very painful.

What I have found is that, as a self-defence mechanism I've learnt to tell people what I think they want to hear. And a lot of that is to protect me and a lot of that is to protect them: I don't want to upset them and I don't want to hurt them and I don't want to spoil the friendship. But that's actually not very honest, because what I'm doing is telling them either a partial truth or an untruth. And because I tend to be very positive and because I tend to be successful, people want to follow suit, so we end up in a web of 'not-truth'. And this is what I'd done with my children—we had to sit down and say to each other things like, 'I don't like it when you do that!' My daughter at that time was very demanding and I had to tell her that some days I didn't want to come home, because I didn't want those demands. Now, when you have a child that's nearly dying, that's not an easy thing to say. But they were the sorts of things that we learned to say to each other.

So you got into new habits in that way.

We did: we learned to disagree and we learned to tell each other the truth.

Has it made a difference?

It's made so much difference, Caroline, I can't begin to tell you. We've gone from being three single people living in a home being polite to each other, to being a very happy, full and rich family who interact and adore each other. Before, we loved each other politely; now we're passionate about each other.

There's choice and there's reality. And what I find, particularly in my work (and everything that I see in my work I see in myself), is that we tend not to see the reality and we tend not to make the choices. I know that's a little confusing so I'll explain it.

Reality is what is actually happening. Very few of us see what is actually happening. As we grow, as children, we form a set of defence mechanisms, a way of looking at the world, which is our way of coping with our childhood. Now, whether our childhood is good or bad, it's never perfect, because we're all brought up by human beings. And human beings do their best, but it will always be imperfect because that's what being human is. So we all develop this way of looking at the world which is our way of coping. Unfortunately, once it's developed, we tend to think . . . we see the world through that, and we tend to think that that is reality. So, for example, if we have a belief that people dislike us, no matter what anybody does we'll think they dislike us. So the reality may be that, in fact, people do like us. Our feeling of the reality, or our sense of the reality, is that they don't. And this happens in every situation. I've seen groups of very erudite businessmen and government leaders act in the most absurd ways which, sitting on the outside looking in, make no sense—until you realise that they're seeing the world not as you see it (which is through your reality), but as they see it (which is through theirs). And because most of us don't know that we're seeing an illusion (because most of us think that the illusion we see is reality), we don't know how we're behaving and we don't know the effect that our behaviour has on the people around us.

And you see this in the work that you do?

Oh, very much.

With senior businesspeople and public servants and so on?

Very much. Most of the problems that I see are very easy to solve on a rational basis. The issues are not generally that hard. It's not that they're not complex—they are; they're complex and they're ambiguous and they're changing. But if you've got a very clear mind and your emotions are not getting in the way, the solution, generally, is not that difficult.

And yet they probably call you in to solve some sort of rational problem, don't they?

Very much, very much.

How do you get past that?

Well, that's what we do: we solve the rational problem. But in solving the rational problem, we have to work with the illusions that get in the way. And the illusions are the sorts of things that get people to stamp their feet and walk out of the room. The illusions are the things that get people to undermine each other, to get people to withhold the truth, that get people to lay traps for each other. So my job, largely, is to help people stop doing that to each other long enough that they can get their rational mind into play and actually solve the issue that they're there to solve—which, once you get the illusion out of the way, is not difficult. The difficult part is getting the illusion out of the way.

Probably the best example that sticks out most vividly in my mind is . . . I was called into an organisation that was going through a very major restructure after a change of ownership. I was working with the top team. There were ten people in the top team, and I divided them into two groups of five and asked them to go away and list the top ten problems that they saw facing the organisation at the time. Then they came back and each group was to report to the other group what problems they saw. The group that didn't have the managing director in it got up and gave their top ten problems and the managing director stood up and said that this was untrue, that these problems did not exist. And everybody else in the room turned around and said, 'But they do! We're your top ten people, and we're dealing with them every day. And we've had two major consulting companies come in and review us in the last eighteen months and these are the problems that they list and these are our problems.' And the managing director said, 'No, they're not. I won't accept it.' Whereupon he got up and he left the room and he actually went and played bowls leaving nine totally stunned (actually, ten—because I was stunned, too) people sitting in the room.

So, what was happening for that man was that he was simply not able to face the problems, because if he faced them, he would have to have done something about them. And at that time, because of the stress of the change that was happening in the organisation, it was overwhelming for him. So he wasn't needing criticism or rebuke, but actually help to cope with the stress that he was facing, and to be brought around to see that help was available from these people in the room. They weren't criticising him, they weren't putting him down, they weren't making him wrong; they were simply saying, 'These are our problems. We're here to help you solve them.'

One of my friends told me the other day how she valued my friendship because I didn't walk away; that no matter what happened I'd always come back and challenge and face the issues and work it through. And it's become so much part of me that I don't even know that I do it, and yet I see that in most people's lives what we do is . . . because we're too frightened to tell each other the truth, because we're too frightened to confront each other with the reality, and we're too frightened to confront ourselves with the reality, it's easier to walk away. And I understand that. I understand that very deeply, because having confronted myself and the close people around me with reality, I know how painful and how uncomfortable it can be.

What do you think are the consequences of a habit of walking away, again and again?

Loneliness . . . a loneliness from yourself. It's like . . . if you walk away, you don't only walk away from others, you walk away from life. And you walk away from who you really are, so you're a shell of the possible. Whereas if you stay and you work it through with the other, with yourself, with life, then you have a richness and a fullness that otherwise you rob yourself of.

Okay, let's see . . . what happens when someone does something that makes you feel angry? How do you see that and what do you do with that?

Well, usually I get angry, but I find a way of expressing the anger—usually not to the other person but to myself. The anger for me is a charge, an energetic charge and I get it out. But then I sit down and I think, 'Well, what is it about that person that I don't like? I mean, what is it about them that's making me angry?' being fully aware that it's probably something about me I don't like.

Recently a friend suggested that I become, in his words, 'more worldly'. And I was very angry, very very angry. And then I sat down and I started to think about what he was saying, and I realised that there was a lot of truth in it. And I also realised that his confronting me was something about *me* that I have trouble coming to terms with. So, after having expressed the . . . it took me three weeks, I might say, to get through this . . . after having expressed the anger, after having looked at the truth in the situation and after having looked at him more or less as a mirror of me and parts of me that I was not comfortable with, I was very grateful to him and was able to turn round and say, 'Thank you for that,' and to maintain a friendship that I would otherwise have lost.

What was his response, by the way?

Delight, just delight . . . and amusement . . .

Really?

. . . amusement that something that he'd said that wasn't of great importance to him had had such a major effect on me.

What would that have been like if there had been some sort of real malice or challenge or aggression in the comment that he had made to you? The same thing? Would you have worked through it in the same way?

Yes, I think so . . .

Because there still might be a mirror-effect for you?

Definitely, definitely. Because all of us are positive and negative. And if I feel I've attracted people into my life that are in some way putting me down, then that's just reflecting very strongly something about myself.

I think we'd like to hear some more about attracting people into our lives. Is that how you see it?

Well, I do. I very much see it that we attract people into our lives. How else do you . . . ? I mean, that's true for all of us . . .

Yes.

I mean, there's the people at the shop that we deal with and the people at the school and our friends, our family's friends . . . I mean, for all of us there's this huge pool of people, so how is it that we pick the ones . . . ?

We choose to engage with certain ones.

Very much.

But are you suggesting that we choose sometimes to become involved with people because they are reflecting back to us something within that . . . . what? . . . that we don't want to face up to or that we haven't faced up to?

Well, there's . . . I don't know if you've read it, but there's a book by John Cleese and Robin Skynner called *Families and How to Survive Them*. And in it he gives an example of an experiment they do with people that are going into counselling training. They put fifty or sixty people in a room who've never met each other before and never talked to each other, and they say, 'Go and find a person in the room that has a similar family background to yourself.' And then when they have couples, they say to that couple, 'Now go and find people in the room that have a similar family background to you', and when they've got the fours, they say, 'Okay, now each take a role of mother, father, brother, sister, or whatever (which they do) and then sit down and discuss your real family background.' And every time this experiment is played, they find that people that had an alcoholic in the family are in a group of four, all of whom had an alcoholic in the family. Or, if there was aggression in the family, they're in a group, all of whom had aggression in the family. Or if the mother died when they were two, they're in a group, all of whom had a mother die when they were in early childhood. And the research is just so consistent that it's hard to believe that somehow people can't 'pick up' the people that had a similar family background.

But why do they want to be in the group with that similar background?

We tend to draw people that have the most to teach us. And the people that have the most to teach us are the people that are most like ourselves, because it's so much easier (and I see this all the time in my work in business), it's so much easier to see your faults in another person than it is to see them in yourself.

So, if I'm feeling angry, it's much easier for me to reflect that onto you than it is to own it for myself. If I don't like something that's happening, it's much easier for me to blame you than it is to look at my part in it. If I'm unhappy or sad, it's much easier for me to blame you than it is for me to say, 'Well, what am I doing wrong?' And so what I see in my work is everyone blaming everybody else. I call it the responsibility-free world: nobody is responsible for anything, it's all everybody else. So there's really nothing to be done about it, apart from whinge and complain, because the alternative is to say, 'Well, what am I doing here? And what do I need to do? And how can I change?' And that's painful: looking at yourself and looking at your own problems and where you've fallen down and what you haven't done right, and your own neuroses (I find looking at my own neuroses terribly embarrassing). It's not comfortable.

But you do it?

I choose to do it. I choose to do it.

Sometimes when we're attracted to someone else, we think we've fallen in love with them . . . ?

Yes . . . we do . . .

You're giving that illusion a bit of shaking here too, aren't you?

Well, there's a wonderful book that I've just finished reading, by Dr Robert Johnson, called *We: The Psychology of Romantic Love*. And he makes this point very strongly: that we, in fact, don't fall in love with another person at all—we simply project what we'd like to be onto that other person and fall in love with ourselves. And then when the other person refuses to live up to our illusion, we get very angry with them and walk away.

It's a very challenging idea, that idea of Johnson's, isn't it?

It's very uncomfortable, particularly if you've done it.

But you find it a satisfying one.

Well, I find it a very liberating one because I've noticed for myself—and certainly for my friends—that this idea of falling in love can be a bit like an addiction. And you end up acting in a way that is neither comfortable nor does it make you feel in charge. And when you realise that what you're doing is simply fooling yourself, then all of a sudden you can make choices and live your life the way you want to, and free yourself of the addiction. So it's a very liberating idea to me.

You use theatre, among other things, in your work—how does that work?

Well, theatre is a very powerful way of helping people see reality. I have found that if I talk to people about reality and illusion, they often don't understand. And if I talk to people about emotion, often people deny they have any, particularly in the business and government world—where we're not supposed to be emotional beings, we're supposed to be rational and objective. So I can talk to people about how emotions get in the way and about how our illusions get in the way and people think I'm talking fantasy.

The actors can act it out and it becomes so obvious and it's so funny, that we can no longer run away from it. So it's a very powerful teaching tool.

Well, what are some of the roles you might portray? And do you bring actors with you or do you invite people from the management group, say, to take certain roles?

I do both. I have a troupe of actors and we go along and they will act out someone resisting change ... or there's this wonderful thing where people say, 'I've told them, I've told my staff what I want and they still won't do it!' So we actually get the actors to tell each other what to do and when you watch this thing in progress you can see why the staff won't do it: because the message that's coming out of the mouth is very different from the message that's coming out of their body language, tone of voice and eye movement. So what people think they're saying is very often different from what they are saying. And the actors are very good at getting this across in a way that has everyone rolling in the aisles and then realising why it is their staff aren't hearing what they're saying.

Really? Even those who have that habit and do it that way?

Very much because it's not *them*, you see, it's the actors. So you can project your own failings onto the actors, see it, laugh about it, and then very slowly come round to thinking that, 'Well, maybe I do this just a little bit.' And that's all we need—it's the beginning, when people begin to realise 'Maybe my staff behaving in this peculiar way has got just a little bit to do with me.'

What are some of the other roles that you find yourself classically reproducing?

There's a thing that we're doing (in a forthcoming workshop) around expectations: where we're using something quite out of the business world, actually, out of male-female relationships. We're showing how people's expectations often stop them getting what they want. Because what we find is that people will come along and say, 'Look, this is what we want to achieve . . . ' and if they head off to achieve that and they achieve all sorts of better things along the way, they don't want the better things: they want what they're there to get. So, what we're trying to show is that if you have a very set view, if you are very . . . tunnel-visioned, I guess, you can miss all the wonder that happens around. So, what we're actually using there is a situation where a man goes to one of these dating agencies and gets a range of women, and the women are magnificent and beautiful and fantastic in every way, but they're not what he asked for . . . until he eventually gets what he asked for and he can't cope with it. So we've used a situation out of the business setting which is one of the things that we try and do quite a lot, too, just to get people to see reflections of business in their own personal lives.

So what would you want to say about that split we seem to have made in our habit of thinking: between that which we are (our being) and how we value that; and our doing, all our performance, our work? There's a real split there, isn't there, in our society?

Well, I can answer that, I guess, on two levels. One is for myself: if I operate from a doing level rather than a being level, I get exhausted; I find that I have a lot to do and it takes me a lot of time and I tend to get fairly exhausted at the end of the day. Whereas if I come from myself, from the fullness of myself, then I actually don't seem to have so much to do. I mean, I get to spend time with my children, I get to spend time with my clients and I get to think through some interesting issues and I get to negotiate some interesting topics and I get to read some interesting bits of information, and then at the end of the day I probably get to go to the theatre or to the ballet or . . . whatever. So, by the time that the end of the day has come, I really haven't done anything apart from being myself and enjoying myself in doing it.

And what I see so much in organisations is that people leave themselves at home and they take a set of skills to work. So what happens is that people in organisations are, in fact, killing themselves on a very real level, on a very base level. In that, if you try and detach who you are from what you do, then you're really splitting yourself in half and leaving probably the fullest, most juicy bit at home.

And another way I look at it . . . it's like, we have energy and we have power and we can have that in a positive way or we can have it in a negative way, but it won't go away. So if we don't bring it out and use it in a positive way, it will go underground and be negative and drag us down and drag our organisations down. And so many organisations I work with are bogged down in the politics, and they're bogged down in the interactions, and they're bogged down in the crises that are simply a response to people pushing down all those positive things or even the negative things, but at least not getting it on the table and dealing with it. So all the energy is going into suppression and to interplay and to politics rather than to actually getting the job done that people are there to do, as themselves . . . coming to work and just getting on with it.

But if I bring my whole self to work, will they like me? If they see all the rough bits and the negative bits and the parts that I don't think are so beautiful—if I bring that to my work or to my relationships, it's a risk.

Yes, it's certainly a risk, and they may not like you.

But I want to be liked, don't I . . . don't we?

Well, I guess that's the problem. And that's something that I've personally been working through quite a lot, because I've always wanted to be liked. What I've found is, as I care less about being liked, I am more liked. And I guess that what happens there is: while we're trying to please the other, they're trying to please us; and nobody is actually pleasing anybody. So, instead of me honestly saying 'This is who I am and this is what I want,' and letting you see who I am so you know who you're dealing with and what you've got before you here, all your energy is going into sussing out what it is that you might do that might please me. And what is happening for me is I'm feeling, 'Well, where is this person? You know, all I've got is this sort of crazy investigating energy that's coming over towards me and no real person to deal with, so how can I like you when you're not really there? Because where you are is over here investigating me.' So there really isn't anything there to like.

So what happens is we play this polite investigative, mutual game which takes an awful lot of time and an awful lot of energy—and often backfires, because if I don't end up being what you think you want me to be or I don't do what I think you think I want . . . you know, it's so tortuous that the energy dissipates, the day disappears and we've got so little done.

Whereas if you just go to work and be you and get on with what you have to do, and I just go to work and be me and get on with what I have to do, when you and I meet, we're meeting someone, we can know what we're dealing with, we can deal with it and get on with it. And our energy actually happens in being ourselves and getting our job done.

So let's stay with the challenge of being myself and being honest and being in the open about that. What are some of the ways, Margot, that you need to be mindful of to keep on doing that, to maintain some sort of equilibrium or honesty? Are there some practices that are in your life that need to be there, to help you get on with this?

I spend a lot of time with myself. I meditate every day . . . .

What form does that take?

I use two forms of meditation. One is a mantra meditation that I do for twenty minutes every day, every morning. And I also use a form of meditation which is basically just sitting: I just sit with my eyes open and I try and merge with the sea or the trees or the flowers or my environment, and really just be very peaceful and do what I call 'coming home'. I just go into myself and get to know me, because there's no way anyone else can get to know me if I don't.

I've done this often with businesspeople and often, when they 'come home', the shock is that there's nobody there, and that there hasn't been anybody there for such a long time. Because the demands of business are such that we're out there all the time, dealing with the clients and the staff and the boss and the children . . . so everything is out there for everybody else. So the shock is that when we do 'come home', often the house is empty.

Just before we move away from that, what's busyness all about then? I mean, people keep so incredibly busy, don't they . . . we? (I can include myself in this.)

Well, what it's about is dealing with the 'out there' issues. So, what we do is, rather than 'come home' and know who we are and operate from where we're going and what we want, we respond continuously to the 'out there', feeling very powerless around that.

It's very interesting (I've done this with a number of groups now)—when I get people to draw a picture of all the outside forces and put themselves in the picture and to 'come home', they feel paralysed. They feel quite paralysed. So from that point of paralysis people hit out and grab what little bit they can, and stay busy around doing that, rather than get on with the fullness of who they are and where they're going and what they want to do.

But why would we want to avoid coming home ... doing the inner work?

Well, it's a bit of a shock to come home and find that it's empty. It's like walking into a house that needs renovation ... I mean, it's much easier to go out and rent a flat than it is to buy your own home and renovate it.

It's less risky.

It's less risky, it's less hard work ...

... *less commitment ...*

... it's less commitment, it's less painful, it's less uncomfortable.

It also means that you're less in control of your own life. Because what it then means is that you're really like a piece of driftwood on the sea, and you'll go where the water pushes you. Learning to 'come home' and to get in touch with yourself and your own power and your own desire and your own humanity is like ... you know, building a huge ship. And anything like that takes time, it takes effort; you don't just snap your fingers and there is a ship. You have to plan it and you have to get the resources and you have to go out and build it. It takes a lot of time, a lot of effort. And, you know, it may not work. The fear is that it may not work.

With my meditation I have a mantra which is three mumbo-jumbo words (I mean it could be 'Coca Cola', it could be anything), which I just repeat silently to myself. And that helps me to ... I suppose, almost go into a trance state, which allows me to go down into my subconscious and come up with a lot of solutions to problems. I very rarely sit down and think through a problem. What I do is I meditate, and the answers just come. What that means is: I often have very lateral answers to problems, and things that I wouldn't have thought of if I'd sat down and thought it through logically. And the mantra—by going into that sort of trance-like state, I suppose—allows me to access parts of my subconscious that I can't get to in a logical way.

So you're suggesting that there is an inner solver of problems below or beneath or beyond the workings of the rational mind, are you?

Yes. Well, that's certainly been my experience and, I believe, the experience of a lot of other people as well.

So, do you pray?

I do. I pray quite a lot. I'm not exactly sure who or what God is. Some of my friends tell me that God is an outside force; and some of my friends tell me that God is your inner core; and my son tells me that he's a blue energy field that incorporates everybody; and I sort of think ....

That's a nice one, isn't it?

I think that's as good an explanation as any, particularly as he was six when he came up with this explanation. I thought 'Well, yes, that's very probably what it is.'

But I find it very reassuring to think that there is a power greater than myself. And I have ongoing conversations with this power.

Quietly or out loud?

No, quite often audibly which my children find embarrassing; they tell me that other mothers don't do this. But I find it very reassuring. It's like going through life with a friend holding your hand.

Is it asking for advice or just sharing your experience?

Oh, it's everything, it's everything. It's asking for solutions to problems, it's asking for advice . . . sometimes someone to get angry with—'How dare you do this to me!' And, knowing that whatever I say or whatever I do is totally acceptable to this unknown energy, it's very reassuring to me.

So there's a feeling of being loved and accepted . . .

. . . and accepted totally.

. . . *whatever you do.*

Yes, very much; total love and total acceptance. So I can say and do and be anything I want, with this energy field.

So, that's also what you think love should be, ideally, between human beings: people being themselves and accepting each other as themselves.

Yes, I guess that's true. When you say that, I'm very mindful that I'm not an enlightened being, that I'm a very human being, and when other people are around me and they do and say and be things that I don't feel comfortable with, I have terrible trouble 'loving' them. I have terrible trouble accepting them totally as they are.

But that is your aspiration?

That is definitely my aspiration.

Margot, in talking about an attempt to be ourselves, is there a risk of being selfish in that?

Well, that's usually the excuse people put up for not doing it. The fear is 'I will become very selfish.' And what I've noticed is that when people start to do this kind of work, they do appear selfish; because, like any new skill, when you start to look in and you start to observe yourself, it takes time and it takes effort, and it does take you away. And, also, if you've been playing a whole series of games with people ('I'll be there for you if you be there for me,' 'If you be what I want, I'll be what you want'), when we pull away from that, we can't really expect the other person to like it. So, initially, the fear is that we will be selfish and we will ruffle the status quo—and, in fact, that's true. But what I've seen is that, over time, people that live this way become much fuller, much more expansive, much more able to give selflessly to other people; because, simply, they have more to give, there is more of them. So sharing it . . . it's a bit like the Magic Pudding—you know, the more you eat of the Magic Pudding, the more comes back, both for you to eat and for you to share. (In fact, there's a lovely part in Norman Lindsay's *The Magic Pudding* where he says he loves to be shared around.)

Yes. So, although you suggest that sometimes we draw . . . attract towards us people from whom we need to learn something about ourselves, there can be the seeds in that, of a more wholesome relationship with another individual being him or herself.

Well, what I've noticed is that as I change, my relationships change. This has very much happened with my children, for example. As I've grown and learnt more about myself, I just feel so much more loving towards them. The things they used to do that annoyed me, no longer annoy me; and the things that used to exhaust me, now invigorate me. So, simply by coming back to me and being more selfish and being more myself, I'm much more able to be there for them.

In fact, I have a rule, as a single mother, that my happiness and my wellbeing are paramount. And, although that sounds remarkably selfish, the reason I've done it is that, if I'm not well and if I'm not happy, I can't be there for my children, and I can't go to work and earn the money, and I can't be there for my clients, and I can't be there for my friends, and I can't be there for my parents. So, if I'm not feeling well and happy and bright and expansive and able to give out, then all the people around me who rely on me simply would be let down.

But, I guess, in the close relationships of family there needs to be some sort of agreement that this is the way we're all going to approach life . . .

Very much.

. . . or you could have terrific conflict.

Well, what I notice is that as I change, the people around me change; so as my children see me do that, that's their role model. And I've noticed that my children are much more articulate now about their needs and what they want and what their limits are and what's important to them. Whereas once, when we were all being polite, they never told me. Now I'm very aware.

Being a single mother and keeping yourself fit . . . what are some of the things you encounter there, some of the things you have to really be mindful of?

Well, I'm very pleased to be, as I call it, 'in a body'. I find that a lot of people that are searching for answers tend to do it in what I call 'an out-of-the-body way'—they spend a lot of their time almost in another world. For me, I'm very pleased to be in this world with both my feet firmly on the ground. So I spend a lot of time doing that: I spend a lot of time walking on the beach, in the bush, swimming . . . the closer I can get to the ground and earth and nature, and actually doing something physical around that, the happier I am.

I also have a rebounder, which I use for all sorts of reasons—ostensibly to get fit, and I get up every morning and bounce—but I think that a lot of that is just a way of charging me up for the day ahead and really feeling the power in my human form. And also to help me express some emotions: if I'm feeling angry, I can bounce angrily; if I'm feeling happy I can skip or I can dance. And I also use it as a form of self-expression . . . so it's very much about being a very human person in a very human form.

In a high-powered job as you have, do you find that you have to fight against being anxious about your planning or worried about what you mightn't have done quite well enough yesterday or something? How do you deal with that? Because it's not an easy job, is it, that you have? It's a very responsible one.

Well, I guess it is, but I tend not to think about that so much as what I'm doing right now. If I sat and thought about where I was going and what I was doing and what might happen, I don't think I'd actually do anything. So what I do is: I do what I'm doing right now . . . like, right now, I'm sitting here talking to you—I'm not planning the workshop that I'm running tomorrow. So I try to do what I do when I'm doing it, and do it as much from myself and who I am as possible, and enjoy it. So I relax into it and be just here. Most of us spend our time worrying about what we did do and didn't do well, or what we will do and what we might do, and feeling guilty about what we didn't do. And all of that removes our energy from actually being where we are and getting on with what we're doing.

And can you take that approach to your mothering?

I do. In fact, I had to learn to do that when my daughter was so very ill;

because for quite a long time there, it was very touch-and-go—and if I had spent my life worrying about what might've happened, I wouldn't have enjoyed what time we had. As it was, she recovered and she's now a very healthy little girl, but for a long time we didn't know what it was, and the choice was: will I fret about what might happen or will I enjoy what I have? And we chose to enjoy what we had.

What are your feelings about the ageing of beauty, for yourself?

That used to worry me a lot. I'd won a number of prizes for my beauty and it seemed to me that that was a very big part of me—I guess, the public face that I showed. And the fear was that, as I got older, obviously this would fade and I'd be less of who I was or have less attention from the world or be less of a person, and it was a real worry for me. But, as I have grown older, I feel so much more content with myself and so much happier with myself and so enriched by an inner beauty, that I feel that I don't really care what other people see, so much as the way that I relate to them and the richness of the relationships that we have and the love that passes between us. And whether they look at me and see a pretty face or not, seems of decreasing importance.

You've had one very close experience with death—your daughter's death. Have there been other experiences that have given you some thoughts about death?

Yes. When I was a baby I came very close to death. I was, in fact, an experiment: I was the first baby in Australia, I think, to have an intravenous drip. It was very much a life-and-death situation and, although it seems a bit like fantasy, I can remember it, there is a flavour of it in my memory. And, also, with my daughter's near-death . . . it was a very peaceful experience and the flavour of the memory I have is of a very peaceful experience, so I've never really feared death. I've feared being maimed, I've feared being incapacitated, but not death because it was . . . the brushes were so peaceful and so reassuring almost, that there was a peaceful haven, and one was really passing from this present experience to another experience. But even . . . I've noticed that as I feel more content with myself, even being incapacitated doesn't hold a fear anymore, because it's just being different, it's just a new lot of learning experiences, it's another way to go. And although it may be uncomfortable and painful—as other things have been—it is just another way.

Often when I'm feeling blue, I write down all the things that I have—the list goes on for pages and pages: I have my children's laughter, I have their smiles, cuddles and love; I have the sky and the water and the boats; I have the trees and the flowers; I have Mozart and Haydn and Rodrigo and Sting; I have Barbra Streisand, Placido Domingo and Whitney Houston;

I have ballet and dance, theatre and film; I have exercise and the beach; I have my friends—their laughter, their trust, their love and their news; I have books and newspapers; I have my work and my clients; I have my poetry and my writing; I have skiing and swimming and bouncing on the mini-bouncer; I have sex and jokes and beautiful clothes; I have a home and a luxury car; I have my education, my excellence, my intelligence, my creativity—I have life.

Fr Hugh Murray

In Vincentian priest and poet Hugh Murray, we meet a man with great enthusiasm for life, and a bonhomie and humour sometimes used to mask a sensitive vulnerability, a man who's been challenged by very serious health problems.

Father Murray's work as a priest, in the example of St Vincent de Paul, has taken a number of forms: teaching, counselling, parish renewal, guiding retreats, drug and alcohol-connected ministry; and presently he's working with people suffering from AIDS, their carers, families, and loved ones.

Hugh Murray is a convivial and popular man, a good cook and accomplished poet.

FATHER HUGH MURRAY: I am very fat. Strangers, forced sometimes to make a comment, try to save my face by saying something like, 'Sir is a little overweight,' or 'Perhaps we could describe you as stout, sir?' The kids I taught were different. The older ones who were close friends just said, 'Gee, you're fat,' and younger ones asked embarrassed mums if I was going to have a baby. I think that one of the reasons God made kids was to bring the rest of us down to size. I used to teach at a boarding school where the kids passed your door after Sunday Mass on their way to breakfast. A kid who loved me well would cheerfully call out, 'Well, that was a lousy sermon this morning' and in my heart I knew he was right. I came down a peg or two.

I wore glasses very early in life and I have the most vivid memories of being called 'four eyes'. At one stage I even wore an occluder, a black eye-mask, and I was very self-conscious about it and, even though I look back with gratitude because it saved my sight, the teasing was awful.

I never had any dexterity with games or sport. I grew, I think, to be fairly facile with words at an early age simply to defend myself against the attacks. I couldn't defend myself physically—I never learnt to fight—so it was my only defence.

When I look back I see myself as being a very shy person. I think I developed this bonhomie exterior to cover up the shyness, but now I like it and it's become part of me, part of my life.

I was a bookworm. I think I'd read all of Dickens by the time I was twelve. Palgrave's *Golden Treasury* of poems was a particular favourite and I remember finding a copy of it forty years later at a bookshop and grabbing it with such glee because it was something from my past.

And what drew you towards studying for the priesthood?

I went to boarding school at the age of eleven or twelve having won a bursary, even though I wasn't really a very religious person. I guess I'm still not if it comes to that. Anyway, I went to this school which turned out to be run by priests. It was quite extraordinary. It was a hot summer's day in 1942 and I knew I wanted to be one of them. As soon as I saw those fellows I said, 'This is what I want to be.' I don't know why that happened and even though my feelings vacillated over the next five years, I always returned to that desire to become a priest.

And since then has there been a change?

Oh, sure, there've been times when I wished to God I'd chosen something else because it hasn't been the easiest life.

I didn't enjoy being a parish priest. I remember an entire church going silent when I said I had hated my time as a parish priest. It wasn't my own parish I'd said it to. We had said goodbye a couple of years ago with some tears on both sides but vast relief for the most part on mine. Thirty-five years a priest and I hated being a parish priest. Of course, they thought I had hated them. Which I hadn't. Some thought I hated being a priest. Which I didn't. What I hated was what it had become: a vocation overloaded with such enormous expectations. I mean, for 200 years in this country we clothed men in black, put white collars round their necks, touched the forelock and then closed up like clams when he turned up on the scene. Or was it the priests' fault? I suspect that it has taken 200 years for us priests to be reckoned as human beings who bleed when we are kicked. I still love being a priest. I love the fact that God seems to arrange it somehow that I'm there where and when he wants me. I love being the instrument of his peace. I love to share the Word. I take the symbolic gifts of bread and wine from all those out there, and I become the instrument for handing back the Lord himself. I love all that. It's just the blackmail of some of the well-to-do that I hate. And I hate the modern capitalist systems of good fiscal management and the very fact that I have to depend on those for some kind of wage. It's just enough to keep me poor and impotent and tempted to say what they want me to say on Sunday because otherwise they don't throw the coins in the hat I send around. Sometimes, Caroline, I wonder if people will ever understand what I mean when I say I hate being 'the parish priest'. That I resent always being expected to forgive and yet rarely feel forgiven? That it's bloody lonely on a pedestal, and very visible, and God help me if I get down for a human touch or a walk in the crowd once more.

So does becoming an ordained priest give you a set of absolutes, a set of certainties by which you will assess all situations from then on? Does being a priest make life easier in this way?

For some priests I think it does, but not for me. I try sometimes to analyse my absolutes and, strangely enough, they come down to a basic knowledge, as distinct from a belief, that I exist. I hold on to that. It keeps me from going mad. And I believe that God exists and that God wants good done. God is benevolent. I've never lost that absolute. But beyond those I'm not too sure about anything. I almost feel the older I've become the less certain I am.

So life is still a process of becoming who you are?

Oh, totally. The skeleton doesn't change and the flesh may vary from year to year with or without the diets, but the psychic diet of cutting a little bit here and building a little bit there and modifying and changing and growing older and growing more experienced in who you are and what purpose lies before you constantly changes. I'm constantly changing.

What moments have there been for you through literature, or places visited, or people you've encountered, that have been moments of fresh discovery?

Simple moments like hearing a beautiful voice or choir can literally reduce me to tears and this emotional effect, and the consequent prayer, becomes very important to me.

Writers, too, like Teilhard de Chardin stand out in my memory of fresh discoveries. There was a stage when Holy Mother Church seemed scared stiff of writers like him. Teilhard was a philosopher, theologian, palaeontologist and, above all I think, a poet; and he gave me a glimpse of what might be the truth. I'm not saying it is the truth, because I don't think any of us can ever really know what the truth is, but his concept of what cosmology was all about and what the world, the universe, the place of the incarnation of Christ, time and space all made sense to me. I don't think anyone else has given me more of a sense of beauty, of something possible, no, of something probable, than Teilhard de Chardin.

There was one poem of his that looms large, called 'Mass on Top of the World', from *Hymn of the Universe*, I think. His whole sense of light is simply marvellous. There's another poem, by T. S. Eliot from choruses from *The Rock*, where he says something like 'O Light invisible, we praise thee. . . ', and it talks about God being light and illuminating. And I find all these sources enlightening.

I'm really not a very pious person, being a born sceptic about most things—I often say I'd need to see a miracle on video-replay three times before I'd believe it—but I remember experiencing what could only be called a personal miracle at Lourdes some years ago. I was travelling in Europe with some married friends of mine and was unwell, having been in hospital in New York. For some reason I was feeling very angry with the Church. I can't remember quite why but the anger was there. At Lourdes I decided to attend Mass in the underground basilica. They'd celebrate the Mass in representative languages, you know, some of it in English, some in German, some in French and so on, but the Creed was always the sung Gregorian creed, *Credo III*. When it came to the part where Christ was tortured, crucified, suffered and died, I had this overwhelming sense of something like a voice saying to me, 'What right have you got to expect the Church to be perfect, if the Christ himself was helpless?'

Even though one part of me says it was simply my neurons firing, I think in some way I do recognise it as being something spiritual. That moment often comes back to me over the years and it's a very important part of my life. I mean, I still get cranky with people, but less so when I recall that time I was, if you like, kicked in the pants by the Lord.

And I am certainly a little less critical of the Church. I still loathe some of the things that happen—and I have got some real bothers about the central bureaucracy that drive me crazy—but deep down she's still Mother to me and I suppose I wouldn't be so critical if I didn't love her as Mother who can carry on in a blousy sort of a way! But the Church is Christ's church and he suffered and it's only made up of human beings who can all be bloody stupid at times. Coming to that understanding and acceptance has been enormously helpful.

So, Hugh, when you go through times of personal suffering, does that image of Christ come back to you and illuminate difficult times? Does it help you through?

Yes, I think it does. I've been fairly sick several times throughout my life. I had a pacemaker implanted about eighteen months ago and the few days prior were pretty frightening, so I've been forced to my knees several times. And even though I'm not yet sixty, I'm coming to grips with the fact that I could die this night. And I think I've come to grips with the concept of relying enormously on God's good grace. I mean, heaven is going to be a gift, it's nothing I've earned. God's grace is good and I've learned to love God and trust him.

I am certain my own vocation is a call to work with him and to be an instrument for him, and even when I really muck it up with my own weaknesses, there is this constant affirmation within myself that God is good and God loves me.

And I think it reflects a lot on the way I try to deal with people. I try not to 'come the heavy' too often! Oh, there are temptations all the time to be powerful and overbearing, but I think the thing that God asks most of me as a priest is just to love people and to stretch some of the rules so that they feel loved.

Hugh, there seems to be in your life a lot of struggle, a lot of pain in some ways. Would you speak to us about the challenges to you, for example, in the celibate life and in living in community?

I often write poetry when I'm experiencing tension and pain, in its broadest sense, and it is a relief. It externalises the pain, and the writing becomes part of the struggle. I write mostly for myself and, I guess, a fair number of them would deal with celibacy in one way or another. Celibacy has always been difficult for me. I'm a person with an enormously strong sexual nature. There was a time, I suppose, when I was a little frightened of that part of growing up, but I know it's part of God's gift to me. I often said I wouldn't ordain anybody who didn't have a strong sexual nature; I don't think people can love unless they've got one. The celibacy part is hardest, especially when you divorce it from sex and put it in terms of belonging to somebody. I think, in the long run, my celibacy means a commitment to God. He's the love in my life. I'm quite sure you can be a priest without having to be celibate. And maybe we'll live to see that happen in the Catholic Church. I don't think I could have survived as a celibate in any way at all if I didn't live in community. To me, community gives me companionship, it gives me family, it gives me home and it's never empty. There's always somebody to come home to. Sure there are lonely times. I stayed over with friends the other night. I like to go to their place to get my batteries recharged. Just being with them and their two children cheers me up because they don't pretend. You get what you see. You see a lot of love and they love to share it. This particular night turned out to be story-night on which the father reads his daughter a story which he must have read about 107 times before now. I passed the wide open bedroom door a little later and saw my huge hairy friend beside this little blonde kid not much bigger than the size of his head and totally trusting him to give her the full dramatic works of the Wednesday Night Story. I remember, Caroline, going off to my bachelor bed thinking how nice it would be to have someone to read to in bed. But if I had, that family would never have had me, and I would never have had them, and the way we love each other and the comfort I bring and the care I get would not pass from one to another.

Of course I haven't got those kids. But I haven't got the mortgage either. Nor have I got the youth any more to read that story week after week like my friend does. Instead I've got the chance to visit and bring my little load of love that tells them they are good to be with. And, Caroline, I can tell you it's been good to hold the hands of people like my friends and to know that my life with its ups and downs has contributed to lots of stories read in bed with love.

What calls you now, Hugh?

Having finished parish work a couple of years ago, I'm working virtually full-time with people who have AIDS or are HIV-positive, and their families. It's a specialised group and there are no real answers. We're just living from day to day.

And what are the challenges for you in this work?

I don't intrude. I can't intrude; but it would be so easy for my school-teacher side to come out and say 'We've got so much to do this year. . . ' and set the syllabus. Instead, I've got to let them be. I have simply to be there, and when they want me, when they want God, I'm there for them.

That's a big challenge for me because I tend to be impetuous. It's been a special grace this year to be able to sit quietly and just be with them. I regret to say that in so many of the cases, because we're dealing with a homosexual group who, at this stage, are predominantly the sick ones, their experience of priests has been bad. Their experience of church has been worse. And when they find out I'm a priest they expect me to wave a finger saying, 'No condoms. . . ' That's sad.

So, I have to work through what's essential to communicate and what's not essential and the fact of the matter is that you've always got to remind yourself these are God's sons and daughters, and he loves them just as they are. There's no room in this work for judgment of any kind. The only judgment I make is how best I can help this person meet his or her God.

I like to think that it's providence. I like to think that Almighty God gives you a little shove, without you knowing you're being shoved, into an area where you'll be of use. It's not the first time I've been aware of this. It can often happen in a priest's life. I don't think about it very often but every now and then I get this . . . oh, I like to think it's a ghostly presence (in the nicest sense of the term!) and that I'm the servant, not the master. And I know that I'm exactly where I'm needed and where I can best serve.

I've met some lovely people. Not just the people who are sick but the ones who look after them. Caroline, you've no idea of the dedication of these people, the community nurses, and volunteer men and women from various organisations. I think some of the women see in these sick men their own sons, or the possibility of their own sons getting as ill, and I'm fascinated by the compassion and sheer hard work of these women. It's beautiful to see.

There are so many different elements in your life, Hugh. I think of you as such a convivial person—you're a good host, a great cook. You're a very funny man. You write poetry. There's music in your life, literature, laughter, so much fun . . .

I think it's part of my nature. I don't ever remember being different in the sense that I was ever dour. There used to be this belief about personality types—the fat being jolly and that sort of thing. I suspect we're also likely to be manic-depressives, too, but basically there's an aliveness about it all. And, again, I like to think that it's a gift, offered and accepted.

Do you see that liveliness as part of vocation? An embracing of life?

Yes, I do. I think, though, if all priests had my nature it'd be rather dreadful for people, but I do think that God's very good the way He makes His selection. I'm glad I ended up a bubbly priest rather than a solemn one. I couldn't bear being solemn. It just wouldn't work.

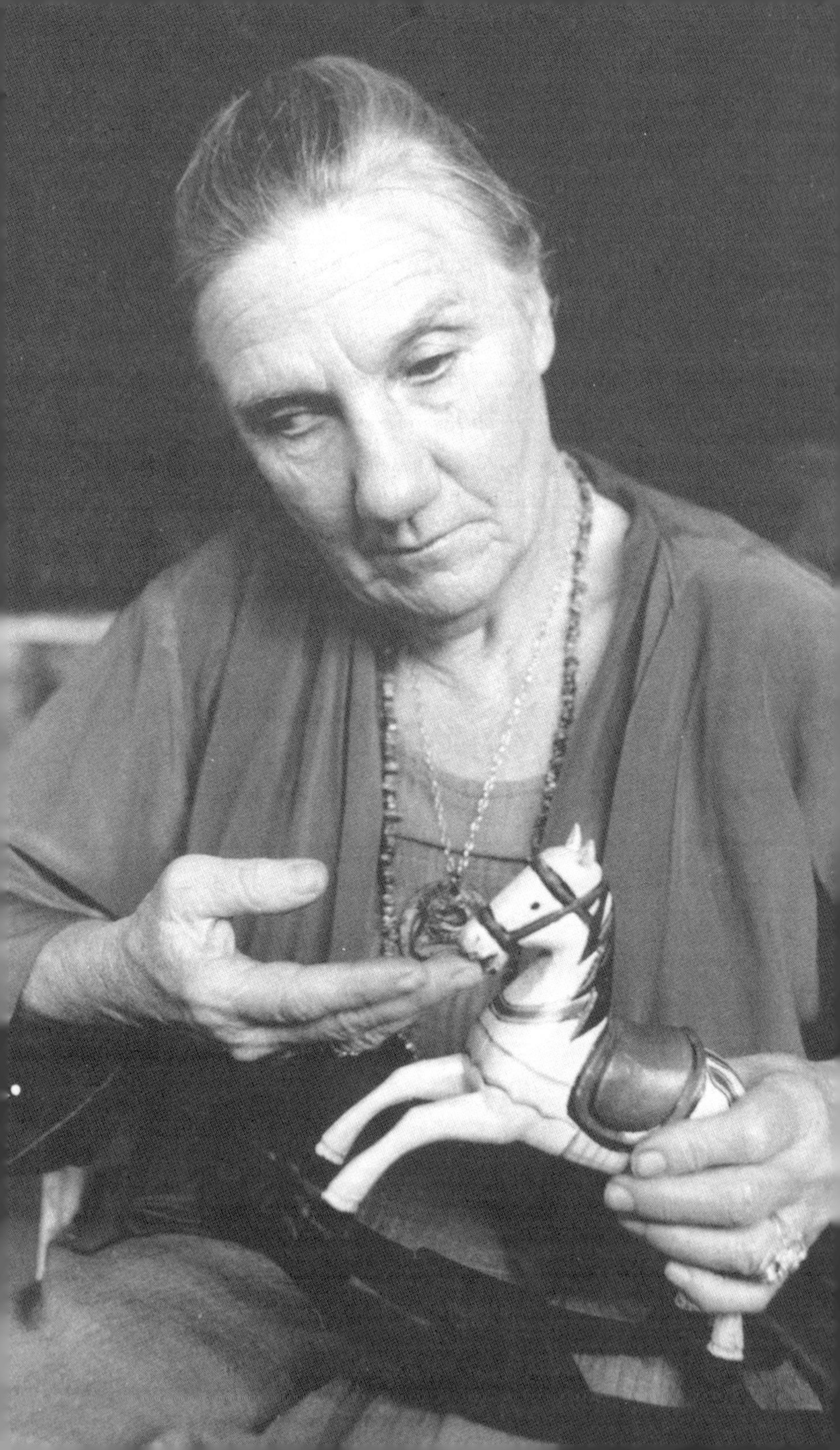

Barbara Blackman

Writer Barbara Blackman sees life as a great poem. She has made a lifelong search for meaning often through the pursuit of art.

She was brought up as a Rechabite—a rather strict and puritanical sect—so it's interesting that Barbara ended up in the bohemian life of Sydney and Melbourne artists.

Even as a teenager at Brisbane High School, she was a member of an avant-garde creative youth group frowned upon by a principal not over-keen on the influence of art.

Barbara recalls seeing as a teenager, the photographs of Belsen after the war as being 'the end of innocence' for her . . . fortunately she discovered the poet Wordsworth at much the same time.

Barbara Blackman describes herself as being an explorer, sometimes catalyst, always lover.

Her searching has taken her to camp out in the remote northwest of Australia; to India; to Queensland to study with Diane Cilento, and to share her attraction towards being a 'Sufi' . . . that is, to live a life guided from within by that which is Infinite.

Barbara is not able to see with her eyes.

BARBARA BLACKMAN: I was an only child and I could never understand people saying, 'An only child is a lonely child.' I accepted solitude as a natural state and I found the world wonderful and people friendly.

But I suppose my childhood had a kind of special quality because I was my own companion. I talked things over with myself and, at four years of age, I discovered the nature of my being. I said to myself—'I am I. There is no other I than me. I will never be anything else but me. But this me that I am is not just my body. My body is kind of acting it out. And I am outside of that.'

What an extraordinary thing to suddenly know at that age, Barbara!

Well, that discovery then—I suppose you would say—governed my life. It allowed me to be brave, in a way, or to be reckless—which is the same thing—because from that viewpoint the experiences that I have are circumstantial and the self beyond that is the real.

So there you are, I lived a kind of double life, a duality—the Barbara that people could see and know, and the inner secret that only I could know.

There had to be a meaning to it, a connection between the two, and I went through my growing up desperately trying to find out what it was. I read things. I listened. I won a gold medal for Sunday School attendance. I bought *Pilgrim's Progress* with the first money I ever had of my own. I struggled and struggled with it, and then, in my last year of school, I got it. I got the book I wanted. Suddenly there it was: T.S. Eliot's *Four Quartets*.

I knew straightaway that here was the book that was telling me what I needed to know. I was sixteen, I could not decipher it. But I recognised it. Imagine how blasphemous I felt saying to myself, 'Well, I can put the Bible down for a while now. This is it.'

It took a lot of sorting out then and has taken half a lifetime to understand. But then, in my youth, I struggled on for the next five years trying to stand my Christian ground armed with Aldous Huxley's *Perennial Philosophy* which is a book of quotations from theologians, mystics, and saints.

Then, when I was twenty-one, I had my real crisis. A huge black hole seemed to open up on all sides and just about swallow me up. The causes were cumulative. I had managed to get myself through university doing Psychology Honours. Let me say that, had I had sufficient eyesight, I should have preferred to study Literature and History. But I was curious about everything and I thought Psychology would give me a good enough set of keys to the castle of knowledge. I was terribly disappointed. It was mechanistic, behaviouristic. The only gleam of light came from my first glimpse of C.G. Jung.

Also, I had kept company with Marxists and tried hard to come to grips with Communism. I wanted to, but I couldn't. Somehow it just would not adhere. So you could say I walked the planks of all the faiths—religion, politics, psychology. Then the ultimate plank: my own body.

I went once more to an eye specialist. He told me that the recent onset of blurring and vision fatigue I had had while studying was an indication that I was going blind—and quite quickly. My eyes were dying. I had not expected that. I felt I was suddenly being given a life sentence for a crime I hadn't committed.

And then, you see, on top of all this—I had fallen in love. I had fallen in love with a painter, with Charles Blackman. What to do? We were both so very young—a pair of little bunnies—but he said he wanted to be a great painter, and I believed that he could be. But then, how could someone going blind undertake to share a life with someone whose life was supersight? So you see, everything seemed to crash all about me like an earthquake of the psyche.

And how do you recall coming through that?

I was reading—in fact just this last week—something that Jung said—(and I paraphrase) 'Just because there is a problem, that doesn't mean that there is a solution.' We, of course, in our so-called scientific age, are conditioned to think that there is. The ancient wisdom points out that the tree cannot grow through the rock. The tree grows round the rock. Very often you don't solve the problems, you transcend them.

By accepting both sides of the problem, the conflict, you move beyond it. Now, you can take this idea a long way and say that Christ was crucified on the cross which is an intersection of a horizontal and a vertical, two forces going in opposite directions symbolically, and He transcended by resurrecting. So I find that when I come up against a problem I cannot solve, I do nothing. I just lie there and wait. I've always trusted the Unknown and It has never let me down. Something you cannot for the life of you imagine or plan for or expect, happens.

And, at the age of twenty-one, what was that to be?

Well, I was just lying about having what you would call a nervous breakdown. I took to my bed with my knitting and chocolates and packets of fags—you see, I was trying to smoke, but I never did learn how—when a friend came along and he said, 'Look here, I'm going down south for my annual holidays. Get yourself up out of all this and come down with me.' So off we went to Melbourne, where he pitched me head-first in amongst wonderful people who became my friends and part of my life.

There were the Boyd family in the 'brown room', Neil Douglas in his garden, the Langleys, John and Sunday Reed holding court at Heide, all the Smiths including Joy Hester in the parlour of Martin's picture-framing, the Eltham builders, the talkers at the Mitre Tavern, Matcham Skipper and the gang from Montsalvat, Cliff Pugh and the Gallery students.

Exactly what happened was this: In those days the train from Brisbane got us into Sydney early in the morning, left to goggle round the spectacular city all day like a couple of country cousins until it was time to grab a pie and peas and get on board the night train for Melbourne. So there we were wandering bravely through King's Cross when who should appear out of the blue right in front of us but Charles Blackman. So there you are. There's the Unknown. We had lost track of each other in that earthquake. But there we were, face to face. We just looked at each other. We knew we just loved each other and our lives *had* to be joined, mingled, mean something to each other.

That happened, crisis transcended—I forgot I was having a nervous breakdown. I did not return home to Brisbane. On my way back from Melbourne I stayed in Sydney.

So you married—and for twenty-eight years.

We had a wonderful marriage and I think we were as creative as possible for each other within that marriage.

One of the fascinating things to me, I suppose, is that, when the time came you both felt for you to part, you did that creatively too.

The Byronic side of it was certainly there—

Then we two parted
In silence and tears
Half broken-hearted
To sever for years

at the same time we recognised we had to give each other up. I do not see our marriage as failing or breaking down. It finished, was complete. Life had to be different for each of us.

Marriages end in different ways. The decision was made, I wrote a letter of resignation to take effect in two weeks time on the day of our twenty-eighth wedding anniversary. That gave it a kind of symmetry. From then on, we were able to try and help each other on our new paths. We became as brother and sister, we are friends. We still help each other. We still love each other. But our lives have moved in very different directions.

How has art been important in your life, important in helping you to find meaning and make sense of life?

Art was always there. My father was a Sunday painter. His pictures hung in the house, although I didn't know him personally because he died when I was three. In my teens I moved among the BARJAI Group, young avant-garde poets and painters. We went together to exhibitions and soaked up the books of the Masters in the Art Library.

Then, for my Honours thesis, I followed up a North American research on 'Painting and Personality' on the diagnostic value of pre-school children's painting. Also, in clinical studies, I looked a little into those areas of some people's lives where, in going through deep disturbances, they paint out their imagery therapeutically.

I felt there must be some connection between these three—the conscious committed artist, the innocent unselfconscious child, and the fragmented adult. These seemed to be signposts and I wanted to take that path of inquiry to find what was their common ground. But it was then that my sight collapsed, so I had to put that search aside.

The personal meaning of life seems to me to be like the image in a form of art.

Life is a great poem and I seek to know how the poem works. With Charles and me it was the wings of our two poems of life interlocked. That's what married us. Art seemed for me then the only way in which that mystery of the poem was being revealed.

Now that my life has moved on out of 'the art world' into another aspect, I think I can understand more what is the common ground between those three moments of art.

Would you say something about that, please, Barbara.

It's hard to put it into words because it is so simple. I think in that early part of my life of which I have been speaking I was what you could call an 'undiagnosed mystic'. One part of me could grasp things directly by intuition. But the other part wanted to be rational and have explanations and precedents. That was the nature of my education and of the thinking of people around me. It is only in the last few years I have had the chance to look at things in another way, to study the esoteric and make sense of it that way.

If we look at the human condition, we see that we live our lives being conditioned all the time. We are conditioned—to take an example—to think we cannot tell the time without reading a clock; but also in ways much more profound. For instance, conditioning to linear time rather than cyclical time. An example of this: we insist that Aboriginal witnesses in land rights stand up in court and give evidence in a sequential historical way, as we do, instead of by song in their cyclical, traditional way of recording events.

Another conditioning is causality where we seek cause and effect instead of seeing effect being the cause of the effect. What I am saying is that there is an area that is unconditioned and that the human spirit, the human psyche, can sometimes dip into it. That's what the young child, the disturbed patient and the gifted artist do—like diving into the deep and bringing up the fish.

I think also that what I was talking about, right at the beginning, the 'me' that is unique, that is in every person, is part of that unconditioned—whether you call it divinity, eternity, the collective unconscious . . . Wordsworth called it 'God'.

Our birth is but a Sleep and a Forgetting
The Soul that rises with us, our Life's Star,

Has had elsewhere its setting
And cometh from afar
Not in entire forgetfulness
And not in utter nakedness,
But trailing clouds of glory do we come
From God who is our Home.

Barbara, what would help me tremendously right at this point is if you can recall particular moments or times when you have had that sense yourself.

Oh very many times, great and small. It's so quick. It is when one just has to do something without time to work out how. One finds the means to do it just out of the need to do it. The need becomes the means.

Well, here's a recent practical example: I was working out a wedding reception event for my daughter and I wanted to use appropriate poems. I telephoned her godmother, Judith Wright, who said there was a poem of hers 'In Honour of Love and Marriages' in such-and-such a book which I could get from so-and-so. While she was talking I reached up my spare hand to the bookshelf where the books are in higgledy-piggledy order and grabbed a book and held it open to the friend beside me. There was the poem. But a moment before, I could not have told you if I owned that book, let alone where it was.

What about when you suddenly upped and decided to go and live in the bush for six months?

Ah—that looked like sheer madness . . . My life was on the turn. My *nuova vita* was starting up. My marriage had just finished. I was in a new place, Western Australia, producing radio programs. I was there at the beginning of Radio for the Print Handicapped in Australia. Life was great. I had gathered a lot of wonderful people about me in Perth working as volunteers on the program. I had leapt out into the Unknown, joined five different societies—writers, broadcasters, Jungians, jazzies, oral historians. But I kept feeling I needed something else.

I needed something fundamental to happen to me. The little inner voice said, 'Lie upon the landscape of your country'. I decided that what I wanted to do was to go away from all I knew and just go camping—go bush.

Probably this had come up from the depths, from something very early in my life. I have said that my father died when I was three years old. He had been a surveyor and, when he knew he hadn't long to live, he took my mother and me to camp with Aboriginal people, whose ways he loved, out on Pumicestone Creek, Caloundra. So we camped with these people and went fishing and cooked round camp fires, and I think we were deeply happy. So that must have been what spoke to me now at this other time of loss and bereavement, which the end of a marriage is. So that's what I had to do.

The decision took shape because the more I was getting to love Western Australia, the more the Perthies gave me the feeling that the real place was up north, the real West.

But all these mythical places—the Kimberleys, Broome, the Gibb River Road—were all so far, such a distance, one needed a long time. And a good car. I had been left with the Range Rover in Perth, this splendid chariot, and so I just had to find the people to come with me. I went around, fired with this idea, waiting to spark off someone. I was put in touch with a man in Adelaide described as a wanderer, a 'white Aboriginal', a good bushman. So, I arranged it all by telephone.

Then people said to me, 'You're mad. You haven't even met this man and you're going off camping for three months . . . ' (turned out to be six months). So I phoned him and said to him. 'What would happen if we got out on the road and decided we didn't like one another?' He said, 'Don't you like people?' I said, 'Yes, I like people'. He said, 'Well, why wouldn't you like *me*?'

He said he had a little half-blood daughter of three coming along with him. We made up the party with another woman, a full-blood from Aurukun in Cape York, and halfway up we picked up a young Italian-Australian scientist who had been working on the Aboriginal Health Program in Arnhem Land; later, another little black child.

We were a funny little crew—and off we went and we had a wonderful, wonderful time. The men were both good hunters. We slept under the stars. We went to remote places. And I was healed.

You stayed out for six months and you were healed. *More on that, please.*

People had said to me, 'You'll get brusied from lying on the ground. You'll get the trots from bush tucker. You'll get sores.' But I knew—I knew from the very first night, when I lay down upon the sands of a dry river bed under the sky, I felt happy—happy in a way I had never felt happy before. Then—the more I got to feel myself one with the old slow time of rock and the near fast time of birds flitting by, the deeper that happiness became. Oh, the places we went to, the silences—the way we were able to pull fish out of the sea and eat them—and the crabs, the wallabies, goannas . . . I had never been part of nature like that before.

And you were healed?

Yes, yes, yes. I was healed of the sorts of fears I might have had as a middle-aged blind person living by myself for the first time—also having had a cancer operation just before departure.

So, Barbara, what do you think about healing now?

You mean in the light of what I was saying about the unconditioned? It comes out of a state of being rather than from an act of doing. My understanding now is that's what Jesus did with His healing. He *did* nothing. He just *was* there, Himself a part of that unconditioned. So He was able to take the wounded, the unwhole person, and dip them into It—in an instant. He wasn't going about it the way a doctor would. Nor does the painter go about making his work of art the same way a lawyer goes about his work. The preparation, the discipline, is there, and then—it happens. It comes into the act as inspiration.

About fourteen years ago a wise old woman, a relative, came to stay with me. She withstood a few days of our household, the pace, the drama, the hyperdynamics, and then she took me to task. She said, 'Your life's in a dreadful state. You run about all over the place, planning, organising every little detail. The emotional atmosphere is stifling. There is no place for intuition.'

Then she taught me the other way of going about things—wanting, willing and waiting; to be clear about what I wanted, to will it to happen, and then to trust and wait for it to happen. Caroline, one of your recent interviewees quoted the Buddhist dictum: 'Don't just *do* something—Stand there.'

And that makes sense to you?

A lot of sense. But it was hard for me to learn that, because I am a very impetuous, impatient person.

Barbara, have you felt stereotyped sometimes as a person who is blind?

Yes. That's another hard-learned patience. Very often people do see me as just that, only as a monument or personification of blindness. That's often the most difficult thing about being blind. Actually I'm not a very good blind person at all. I've failed Braille from the age of twelve. I don't have mobility, I don't go scampering around the streets by myself. I've never had a seeing eye dog—I think the RSPCA would not allow any decent dog to be led along my dance.

But I think a terrible fear of blindness lurks deep down in the heart of most people, and this is what they pre-empt into what they see of me. So they put up a barrier that becomes a kind of blockage for me.

For instance, one of the experiences I love is that of walking into a room full of strangers, strangers with whom one shares common interests. It's so exciting to feel one is going to meet new and interesting people. I went recently to a weekend conference of the Oral History Association in Sydney. The taxidriver delivered me to the door. I just stood there with my white stick. Gradually people came up and we began talking to one another. But it can happen that, in a situation like that, someone, well meaning but unimaginative, can come up and grab me and take me over, super-protect me, and almost at once start asking, 'Now, how are we going to get you home?' They are just seeing me as a problem.

How much memory do you have of things seen?

I suppose I do live on my early visual memories. I shuffle my pack of remembered images and pull bits out to make up the picture that fits a description being given to me. But the visual references become less and less important. I forget to ask what my friends look like and to sketch a visual. Someone read out a newspaper article recently in which a close long-standing friend, now in the political arena, was graphically described. It was a wonder to me to find out that he was balding on top, had spectacles and a neat goatee beard. But then, I might well forget it and go on happily with my own kind of schematic image of him.

So, you encounter people in a different way?

I suppose I must. I think I am a worry to people who have invested a lot in their appearances—and I don't see them . . . I think I make them feel a bit uneasy and they start to pity me. There's the rub.

Interesting. I hadn't ever thought of that before. Your life is so rich. It's so full of incident and search and quest. I hardly know where next to dip in. But I'm going to dip into India, 1982.

Ah—India was wonderful to me and taught me so much. Again, I went on impulse—and found myself for the first time on the inside, as though I had come in from outside, to where I could drink at the well of eternity. I went to Bombay to the International Transpersonal Conference on 'Modern Science and Ancient Wisdom'.

A palace of a hotel, 1,000 people, a week of papers, discussions, meetings, minimal sleep, great speakers on both sides—Fritjof Capra, Rupert Sheldrake, June Singer, Virginia Satir, Mother Theresa, Muktananda, Bede Griffith. Then, in a small group, for ten days a trip through to Delhi via the temples, the caves at Ellora and Ajunta, the abandoned edifice of Fatehpur Sikri, the Taj Mahal, right up to the Red Fort at Delhi and the amplified voice of Mahatma Ghandi speaking for his people.

What India taught me was Both. Not Either/Or but BOTH. In our culture we are so strung up on 'either/or'—we are conditioned to right-wrong, good-bad, life-death as being opposites, in conflict. It's the two sides of the penny. India helped me to understand about accepting both sides of the crisis. The penny itself is what is within the two sides, and we have to live within the paradox. Life is the reconciler. The more one reconciles things within oneself, and outside, the more one becomes part of the whole—the unity, the harmony of the whole.

It sounds from that as if Jung might still be a useful companion for you?

A great well—yes.

And also, haven't I read somewhere in your writing that you felt Jung was the psychologist who had some insight into art?

I wish I could quote the passage to you exactly where he likens the artist to the tree whose roots go down deeply into the common unconscious and bring up through the foliage the flowering image.

Where are you now in your thinking? What are the threads of your life now?

You're asking me what I'm doing now. I do some work for the Australian National Library on their Oral History Program interviewing distinguished people about their lives. I kind of take down their autobiographies on tape. That's a great privilege—to go through people's lives with them. I'm a bystander while they look back on what that life has been.

And building?

Caroline, we've spoken about two crises in my life, times when my life changed shape radically. I feel now that I am in my third third of life. It may be the longest third, it may be the shortest. But it is different from the other two parts. I feel that by now I must have learned a few things along the way—if I'm going to learn anything at all—and I have certainly gained a few things materially from what I see as a blessed and lucky life so far. Now is the time to lay these things out and use them and invite others to share them.

I've been able to buy a hundred acres of bush down south, 'real tiger country', lots of rainforest, not too far from the sea. I live now in a present-day kind of marriage with a philosophic Frenchman, a student of the gnostic tradition, and we have built our place upon this land.

It's made of stone, mudbrick and wood. I think, Caroline, you might know Chris Nash, our builder, who built the well-documented monastery at Stroud when he was a Franciscan brother. He has made a triple saddle-back kind of roof. People say it's a 'temple in the bush'—and that goes along with what we want the place to be.

Caroline, I know now that what is most wonderful for me in life are people, study and the bush. So here we hope to put these three together, removed from the rest of the hurly-burly of life. Ours is a house of hospitality, contemplation and study. It's no institution—no brochure—it's a feeling, a centre, a magnet. People will come here who want the quiet in which to think, write, compose, and we shall work and cook together, and gather around the fireside to read poetry, listen to music, study texts.

Sounds a bit like Diane Cilento's Karnak—in that spirit. So can you explain a little about the practice of Sufism?

I heard a lecture by Irene Tweedy, an English woman who studied Sufism in India, and I'll quote her: 'The aim of Sufi training is to live a life guided from within by that which is Infinite.'

And that has meaning for you now, as it has had for many years, from what you've said?

Surely. I couldn't possibly work my life out just trying to make things fit from the outside. I really couldn't. I really wouldn't know what to do next . . .

. . . *if you weren't listening to what is happening within?*

I have to trust that—like walking on the water. I couldn't get about my gypsy travelling life without trusting there to be a friendly arm, a timely word.

Barbara, and where is God in that now, if anywhere?

God's everywhere. God is the well, and the fountain—the effusion of love that is everywhere—within and without.

Emma Pierce

This talk will offer hope for anyone going through a personal crisis, whatever the nature of that crisis.

It's a story to bring comfort into darkness, to remind us of our inner strength, a story about awful isolation and about healing. It's about the cures that don't work, the experts who try but who don't know the answers and about the power of human faith. It's a story about madness and coming back from madness.

Picture an intelligent woman who'd won top marks in some subjects at school—a married woman with three children and an authoritarian husband with a foreman's job in forestry which kept him away from home during each week, a husband with rigid ideas, a violent temper, a terrible objection to his wife's Catholic religion and to his children being educated in that tradition. The marriage became a battleground with the wife submitting to the husband and his sexual demands because she believed her religion said she must. She feared her husband, but in obedience she continued in a desperately unhappy life. Gradually she went mad, and there began years of grotesque hallucinations, loss of meaning in life, and terror. So this is the compelling story of a woman who's been in the abyss of mental illness and who has come back to write a book to shine the light of reason on the taboo of madness.

This is Emma Pierce's story.

EMMA PIERCE: I think the most formative thing in my life was being sent to a Catholic boarding school. I came from a non-Catholic family and I was quite intrigued by it. I always had a very analytical mind, and pondered many things that probably children my age didn't normally ponder—maybe I was mad then, I don't know. But I began to argue furiously with my father to allow me to become a Catholic which he eventually allowed when I was twelve. That religious conviction marked my entire life. I'm not rigidly Catholic at all. My friends say I'm a liberal Catholic. I tend to think that means being a more compassionate, understanding person. I certainly don't think that the only people who get into heaven are Catholics! But yes, the upbringing with Dominican Nuns and conversion to Catholicism were massive steps for me. And even at twelve years of age, I think I appreciated the step I was taking.

And then your Catholic conviction was to prove to be a tremendous stumbling block in your marriage?

Yes, it was. I think I was fortunate in not making the mistake of 'throwing the baby out with the bath water' when it came to my Catholicism. I think a lot of Catholics make that mistake.

I grew up very much on the kind of hellfire-and-brimstone idea of rules and regulations and if you broke them you were damned for ever more. I grew up with this very frightening image of God and religion and it took a lot of growing on my part to be able to see past all that to the forgiveness . . . the compassion . . . the understanding . . . the realisation that it was Almighty God who made human nature. So if He can't understand it, who else can? And no matter how beautiful marriage was intended to be, it isn't always that way. And I had to find that acceptance within His understanding.

I think it was an old parish priest who taught me something special without even knowing it: 'What is moral appears to change, but it never does. If you examine what is moral, it is that which is just and loving for all concerned, and that can change.' It's both moral and just to stand over your three-year-old and say, 'Eat your peas!' but you wouldn't stand over your thirty-three-year-old and say 'Eat your peas!' It's no longer the just and loving thing to do. And I ultimately came to the decision that, yes, my marriage was over. Even now, twelve years later, I look back and think, 'It was just and loving for all concerned'—for myself, for my husband and for my children. I think we all benefited from it. That's not to say I advocate divorce or marriage break-ups although I do think we go into marriage a little easily. Strangely enough religion is often a large part of personal breakdowns. And I've never met anyone who broke down who didn't run into God as a big question mark. He always is.

The way I look at it now, going mad is the best thing that ever happened to me. And I know that sounds a crazy thing to be saying but there were so many things I would never have learned any other way.

Going mad is like being taken apart, right down to the foundation. And then you re-create. You go right back to the wire and start all over again. And then you begin to realise that who you are is not a discovery but a decision.

People go through life thinking, 'I have to go to an analyst and find out how I think and what I say and why I do this, and who I am etc'. No you don't! You know yourself if you have the ability to be honest with yourself. You know yourself far better than any other human being could possibly hope to know you. All it takes is the courage to be honest with yourself, to stand naked before God and say, 'This is who I am'. And that's who you are.

I went through the processes of analysis and group therapy with the assumption that self-awareness brings about change. But it's decisions that bring about change. Self-awareness is a value to the extent that it makes you aware of what choices you've got. But to say, 'Look, if you discover this about yourself, that will change'—is a load of bunkum.

Would you take us into the experience of feeling that you were going mad; what that was like, and perhaps something about the treatment that was offered you?

At first I denied the feeling of going mad. I found it very hard to come to terms with the fact that I was going mad. I got through the delusional thinking still trying to convince myself that it wasn't happening.

Delusional thinking?

Thinking I was a vampire which was terrifying. Everyone has funny thoughts that occur to them, and you think, 'Oh that's ridiculous' and you push it aside and that's fine. But a delusional thought (and you've still got that ability to recognise it as a delusion) is a mind-driven conviction that you start to fight. You become terrified to wake up and begin thinking because you know what's in your head and you don't want to think it.

I've heard it expressed by many people in the same situation, that if you could simply open your head and cut out the parts that thought that way, you'd be all right. And it's this feeling that your worst enemy is at home, in your own head, that no matter what you do you can't get away from what you're thinking, that is so terrifying.

At first I went to a psychiatrist and then into a mental institution with the closest thing to a 100 per cent conviction that these people could help me. The devastating thing was learning little by little that the most helpless people in mental institutions are the experts.

When I was in the mental institution, I actually made a deliberate decision—God knows I was bombed out on tranquillisers, shock therapy and God knows what—but I actually made a conscious decision: 'I can stay here and be mad or I can go home and be mad, but there's no way anybody here has got any way of helping me.'

So I decided that I'd go home and be mad, or at least I'd give it a go.

I found the treatment in the institutions humiliating. I was consistently patronised, as was everyone else in there. I had no compassion for anyone else. As far as I was concerned, all the other inmates were really mad but

I was just sick. It took me years to discover, after meeting many people who'd spent years in mental institutions, that it's a conviction that first strikes every patient—that everybody else is mad but somehow you're just sick. You have an idiot idea of what madness is. And really the idiot idea comes from the textbooks and the psychiatrists. And this idea is that somehow something suddenly goes bang in your head and you go mad overnight. But you must appreciate that you go mad the same way you do everything else—a step at a time. You learn how to be crazy and you can unlearn it.

Were you frightened while you were in the institution?

No, I don't think I was frightened but I went from being hopeful to being sceptical . . . cynical. I fluctuated between believing what I was told and not believing it. A lot of the analysis seemed illogical. I was then told, 'Well, how the heck would you know? After all, you're mad and I'm the doctor. I know best'. And how I struggled! Looking back now, I know that I was treated to the best of their ability. Sure, there are inadequate, threatened, insecure little human beings in every field and we had our share of 'power mongers', as I call them, in mental institutions. But I don't see these people as being big bad ogres, just people with problems . . . problems just as big and sometimes bigger than the inmates at mental institutions.

By and large the professionals do try to help. I guess what hurts is that they really don't know how to help and I find them now resisting the knowledge that it really is simple—not easy, by no means easy, but definitely simple. The constant diagnosis is that it is a 'physical illness'. I will make a categorical statement and say that even after 500 years of mental illness research, they will never connect it with a physical cause. I'm not talking about epilepsy and actual brain disorders. I'm talking about the agonising loss of personal value, of living without a sense of worth and meaning. To say that you were born with a predisposition to being unhappy is crazy!

If a man loses his arm we say, 'That's okay, you can find a way to cope without it.' If you're born without sight, 'We'll find a way to cope with it.' To all and sundry anywhere, in any endeavour, we say, 'Look, if you really want to do it, you can overcome this.' And yet to the people who have lost hope and meaning, we say, 'There isn't any!'

I think it's got to be a case of 'physician heal thyself'. If you've no hope and no faith or no bright future to hand to a patient, leave him alone—you've got nothing he needs.

So the range of treatment given to you over this period of years was analysis, treatment with drugs, and electrical shock treatment. What do you think were the effects of all those things upon you? How did you come out of it all?

I came out of it as close to a vegetable as a human being can get without actually turning into one. Look, I think there is a place for chemotherapeutic drugs. I needed a rest from my own mind. Overall, I've no objection to the use of chemicals and tranquillisers. What I do object to is being told, 'You must take these for the rest of your life. You can't cope without these.' Now for a period of weeks or months they can be helpful, they can give you a rest. Sure they dull your mind but sometimes that's helpful. Then I think you've got to be brought off them slowly and given some direction. You have to start taking control of your own life.

I went home with my memory gone and that was frightening.

Was that from the shock treatment?

Yes. That was terrifying. I can't describe that kind of terror but people who have been through it will understand. I lived in the same town for fifteen years. Several times I had the experience of going downtown and coming out onto a street that I knew but looking around and thinking, 'God help me, where do I live?' I knew that I lived close but I didn't know in which direction to go. It was worse than being lost. Because when you don't recognise a place at least you can say, 'Okay, I'm lost!', but when you know that you recognise things but you're confused, you think, 'What is happening to my head? What on earth is happening to my mind?' and when you've been through all the delusions and hallucinations and God knows what, you lose credibility with yourself, and that is devastating.

It's frightening! It's no consolation when people say to you, 'Your memory will come back', because so much has left you that hasn't come back, and you find that you really can't rely on it anymore and you walk away and say, 'Well, yes, they must know', and then you think, 'But they didn't know before about this, nobody has ever cured this or that.'

Side-effects from drugs have got to be taken into consideration far more than they are. I see people even today walking around 'bombed out' and in peculiar physical positions. At one stage I was on an anti-psychotic drug that had the effect of dropping my head to the left side and I would straighten my head but I had to think hard to keep my head straight and look ahead of me, and if I walked down the street I had to keep concentrating to keep my head straight in front—and it's very hard to do that for any period of time. And every so often I suddenly realised that my head had dropped again because I'd discovered I'd be watching where I was going out of the corner of my eye. That was humiliating. I used to run home and literally run into a corner behind a lounge chair and sit on the floor and cry and think to myself, 'My God, not only do I have to be mad, they've got to make me look mad'. There's not sufficient concern, compassion, and understanding for what the insane person is feeling. There seems to be a general acceptance that they can't think like human beings, they can't feel like human beings, and they can't behave like human beings. The one thing that's never ceased to amaze me is, not only did my feelings never cease to be human, I never met anyone who went mad whose feelings weren't always human.

When someone is talking about you when you're in the room, you feel it. I used to get things like, 'Oh, she's been a very good girl today, doctor, she's eaten half her breakfast.' You fluctuate from intense anger to absolute despair and think, 'Well, why wouldn't they treat me like a kid, I'm mad'. And you can't even stand up in your own estimation of yourself. There's no consistency to your thinking, to your feeling, to your behaviour . . . and you know it.

This all happened years ago, didn't it?

Yes. I broke down about sixteen or seventeen years ago and I suppose I got back on my feet about fourteen years ago.

So, after the chemical treatment, analysis and so on, was there still that feeling of the vampire; of the fear that you would hurt your children; of the panic of the absolute lack of meaning?

It floated in and out. My daughter was once asked what was her strongest memory of me in those years and she said, 'Oh God, mum was forever in bed.'

I slept and I slept and I slept. I was on three different tranquillisers and anti-depressants. I slept at least twelve hours every night. I slept three or four hours every day. The rest of the time I just sat in the corner and prayed to die.

As to what I thought . . . I didn't really think much at all. When I wrote *Ordinary Insanity*, I went back through an old blue folder of all the things that I had written in those years and there were just ramblings and disjointed words and sentences. I've no idea what I meant.

There are other instances when my mind was clear and I can make out what I was writing and what I meant. And there are some things in the folder that I was slightly startled and astounded to find which were beautiful, philosophical trains of thought that God knows how they got under my pen.

But I think that the tranquillisers probably helped me in that short period. But being on them for such a long period made it difficult believing in myself and putting my life together. One of the problems that they caused was addiction. I hear all the dramas and traumas about heroin and cocaine and I think, 'I wonder does the world appreciate how many legal drug addicts there are?' Drug addicts who are 'bombed out' on prescribed drugs, and God knows I was! And coming off them is a tremendous battle. And you think, if this was given to me as a healing measure, it is destroying me.'

I took months to come off tranquillisers and I feel the battle shouldn't have been necessary. Even though I grew and gained from each battle, I think life has enough tough obstacles without creating others.

Can you recognise the main turning points in that period?

The first turning point was a belief that total recovery from mental breakdown was possible. And I would consider myself to be one of the very lucky ones because I absorbed that idea in one massive dose. I've watched hundreds of people over the nine years that I attended a group called 'GROW', develop this belief over a period of weeks and months.

I went to a public meeting where two people who'd broken down twenty years ago gave their personal testimonies and I walked out of that meeting realising for the first time that, while I had spent all my time running around doctors and psychiatrists and treatments looking for a cure, I didn't really believe there was a cure. What I was looking for was for something to make me feel better. But I walked out of that meeting convinced (and I've never lost the conviction), that absolute recovery was possible.

I was diagnosed as having a chemical imbalance. I don't know if I've still got it and I've offered myself for testing but nobody seems to want to test me. But anyhow, according to them, I had a chemical imbalance and would have to take pills for the rest of my life tra-la-la. I haven't popped a pill in fourteen years and I'm still here and I don't know if I still have the chemical imbalance but it's not affecting my life. But the conviction that I could be cured was vitally important.

Getting into a 'GROW' group helped. I made a decision quite consciously that for six months I would do everything I was told without question and wouldn't argue, because one of the faults you have when you go mad is you analyse everything. Even people who don't normally analyse begin to analyse. You've lost the meaning in your life; you've lost everything and you start looking for answers so you begin to analyse. I decided I would do as I was told. Which was just as well because there were many times I thought the 'GROW' group didn't know what they were doing. It all seemed too simple, too ordinary and it just didn't match any kind of treatment I had been through. Being told things like, 'Go home and make your bed'.

Everyday activities

Yes, what a lot of rot! What's that got to do with somebody being crazy? But it worked, so I was very fortunate that I made that very conscious decision to do as they said. It stopped me from giving up many times. By the time the six months were up I knew I was on the right track. There was no going back.

The other tremendous stepping stone for me was losing my youngest son one day. It was only for a couple of hours but that was enough to take me apart in the state I was in. At that moment, I discovered that I could love with total 100 per cent selflessness. I had never stopped to think 'Am I loving? Am I not?' If someone had said, 'Do you love your kids?' I would have said, 'Yeah, sure! Doesn't everybody?' But that incident made me realise how tremendously I love not just my youngest child, but all of my children and the reward from the knowledge that you can love like that is unbelievable. It's greater than a feeling of being loved by anybody—just that you can love.

I often think about the story in the Old Testament, when God said to Abraham, 'Take Isaac up on the mountain and sacrifice him'. Now that had never made sense to me. I used to think, 'You're a bit tough, God!' After all, if he was on Abraham's side he would have known what Abraham was going to do. But now I understand the very point: God knew what Abraham was going to do. What God did was to give Abraham a tremendous gift by letting Abraham know that he loved and that he loved his God very much. Abraham must have come down from that mountain ten feet tall . . . and I felt like that. That I could give, that I could love and not want anything in return. I'd never realised I could love like that. And that's a tremendous gift. If nobody ever loves me again, as long as I live, I could live on that knowledge. It was a tremendous step and I don't think at the time I realised what a huge step it was.

And do you think it had a lot to do with what we call 'sanity' and 'meaning'?

Absolutely. We ask what causes insanity? I would put it down to two words—'misplaced importance'. If there's a single cause for insanity that's it. And when you look around you and think about it logically there's no psychiatric voodoo attached. Misplaced importance full stop. We hear about things like shootings on US freeways by people who got mad just because somebody cut them off and you say, 'Such a little matter', but when you think about your own life, it's the tiny little things that really upset you. You get in a flap because you're running late for a meeting or your hair isn't right. I had a friend who said he once spent a whole hour at a party sitting in a corner terribly dejected because he looked down and happened to notice he had mud on his boot. It's these little things that get people intensely upset. If you've got your priorities in order, and you consistently work towards them, you're never going to go mad. But that working toward them must occur daily. Every single day you're tempted and you fall into temptation. I know I do. I laugh and say, 'I'm a retired maniac' and then I say 'Hang on, I'm really just semi-retired'. I still do crazy things. But every time you're tempted to get into a flap about something—to get upset because something isn't done—or isn't done perfectly, stop and think, 'Just how important is it?' And when you look at it in that light it seems different.

We've got to get back to love. Love's the most reasonable thing on earth. If you look down through history to all the un-loving incidents, they don't make any sense—they're destructive . . . they're devastating . . . they're degrading to humans. But if you look through the loving incidents . . . they make sense, they're reasonable. I think it's the mind of God making itself manifest in the world. And if you do what is reasonable, it's always loving and if you do what is loving, it's always reasonable.

I remember going through a kind of growth process when I was learning to be sane again, where I would use reason to find love. But then you get to a point where you use love to find reason—it reverses. I mean, you can look at a dying Christ hanging on a cross and think what I thought when I was terribly sick—that He was a mug. What was He doing hanging up there for a bunch of jerks who didn't care two hoots, who didn't want to know about Him and couldn't care less about His love or anything else? And you think, 'You're crazy! Why would You give Your life for that?' But He did because He loved enough.

I think it's the love in essence that makes the unreasonable, on the surface, reasonable. So there's a kind of growing process where you use reason to find love and through your love you find reason.

And what has happened with you and the Church or with you and God?

God and I get along fine these days.

My growth process towards God was a long one. I went through an experience which I related in *Ordinary Insanity* where Christ frightened the hell out of me.

What was that experience?

It was in a church. I often sat in the church, not to pray but to just wonder about God. And I always used to sit near the door—I was terrified I'd get locked in. I was looking at the crucifix and thinking—pondering, and I suddenly remembered Christ's dying words, 'My God, My God, why have You forsaken me?' And in my desolation I felt Him reach out and touch me—not in any 'God up there, pie in the sky' way, but with complete humanity. Suddenly He touched me as a human being. I felt a compassion I didn't want to feel. I felt a fear of Him because He was Almighty God and He shouldn't feel the same way I felt and I could no longer say, 'You don't know how I feel', because suddenly I realised He did.

Realisations and emotions flooded in. I ran all the way home. I was terrified and it was a long time before I could attempt to go near Christ again. I didn't go back to a church for ages. If I prayed to God—I cut Christ out of my mind. I couldn't face Him.

This man lived to show me how to live and I was making mince meat out of His example. I didn't want to go near Christ. I was well on the way out of my breakdown and into recovery before I felt comfortable about re-approaching Christ.

I would lie awake at night and go through all the Bible stories that I'd learnt as a kid but visualising them in today's terms. I wondered what colour hair Christ had? What colour eyes He had? What was His favourite dish? What was His favourite colour? Did He like dancing? The Gospels are so devoid of emotion (I can understand that they need to be), but I used to wonder if the Apostles would see someone walking down the street with the same slant as The Master. Did they miss His footsteps coming up the street? All the little human attachments that He had and that we forget when we've got this Almighty God up there loving us but in a disjointed, detached kind of way. But when we've got an Almighty God with His two feet on the ground, grubbing in the mud like the rest of us, suddenly He becomes very human. Suddenly He's there—tired feet and all and just so human and loving life. I guess I fell in love with the little Jew. And if that's mad that's fine, I don't mind being that kind of mad, but that was the growing process.

As far as the Catholic Church is concerned, I never left the Church and I never intend to. I think my first ideas of 'having to stay married otherwise my mortal soul will be damned to hell' weren't right—God's not that tough. These days when in a situation where I'm fighting with my conscience about things, I just think, 'God's at least as good as I am' and that's not hard to beat.

Emma, right through your experience, there is writing. There is the written expression of what was happening and it makes an extraordinary record of you over the years. Records of you losing yourself, finding yourself, and there's one especially important piece of writing that means a lot to you—

Yes, my first step towards recovery was a little piece I eventually called 'My Lifeline'. I wrote it when I committed the first selfless act that I'd committed in many years.

I used to keep my daughter home from school on very black days when I felt I just couldn't cope any longer. I suddenly realised I was going to keep her home from school this particular day and I realised that while I wasn't doing much as a mother the least I could do was to get out of the way and let her teachers do something to equip her for life. But the moment she walked out the door I began to panic and to stop myself from going out and calling her back, I picked up an old piece of paper and a chewed up bit of pencil and I sat down on the floor and I wrote. I wasn't trying to write anything, I was simply writing to stop myself from dragging this kid back home again. And the piece was ultimately called 'My Lifeline':

> Deep it is and dark,
> desperation waves heavily.
> The sun is dull outside,
> The clouds are thick around.
> I reach out and feel nothing.
> My deepest self is troubled.
> I feel fear and I'm afraid
> and it is nothing out there
> it is here
> inside,
> in me.
> I fear myself, my weakness.
> I fear what I am and what I'm not.
> There is only one straw to clutch at.
> Sometimes it's thick and strong,
> sometimes it's so thin, it's almost lost
> but at least it is there.
> A Being who defies description
> who must be good.
> Look at the beauty of nature
> and I am here, a part of it.
> I was meant and designed to be.
> Of this great universe, I am a part.
> More than the sun and moon.
> And I am not a necessity,
> not in the fullest sense.
> Therefore, I must be a 'want'
> and if this great Being wants me,
> who am I to argue.

That was my first acceptance of any kind of hope in my life. It was the first time that I had an emotion that I felt I could trust and I have no explanation of why, except that it was some intrinsic knowledge that the hope that I felt was real—and it has never left me.

To get hold of an emotion—a feeling—a knowledge—an intrinsic something that you can rely on, that no one can take from you, is the starting point on the way back to sanity.

So can you distil the essence of meaning now? What is this central thought or idea of feeling, of knowledge, that you have at heart now?

The central feeling is that the infinite Being that created the universe, created me with love and still loves me. He doesn't often love some of the things I do, but He never stops loving me. And to me, irrespective of what happens in my life you know, whether I'm rich or poor or fat or skinny or whatever—that love's there and that is an inherent intrinsic value nobody can take away from me. To me, that's the foundation that I'm now standing on. Please God I'll stand on it 'till the day I die. I find people whose foundation are the things of this world, are in danger. If your foundation is in your money, status or your marriage or whatever, you are as safe as that is: if your marriage goes—you're gone! If you lose your money and your power—you're gone! But if your foundation is something out of this world, intrinsically you're the only person who can shift it.

So, for you that was always true, but you forgot it and in that forgetting went mad, or you couldn't realise it and through that inability to realise you went mad. Is that something like it?

Yes, I think so. It was something I had to realise. I don't think it was something that I forgot. I don't think I every really learned it because if I had learned it I wouldn't have seen this rigid scorecard as if God was going to squash me like an ant if I stepped out of line. I think it was something that I needed to learn and I'm still learning. We think we've arrived at some understanding between ourselves and God but we've got to appreciate that we're never going to comprehend the mind of God and understand, for example, why He'd love pathetic little creatures like us. But the understanding keeps on growing into different spheres. My relationship with God today is different from what it was five or ten years ago and I dare say I hope in twelve months time it will be different again. When I was coming out of the breakdown, I used to laugh and say God must be on the GROW program because He was improving too.

Is the GROW movement and the regularity of GROW meetings to keep you in this knowledge, to help you keep your feet somewhere solid and real?

I think the GROW program as a whole, while there's a lot of spirituality in it, doesn't rely on spirituality for its mental health. I don't think God meant anyone to be unhappy. God found his way into the GROW program the way everything else in the GROW program found its way there—it worked. It was a question that needed to be answered and it was answered. I find a lot of people coming to GROW with a kind of hate for God. I went in with a tremendous resentment towards God—we certainly weren't friends. The fact that God is a huge question mark in the mind of every insane person I ever met says something about where we all stand. Most honest people would admit to having asked the question, 'Is there or isn't there a God? And if there is, what's He like?'

And I used to say in the groups that didn't believe in God, 'Look you don't have to pray with conviction, just pray with sincerity'. There are a heck of a lot of captains in sinking ships that send out an SOS just in case someone is listening. By the same token, if you honestly don't believe there's a God (and I don't think that there's anyone that's convinced there isn't), don't bother talking to Him, because it's like chatting at one end of the telephone knowing there's no one at the other.

But I would find it very difficult to accept that a reflective mind didn't question. I would find it very difficult to believe that a reflective mind would accept categorically that there is no greater being than humans. That just doesn't make sense. There's got to be an author of life somewhere . . . the difficulty might be deciding what He's like.

So what has been the point of it all? What for you now is the meaning of it all? The experience of abject fear—hallucination—terror of hurting your children—pain—suffering—treatment that hurt you physically and mentally and then coming out the other side: how do you now make sense of all that?

I find that it's been a growing experience. I don't look at it as a breakdown as much as a breakthrough to better living. It's given me, I suppose, in a sense, a mission in life, which is why I've written *Ordinary Insanity* and I'm still writing. I hope to produce another book soon.

I hope to give sufferers and healers alike an understanding of what mental illness is and how to deal with it. I want the medical profession to stop and think how would they like to be on the receiving end of the diagnosis. To see that they don't have a shred of evidence to say that the cause of mental illness is physical. That there are effects on the physical body is undeniable! If I won Lotto I bet I'd have a chemical imbalance! They say manic depressives have eleven chromosomes and thirty-five different chemical imbalances and God knows what and they probably do but for all the inquiries I've made, none of these manic depressives were tested for chemical imbalance before diagnosis.

We know that if you pat a pet it brings down the blood pressure—you can't separate mind and body, but there is not a God in existence that would create even one human being with a predisposition to being unhappy and that's what mental illness is ultimately.

If you know that you're seeing the world upside-down and you're told you can come to terms with it, you live with it. When you don't know what is real, and you know you don't know, then you're in agony.

People can deal with anything once they know what it is. But for people dealing with a lack of knowledge of what is real—they suffer.

No one is so crazy that some part of them doesn't know it. God did not create us that way, nor did He create us with a predisposition to being that way.

What I most want to do with the rest of my life is to help people out of the same hellhole and prison that I was in, and to say to them, 'Don't believe you were born this way and can't help yourself. God didn't create a human being who wasn't able to help themselves. He's not that kind of a God and we're not that kind of being.' You know, we can inherit instinctive thought or 'primary thought', as I call it. We cannot inherit reflective thought. It's choice and that's where madness is—in decision-making. It's in the emotion and we don't inherit that—we choose who we are. And if we've gone off on the wrong track—fine! We can turn around and come back. You know, there's nothing unforgivable about what any of us have done, we can go back and put it right. And it's within our power to do so. It's not in anybody else's power and it's certainly not in any chemical balance.

And although we're talking about severe mental breakdown and all the labels that are given to it, are we also talking about loneliness—about isolation—about the feeling of alienation that many people do in fact suffer from now?

What I've tried to do with *Ordinary Insanity* is to explain that going mad is a process. So is going through feelings of loneliness—isolation and so on. That's part of the feeling of first starting on the downhill run. I'm not saying that everybody who feels lonely is going mad. That's part of our common human condition. But certainly people who are suffering from isolation and loneliness suffer and that's a massive problem and there's a way through it. There's a way to learn to be comfortable and at home with yourself and to view the world through eyes that are sufficiently loving to make life jolly worth living, irrespective of whether you've got a partner for life or plenty of money or a job or whatever!

You know, Malcolm Fraser was dead wrong: life was meant to be easy! One little Jew did all the suffering and He said, 'I came that they could have life and have it more abundantly.' Now if He didn't mean the joy of living—what did He mean?

I think we were all meant to strive to be happy. I think it's a bit of an insult to God to walk around with a long face. It's like saying, 'Listen this is a crummy life you've given me.'

I remember a story of St Theresa who was having a bit of a go at God and said, 'This is a bit of a rough trot you've been giving me the last few months', and He said, 'Well, that's the way I treat all my friends', and she said, 'Well, it's no wonder you've got so few'. I feel at times I can really identify with that and say, 'Hey, this is a bit of a rough trot, Son!'

But I suppose if God had another way of bringing us to Him other than suffering, He'd use it. I don't think there's any other way us human beings will ever learn anything—we seem to have to suffer in order to grow.

Judge Marcus Einfeld

Mr Justice Marcus Einfeld of the Federal Court of Australia, was first President of the Australian Human Rights and Equal Opportunity Commission; formerly a Queen's Counsel who appeared in many of Australia's most famous legal cases, including the Ananda Marga Three, the Social Security Conspiracy case, Mr Justice Lionel Murphy's Parliamentary Enquiry, the Bartons, the BLF, *the Mudginberri, and many others.*

Marcus Einfeld has been an outspoken champion of the cause of the powerless—like people claiming injustice at the hands of unscrupulous police giving untrue verbal evidence against them. He's travelled widely to build bridges of understanding and communication between people of the Third World and those of Eastern and Western countries. He negotiated with the then Government of the USSR *to secure the emigration of scores of Soviet Jews and others seeking to leave.*

He's worked with a number of international bodies especially in the area of human rights and at home he's been active with the Council on AIDS *and other service organisations.*

Judge Einfeld is the son of a widely respected, crusading former New South Wales Labor Minister for Consumer Affairs, the Honourable Sidney Einfeld.

The judge is a family man. Two of his children are still very young. Yet he keeps up a gruelling schedule in public life. What is it that drives him to work so hard for a more humane and just society?

JUDGE MARCUS EINFELD: My father is known to many people because of what he believes in. Almost despite his political associations or affiliations. No doubt the sort of man he is influenced his political associations as well but he is a man of very remarkable human qualities. When he was in public office, he used sometimes to comment that he was terribly upset because he'd failed to do something that he'd aspired to and not achieved. I would say to him that people out there were very uplifted by the fact that you tried, not so much whether you succeeded. Everybody realises there are limitations on what can be done. But he is a man who was able to inculcate into me, as into a lot of people that he mixed with, a genuine feel for people and a recognition that there are a lot of people out there who are battling and who are supported by nobody. I don't mean financially supported but emotionally supported who believe that there is somebody in there who is fighting for them. These are very difficult times in our society. My father was able, I think, to generate a general belief that he is a fighter for rights and for decency and for honourable behaviour and for a recognition that many people are wronged in this community. I learned a great deal from him. I think more than any other single person that I know of.

And Judge Einfeld, in your case, if your father and his ideas and his drive and his sense of justice was the source of your own tendency in that direction, what fuels it? What keeps it going now, do you think?

The recognition that it is the right and honourable thing. The recognition that the cause that my father espoused is a proper and just cause. People demand eloquent advocates for justice and humanity. The cause that keeps me going now is the extraordinary incidence in our community of injustice, and you certainly do have to have the commitment. I can't tell you precisely when and where I got the commitment. I know I've always had it and I was always determined that if the opportunity presented itself or if I could make the opportunity happen I would serve the cause of justice and humanity in the widest sense, and I did so at the Bar. I took cases which were relatively unpopular and often unpaid or underpaid, which gave me an opportunity to pursue my inclinations in this direction.

I left the Bar in 1972 because it was not giving me satisfaction—it was providing me with a living, but not much else. It wasn't providing me with humanitarian stimulation of the kind I wanted. I found myself reading only law books and law briefs and what I wanted to do was go out and help people and read more widely and cover fields that I would not otherwise cover in the course of a law practice where you very much depend upon what comes in through the door. You don't choose the briefs—you have to wait for them to come. So I went off and did international work for five years so that I could get exposure in a much more general and much more humanitarian area.

Did you enjoy that?

Yes and I would do it again if I had that time over. I might do a few things a bit differently but basically I did enjoy it. I was exposed to international human rights and humanitarian law through UNESCO and the United Nations and the UN Commission on Human Rights and other bodies of that kind, World Health, and the International Red Cross. I managed to meet a very large number of like-minded people and many people who were not like-minded, but that also helps to stimulate you. I also went out in the field and I saw people in Africa and in Asia and in South America who were really in desperate straits. They had no one to defend them. I saw women deliver their own babies in the fields of India, and get up and continue the cotton-picking or the tea-picking which they'd been doing right up to the birth. I saw people starving and in hopeless circumstances, with children in unbelievably bad states of malnutrition and ill health. These were in thousands, even tens of thousands of people.

And it seems that there's no choice for you on seeing these things but to respond.

Yes.

Is this a feeling of anger? Is it righteous anger, or how would you describe that response?

Not righteous anger, it is frustration that the world has allowed it to happen and that I can't do anything massive to change it. Although it is very often the case that people say, 'Well what can I do, what do you want me to do?' For myself my answer is that however difficult it is I do not have the right to remain aloof from it. I recognise that it's very difficult. Progress is very slow but I cannot live with myself if I don't try. I felt that in the 1970s when I went overseas. I took a massive cut in earnings. I feel it now when I have taken a substantial cut in earnings. I did it at a relatively young age because I felt the need, again, to go outside my own narrow confines of my own survival and of the survival of my own family, and get out and do something for other people.

Do you believe that there's an element in you, the Jewish heredity, which gives you a special feeling for injustice, a drive to want to do something about injustice?

No, I wouldn't want to be as arrogant as that in Jewish terms. There is a belief, and I think it has some justification, that Jews have a certain heightened sense of justice and humanity born of the extraordinary sufferings that multiple Jewish generations have had to bear, but, I don't think Judaism is a repository of particularly humanitarian people. I think there are many Jews who are motivated by whatever it is they have learned and whatever it is they have inherited they put into humanitarian pursuits.

And some of that is true for you?

Yes, I think so. I don't think anybody can deny the effect of their background.

As someone who works very hard and in various ways to help, how good are you at receiving help from others?

I think, not very good. I welcome and look for support and assistance and stimulation and ideas, and I depend on them. Perhaps I am not as good at being able to extract that sort of response from people, as I am at giving it or offering it.

When you're in need is it easy for you to accept somebody else helping you? When you're in pain or when you experience suffering?

I'm much better now than I was because my wife of three years has done a great deal to reverse what was the position before. I think I was much more self-contained and inward-looking than I am now. Because of the things which drive me there's not a great line between yourself inside, and yourself outside. I genuinely believe in all the things I'm doing. I'm not an advocate because I'm a paid hand or a hired gun, I am doing what I want to do. I enjoy it and I have a sense of mission about it and because it comes from inside me it reflects what I genuinely believe in relation to my own life and that of people dear to me, as much as it does for the world at large. So I don't know that there's a very clear-cut line between these things. The only question is whether, in relation to my own personal views as they affect me, I open up and let others come in, as it were. I think I do probably in a family sense but that's about it.

Have you a faith in God?

Yes. I don't know that I could define precisely what God was, or is, but I certainly have a faith that there is a divine, superhuman entity which has a significant role to play in guiding our lives. I'm not quite sure to what extent, and I certainly don't believe that He or She is directing everything we ever do and think, but I think there is a moral guidance, divine guidance, yes.

And is God a judge?

I doubt it. Not in any sense that we can understand. Certainly not the sort of judge that we define. Or a judge like me and my colleagues who listen to evidence and decide whether the law has been complied with or not complied with as the case may be. I don't think it's a moral judge that would say, when you're bad, that's the end of you or that's a black mark against you and all these marks add up. I don't think it's quite as corny as that. I think it is beyond our capacity to express in language which is applicable to our daily lives. It's a different sort of concept.

A mystery in some ways?

Yes. Mystique more than mystery.

You don't mind that?

No. I accept that there are questions we will never be able to answer. I used to worry and think about it a lot. Why was it that we can't answer these questions? Why did the Holocaust happen? Why, for example, are these poor children in the Sudan allowed to die? Why, when the rest of the world is so rich and when the European countries have mountains of bread, butter and wine and anything else that you name, and when Australia can't find markets for its wheat and its wool? Why can't we give it to these people?

What stopped you asking the question?

I asked the question all the time.

But what stopped you asking the question?

Nothing stopped me asking it but I recognised that I can't answer it, and that the answer exists somewhere and in a way which is beyond my capacity to provide the answer. I've raised these in international forums, I've said that in UNESCO and the United Nations. Why? And, of course, no one addresses the answer, no one will be able to give you the answer. I walked around Brussels trying to beg the European Community officials to let me have some of the food that was going to be thrown out. I'd say 'Just give it to me, under the lap, if you like, don't tell anybody, but just let me take it to Africa or India and give it to people.' They said 'Oh well you can't do that because you didn't fill out the forms and we haven't passed the resolution' and so on. I just walk away holding my head and cry and sound out about it when I make speeches, but I haven't found the answers. Maybe God has the answers, I don't know what they are.

Do you have a feeling of urgency that there is a great deal to be done?

Yes, That's why I went overseas in the 1970s and that's why I took this job now. There is an urgency and we cannot stand back. The Psalmist said words to the effect that, 'it is not thy duty to complete the work, but neither art thou free to desist from it'. I can't hold back from trying. I have to be satisfied that at the end of my time that I've done what I could and I've tried to stir others into doing what they can. If we all pull together, we can do a lot of things. Australians in particular can because we live in a fantastic country, a wonderful country. We have wonderful advantages that other people don't have, even people in countries we would regard similar to ourselves like Britain and Europe, and the USA for that matter.

We can do things. It is not right that we are impotent, but I must try. The answer as to why everybody doesn't try or why we don't succeed or why I can't supply the answers, I don't know, but I've still got to try.

Judge Einfeld, does that feeling of urgency, 'that there's so much to be done', rob you of peace?

In a way, yes. In the sort of peace that you're talking about, yes. I have my peaceful times and I certainly enjoy my family. I enjoy entertainment, and I like going to sporting events. I like having holidays like every one else, not that I seem to get too many. There is a sense of urgency robbing you of the opportunity of ever completely relaxing. If I go for a holiday skiing I relax for a week and if I go for a holiday swimming or fishing I relax for the time I'm there, but as the time is coming to an end, I'm beginning to feel jazzed up again ready for the fray. A week is not really a long time because it takes you the first two or three days to wind down, by then you're nearly at the end and you're starting to wind up again. There is a certain sense of interference with peace, but I suppose I get my peace very often from doing what I'm doing. I mean if I've done something towards my aim and I've done it well, or it has managed to achieve a result then I feel a sense of elation at that, even though it might have been extraordinarily tiring.

Do you make any time in your life for prayer or for meditation or for reading?

Yes, I do make some. It's not enough but I'm anxious to try and order my priorities a little more to make a little more time.

Because children help you re-order your priorities a bit I suppose. Are you enjoying that?

Yes I'm enjoying both of my small children, as I enjoy my older children, but they force you to re-order your priorities. In that sense my wife is very understanding and bears the major burden, as many wives do.

Do you learn from your children?

Yes. Little children from whom you can't learn terribly much in a sort of intellectual sense, but you learn a great deal in respect of yourself, of what's important in life, and how they depend on you, and how your presence is important, and how they make you feel a sense of elation in itself. I think that's a very important thing. In many ways it is selfish to have children because you are doing it for yourself, not for them. I mean you are bringing them into a very uncertain world, you are in effect telling them that they're there and you'll look after them up to a certain point but then they're on their own. So you really do it for yourself I think. It's important that one shouldn't lose that sense of selfishness in relation to children. They don't get a say about whether they come into existence. You make them. Then you have an obligation to try and give them a bit of a go but beyond that they're on their own. I think that one should never overlook the personal selfishness that's involved in having children and therefore, to get the benefit to learn from the experience in that way.

Judge Einfeld, your work has taken you into contact with people who have been through a great deal of suffering; from people who are not allowed to come out from behind the Iron Curtain, to prisoners, helpless and powerless people, who feel that they have been imprisoned in this country, wrongfully. So you've seen a lot of suffering. I wonder if you could say something about suffering?

It's very difficult for people who've had my good fortune in life to identify easily with people who've suffered from things which are virtually impossible to re-create in ourselves. When I have been to prisons and I've been to them in Australia and I've been to them in the Soviet Union and I've been to them in other countries, there's a terrible feeling when that gate shuts behind you, even though I know that I'm going to be allowed out half-an-hour later or two hours later. When I ask to be allowed out, I'm going to be allowed out.

A feeling like what?

A feeling like the world is virtually coming to an end; that you have no hope; that these places are appalling places. I mean the idea that a Soviet prison is in some way vastly worse than our own prisons is quite wrong. Our own prisons are appalling places. Now that may be because there are no votes in prisons and again it may be for all sorts of reasons, but no one should be under the misapprehension that prisons are anything other than appalling places. There have been some developments, which have improved the situation, but by and large they are terrible places to be in. Long Bay is just an awful place; Pentridge is just terrible. As regards people in impossible circumstances, unequal circumstances, you can take that across the board, you can take those lads from the Ananda Marga, who were in gaol for a crime for seven years, for a crime they didn't commit. You can take Dr Sakaroff and his friends who were put away sometimes in prison and sometimes in internal exile (which is near enough to prison) for crimes which you can't define. They're called 'anti-State activities' or 'anti-Soviet activities'. What they did was they announced the fact that people should have rights, that they should be able to vote, and they should be able to travel, have freedom of thought, and be able to have plays and artistic performances and art itself, which was critical of the establishment, that's what they went to gaol for. Dr Begun, for example, whom I met in

Moscow last month and whose case was given worldwide publicity on the front pages of newspapers, was in gaol for seven years in a prison camp for having taught Hebrew to children. This is positively monstrous.

What do you think is the effect on those people of this suffering, of this injustice?

It is incredible to meet such people and find that they survive the experience. I have said publicly on many occasions, I wish I could be as confident, that I would have emerged in the way they've emerged. Dr Begun could be anybody's father or grandfather, one of the loveliest men I've met. I sat with him and had a cup of tea and piece of apple. Soviet families don't have food like we have so you sit and have quite modest food in an extraordinarily tiny modest apartment which is one room, crowded for three people. Wonderful people, his wife is a very small woman of sixty or late-fifties, but a strong, wonderful, beautiful woman, with strength about her. She could stand up and get bashed by the KGB thugs outside the Kremlin, together with some Western journalists for protesting that her husband should be let out. Very courageous, wonderful people.

So in a way this inspires you, I mean in an obvious way this inspires you? The suffering and the way people overcome this?

When I think of what little I do in comparison to what they do it's unbelievable.

But how do you account for it? What do you make of it? What do you make of this victory?

The supremacy of the human spirit—people will fight if they're given a chance, and given half a chance to strike back at their oppressors will do so, and will do so honourably. We should give them every conceivable support and we should do it in our own society. The people out there, who are denigrated by the far Right or the rich or by the other intolerant people, don't want to be supported by the welfare state, to live on social security. I'm talking about the vast majority of people. Of course there are exceptions and there are people around who try to trick the system, but the vast bulk of Australian people are honourable, decent people. All they want is a fair chance. Society owes an opportunity to every member of our society who pays taxes or is a law-abiding member of our society and that's what we have to make available. That's the sense of urgency as there are a lot of people out there who are growing old without that opportunity. There are a lot of children within yards of this very studio, who are homeless and are selling their bodies because they have nowhere to go; who are injecting their arms, because they have nothing else to do and because they're in the midst of other people who do the same thing. There is an urgency, but we have to save these people, they're all Australians, they're all our fellows. I'm not going to write-off whole generations of people, while we wait till we get the economic society back into order, because as everyone knows, we're not likely to do that and certainly not in the short term.

Are we likely to do it through a change of heart as individuals?

Yes. That's our great hope, that's what we've all got inside us, the capacity to change our direction and to change our emphasis. We've all got to battle to survive. Everybody knows that you've got to earn a living, you've got to pay the bills and the rent and the car registration and everything else, and we've got to educate our children. But there is time in every person's life to apply his or her mind to the affairs and well-being of others. If we all gave an hour a week or an hour a fortnight or an hour a month to helping others less fortunate than ourselves or to at least involving ourselves from our own self-respect in the affairs of others less fortunate than ourselves, we would not only be a richer country, but we would all have unbelievable richness inside ourselves.

The language of
is
colours

Alice Fitzgerald

Alice Fitzgerald was told by her doctor that she had cancer and only a very limited time to live. I visited Alice at the Eversleigh Hospital, run by the Anglican Deaconess Institution. Eversleigh's famous for its skilful and sensitive service to people with life-threatening illness. It was a sunny morning with a cold westerly blowing; the gardens were bright with cinerarias and camellias. Inside, a cheerful atmosphere, calm, and a warm welcome from Anglican Deaconess Miss Joan Hartley, Eversleigh's Director of Nursing.

Alice had suggested morning was her best time, so producer Stephen Godley and I arrived at 10.00 to record a conversation with her for The Search for Meaning*.*

She was small and tranquil, beautiful in middle-age, sitting in a wheelchair.

I had been told that she'd had a tremendously active and creative life. She had brought up three children, had one career in advertising and another as a health educator. Now she was said to be dying, yet she seemed full of serene life and, even in this hospice, still a powerful resource for the visitors who came to her.

I was hoping that I would know what to say to her. I was hoping that she would tell us what it's like to be near to death. Was she afraid, or lonely? Were there things she had not had time to complete? Could she bear to leave a life lived generously, with daring and exuberance? What were the most important things she had learned from sixty years of living? What sustained her now, what made it bearable? Might she be religious, or humanist, or possibly in a despair devoid of meaning?

Fear of death is said to be one of the scourges of the western world. What insight might we gain from someone forced to contemplate death as a present reality?

As it turned out, Alice Fitzgerald was suffering most from culture shock. Her most recent of many adventures had been to teach English on the Russian island of Sakhalin in the Sea of Japan between Hokkaido and Siberia. She was forced to return home when she fell on the ice and broke her hip.

ALICE FITZGERALD: I might say that I came to this hospital kicking and screaming and not wanting to be back in Australia and not wanting to be in hospital care. Part of that was because I had felt so comfortable and at home in Russia, and part of it was because I felt that I had coped well without any sort of medical treatment until then, and I wanted to go on not having interference from a medical point of view.

I've been here for about four months and I have not had any kind of interference. All I've had has been sustenance and help, succour, offers from every point of view to allow me to proceed and do the things that I want to do in a way that I feel is appropriate. And because of that I've not only stopped kicking and screaming (laughs), I've learned to accept quite a lot of things that I think I didn't accept before.

Would you feel able to say what is the condition of your health, why you are here?

I was diagnosed about a year ago, in May 1993, with cancer, having been given a prognosis of about two months, possibly to two years, and told that there was no way I could survive. The cancer was in my liver, possibly other parts of my abdomen, and there was secondary cancer in some of my bones. When they diagnosed they offered me treatment. They also wanted to 'open her up' (laughs) and I said, 'No, no'. They wanted to know why not, and I said I would prefer to live healthily on the level that I was rather than recovering from so-called treatment. The doctor thought I meant 'I want to die', but he finally realised that I meant 'I want to live, and that while I'm alive I don't want to have to take on extra burdens', like the burden of recovering from an operation, for example. Nothing could promise me any sort of cure and so, with that in mind, I had already applied for a job teaching English as a second language in Russia, and when I got home from the hospital after all the various diagnoses there was a letter saying, 'Yes, you can have the job'. And I thought, well, if this isn't a message from God I don't know what is. I rang the doctor and told him and said I would like to go and did he see any reason why I shouldn't. He said 'No, but I think you should inform the people who are going to hire you.' I did that: I telephoned Russia and asked if I could come anyway and they said 'Yes'.

I thought, this is just wonderful. And after that, every door opened. I even had time and money enough at that particular point to be able to make a trip to the United States, where my original family is, and to take two of my children who'd never met their relatives. So I did a bit of closure there and had a wonderful month or so saying my goodbyes and mending fences, and that was absolutely the best thing I've done for years.

Then I went on to Sakhalin, and everything that happened in Sakhalin was so right. You know, people talk about hardship in Russia and so on. There was never hardship; there was discomfort and there was inconvenience but there was never hardship. And all of the things that happened seemed to proceed, in a way, with a will of their own to provide for what was being asked. I was writing curriculum as well as presenting the work.

And what do you make of that fluency with which things seemed to happen during your working time in Russia?

Oh, it's one of those things that I can only see as God-directed. I have no way to put it any place otherwise, and I do know that throughout my life I've discovered that if there's something that I want to do and it's in a particular direction and I haven't done it before, if I put my head down like a bull and gore my way through (laughs) it doesn't turn out right, and often I don't end up doing the thing that I thought I wanted to do, but something else. Eventually I realised that the 'something else' was the thing that I was supposed to do and that I should have been spending my energy on, and so when all the doors open and something happens like this and it's right, I can only say, 'Well, that is what I was supposed to do'.

Can you, then, think of the cancer in any similar way? I mean, how are you making sense of that?

For me the cancer is something that I gave to myself out of years of misunderstanding, years of choosing a lifestyle, I suppose, that was, if not unconventional, at least very hard, because I set out to live in a way that could only provide truth.

I was very young when I left home: I was seventeen, and even then I think it was God who must have guided me to know that I wanted to find out what was true and I wanted to live by that. In the world that we live in, although we're told all the time how free we are and how truth is available if we want it, that's not true. We aren't free, and I wanted to free myself of those things that impede fulfilment of potential. And that doesn't make you very popular sometimes with the world at large. When I was a copywriter in the advertising business, for example, one of the things that I always refused to do was to write anything that wasn't true. Now, that's a big task, especially in consumer advertising, and there had been times when I either wrote a little paragraph or stood up on my metaphorical soapbox and announced what I thought about a particular product. I always said, 'I will write it, but I won't write it untruthfully'. And the interesting thing is that I never got fired from a job for that, but the penalty is that it doesn't endear you to the people who are willing to do the thing that isn't truthful. And so it causes imbalances in your life and I guess those are the kinds of things that have been penalties for having that quest always behind me and behind everything that I did.

Are you suggesting that the quest for truth has led you time and again into situations of conflict, or having to make a stand, and that there is, in fact, some connection between that and now having cancer?

I guess, yes, that is what I'm saying, in a way: that very often there was internal conflict concerning those kinds of things. I had to determine for myself whether or not I was just being a troublemaker or, in fact, there was something about justice or truth that was actually at issue. I had also to deal with the kinds of conflict that were put up by other people who didn't like people who disturbed their equilibrium, disturbed their status quo.

What is the source of the desire to make this quest for truth?

From the time I was a very small child I know that there were things that happened that were so pointed that I had to say to myself, 'I will not be like that'. One of those things happened when I was less than three years old. In our house—in New York—there were little vestibules between the front door and the outer door so that you don't get too cold or too wet as you come in on snowy days, and in our little vestibule there was an icebox—it was just before everybody had refrigerators—and sitting on top of the icebox was a dozen eggs in an egg carton. Somebody knocked at the outer door, and my mother answered the door and I went with her, holding on to her skirt—I can remember the feeling of being very little and being at her knees. There was a very tall black American at the door and he asked for something to eat. He said, 'I haven't eaten for several days; I'm very hungry, and I have no money. Will you give me something to eat?' And she said, 'No, go away, I don't feed beggars', and threw him out and went back into the house with me and stood there at the door for a few minutes. Then, just to test whether or not he'd actually gone, she opened the door into the vestibule and looked around at that little tiny room and she saw that the eggs were gone from on top of the icechest. She said to me, 'That terrible man, that bad man, he stole the eggs', and I said to myself, 'If she had given him some he wouldn't have needed to steal them'.

So, incidents like that thread all through my existence from the time I was very small, and I don't really know if everybody has those things happening in their lives—and I think they probably do—or if it was unique to me. All I know is that most people put it away because they feel that they can't do anything with it and I, for whatever stubborn reason I had (laughs), I didn't put it away, and I wanted to be concerned with justice, in particular. I suppose I should have been a lawyer (laughs).

Do you think so?

I don't know.

At the age of seventeen you left your New York home and what I gather was the demanding authority of your mother to make your own free-spirited, unconventional way in life.

I recall saying to myself each morning on the way to my first job, 'I must be tough, I must be tough'. It may be that preparing myself to be tough was the beginning of preparing myself to have cancer, because I'm convinced that cancer is given to oneself, partly by living style, attitude and diet, and the pollutions that we live with. I think people in Third World countries haven't had as much cancer, and as varied cancer, as the rest.

Apparently, no. Can you remember leaving home? What your mother said to you, for example?

Oh, yes, well, that was a rather traumatic incident. My mother, of course, disapproved totally. I remember sitting on the bottom step of the steps in our house, ready to go—my bags were packed. My father, who was a very gentle man and a helpful man, had said that he would drive me into the city where I was going to live with a friend, so he wasn't against what I was doing at all. But my mother was crying and was wanting to know what is it that a nice girl would want to do away from home that she can't do at home. And I remember saying to her, 'I have to find out if everything you've taught me is true, and if it is then I'll live by it, and if it isn't then I'll live by what I find out to be true'. And I have, in fact, tried to live my life by that prescription.

Could she accept that?

No, not at all.

What did she say?

She said, 'Well, would I have taught you anything that was wrong?', and I said, 'You taught me what you knew'. That was all I could answer; that was the best I could do. What she understood from that I don't know, but I've never been the good child of the family (laughs).

What is your earliest memory?

A very insignificant memory, but a very sweet one. It was before I could walk. I remember being in my cot in the bedroom downstairs and I remember my father coming and lifting me out of the cot and carrying me upstairs to where the rest of the family was. It was very sweet. It must have been early morning, and I can see the shadows and the light as I think of it. Nothing happened, that's the whole memory, but I must have been very young, because I'm told that I could walk, at least holding on, at the age of six months, so it was a very early memory.

Have you been close to your father? Has he been a significant influence in your life?

My father was . . . I guess you could call him an intellectual of sorts, but he was a very sensitive man. He was an artist, he was humorous, and he was very supportive of the things that I wanted to do. That was an interesting thing, because he wasn't a man of great courage or power; he was, in fact, fairly powerless in our household. But I can recall a number of incidents when, with just a word or just the touch of his hand on my back, he was saying, 'It's all right, I'll help you', or 'You can go in this direction, don't worry'. He said to me after I had left home—because my mother would ring me periodically and cry and tell me to come back home—and he phoned me once at work and said, 'How would you like to have lunch with an old man?' I said, 'All right', and we had lunch together. And he said to me 'Don't worry about your mother. I'll look after your mother and you go ahead and do the things that you want to do'. And I felt that that was just the most wonderful thing he could ever have done, particularly because my mother's influence was not benign but was very strong. When I was twenty, having already been away from home for three years, I went back to visit. He was sixty, and he looked at me and said, 'You know, Alice, I'm sixty years old and I've never done anything in my life that I wanted to do'. And I thought, Oh, God, this is tragedy; I'm not going to be sixty having never done anything that I wanted to do. I suppose that influenced me also to go ahead and try to do the things that I felt were right.

How old are you now?

I'm sixty. Yes, that same age.

Is that significant to you in any way?

I don't know. It's maybe a time when awareness came to my father and I think I've been growing in awareness for a long time. But certainly this illness has caused a lot of thinking to coalesce and maybe the age is significant; I don't know.

It's so curious, sitting here speaking with you in this hospital where people are dealing with life-threatening illnesses as, indeed, you have been, and knowing what an adventurous life you've had: two careers, brought up three children, and I want to ask more about how you're dealing with it—what is sustaining you, what are you thinking about?

Yes, well, I think probably the most significant thing that I ever did in my life was to become a member of the Baha'i Faith. I had spent many years calling myself an atheist, and then later agnostic but about eighteen years ago I became a Baha'i, and that has been the most life-sustaining, intellectual, spiritual, all kinds of adventure of my life. It sustains me and it gives me hope and it gives me courage. It gives me a direction, and it gives me a code of living that I couldn't have had otherwise.

When I was about twenty-eight I sat down to write a book and every morning I would discipline myself to write. So I'd spend three hours at the typewriter and then do other things for the day. And, of course, I was continually reading philosophy and reading religion and discussing all kinds of imponderables with people—that was my bent and I did that all the time. One day, while I was writing, I looked up from my typewriter and it was as though something happened: I saw something. I didn't see something with my physical eyes, I saw something with my inner eyes, and when people talk about 'the scales fell from my eyes' or 'the veil came away from my eyes', I understand that perfectly, because that's what happened. I had been in so much difficulty at that point in my life for a variety of private reasons. I wasn't coping and I wasn't solving my problems, and I had invented a little prayer. I didn't know whether or not there was God and so I would start this prayer by saying, 'God, if you're there, give me courage, give me wisdom, give me knowledge, give me understanding'. It became a little mantra and I kept saying it over and over. I would say it when I woke up and I would say it when I went to bed, and I would just say it all day long. For months that went on. And so I think that this incident that happened while I was sitting there at the typewriter was the answer to that prayer. Suddenly, I knew things that I had never suspected I knew; I could see things that I didn't know that I could see, and I saw myself as . . . the only graphic description I can give of this is as a mote of dust. You know when you see dust falling through sunlight?

Yes.

Well, it was as though there was a ribbon of sunlight going in an ellipse and I was one of the specks of dust in that ribbon, going round and round, and I could see myself as part of everything that made me one with everything and also as nothing—totally insignificant, just a bit of dust.

In later reading, and certainly from earlier reading, I can only relate that to the Buddhist concept of nirvana, but it was the most life-giving experience I could have imagined, and it changed me completely. Absolutely nothing changed outside of me, but I changed so significantly that I was happy instead of being miserable (laughs). I could cope with everything and things didn't touch me negatively that had touched me before. And yet out of that and I stayed in that state for several months—it was absolute bliss, it was just heaven. And I stayed in that state for quite a few months but I knew all that time the one thing it didn't give me was a code for living. It gave me a knowledge but it didn't give me a code. And so many years later when I found the Baha'i Faith I thought, oh, this is the code. This is where it rests.

What is the essence of the code that satisfies you in the Baha'i Faith?

I suppose it's that one should live by what one says. The essence is that it creates unity. It believes that there's one God, one mankind and one religion. And in order to make that a livable creed one has to do what one says. And that code is then given in all sorts of very fine laws, like the requirement for a Baha'i to not be prejudiced or to have equality of men and women, or equality of religion and science and compatibility of religion and science.

So Baha'i and you were obviously a good match.

Oh yes.

You brought your own understanding to it. It sounds as though they met well.

That's right. And perhaps if I had met the Baha'i Faith earlier I wouldn't have recognised it. But I was ready for it then and it was given to me and I felt enormously lucky. And that's what sustains me now. I've never looked back from that.

Now that doesn't necessarily give me the specifics of how I think, because as a Baha'i I'm not required to think in a confined way and so that allows me to think as broadly as I like on a variety of issues.

Are you feeling in any sense trapped now, knowing that you have been severely ill, knowing there might be a limitation to the remaining time of your life?

Oh, no. This so-called death sentence has been the most liberating experience I can think of: it's wonderful. In a way, what I can see is the door, the door that's standing there just waiting for me to go through it. I said to somebody who is terribly worried about my happiness (laughs)—they thought that I should want to fight against death—and I said, 'When you have your boarding pass in your hand (laughs) you don't want to stop the trip, you want to go on'.

Is that how it feels?

Yes, yes, this is something so wonderful that I'm going to. I see death as the goal of life, death as the reward of life, and of course, every religion has always told us that but we don't listen, we don't hear what it's saying. So we say, 'No, no, no, everything but not that'. Yet the moment you're born, you're born to die, and that certainly must be the end of a good life—whether good or bad we're all going to die—but it seems to me that it's given as a reward for a lifetime of living. This lifetime of living is supposed to be a teaching experience, and if you learn those lessons well then you'll be happy when you reach the door and can go on into the next world. I guess if you haven't done the things that you felt you should do, well, then it makes you ask for more time. But I don't want more time: I don't need another five minutes; it doesn't really matter at all. Because I've spent my life doing the things I felt I should do.

And you began with a quest for truth. Do you feel that that has been satisfied?

Yes, yes, I do. There's a tremendous lot more that I can learn and a tremendous lot more that I can do, but I feel vindicated: I feel that my life has been spent well.

And you speak of a doorway.

Yes.

A doorway to . . . ?

A doorway to the next life. A doorway to whatever is beyond. A doorway to . . . Heaven? Ah (laughs), I don't know what. I guess part of my individual thinking about certain questions, whether they're Baha'i or Christian or any other religious questions, is, what is the next life? I see very strongly that the essence of me is not my body at all: the essence is something that's within. And I've always felt that way all my life . . . like I'm having a ride in this car (laughs) and looking out through my eyes, and that essential me can't be destroyed because it isn't material. So what happens, I think, when you die is that the body disintegrates but the essential you continues. In fact, there's a very lovely description in the Baha'i writing where Baha'ullah says the body is like a cage and the soul is like a bird, and when the cage breaks the bird can fly. And that's exactly how I feel: that this is freedom, this finally is the ultimate freedom, to die. And I wouldn't want to hang on. If I hang on it's a penalty rather than a reward.

What, in clinical terms, is the condition of the cage, as you speak of your body now? I mean, you've had a broken hip?

Yes, I have an unsecured broken hip. When I went to Russia I fell on the ice and broke my hip, unfortunately, and it couldn't be put into a cast or a splint because of the other cancers that cause acidic fluid to develop in my abdomen, and so a cast could never be any size because this fluid has to be tapped regularly and I go up and down in size (laughs). So I've been living with this unsecured broken hip since I fell. I have been told that it won't heal because the bones all have cancer in them.

Are you in pain, Alice?

I am sometimes in pain, but one of the purposes of this particular hospital is to provide palliative care and part of that is to keep the patient pain free.

Is that possible?

Very successful, very successful. Morphine is the basis of that; a combination of morphine and Panadol, would you believe! (laughs) But it's very good. If it doesn't work and I do feel pain, then they give me what's called a breakthrough dose and that alleviates it within an hour. So it's very good. That's one part of it. The other part of it is that I may have been given a reprieve because my leg is doing things that a broken leg, broken at the neck of the femur, shouldn't be doing. It's bending in ways that it has never bent, not since I've had the fall. I guess I'm getting better, much to the consternation of the doctors!

It's hard for them to understand it medically?

Well, they've said that the only reason it could possibly get better is that either it's due to the treatment that I've had—and I haven't had any treatment—or due to other causes.

Other causes . . . now, there's a phrase!

Other causes! (both laugh) I asked them if they wouldn't like a miracle or two but they wouldn't like a miracle at all (laughs).

And what do you think? Do you want to label it?

No, I don't want to label it, necessarily. Once again, I do think it's God's hand working. I feel, in a way, having just said that death is a reward, that maybe my reward has been taken away from me, and that's a bit difficult to live with—much more difficult to live with than the thought that I'm actually going to die. If I thought I was going to die tomorrow I'd just pack my bags and go (laughs).

Really?

Yes, yes. Because I felt I had done the work I was supposed to do. But what am I supposed to do now? I keep asking God.

And yet, one of the things that's happening while you're here in hospital is that many people are coming to visit you.

Oh, yes.

I mean, I know that you have become a resource for many people. I don't know if you see it that way, but that's the way it is seen by others. Could that be part of what you're supposed to be doing now? I don't know . . .

Yes. The only way I can see it is that that may be true, because even while I was still in Russia I can't tell you the numbers of people who came to visit me after I fell. They literally came by the dozens. They came and brought food and asked me to tell them what I knew about life and living and the Baha'i Faith—not necessarily in that order, not necessarily the Baha'i Faith, but about life and living. They said things to me like, 'You've changed my life', and I really don't understand that—it's a terribly humbling sort of thing to have said to one, because I don't know how I did it and I can't reproduce it (laughs). I don't know how to change somebody else's life and I don't know what it is that people are seeing in me, but people have said so many things of that nature that I can only conclude that my role now must be to teach something to other people.

Well, it's fairly well documented, that fear of death in western society is one of the greatest influences on the way we live our lives.

Yes.

You don't have that.

No, I don't.

Perhaps that is an extraordinary message that you communicate.

Well, maybe it is. Baha'ullah said, 'I made death a messenger of joy for thee; why dost thou grieve?' I believe that totally. I don't just believe it because I'm repeating it parrot-like: I'm saying it out of life experience that tells me that that's absolutely true. That this messenger of joy . . . maybe the messenger of joy has come to say it's not very far off but not quite yet.

Have dreams been any part of your understanding or of clarifying your understanding?

Yes. Off and on throughout my life I've had significant dreams that have changed the way I've thought or the way I've behaved. But when I was diagnosed with cancer last year, as soon as the diagnosis was made—and I was quite surprised, even though in myself I knew that it was true, I was surprised and a little bit, oh, I don't know if shocked is the right word, that's too strong. But I didn't feel terribly good about it at first and it didn't take a full day to stop feeling negatively, and that night when I went to bed I had two dreams. In one of the dreams I saw a tower, a sort of dark blue tower made of strips of metal exploding against the night sky, with orange flames coming out of the top of it, and people way down on the ground running and running in all directions. I was running, too, and everybody was in panic but I wasn't in panic, and right beside me there was somebody running—just off to my left and slightly behind me—and I knew he was there; he was there all the time with me but I couldn't see him, and then that was the end of the dream. And then later, towards morning, I dreamed the rest of that dream and it was that there was a group of people sitting in some kind of hall or cavern—some dark, unfurnished place where there were just benches around the walls. There were children playing on the floor and there were adults sitting on these benches consulting about how to carry the world on, how to create a new world from the one that was being destroyed. And just beside me was this person, also protecting me and being there, but I couldn't see him. He was always there and I couldn't see him and he was always protective in both dreams. And when I woke up in the morning I knew, and I said that those dreams had told me what I must do: I'm protected and I must go and teach, not necessarily the Baha'i Faith, I must teach whatever I can teach to everybody for the rest of my life until I'm finished. And so that really was a very important couple of dreams that I had—very significant.

What would you say is the essence of 'what I must teach'?

If I said the Baha'i Faith I would be telling the truth, but it's more than just the rules of the Baha'i Faith or the history of the Baha'i Faith. I think it's something about living without fear; I think it's something about living with integrity. I think the most important thing that I know, and so many other people don't know, is that you can live truthfully, you can live happily truthfully, and that it doesn't matter what other people say. What matters is that you and God have the relationship intact and have it right. I think that's the truth.

Does it mean, Alice, that you are never fearful now?

No, I don't think I can say I've ever been not fearful. It's a strange thing. I live without fear in the sense that if there's something that I see needs doing, or that I feel I want to do for some good motivation, I might be terrified of doing it. I might say, 'Yes, well, I'm going to Russia now, bye-bye!': that all sounds very glib and, in fact, it's too easy like that. I'm going to do it but I'm really scared, I'm really afraid, and I don't know how I'll do it, and here's another thing I've never done before and I'm not really familiar with what I'm doing, but I'll do it. Now, once you've taken that first step and you say, 'I'll do it', you don't put your head down and gore your way through. What I say is, 'Please, God, do this for me, because I don't know how to do it myself'. And that takes away all the fear. Then, whatever happens you can accept, because you don't have to deal with it, in a sense. You have to continuously put it back into God's hands and then you get the guidance and then the right things happen around you.

And is that true of the cancer, too? Is that how you think about it—'Please, God, do this for me'?

Well, I haven't asked Him to take away the cancer at all. In fact one of my friends recently said, 'Oh, this Baha'i community is praying for you'—and I know that literally all over the world there are Baha'is who are praying for me—and I said to this friend of mine, 'Please tell the friends to stop telling God what to do. He knows what I'm supposed to do, and if I'm supposed to die let me go. I don't want to hang on and stay here, and tell them to stop praying for me.'

It sounds as though that's an important thing for people around you to understand, too: let me go, I need to go, let me go.

Yes, it is.

Do you feel some hanging on through love, through affection, through fear?

Oh, there are a lot of people hanging on to me.

What does that feel like?

It feels not very good. It feels that people are impeding me, in a way unintentionally, and it's a responsibility, it's a terrible responsibility, because it's like having about five hundred children (laughs)—too many and too much—and I don't know what to teach them. In that same sense I don't know how to serve them.

But this is so helpful to me, to hear this. What is it that someone could say to you that would be releasing and loving and not clinging?

Ah, well, you are being releasing and loving and not clinging. You're saying, 'Yes, I understand what you're saying and I think that's wonderful.' You're not saying, 'Oh, no, please stay around, we need you.' All of these people saying, 'We need you, Alice', I'm not too happy with that. But if somebody says, 'That's wonderful; go your way', then that makes me very happy.

In fact, I haven't said anything like that. All I'm doing is listening.

Yes, I know, but you are saying that, anyway! (laughs) I feel that that's what you're saying.

Are you lonely sometimes?

Ah, I think one of the factors in my life that's been terribly significant has been loneliness. I was lonely the day I left home, I was lonely in the years that I was learning how to be a grown-up. I remember at the age of twenty-one looking at a friend of mine and saying, 'Where are all the grown-ups?' We hadn't turned into them and we couldn't find any (laughs), and I think I'm still looking for them. I think this quest for soulmates, if that's what it is, is very difficult, because there are not very many people with whom you can deal on an equal level because a lot of people just think I'm a bit of a nut (laughs). Those are the people who don't agree with what I'm about, or feel themselves less when they hear what I'm saying, for some reason. I don't ever want to make anybody feel less: I think my job, if I have any job, is to empower other people, and I guess that empowerment comes to yourself as you do things and see them successful, and the loneliness comes, I guess, when you're bashing your head against brick walls. There's been a tremendous lot of loneliness in my life: raising my children by myself, for example, for twelve years with no relatives and no extended family was a very lonely experience. There've been lots of times when I've been lonely, but I don't feel lonely any more. I think maybe since I've become a Baha'i I haven't felt much loneliness.

Have you a sense that there will be some sort of reunion of kindred spirits or soulmates when you go through the door?

Oh, yes, absolutely! I'm sure that there's . . . I feel that going through that door is actually going home, and I feel as if I've never been at home and so that's where I'm going.

What are some of the other important things that you've learned in a lifetime of doing and thinking and adventuring?

When one is very young, obviously the most influential people are the family. And teachers: I found teachers were very important to me; two or three teachers in my early years, even in primary school, and then in high school. And they were people who, in some way, said 'Yes, you can be you'. I think people have a choice: when they get to a certain age they can begin to say, 'Well, I don't have to be what my mother or aunt or grandmother wants me to be, I can actually become my own true self'. Part of that is a being who is able to love and who is able to trust, and we live a lot in this society with neither love nor trust. I think that's very significant: people are frightened of loving and trusting. They're frightened of God, they're frightened of lots of things, and many times I think it's because their own role models taught them incorrectly and they didn't take the trouble to find out whether or not there was something else to be or do.

You are a thinker, aren't you? It seems almost as though it's been a lifetime of working things out.

Well, yes, it has been, it's always been working things out, on and on. Yes, and part of that is because of being lonely and part of it's because of needing to have integrity and so on. I mean, I've changed direction on a number of occasions because I've found that I was not doing what I thought I was doing, and had to chide myself and change a bit. So I'm not all peaches and cream! (laughs)

Are you getting tired now?

A little bit, yes. The only thing that I wanted to say is that people who demand that other people conform to a standard are really asking for a sterile society. I think the way to build a dynamic society that's ever-changing is to allow people not to conform, but to behave responsibly and to become fulfilling of their own potential.

It's been wonderful speaking with you: so encouraging and so clarifying. Is there any music which accompanies you in your thinking, or in your belief?

I suppose there are certain pieces of music. I love music. I don't like music all the time, I like silence. There's one piece of music that I heard many, many years ago at the same time as I discovered Beethoven, and Beethoven's Seventh Symphony became a favourite of mine. But also at that time there was a piece by Villa-Lobos called *Bachianus Brasilieras No 5*. It just reaches me; it touches me very deeply, and it's a very mystical-sounding piece of music.

When we turned off the tape recorder a welcome tray of late morning tea arrived, and so did a stack of large, flat, square parcels addressed to Alice. They were her watercolours, pastels and pencil drawings back from the picture framer: delicate, finely observed studies of the human figure and of leaves and flowers. She said that painting and drawing have been a help because they take up all her attention, focusing the mind on the task in hand and leaving no space for any distractions or concerns.

It was exciting to see the beautiful, lively works of art emerge from their brown paper wrapping to surround Alice's wheelchair and fill the small room. There was one extra package. Alice opened it curiously to find a present from the picture framer: a box of coloured pencils and a sketchbook of best quality paper to encourage the artist to continue.

Kevin Gilbert

There is a sense in which Kevin Gilbert has always been a displaced person: born on the fringe of mainstream society, orphaned at an early age; raised largely in institutions; primary school education only; in teenage the roving life of the seasonal worker; and then, for many years, brutally treated in New South Wales prisons.

In another sense, through his Aboriginal view of life, Kevin Gilbert has always belonged, and always been a free spirit in the land of his ancestors.

His story reflects much of the tension between black and white in Australia, in the past 200 years. His mother was Wiradjuri, a central New South Wales group. His father Irish-English. To judge from Kevin's fine appearance, they must have been a striking couple.

During the later part of his imprisonment, Kevin began to write and to paint. Much of this creative outpouring was angry and he is still outspoken today, hurt by the suffering of the Aborigines, but also offering a wider vision of a more compassionate Australia for all to enjoy. The latest book of Kevin's work is Blacks on the Edge, *with Eleanor Williams, (Hyland House). He is the editor of a collection of poems by Aboriginal writers,* Inside Black Australia. *Perhaps as we read Kevin Gilbert's story, we might contemplate the traditions he represents: the 40,000-year history of his mother's people in this mysterious ancient land; the wit and gentleness of his father's people in those green and misty islands on the other side of the world.*

KEVIN GILBERT: The Lachlan River, interestingly enough, is the old Kalara River—that's the Aboriginal name for it: 'the ever-flowing river'. I was born on the banks of the Lachlan River in a tent. I just remember the early years; I was the youngest of eight children in the family, and I remember the children and the animal life, fishing, fish jumping in the river, Aboriginal relatives coming and visiting, and then the big occasion of going across to town. We had to cross the Goobang Creek over the Chinaman's Bridge and we had some friends in the early years in the Chinese market gardeners and the little Chinese shop; they were always warm, flowing people. The rest of the Aboriginal people were over on the Aboriginal mission, which is like a refugee camp. My other main family, which is my grandmother and aunties and uncles, refused to live on the mission so they lived on the lagoon, called the Murie. These were very early and precious memories, that they maintained their independence from the government mission.

All the other children were at school and I used to play on my own on the river banks, and there was only my mother and I most of the time so there was a very close bond. We lived out of town, of course, and my mother used to take in washing at the local butcher's and I'd accompany her when she was doing that. We found town alien. It was like walking into an enemy city, if you like, each time. We were much different than the . . . we could feel the attitudes of white people.

There must have been the most extraordinary dislocation from those years that you've just described, to what would happen next—when both your parents died. You were only . . . what . . . seven?

Yes, I was seven. We were at Leeton at the time and then suddenly orphaned. My eldest sister, who was about eighteen, took over. My brothers had just enlisted (one was sixteen—he was the youngest commando in the War). So we found it very difficult. We had a policeman who was a sort of guardian or trustee of the family, and of course the older girls found this fellow was watching the house, and all that sort of thing. We had very hard years, yes. And, of course, when I started school there, we had all of the attention of white children. They used to stone us and we used to fight them down. I used to get them one by one and sit them on burrs, and different things like that. So we learned to survive at a very early age and were brought up in a fairly hard world.

When I was about eight I went to an orphanage and two of my other sisters went to an orphanage and, of course, those early years taught me a lot about this society and about justice. And the school system taught me about the real standards of hypocrisy, if you like: we were taught to stand up and sing about justice and democracy and 'Britannia Rules the Waves' and 'God Save the Queen'—and I knew the Queen had stolen our country, that they had become Crown lands by a lie, a lie of *terra nullius* (that is, wasteland and unoccupied), and I knew that my people owned the land, that we were sovereigns in our land. I saw the brutality and the starvation of Aboriginal people. There was no Social Services in those days: there was 7s 6d a week rations for families. So we saw all the inequality. And that continued, where we had no rights, for many, many years.

And as you saw these things and began to have a greater insight into them and an understanding of them, what were the feelings inside?

I knew my personality. I knew the stories of my people. I believed in the law of the Aboriginal people and the society, and I was able to make comparisons. There was an anger towards the lies of white society, although I met a lot of good white people. We used to have the Salvation Army people come around, singing their songs and talking about some of the good things and they were quite helpful. On the other hand, when we went to town and we saw these Christians they were talking about (and, of course, we believed all white people were supposed to be Christian), we saw all the wrong things, and that helped us make our assessments. And those assessments weren't wrong—that something had gone awfully wrong with white society.

As an Aboriginal youth in those days, there was no vote for Aboriginal people; there were no drinking rights; apartheid was a fact of life. I had no education because teachers in my day believed that Aboriginal people should only have fourth-class education to count their money and to become servile to white society. So most of the time I was out of the classroom, cleaning the yard; or wagging school because I hated the place. Then, when I married, I had to establish a family; I had to try and earn for a family. So I thought the only way I could do that was to become a fencing contractor, to work my way to managing a sheep station. I knew I had the ability to do any of these things and I started working in that manner. Going along, with all of this hardship and pressures on my family, I got drunk on one occasion and there was a fight in my family—and as a result my wife was killed. I was charged with murder, and I went to the Dubbo Courts and received a sentence of penal servitude for life and, though I don't raise any great quarrel with the situation, I spent fourteen and a half years in prison. I've got no claim on it, because I do believe basically in the principle of the law, even if it's a hard law; that it must be applied and that life, in itself, is sacred—and that's all life, not just human life.

The prison system was very brutal—not so much because of the prisoners, although some of the prisoners had very brutal backgrounds: it was made more brutal by the brutal guards and, of course, I ran into a fair amount of trouble (trying to escape, trying to get out of it, trying to get an appeal on my case), and ultimately I was transferred to Maitland Jail. I was always interested in writing, so I wrote a sixteen-page exposé on the corruption of the guards within the prisons and the prison system. I also had, amongst those papers, many other loose sort of plans to escape, and those writings were found in my cell and I was very quickly removed to Grafton, to the Intractable Section. I was possibly one of the few prisoners that ever went to Grafton on a non-violent charge. So I spent five years and seven months there, and, again, I saw a heightened injustice. If you missed a step when you were marching you'd suddenly get a baton smashed on the back of your neck; you'd be knocked to the ground and you'd have four or five guards come in and beat you. The guards would strip you off and make you bend over, look around your anus, look around your testicles, just to try and denigrate the personality. And then you could be abused, or smacked in the mouth, knocked over, kicked, at any time.

So this was the great reform system in New South Wales. I reacted to that, so I used to abuse the guards and stand at attention while they were beating me. Luckily or unluckily, I came through that, and when I did return to Long Bay, there were changes in the prison system. I started writing poetry and doing art work, and people became interested and Peter Luck did a program on 'This Day Tonight'. And all of those things gradually brought about a change, so that I was released on parole.

Was there also some spiritual strength that you drew on during those years in prison?

Yes. Right from our early beginnings we were taught of the sanctity of the total life around us. There's a difference in the white appreciation of . . . creation, if you like. Their belief is that man was created from clay, and out of this substance he took an ascendancy, or a superior position, over all other things. The Aboriginal way is that everything created is equal and sacred: that the soil, the clay, the rocks, are all sacred within, say, creation; and that all have a personality, a distinct personality. I had the strength of knowing that my creator is not above me somewhere, but is always with me; that, whatever the substance around me, that creation flows to me, through me, within me; that the universe is a part of me, as I am a part of it. And I think that once you know that, there is no fear, as such: there is a complete belonging, and life and death is just a constant flowing, that there is no real change.

Does that mean that even when you were actually physically imprisoned and being beaten and treated so cruelly, there was a sense of freedom, somehow?

Yes, there was a sense of life and freedom; that this was only man imposing his very narrow and very bigoted view, his very minimal power and arrogance upon the world; that this was not what the real powers of life and the real powers of personality are; that there is a continual flowing, a continual renewing within that.

One of the things with the Aboriginal community is that you see the old tribal people sitting down by the campfire, playing the didgeridoo, and 'yackaaing'—which I've spelled out a little in a poem.[1]

At night, as I sit by the campfire,
The Great Serpent Spirit, a star,
I sing songs of love to the Presence within
As It plays with the sparks of my fire.

So, this presence is an ever-flowing thing with me. There's no need to meditate distinctly; there's no need to go to any church; there's no need to think spiritual or religious thoughts. There's a constant flowing of life and we are very much a part of that life.

I think that there is an evolution of consciousness in the white world that is slowly coming to recognise the greater depths of this. There is a total evolution of consciousness, and I believe that that consciousness will ultimately win, because that consciousness is the universe—it's the personality, the total universal personality within the world, within the universe.

So, it's quite possible for you to think of yourself as being related to me and to everybody else?

Oh, yes, to everybody else and every thing. I'm a tree, and the tree is me, and I have no more importance than a tree. In fact, it probably has greater importance than me, because of the benefit and the value that it contributes to life—whereas our contribution is very minimal, and it's only a flash of time. And in that flash of time we achieve or we live our life selfishly, exclusively to ourselves; or we give our life to the generations that are to come and we use our life to the law of that creation and to the benefit of everyone; and we also relate to everyone.

Then what do you think creativity is—that creativity which allowed you to write with such passion, such vigour, such clarity, in your poems, your plays and your other writing? That creativity was to flower, it seems to me,not necessarily out of the pain and suffering you had in prison—I don't know, please tell me—but at least within that environment. What's to be said about that?

I think that flowering and the creativity has been always within me, and that it's within everyone. Finding an avenue for releasing that . . . everybody has talents and nobody is superior to anyone else: everybody has a contribution to make. And that was my inner contribution, if you like, that had to flow for justice, for people, to try . . . I couldn't

1 From *Inside Black Australia*, edited by Kevin Gilbert, Penguin Books Australia, 1988.

write—I had a fifth-class education—extremely limited. I couldn't write: I had to write for what I believed in. I couldn't paint: I had to paint for what I believed in.

But you learned to do those things in prison!

Yes, I learned to do those things because I had a statement to make, and whether that was in prison or outside . . .

It would have happened anyway, would it?

. . . I would have made that statement. And it would have been sooner or later, because that was the only means by which I could, as a person, take my part in ending the horrors that I saw and the horrors that I still see. I see Australia as having to work towards a new beginning. After 1988—what? More racism, more plundering of the land, more human isolation?

And that's working towards a new beginning for the sake of, I think you were suggesting, the white Australia and *the black Australia.*

Yes, white Australia must learn more about the land, accept the history of the land and the people, and really start identifying themselves and their generations, all the future generations that are going to come. There is an incredible amount of isolation in the white community: for instance, 1,400 youths committed suicide last year in Australia . . .

You mean that people are feeling a personal isolation and loneliness?

White people—a personal isolation and loneliness. There are 400 young women who died—suicided. Now, there is isolation because people haven't learnt to belong; people haven't been able to develop their culture with the land. Nobody should be homeless in this land, and yet there is an incredible amount of homeless people. You cannot build a nation until there is a national spirit, until there is a national identification.

Are you suggesting that a healing needs to take place for the newest comers to this land—that is, those who have come in the last 200 years—some sort of healing for them, that will take place through a closer identification with the land?

A closer identification with the land and with the better part of our nature. To fulfil a dream, a dream of democracy, or justice, or honour, you have to meet those requirements: you have to actually work. You can't be a religious person unless you practise those acts, unless you are committed to acting in a good manner. And I think Australians have to act in a good manner and a responsible manner to the land—to the management, to the heritage of the land—and develop their personality more in line with the land and with all the people in the land. Australia is a very, very good country rich in resources, but very poor on the people side: and that imbalance has to be rectified.

Do you think that many of your experiences in life have made you a compassionate person?

Yes, well, I think I was born that way. I think, like most Aboriginal people . . . one of our weaknesses maybe, is a humanity, a softness. One of the things that has stopped us from retaliating against the brutalities we've met is the respect for the lives of children and women. We're unable to carry out those types of terrorist acts, if you like, that may help to bring about a political solution. But I'm a poet, so I have a very soft, compassionate area within my personality—and I think the land has this, as well. All the Aboriginal people I know have the traditional compassion and identification with all life, all people whatever their position—except the positions of arrogance and isolation.

So, you are describing this weakness or this gentleness or this softness as a strength, in a way, aren't you?

Yes, it's a continuation of strength. Yes, it is a strength.

When you're communicating with me, for example, is the fact that you are looking at a white face and that you have suffered very much during your life at the hands of white people—is that a great barrier to us communicating, for you?

No, not really. Aboriginals talk about white society (you know, 'The whites are doing this to us, the whites are doing that to us') . . . and, sure, we hate white society, but when we meet individual people you're no longer white to me. You are flowing to me at my level, and when I go from here and I meet other people who are flowing to me at the human level, I take in their personality. The colour of their skin means nothing.

Kevin, you've enjoyed a good deal of notoriety as a poet. Does it feel like that to you? Do you feel like a successful writer? Or does success have some other meaning for you?

In our community everybody has an equal place, so that while I can write and I can write a poem, one of my fellow Aboriginals can throw a spear better than me, can run faster than me, can swim better than me—probably swear harder than me! So there're all of these various things and success in terms of being a writer or a poet has no great meaning. I'm only just another person in my community, using my ability in my way to feed the tribe—it's like tucker to the tribe. And all the other Aboriginal people around me are doing their thing to feed the tribe, get tucker for the tribe. So, I'm doing my part as well as the next feller.

So what is a successful human being in your estimation?

A person who uses every moment of their life in a caring way, a responsible way for other people; who tries to earn their breath of life in this land—their breath of life being their contribution to the people around them, to themselves and to the world. It's a very short span of time that we have, and every moment of that should be used in flowing, loving, caring and bringing about those types of changes we need.

And how do you contemplate death?

I can't see any real cut-off point: it's just another continuous flowing in my life. I will always be a part of the land and my spirit will be a continuous flowing. In the Aboriginal community we have very special trees. Budjarng, a tree named after your grandmother, and the rocks. There's a continuousness there, and my soul won't go up to some elevated or some cast-down level: I'm a part of the continuous spirituality and personality of this created universe. It's all a total, a sum total.

So, you won't keep this body and go into another dimension, will you?

No.

But your soul . . . ?

The whole spirit will flow and mingle into its home and then whatever form it comes out in at some later stage will always be a part of this earth, which is the main focus. We'll go 'from ashes to ashes and from dust to dust' and we'll flow back into the earth. But there's something *more* than ashes, something *more* than dust—the personality, the spiritual personality, will flow into that which is the total.

Would I be right in thinking, then, that there's no need to fear death?

Oh, there's no need to fear death! No, death is just . . . it's not even a long sleep; it's a new phase; it's just a continuous phase of our life, and has to be accepted. We can't escape death, so we've got to accept it. It is a continuous flow, like a river flowing into the sea. So *we* will flow into the sea.

Kevin, have you any forgiving to do, of people who have hurt you, who have been cruel to you, who have beaten you?

No, not really forgiving, I don't think. People are always responsible for their actions. And this is one of the things about Aboriginal law. It's pretty clearcut; people must take responsibility for their actions. And it's not up to me to hold judgment on them, if you like. Where they've inflicted deep hurt on me, especially some of those guards, my nature is still primitive enough to welcome the opportunity to meet them in the bush some time, alone, without witnesses—I'm still primitive enough for that. But there's no need for me to forgive them, because their conscience sooner or later will affect them, and, if not, the generations will judge them, and their whole loss . . . they have their own executions, their lifestyle . . . the unhappiness at the end of their lives—that seems to be the sole judge.

Do you hate anybody?

Not really, no. No, I hate injustice, I hate the perpetrators of injustice, I hate people who abuse power—generally. But, no, I don't believe I hate anyone in particular.

When the white man took his bloodied boot
From the neck of the buggered black
Did you expect some gratitude
His smile 'Good on you Jack?'
When your psalmist sang
Of a suffering Christ
While you practised genocide
Did you expect his hate would fade
Out of sight with the ebbing tide?
In another time, another age
If fate had reversed the play
And a hard black boot pressed on your white throat
When released—what would *you* say
Friends and pals forever together in a new fair dawn?
Or meet like you and I shall meet
With flames and daggers drawn.[2]

Do you feel yourself more to be Wiradjuri, or Australian, or just a human being of the world? What's your strongest identification?

Wiradjuri—Wiradjuri being my central personality, flowing to the whole of the universe—and that means everybody in the world. I have a responsibility within my land and also for everybody within the total land of Australia and throughout the world, because we all have a common destiny these days, and we can avert a common tragedy, and we can all generally grow together. Or we can neglect to take full responsibility for the nuclear war, nuclear warheads, American bases, infiltration, human abuses, the abuse of human rights—and we will end up in something that's not worth having, anyway. Or we can take responsibility and make this whole world

2 From 'The Flowering . . . ', Kevin Gilbert, *People Are Legends*, University of Queensland Press, 1978.

a place fit for all of us to be able to share together and live reasonable lives. I don't mean rich, affluent lives: I mean to not be isolated, to find welcome wherever we go, to find pride, justice, honour. And we can do that.

May I ask you, finally, to reflect, if you would, on suffering—the suffering in your life?

Suffering is at many levels. One, the personality ego suffering is the one that is the most excruciating. Where the ego is denied, unable to find direction, is repulsed by somebody, either in a caring way or in a loving relationship, or not able to assert itself, all the self-doubt that is in the mind is the greatest suffering of all.

Most often we find that we don't act as we are: we don't act according to our personality, but we act to a programmed idea of how we think other people should see us, how other people would expect us to react, so that even at the communicating level we are unable to communicate our personality, our thoughts and we are frustrated at that level. And that causes, possibly, a lot of the deepest suffering of all, because from that inability to communicate and knowing our inner personality, we start feeling that we're crazy, we're out of step. What's wrong with me? Am I going mad? Am I ugly? Do I think horrible thoughts? And that is the greatest cause of individual suffering.

Have you felt that sort of suffering?

Oh, yes. Yes, very much so, especially in the areas of caring for someone, my own sexuality, the inability to approach people even at the common-day level. When you suffer at the hands of other people like prison guards, police, society itself, then you can shove the blame sideways a little: you can say, 'Well, it's them. They're out of step. It's their fault,' and you're not able to relate it to yourself so much, so it doesn't become quite so painful. Through all my years of suffering I managed to realise, work my way through my own identity crises, if you like, my own problems in communicating.

But one of the joys of communicating, I suppose, is to feel understood by another person, especially in a personal relationship, a friendship, or whatever; and if we don't feel that sort of acceptance, is there loneliness in that sometimes, for you?

Oh, yes. Yes, I think, essentially, most human beings are lonely; there's an essential loneliness. Because humans can't always meet human needs, even in longstanding relationships within family, within marriages. There's always an isolation and a loneliness; there are always secret places, there are lonely crags within a personality.

You think that's true for everyone?

I think it's true for everyone, yes. I'm more of a solitary person now. I don't live in the Aboriginal community. I don't espouse the company of men too much: after being in prison for fourteen and a half years with men, seeing the rawness of nature, I don't admire mankind—man—all that much and I don't espouse his company all that much. Women are a different matter, of course, being a male! And I find more compassion and a greater sincerity, more caring for the nation and for children amongst women, as well. But there's loneliness there, yes, and I think everybody has that type of loneliness.

Do you have a yearning to have that loneliness assuaged? Do you think that loneliness can ever be satisfied?

No.

Does that happen in the next life?

No, I think it happens on fortunate occasions, when you meet a personality . . . or that happy instance when you flow for a brief period of time. I think life is like that: by your personality you can allow that moment of isolation to develop into almost a full-term thing; or you can 'group' yourself together, accept that isolation and loneliness comes, and then wait for your next period of flowing. I think we are like tides of personality—we ebb and flow—and I think that's one of the great things that people need to recognise.

Magda Bozic

This is the story of a journey, which can be appreciated at several levels; it's the story of an enforced departure from a beloved country, of landfall in a strange place; of making a new home; of faith and family; of growing older—and finally of return to the birthplace. This is a story with meaning for anyone who's ever had to leave home and familiar faces.

But it's also the story of everyman-and-woman ... the story of the journey which is life, a deeply personal telling which is also universal.

The eloquent story-teller was born in Hungary. Her name is Magda Bozic. She left her homeland after World War II, to make a new life in Australia, living in Canberra and Darwin. Her contribution to the new life in Australia has been recognised with an award, but she prefers that not to be mentioned, so I suppose I must not name it. The story we now read begins in Budapest—Magda a young woman—the time, late 1930s.

MAGDA BOZIC: I was lucky to be young enough to have a few marvellous pre-war years, when there was such a flourishing of the arts and there was creative spirit all over Europe as well as countries like Hungary in art, in opera and operetta, and in the marvellous cabarets. There was tremendous humour and wit and 'sending up' the danger to a point where you could laugh for half-an-hour, if not longer, about it and that was such a redeeming feature of life to be able to exchange a joke over the most dreadful things in life.

Remembering the years before the war really is a contrast with what happened after the war. One so vividly can recall the warm spring and summer nights walking along the Danube and talking excitedly about a marvellous night at the theatre, of some great production, and going to a coffee shop and going on *again* with talk and more talk. Walking home under the stars and stopping at the bridge and watching the barges going down on that dark river, and chestnut trees in full bloom in the springtime. Walking home on a snow-covered street with the snow falling again in the middle of the night and it's so quiet around you, everything, and all you can think is life is so beautiful. But you don't really verbalise it, you just feel it—you belong to this world, you are part of all this wonderfulness that is around you.

But then war arrives and until that moment history was a subject in your school curriculum, or it was the chronicle of distant heroes doing heroic deeds and having streets and parks named after them by a grateful posterity. When the war arrives to your doorstep history suddenly has an evil human face and it becomes an insidious force that takes over your country and the destiny of the world and you look around. Overnight, for millions of people, the idea that they can live and grow old and die in their own country becomes a luxury, a wishful thought, all dressed up nowhere to go ever again. It is then you understand that history is not just a subject in your school curriculum but it is your own destiny, once you live in what the Chinese call 'interesting times'.

You were a young married woman.

I was a young married woman and then in the war my husband went to Russia where he was killed. We went down to the air-raid shelter with the family when the war and bombing started in earnest in Hungary and two of the family died there in that air-raid shelter, my father and my sister. My mother and I were the survivors. When we came out from the shelter we walked around and we looked at Budapest. Before the bombing, it had been such a beautiful city that it sang, your heart sang when you walked along the main avenues and up in the hills. We came out of the shelter and we really didn't know where we were because there were in the streets rows and rows of collapsed buildings and ruins, including our own home. There was absolutely nothing, a burnt-out shell and we wept and wept for a life gone forever, not our own personal property and not our lives, but the life of Budapest as it was in those few precious wonderful years that we had known before the war.

Nostalgia is such a treacherous friend and travelling companion because when you go back, as I did go back after twenty years away from Budapest and from Hungary, you go back and you carry in your mind that precious moment, those treasured hours, the way life was once and could never be again. And you go back and you look for it and you carry it in your mind and you look at the place and you want to find it. At odd moments it comes to you and it talks to you and then it disappears again in your life. And then you realise it's gone. You have to step out, start life over again, that world is not there any more. Civilisation as we have known it, has gone. And so a new life starts in Australia.

What of the day you left at the railway station? What happened then?

When you think about the crisis point in life very often you can't put them into a tidy order and say, 'This is a crisis', and put a red ribbon around it. When you leave your coutnry forever, and people say, 'Aren't you lucky you were able to leave', you want to say 'Why am I lucky that I was able to leave the country I loved and never wanted to leave, why do I have to be lucky for that?'

The full impact hits you when you are on the station with your luggage and there you stand. You suddenly look at the people around you with whom your whole life was a network, with whom you went through all that life meant to you, love affairs, happy moments, terrible times, awful grief—but it was all shared life. This small crowd of people stand around you with their awkward little presents. And you suddenly realise in that moment that they are thinking the same thing, they hardly dare to look at you and you at them. You are thinking just let's have strength to get through that five more minutes, but you break down and you weep because there is no way in the world that you can pretend any more. The time is too strong; it grips you. You get on that wretched train and it slowly, slowly moves away. They are standing and waving to you and you know you can't touch them any more. You still see them, fading slowly into the background and then you look around and you are on your own.

That chapter which was the first half of your life ended in a very visible and dramatic way on that railway station. There is a full stop. You haven't got a clue what is ahead of you, because you don't know the rules of the games any more. You have no idea what Australia looks like; what is waiting for you there; what sort of people are there. How am I going to talk to them, I am leaving behind all the language rituals, my strength and joy in life which made me communicate, which built bridges, which broke sometimes and blew up bridges as well, but it was all there all the time, it's gone now. I left it behind. I am naked so to speak in the world.

From being one person with a language, with home, with friends, you step ashore in another place and you're a migrant. You don't speak the language, you don't have friends, you cannot say what you want to say but you nod and smile and feel awkward and be silly but you cannot be yourself, because that person (who is you) cannot communicate. The decision I had to make was either would I stay within the little group of people, my own compatriots and we'll spend the time working out who is who, who was who, who will be who, and talk about immigration and so on . . . or, I would go out and find Australia.

I didn't know where Australia was, the only thing I knew was that the Sydney Harbour is the most beautiful place in the world. I still think it's the most beautiful place in the world, I make a pilgrimage every time I come to Sydney, just to pay homage to this wonder of the world. Then that was all I knew about Australia—that there is one beautiful thing about it, so I had to go out and find it for myself and when I ask people where to go and how do you find Australia? They said go to Canberra. So I went to Canberra—a dreadful place, a collection of paddocks and flies and loneliness and magpies picking your brain every spring, but there was a compensation. Have you noticed that life always offers you compensations? Takes one thing away from you and you don't know why but it brings you something else and it turns out to be a wonderful gift and you take it up and you go on.

And what do you make of that, is that some sort of divine plan or luck or fortune or?

No, it's cause and effect. I am a great believer that we are carrying in ourself our salvation and our damnation in so many ways. You can either sit down and say, it's all in the lap of the gods. It all happened to me but I can't do anything about it—this is how life is. Or you can say no, this is not how life is. You look at half a glass of water on the table and you don't say this glass is half empty, say that it's half full and pick it up and enjoy the fact that you've got half a glass of water. Don't cry that it's half empty.

So you've always had that optimism, that hope that something would come next?

Oh not optimism so much as to take it on, to not let life sit on you.

To accept the challenge, to go forward?

Just to be like a rubber ball. You know how you push a ball down and the harder you push it down the higher it jumps up again. It's just that feeling that I have to try and get up and pick up the pieces and go again and make some kind of sense of these pieces.

Canberra made no sense except that I happened to run into a circle of wonderful, wonderful friends who really did save my life at that time of great despair and loneliness. They were so very similar so suddenly it was a group of people and it was a wonderful time. There was no hierarchy. I got a typing job in one of the government departments but I lived in the hostel together with all these very lovely people who worked in all walks of life. By now they would be all separated in their ivory towers in their tickey-tackey houses and University House and they wouldn't even look at me, but luckily there was not enough accommodation, so all these interesting people were all mixed up in that wonderful 'melting pot'.

Tell us please about meeting your husband in Darwin.

You want to hear about romance? I went up to Darwin because at the typing pool the chap in charge came in and said, 'Does anybody want to go for six weeks or three months to Darwin?' The girls said 'You must be joking!' And I said 'Why? Where is Darwin?' They brought out a map and they showed me. From Canberra to Darwin is the distance of half of Europe or more and of course I wanted to go. They gave me a lovely farewell and put me on an aeroplane. That was my introduction to Australia, farewell ceremonies of little afternoon tea and presentation of gifts which made me feel very important. Do you remember the DC3?

Yes.

Going like a yo-yo up and down for ten hours, it was like a milk run. It stopped everywhere to deliver letters.

But that was real flying.

But to look down on this Australia and for the first time to have a visual understanding that this is not a small country of tidy little meadows. It is wide, huge! The beginning of the world, biblical country almost in its austere, terrible loneliness as I looked from that aeroplane, which was not as high as aeroplanes are now so it was possible really to see all that.

Then I arrived to Darwin and that was the most marvellous adventure of life. Darwin nearly forty years ago was not that tidy nice town which I believe they are trying to turn it into now, making it into another Canberra. It was such a beautiful place with poinciana trees and the frangipani perfume which followed you wherever you went, and then I got to know, in the hostel, all sorts of lovely adventurous girls who knew all sorts of lovely adventurous boys and on the motor bike off we'd go out into the bush and crocodile-shooting. Can you imagine crocodile-shooting?—Leaving the coffee houses of Budapest and ending up with a gun on my shoulder, being told, 'Now, shoot between the eyes'.

And I wrote home these letters to my friends and one friend wrote back reminding me I used to be scared stiff of a little Pekinese dog in her backyard. She asked what is crocodile-shooting? So I wrote back, 'This is all another game, played by different rules'. It was all so, so wonderful.

One day I met my husband through one of the Australian girls who knew a couple of foreigners working in Darwin and she said, 'I met a Hungarian and he will come along'. That Hungarian chap came along with a tall marvellous-looking chap who spoke very little English and that was to be my husband. Of course we didn't know that at that time but it was very romantic, marvellous and also it was that we were terribly lonely and therefore all this romance was magnified by that sense of being drifting together and having feelings for each other and singing and reminiscing. Even so it was in terrible broken English.

He was not Hungarian, was he?

No, he is a Croat, comes from near the sea. I come from an inland town so it was in so many ways two totally different backgrounds finding out a little, not an awful lot because our language was not all that fantastic. But anyhow we met and married there. Then we came to Canberra which was still as awful as ever, but he got a job he liked with the Ionospheric Prediction Service. I got a job at the university which was wonderful, because I could rely a bit on that ancient Greek and Latin which was part of my high school curriculum at home and that was the reason why I got the job. So never say that any education is useless, it might happen that twenty years later it may save your life. There I met people who were still my friends and who were like a family closing almost around me and keeping the cold wind of Canberra away from me. Also friendship is the great salvation of life, tuning into other people's lives and sharing without judgement, without getting involved in other issues, other interests, other incompatibilities. We receive a consolation prize in life. We get all we need to carry the other problems.

After being married and working in Canberra I had my marvellous son. Growing up in Canberra was a very easy, very lovely affair because there were good schools and good kindergartens. It all made life so much easier. This is the great trap of Canberra as people are not there because they really love to be there but because the facilities are there or their jobs are there. It's almost like the difference between a love marriage and a marriage of interest. If you talk to people in Sydney they say, 'I hate the damn place but I couldn't live anywhere else'. In Canberra they say 'Oh, you know it's such a good place to be; that it gives you material advantages and this and that', but nobody says, 'I'm here because I couldn't live anywhere else.'

Would you say something about what it meant to you emotionally and perhaps spiritually to have your son?

Everything, absolutely everything, not because he was my son but he was such a nice kid anyhow. Through him I really could get gradually identifying myself with the country, which was almost impossible because by having friends you are exchanging ideas, you are communicating on a different level, it's not living in the country as such. But when you have a kid and you push the pram down to the old Civic and the greengrocer says, 'How is the kid today?' And you know the people, they stop and talk to you and they talk to the kid. We had a marvellous kindergarten teacher who saw that the great problem for me was being lonely and isolated, and she gave me a lot of love and understanding. The schools again were very good and easy, within walking distance, at the corner. Gradually through the activities of the schools, the canteen, the plays the school put on, we really got involved. Slowly, in an imperceptible way we became absorbed in understanding other ways of thinking, other ways of living and the essential, basic, common, human identity with others in spite of superficial cultural differences. These didn't matter any more because again a different kind of friendship on another level was formed with all these people. So my son meant to both of us, to my husband and me, that link which is very hard to forge with a community where you did not have your own childhood memories and your own roots. So as he grew up we really grew with him and opened that window to that domestic Australia that I had no idea about it, exchanging recipes and chatting at the clothes line. Going out at night together with all the neighbours, we'd take scones and food in a basket, and light a fire and let the kids run around. New memories were superimposing themselves in a new term of references, about joys, the day-to-day life. So gradually one is receding and you build over another one.

When you grow old and you look back, then you are looking back on two pasts and the ghosts of these two pasts are talking to you in two different languages, because they are built on the top of each other. This is what all migrant life is about. We are carrying with us two pasts, one in another language and in another world. The other one as we are living our daily life we are building over that previous past, the two together are our life and are our term of reference to life.

So what do you think now after all your experience of the human being, the nature of the human being and the human spirit. Do you see a pattern? Do you see a purpose? Or does it seem haphazard?

I see that the good perpetuates itself. Never say, 'It's not worth doing a good thing', no matter how little. Things that women and men are doing in the community all have significance. If all the millions of good people worldwide carry on believing in the inherent value of being good for no other reason than because we are human beings; and look on every human being having no categories and barriers, but to accept and cherish the diversity and the humanness and the kindness and the goodness in the world. If we would have let that go during the war, when we seemed to have nothing else during the German and Russian occupations we would have let that feeling of believing in the humanness of the human being go and we would just believe that, 'Here it is, the jungle took it over'. The local flag bearers were often worst because the rules of the jungle were on the streets. We couldn't have survived, and we could not start a new life because it would have dehumanised us too, and you must believe. You must carry on with hope that there is always another day and that day might just see the end of some terrible evil suffering in the world if everybody just does something. You must never give up hope.

Does this philosophy of life you have stem from an understanding that we are made in the image of God? What is the source of that goodness?

I don't know, I cannot carry the meaning of words beyond their meaning, I don't know that when you say 'God' and when I say, 'The goodness in human being', if we are not talking in fact about the same thing. I suspect we are, and therefore I don't know where it comes to Earth but it is in everybody. Nobody is born wanting to be evil. If we give up the goodness that is in all of us, that's evil, because we let go that feeling to stand up and be counted. Where somebody is suffering or in trouble, even if it is inconvenient perhaps it is worth helping.

I talk so much to older people as I am growing older and many of my younger friends are still working. So I gradually get to know a new country, another country called 'Old Age', and there when I talk to people I suddenly discover that sense of insecurity which comes from society changing. Violence is worse than it used to be. People don't dare to leave their doors open the way they used to. Everybody has two or three locks because there is a feeling that society is, in some imperceptible way, tolerating more and more violence.

I asked a friend, 'Why don't you go for a walk in these beautiful spring evenings?', and she said, 'Are you mad, you're obviously not living in Sydney, no one dares to go out to walk at seven o'clock at night and watch the stars, somebody will snatch your bag or knock you down or . . . .'

Now, these are the terrible things that every one of us should protest against by standing up and fighting to voice our feeling about it. It's no use to have these silent, repressed anxieties. Politicians keep ear-bashing us about nothing else but whether we will get a dollar more or not. Australian society is worried about other things as well. This is an insult to the voters and they are ignoring all the other issues that the average Australian would like to know for their kids and for the future of Australia.

What else is to be said about getting older? What other feelings have you about that?

Getting older so far is a wonderful experience. It feels as if you went on a long journey and you were carrying a heavy bag which was full of little parcels: ambition and expectations and wanting to be young first, or beautiful, or to be loved, or to achieve things in life—like a supermarket where all these things are labelled with what expectations our parents, the world, our friends, our profession all have for us. Then comes this wonderful day, even so it's a very painful day, when you leave work. It is almost as tragic a day in your life as it is when you leave your country, and that is really what you think of in terms of crisis points in life.

I was working in the Human Rights Commission, which was a marvellous experience. I had several other jobs with all sorts of tricks after I retired. You're automatically supposed to be senile from Tuesday afternoon to Wednesday morning and can't get a job, so I didn't tell my age and got over the jobs. At the Human Rights Commission I had this tremendous conviction and commitment to be able to say that in Australia we have nearly 150 different nationalities (and I don't know, 70 or 80 different religions). Children in the schools, in the kindergartens, are often coming from homes where the parents are from countries where repression, persecution, (totalitarian regimes therefore), are common. Those children from the day they are in the community should get some idea, regardless what they hear at home from perhaps 'different way of thinking parents', about what human rights are, be told that we are all equal, that none of us is better or worse on account of anything, than the other, and if they learn it in the school, it can't be taken away from them. Some will dismiss it and a lot will remember it. The lesson of equality will be in the pattern woven in that magnificent carpet which is that person's life.

Now, returning to the subject of old age: so many things at various stages of life are so terribly important that we hang on to them and feel tense about them. Once you've got over the sadness of being out of the workforce you gradually feel a sense of freedom that your life (for the first time in your life in a sense), is yours and it is a beautiful feeling. You can go for a walk along the beach for hours and watch the seagulls dipping down in the sunset. You are not thinking about, 'I have to pick up the kids, prepare dinner, do the washing, I have to do this and that'. Your life is yours! You can think, listen to music, listen to articulate, beautiful programs. If your eyes are bad as mine because you are old aged, then again you look around again for new openings. One of them for me is some marvellous friend reading on cassette the book that he thinks I would like to read. I have a cassette library. so I just ignore my book library, and walk up to my cassette library. When one door closes there should be another door that you slowly open and find your way to other pleasures that replace the ones you can't have. You just have to know the difference and accept it. You can't go on being sad about the things you lose because you are growing old. This wonderful interesting universe is full of beautiful things as well as with awful things. You are free now just to pick up the beautiful things.

Let me for just a moment go back to tell you about the day when I left work at the Human Rights Commission. I decided that I will just sneak out at the back door, because you know, this old romantic idea we all had in Europe, in great love affairs and what not, that you just walk away and you tell that person, 'Don't look back . . . I am going' you know, that was always a part of life. When I left Hungary, I made a New Year's resolution and I said to myself, 'Never again will I have a farewell organised in my life. I will just walk away and don't look back. I cannot bear the thought of another farewell, I really cannot.' So, I said to myself, 'I will quietly walk away in the middle of the afternoon'.

In the next room, as I walked in just to say, 'Ta-ta, see you tomorrow', there was a long table set with a white tablecloth and there were roses, just dropped here, there, everywhere, single roses the people brought in from their garden, perhaps with a little note, perhaps not . . . and there was a very old little gramophone, do you remember that very old His Master's Voice?

Yes.

And somebody just turned on that gramophone, and there was a Hungarian voice singing, 'It is late autumn now, the leaves are slowing falling and goodbye to all that, that was the summer'; and there were people all around me and that's how they said good-bye to me. Isn't that lovely? So once again the good-bye was really a very heart-wrenching good-bye but of course I meet them and so it was not a total loss as it was the first one.

And one day you went back to see again the land of your birth?

There was one day when there was a real big snow fall in Canberra and I walked out and walked through the bush and saw the snowflakes falling down and I thought, 'I must go back'. I haven't seen snow all those years and I just want to go back. It all brought it back.

I had a great and wonderful brother . . . and he and my husband said, 'Of course you have to go back'. They understood. This was an issue I had to face.

I went back to Hungary and after twenty years waiting, there is written up on that airport in glittering letters 'Budapest' and I stepped off from the plane clutching all the presents I had for everybody and next to the waiting room was a waiting platform. It's there my friends were all standing there. The babies they were holding in their arms when I left Hungary were now young women and they were holding their own babies. There was this whole clan, this whole tribe. They are shouting and they were waiting for me. It was an *incredible* moment of time. When you live life so absolutely, to its fullest intensity, and dream about something and it comes true, you realise that moment that this is it. I walked slowly as if my legs were lead, because I thought, 'this would never happen again, the next moment already would be a past history of that previous moment'.

It was such a mixed, wonderful trip really. When I came across something that spoke to me in the same language, I wept and wept and wept every time. I remember walking up to the hills. There was an old oak tree and I found a heart, that heart which was my 'great first love of life' with an arrow across which we were carving out. Suddenly there was a war. Millions of people died, the city collapsed, but the big oak tree stands there, with a heart and a cross in it. Details like that really wring your heart. You walk up to the hills and look down on that city and from there is this misty outline of that place that you love so much. I had returned.

I started to walk around and into the shops and I talked to people and I was a tourist, a stranger. I didn't know anybody except two or three people, and perhaps their children (in a way of remembering them more than in reality), but beyond that small network, I didn't belong there any more. New generations of people had grown up, they thought differently, living in a different world of experiences, and to them I was a tourist. And so I walked around and just let the memories and the reality mix in all sorts of strange ways. When I used to walk around in Canberra in the paddock and think about Budapest; now I was walking around Budapest thinking, 'What are my son and husband and my friends doing?' It is confusing.

Life for a migrant, and perhaps to most of us in so many ways, consists constantly of incoming messages from life. You gain things and take away things from you and you can't assess what was success and what was failure and what was gain and what was loss. It's a circle—it's all part of the same game. You need this double experience of what comes to you, whether you like it or not. Make the most of it. What happened to be my life in the 1980s or 1950s or 1970s, in Europe and then in Australia, first a human being, and second perhaps as a migrant, is part of the circle. I have many Australian friends who are very, very close to me and we share absolutely all our life events with each other. There are millions of migrants out there whom I have never met and never will meet whose experiences and language set them apart. But with all these migrants I have one experience in common: that at one moment of history we all had to leave our country that we loved and never really wanted to leave. We had to leave behind our language and all that was dear, that made sense, to start a new life. That is a thread that ties us all together in a common experience and it's there. So in a way other threads, other times are with my Australian friends who did not have this experience but nevertheless we are all one family and cannot be otherwise, if we want to be one nation.

'This book provides an original perspectiv[illegible] aspects of dyslexia and will be welcomed by professionals working in the field. It provides a refreshing addition to the plethora of books focusing on the theories and causes of dyslexia and complements these by turning to the important question of what it feels like to be dyslexic.'

– Professor Maggie Snowling, President, St John's College, University of Oxford

'This is an important and much needed book – the emotional impact of dyslexia has been neglected for too long. In this comprehensive and accessible analysis, Neil Alexander-Passe skilfully draws upon contemporary theory and research from a range of disciplines to explore what we know and what we can do to best support the well-being of those living with dyslexia.'

– Professor Neil Humphrey, Director of Research for the Manchester Institute of Education

'This book provides a comprehensive picture of the many manifestations of emotional and affective domain challenges that might be encountered by dyslexics. It uses a wealth of pertinent research to provide a comprehensive background for understanding these problems and proposes a structure to manage and overcome them.'

– Steve Chinn, author of Addressing the Unproductive Classroom Behaviours of Students with Special Needs, *founder and former Principal of Mark College for dyslexic pupils, Chair and co-founder of the Council for the Registration of Schools Teaching Dyslexic Pupils (CReSTeD), Visiting Professor, University of Derby*

'It is our responsibility as advocates for dyslexia to ensure that the next generation of dyslexic children have the opportunity to express their strengths more fully, with greater understanding and support within school and society for their difficulties. This book can contribute to this recognition.'

– Emeritus Professor Angela Fawcett, Swansea University, Honorary Professor, Sheffield University

DYSLEXIA AND MENTAL HEALTH

of related interest

The Self-Help Guide for Teens with Dyslexia
Alais Winton
ISBN 978 1 84905 649 6
eISBN 978 1 78450 144 0

Creative, Successful, Dyslexic
23 High Achievers Share Their Stories
Margaret Rooke
Foreword by Mollie King
ISBN 978 1 84905 653 3
eISBN 978 1 78450 163 1

Addressing the Unproductive Classroom Behaviours of Students with Special Needs
Steve Chinn
ISBN 978 1 84905 050 0
eISBN 978 0 85700 357 7

Self-Harm and Eating Disorders in Schools
A Guide to Whole-School Strategies and Practical Support
Pooky Knightsmith
ISBN 978 1 84905 584 0
eISBN 978 1 78450 031 3

Count Me In!
Ideas for Actively Engaging Students in Inclusive Classrooms
Richard Rose and Michael Shevlin
ISBN 978 1 84310 955 6
eISBN 978 0 85700 377 5

A Practical Guide to Mental Health Problems in Children with Autistic Spectrum Disorder
It's Not Just Their Autism!
Khalid Karim, Alvina Ali and Michelle O'Reilly
ISBN 978 1 84905 323 5
eISBN 978 0 85700 697 4

DYSLEXIA AND MENTAL HEALTH

Helping people identify destructive behaviours and find positive ways to cope

NEIL ALEXANDER-PASSE

FOREWORDS BY MICHAEL RYAN AND PENNIE ASTON

Jessica Kingsley *Publishers*
London and Philadelphia

Drawings at the start of Chapters 1–11 were drawn by
Catrin (Cat) Bywater and are reproduced with permission.

First published in 2015
by Jessica Kingsley Publishers
73 Collier Street
London N1 9BE, UK
and
400 Market Street, Suite 400
Philadelphia, PA 19106, USA

www.jkp.com

Library of Congress Cataloging in Publication Data
Alexander-Passe, Neil.
Dyslexia and mental health : helping people identify destructive behaviours and find positive ways to cope / Neil Alexander-Passe ; forewords by Michael Ryan and Pennie Aston.
pages cm
Includes bibliographical references and index.
ISBN 978-1-84905-582-6
1. Dyslexia--Psychological aspects. 2. Mental health. I. Title.
RC394.W6A45 2015
616.85'5320651--dc23
2015016721

British Library Cataloguing in Publication Data
A CIP catalogue record for this book is available from the British Library

ISBN 978 1 84905 582 6
eISBN 978 1 78450 068 9

Printed and bound in Great Britain

CONTENTS

FOREWORD

Michael Ryan

Pioneers in the field of dyslexia observed that many children with learning disorders struggled with anxiety and depression. The neurologist Samuel Orton (1937) was one of the first researchers to write about the emotional reactions some children have to dyslexia. Later, Richard Lewis and Alfred Strauss (1951) identified emotional problems as a symptom of certain learning disorders. On the other hand, early psychotherapists such as Phyllis Brett Blanchard and Virginia Axline postulated that reading disorders were caused by emotional problems. Research has demonstrated that dyslexia is not caused by psychiatric disorders. Instead research indicates that as many as 20 per cent of children with dyslexia also suffer from depression, and another 20 per cent suffer from an anxiety disorder (Willcutt and Gaffney-Brown 2004). Equally important are the data that suggest that when an individual demonstrates this kind of comorbidity both disorders are more severe and more difficult to cope with (Willcutt and Gaffney-Brown 2004).

The first developmental task asked of a child outside the context of the home is to learn to read. Eric Erickson has theorised that failure during this period (five through ten years) produces feelings of inferiority rather than feelings of competency. Therefore, reading failure interferes with the individual's development of a positive self-image. Furthermore, dyslexics are more likely to demonstrate deficits in social abilities and social skills. These deficits put them at odds with their peers and family at a time when they need support and empathy.

Finally, dyslexia often produces many inconsistencies in the individual's life. Dyslexics may be gifted in some areas and have significant deficits in others. Furthermore, their cognitive skills in certain key areas fluctuate over time. This can produce what appears to be an intermittent disability, which makes it difficult for the individual to understand and compensate for their problems.

Although these emotional conflicts are caused by dyslexia, they can develop a life of their own. For example, a dyslexic student could develop test anxiety because of her reading problem. After the reading problems are remediated, she may still fail because of her overwhelming anxiety during tests.

Furthermore, it is not uncommon for highly successful individuals with dyslexia, such as a hospital chief of staff or a powerful CEO, to experience ongoing shame, anxiety and feelings of inadequacy. Even though these individuals' achievements have earned them a place at the top of their fields, they are terrified to go to work each morning. They often feel like frauds and unworthy of their success. They struggle with both the fear of failure and the guilt of feeling that they're pretending to be someone they're not. Until we have a comprehensive understanding of dyslexia and the feelings that it produces, our ability to help both children and adults will be limited.

Unfortunately, there is very little written about the connection between dyslexia and emotional disorders in either the clinical or scientific literature. It is gratifying to see the research on phonological awareness has mushroomed in the past 20 years, however, interest in the comorbidity between dyslexia and psychiatric disorders has not followed suit. We know even less about how individuals with dyslexia cope with these painful and damaging feelings.

The present work is a significant contribution to the field. Using research and personal narratives, the author describes dyslexia, how it affects an individual's development, the painful feelings produced by dyslexia and how dyslexic individuals can cope with these painful feelings. In fact, he offers a comprehensive model for understanding the defence mechanisms used by dyslexic individuals. Here, the author offers a unique contribution to our understanding of dyslexia. The stress and feelings caused by dyslexia have been identified in other works: this book goes farther. Not only does it suggest some unique defence mechanisms such as self-harm that other theorists have not associated with dyslexia, it also identifies positive coping strategies that many dyslexics use.

Thomas Edison might be one example of someone who learned to use these positive strategies to cope with his dyslexia. A number of biographers have marvelled at Edison's ability not only to overcome his failures, but also to learn from them. It may be that his extensive school failures helped to prepare him for a career that demanded persistence in the face of numerous failures.

Neil Alexander-Passe has done a remarkable job of presenting both theoretical and practical information in an easy-to-understand way. He handles very complex and difficult problems with sensitivity and offers concrete suggestions. This work will be an excellent resource for both the researcher and the clinician. It adds to our understanding of dyslexia and how real people cope with this devastating condition.

REFERENCES

Blanchard, P. (1928) 'Reading disabilities in relationship to maladjustment.' *Mental Hygiene, 12*, 772–788.

Lewis., R, Strauss, A. and Lehtinen, L. (1951) *The Other Child: The Brain-Injured Child.* New York, NY: Grune and Stratton.

Orton, S.T. (1937) *Reading, Writing and Speech Problems in Children.* New York, NY: Norton and Co.

Willcutt, E. and Gaffney-Brown, R. (2004) Etiology of dyslexia, ADHD and related difficulties. *Perspectives, 30*, 12–15.

Michael is a clinical psychologist specialising in both child and adult psychotherapy. He began his career as a special education teacher in a preventive programme for dyslexic children. He completed his clinical training at Colorado State University and the Devereux Foundation. He developed one of the first college programmes for learning disabled students at Colorado State in 1980. He was educational director of Larimer County Mental Health in Fort Collins, Colorado.

Since that time he has been in full-time private practice. Specialising in learning disabilities and attention deficit disorders, Dr Ryan has lectured and published widely on learning disabilities, attention deficit disorders (ADD) and testing and measurement. He has taught at the graduate level at Aquinas College and has been on the editorial board of Annals of Dyslexia since 1985.

He is the former vice president of the International Dyslexia Association and the current president of the Michigan branch of the International Dyslexia Association. Furthermore, he has been a consultant to the governor of Michigan, the Michigan Department of Education and the Air Force Academy.

www.dyslexiadx.com

FOREWORD

Pennie Aston

When I trained as a counsellor I had not yet been diagnosed as being neuro-diverse. I had enjoyed a very varied, creative career that had been extremely fulfilling but somewhere in the murky depths of my heart lay an injured student trying to work out why she just could not pass exams. You do not need exams to be a performer, or a gardener, or a presenter or any of the various other occupations that wove decade by decade into the tapestry of my working life. You do however need to pass them for counselling. You need to write lots of long essays, be able to explain yourself articulately, and be able to remember lots of names, dates and jargon. Somehow I managed. The spare room for the revision period was turned into a mini-library, the family was expunged for a fortnight, the walls got covered in mind maps and I devised mnemonics and cartoons that helped me to remember. I was one of the lucky ones – a stealth dyslexic. Although not able to learn in the way I was taught at school, I was bright enough to have devised different strategies through the years so that, when I was in a calm state of mind, I was able to learn and relearn so that facts and figures stayed in my memory. I also had the support of my family both financially and practically to be able to take time off to apply myself without distraction.

As my career progressed and different pressures and demands arose, I slowly realised that dyslexia is so much more than a difficulty with reading and writing. It can impinge on every aspect of life and have a devastating and long-term effect on self-esteem. As a parent of a now grown up dyslexic child I have watched and learned as strategy after strategy assisted being able to read and write, but no strategy existed to enable understanding of or do anything about the sense of isolation, the different way of processing information, or to deal with the incremental anger at misunderstandings and judgements meted out past, present and – anticipated with great anxiety – the future.

The emotional repercussions of dyslexia can be presented in so many convoluted ways because it is so idiosyncratic. It is understandable that non-dyslexic people are more comfortable considering it as no more inconvenient than 'being a bit short-sighted' as one person told me. However, on a day-to-day basis many dyslexic people are dealing with a cocktail of poor concentration, memory lapses, emotional dysregulation and sensitivity to noise, light and texture. This lies in tandem with feelings of shame, embarrassment, guilt and fear of limitations being found out. At the same time, dyslexics can be inspiringly creative, often with an innate ability to problem solve and a vibrant visual recall. Being dyslexic is like being on a seesaw of ability and disability, never quite knowing when a mind full of ideas will disintegrate into a mind full of blankness and confusion. It is no wonder that many end up suffering from an unrelenting generalised anxiety that can escalate to full blown Post-Traumatic Stress Disorder, depression and despondency triggering adverse emotional coping strategies.

That is why I am so pleased that Neil is addressing this long ignored topic. As a counsellor specialising in the emotional repercussions of dyslexia, I believe dyslexia is inextricably woven into self-image, self-confidence and self-esteem. It impacts on everyone – not just the dyslexic. For the individual, it is trying to make sense of where they belong and are cherished in the world. For the parent, it is dealing with a child who either doesn't think the same way as you or presents with all the aspects you have worked so hard to overcome yourself. With no teacher training on dyslexia awareness, school can be a minefield of fighting for access to the right support, which challenges the teacher's faith in her ability to teach. The ravages of the emotional turmoil that can ensue may lead to seeking help from a counsellor. With no dyslexia awareness in counselling training, counsellors may well not appreciate what 'being dyslexic' may mean. Not in terms of literacy, but in terms of the emotional landscape that can be expressed through adverse emotional coping strategies. Understand the dyslexia. Understand the dyslexic person and you will understand the presentation.

Pennie is an expert counsellor, trainer and supervisor in addressing the emotional repercussions of dyslexia. An experienced and skilled facilitator of positive change in both individuals and organisations she has worked in the therapeutic arena since 1999, preceded by a 20-year career in television and the performing arts. As a result Pennie has exceptional understanding of the needs and dynamics of people, organisations and the relationships and structures within which they function, particularly where dyslexia can impact on behaviour and the emotions.

As a writer and speaker on the emotional repercussions of dyslexia and other neuro-diverse conditions, Pennie provides her services to a number of high profile clients in the corporate and not-for-profit sector, as well as to schools, further and higher education establishments. She is an independent provider of supervision and training to professionals on dyslexia awareness, professional conduct support in relation to dyslexia, dyslexia emotional support, one to one and group counselling. Pennie also provides forums for continuing professional development on a variety of topics from practitioner wellbeing through to creative artistic expression.

She is currently developing a programme on dyslexia awareness training for counsellors and counselling skills for dyslexia tutors, and is a presenter for dyslexic success and celebrated hub on creative dyslexia counselling.

www.grooops.com

INTRODUCTION

This book is the culmination of 15 years of my experience researching dyslexia and the emotional difficulties that can manifest as a result of dyslexia.

Whilst many would argue that dyslexia is a learning disorder or disability, others would argue that it's a learning difference, with the difference being what makes certain individuals stand out in society. Thus the question can be posed: is dyslexia formed by society or by neurological deficits – or, in other words, by 'nature or nurture'? This book aims to investigate this question as it is through perceptions, both those of the non-dyslexic members of society and the dyslexics themselves, that the image of the dyslexic is created.[1]

Everyone is concerned about their health, and mental health should be no different. The ability to deal with life's events in a balanced way is important. However, if life's events are perceived to be stacked against you, the ability to retain mental health is even more important. Life through a dyslexic's eyes can seem very unbalanced and their challenge to regain balance and develop positivity is a life-long journey.

This book begins by delving into what is dyslexia, and questions the varying definitions, diagnosis, prevalence, cognitive theories, assessment and, finally, interventions. What seems clear is that difficulties are present in 10–20 per cent of the general population, and whether it is called a reading disability or dyslexia, the learning deficit remains and the challenge educators face is to create best

1 The term 'a dyslexic' is used throughout this book as it is the term most dyslexics choose to describe themselves.

practice interventions to reduce negative behavioural or emotional manifestations.

Chapter 2 discusses the dyslexia lifespan, starting with preschool/ nursery, primary school, secondary school and all the way through to adulthood. As dyslexia cannot be cured, individuals develop a range of strategies to minimise difficulties, so on the surface they can seem symptom-free. However, the experience of growing up with dyslexia is made worse by a lack of public understanding and knowledge, which can delay identification, diagnosis and intervention, resulting in dyslexics suffering from educational and emotional neglect for most of their mandatory education.

Chapter 3 examines difference, disclosure, stigma and labelling. Dyslexics notice their differences very early on, and the fact that they learn differently, along with unfair comparison to non-dyslexic siblings, can mean the situation worsens. The chapter moves on to look at the issue of disclosure. Many children and, even more so, adults fear disclosure to friends, family and more importantly employers of their difficulties, which can trigger perception of or real discrimination in the workplace. Stigma is discussed, looking at how dyslexia is perceived in society, and how the lack of general knowledge about dyslexia can lead to discrimination and misunderstanding, increasing the effect of dyslexia on an individual's ability to perform tasks in the workplace.

Labelling can be both negative and positive for individuals, as externally a label can reduce opportunities offered, but internally a name for what has caused many years of hardship can aid improvements in self-image. In many cases it means that individuals can see they are not in fact stupid, but intelligent and misunderstood.

Chapter 4 looks at the dyslexia identity, as only through awareness of personal difficulties and a label can a negative personal identity be transformed into a positive one with an understanding that the difficulty/difference from dyslexia is not life limiting and that the person is more than just a misunderstood label.

Chapter 5 looks at self-belief in dyslexics. All individuals develop an image of themselves from a very young age, based on their self-perception (self-esteem) compared to the feedback they gain from others. On entry to school dyslexics are faced with peers and teachers who are able to outperform them on even basic tasks, and they see themselves as lacking. Shame, self-esteem and dyslexia are discussed, looking at how dyslexics begin to withdraw to defend themselves as they are different and unable to attain the same educational achievements as their peers.

Chapter 6 focuses on understanding how dyslexics experience threats and manifest fear of situations. Stress is caused by trying to reach the perceived average standards and falling short in many cases, and dyslexics feel anxiety at the thought of similar situations that may present themselves, especially in school, highlighting their difficulties, e.g. reading aloud in class. Anxiety can severely affect an individual's ability to try new tasks in an environment that has been threatening in the past (e.g. the school classroom).

Chapter 7 presents research on how dyslexics cope at a range of ages and in various situations. From early on there are dyslexics who are supported as learners and will not see any barrier to their potential; other groups, however, tend to recognise their difference and will withdraw from threatening situations leading to self-created isolation, depression and, in some cases, mental illness. The third general group is more pragmatic and will, with the help of parents, develop non-academic abilities to offset any difficulty in school. Such individuals develop high self-esteem through mastery of skills that others find difficult, e.g. art and design, engineering, sports, music and drama. These are the skills that need to be nurtured to develop satisfying and suitable careers for dyslexics.

With an understanding of dyslexia provided by the earlier chapters, in Chapter 8 the reader is then led to a discussion of defence mechanisms and coping strategies, their theoretical background and how they relate to dyslexics, both children and adults. A hypothetical 'dyslexia defence mechanisms' (DDM) model is provided to help readers understand both the emotional and behavioural coping mechanisms that dyslexics commonly use in response to learning threats.

Chapter 9 looks at the pre-defence mechanisms, which, according to the DDM are used as the first line of defence in dyslexics who feel threatened whilst learning. In many cases this is enough to let the dyslexic perform as per their peers, however, camouflaging their true potential, hidden by difficulty in spelling difficult words.

Chapter 10 discusses emotional defences – one of the two main defence mechanisms in dyslexics, according to the DDM. These are broken down into mature, immature and extreme mechanisms, and the chapter investigates how emotionally dyslexics cope with threats. Regression and hypochondria are used as immature mechanisms to return to a safer, less threatening time in their lives when they were cared for as infants. Research evidence is presented on extreme mechanisms, with self-harm and attempted suicide being extreme means used to regain some control over their lives.

Next, Chapter 11 examines behavioural defences as, according to the DDM, they offer alternative means to deal with perceived threats in the forms of task avoidance, distraction and school refusal/ school phobia to avoid threatening situations and tasks at school. In extreme cases, the dyslexic uses criminal activities and drug abuse to deal with a society, building (e.g. schools) or individuals (e.g. teachers) they feel threatened by or excluded from.

Chapter 12, on Vulnerability to Depression, discusses the nature vs nurture argument. It looks at risk and resilience being two sides of the same coin, and whether there are risk factors (e.g. genetic, environmental, educational) that may affect a dyslexic's vulnerability to depression. Tackling hopelessness as a risk factor to depression is also discussed as a means of producing a positive life journey.

Chapter 13 looks at learned helplessness and resilience, with the aim of understanding why many dyslexics, both children and adults, withdraw and perceive themselves as unable to cope with a word-based society that holds literacy and academic achievement in such high regard. As a solution, the development of resilience through conversational attributional readjustment is proposed in the face of continual failure; as a means to compartmentalise their difficulties from global to specific, so that individuals can be transformed into those who experience success, and can plan self-improvement for continual high self-esteem.

Chapter 14 wraps up the book with a discussion and conclusion chapter. It pulls the book together linking the mechanism of self-preservation used by children with the need for parents to uncover their child's difficulties for teachers to see. It also proposes that schools take an active role in supporting the emotional effects of learning failure.

The appendix provides some details of the author's book *Dyslexia and Depression: The Hidden Sorrow*, from which came many of the quotations used in this book. It is a study of 29 dyslexic adults, looking at their life stories and how they have coped despite or because of their dyslexia. Quotes from this study are used throughout this book, and you may refer to this Appendix to gain greater understanding of the methodology used to gain such quotes and data (qualitative and quantitative).

As a final note, the book details the struggles that many dyslexics face throughout their lives, but specifically as children in mainstream education. Whilst many profiles of suffering are indicated, it is only through books such as this that lay bare how dyslexics are tortured by society (perceived or real), that dyslexics will be better understood.

Many dyslexics do not talk about their educational neglect, they keep quiet as they are ashamed that they suffered in an environment that most succeeded in. Only through talking, as many of my research participants did, will their stories be heard and healing can begin.

I would like to thank my wife and children for their understanding. Whilst they are not dyslexic themselves, they have seen how dyslexia can affect those around them, in so many illogical ways.

Chapter 1

WHAT IS DYSLEXIA?

INTRODUCTION

This chapter will review the condition called dyslexia; although it is also known by a number of other terms, it is agreed that it affects skills such as short-term memory, reading, writing and spelling. The chapter reviews definitions of dyslexia, its causes, identification paths and possible interventions. However, this is only a start to understanding the various facets that make up an individual with dyslexia.

What is clear is the lack of clarity on what dyslexia is, which leads to a lack of understanding in the wider community.

THEORETICAL CONSIDERATIONS

Dyslexia seems to be going through an identity crisis at the moment, and this stems from differing definitions of the condition. Even using the term 'condition' is likely to antagonise stakeholders as many see dyslexia as a disability, while others see it as a learning difference.

The word 'dyslexia' was first coined by Rudolf Berlin, a professor of comparative ophthalmology in Stuttgart, Germany (Wagner 1973), to describe a word blindness, from the Greek roots 'Dys', meaning difficulty and 'Lexia', with words. In 1886 Pringle Morgan documented the term and condition in the *British Medical Journal* (Snowling 1996). Since then numerous medical and educational professionals have sought to understand the condition, its origins, its cause or causes and its treatment.

The term dyslexia is argued to be problematic as it is not universally used; with other terms also used to define reading difficulties:

- specific reading retardation
- reading difficulties
- specific reading difficulties
- reading disability
- learning disability
- unexpected reading difficulty
- specific learning difficulties.

Brown *et al.* (2011, p.296) argue 'that without an agreed definition that can be implemented reliably and validly, understanding the nature, causes and best treatment for reading difficulty is unlikely. Similarly, an agreed definition is essential for practice'.

If researchers, educators and practitioners can't agree on a name for the condition, then it will be hard to combine research due to disagreements about the origin of the difficulties. Rice and Brooks (2004) and Fitzgibbon and O'Connor (2002) agree that a universally agreed definition and explanation remain elusive. Fitzgibbon and O'Connor suggest definitions to date have been subjective and too broad, and serve self-obsessive purposes. Let us now examine the difficulties.

MEDICAL DEFINITION

A medical definition can be found in Stein (2001):

> A complex biologically-rooted behavioural condition resulting from impairment of reading-related processes (phonological skills, automatized lexical retrieval and verbal short-term memory, in any combination) and manifest in difficulties related to the mastery of reading up to the level of population norms under the condition of adequate education and a normal development environment. (p.24)

Stein clearly points to adequate education and a normal development environment as key aspects of the diagnosis process; however, both are highly subjective and what constitutes adequate and normal is open to debate. The cause has been linked to biological factors causing impairment, however, it is through manifestation that it is recognised; thus impairment must cause a delay before diagnosis is possible – a child must fail before help is even considered.

CONTINUUM

The definition by Dyslexia Action (2013) describes dyslexia as having both descriptive and causal factors:

> Dyslexia is a specific type of learning difficulty that primarily affects the skills involved in accurate and fluent word reading and spelling. Characteristics of dyslexia include difficulties in areas such as phonological awareness, verbal memory and verbal processing speed. Dyslexia is best thought of as a continuum, not a distinct category and there are no clear cut-off points... It is biological in origin and is defined as a lack of phonological awareness, which is an ability to convert letter combinations to sounds and vice versa.

The concept of a 'continuum' without any 'cut-off points' is unhelpful in the assessment of a condition, and lends a hand to those who question the ability to define a condition that many see as being indistinct from general poor reading ability (Elliot and Grigorenko 2014).

The Rose Report (Rose 2009), a UK-sponsored government report on dyslexia (specific learning difficulty – SpLD), is perceived by many to be an influential review of available literature, and defines dyslexia as 'a learning difficulty that: primarily affects the skills in accurate and fluent word reading and spelling'.

The Rose Report goes into more detail:

- Characteristic features of dyslexia are difficulties in phonological awareness, verbal memory and verbal processing speed.
- Dyslexia occurs across the range of intellectual abilities. It is best thought of as a continuum, not a distinct category, and there are no clear cut-off points.

- Co-occurring difficulties may be seen in aspects of language, motor co-ordination, mental calculation, concentration and personal organisation, but these are not by themselves markers of dyslexia.
- A good indication of the severity and persistence of dyslexia difficulties can be gained by examining how the individual responds or has responded to well-founded intervention.

(Rose 2009)

However, this report has been criticised in the UK parliament as being 'so broad and blurred at the edges that it is difficult to see how it could be useful in any diagnostic sense' (House of Commons 2009, para 71, p.26).

Fletcher and Lyon (2010) offer three primary reasons why dyslexia is hard to define:

1. Dyslexia is an 'unobservable construct' meaning that attempts to measure it are imperfect and people suffering from the disorder cannot objectively report it.
2. Dyslexia is 'dimensional' meaning that there are varying degrees to which individuals may experience difficulty, from minor, severe and in between the two.
3. There is great disagreement from practitioners and psychologists about what characteristics to include and exclude.

(Fletcher and Lyon 2010)

Whilst there is general consensus that the core difficulty in dyslexia is difficulty decoding text, Fletcher (2009) contends that in dyslexics their difficulty tends to be with decoding 'single words', whereas those with general reading difficulty have fluency and/or comprehension problems, but not with single words. Dyslexics are affected by all these aspects and experience a 'bottle-neck' of problems coping with text. The emphasis on single words is based on dyslexics being unable to cope well without continuous text and semantic and syntactic knowledge to help them decode words (Fletcher 2009; Vellutino *et al.* 2004).

UNEXPECTED DIFFICULTIES

The definition by the US National Institute of Child Health and Human Development (US-ICHHD) is more detailed:

> Dyslexia is a specific learning disability that is neurological in origin. It is characterized by difficulties with accurate and/or fluent word recognition and by poor spelling and decoding abilities. These typically result from a deficit in the phonological component of language that is often unexpected in relation to other cognitive abilities and the provision of effective classroom instruction. Secondary consequences may include problems in reading comprehension and reduced reading experience that can impede growth of vocabulary and background knowledge. (Lyon, Shaywitz and Shaywitz 2003)

This definition states the difficulty is phonological at root, and must be compared to normal abilities. Whilst it is possible to measure the phonological deficit in relation to the individual's other cognitive abilities using standardised instruments, the measurement of 'effective classroom instruction' is extremely hard to measure and there is no standardised way to teach. So in this case 'effective' is a subjective judgement.

Stanovich (1992) suggests that definitions are generally designed to serve different groups:

- scientific definitions follow strict scientific criteria for research
- education definitions determine the allocation of additional education resources
- advocacy definitions aim to gain formal legislative support.

(Stanovich 1992)

SPECIFIC LEARNING DISORDER

Each definition above is robust to a different degree; however, they are unhelpful to educators and to those who aim to compare a single condition across a broad population sample.

The draft revision to the fifth version of the American Psychiatric Association's (APA) 'Diagnostic and Statistical Manual (DSM-V)' originally suggested the term 'learning disorder' should be replaced with 'dyslexia' to 'render APA terminology consistent with international use', describing 'difficulties in reading accuracy or fluency that are not consistent with the person's chronological age, educational opportunities, or intellectual abilities'. However, its final version (APA 2013) now uses 'Specific Learning Disorder', based on the reasoning that there are disagreements in the international conceptions and understandings of dyslexia (and other conditions) (Tannock in Elliot and Grigorenko 2014). It is argued by Elliot and Grigorenko (2014) that attempts to find a single definition have been hampered by factors of inclusivity, some definitions have been criticised as being too inclusive and others too exclusive.

APA (2013, factsheet) reasons that the new term:

> is now a single, overall diagnosis, incorporating deficits that impact academic achievement. Rather than limiting learning disorders to diagnoses particular to reading, mathematics and written expression, the criteria describe shortcomings in general academic skills and provide detailed specifiers for the areas of reading, mathematics, and written expression.

The APA (2013, factsheet) definition notes:

> Specific learning disorder is diagnosed through a clinical review of the individual's developmental, medical, educational, and family history, reports of test scores and teacher observations, and response to academic interventions. The diagnosis requires persistent difficulties in reading, writing, arithmetic, or mathematical reasoning skills during formal years of schooling. Symptoms may include inaccurate or slow and effortful reading, poor written expression that lacks clarity, difficulties remembering number facts, or inaccurate mathematical reasoning.

POLITICAL DRIVERS

Kauffman, Hallahan and Lloyd (1998, p.276) argue that strong political drivers have 'overwhelmed' scientific considerations, which has resulted in terminology that is 'defined loosely and treated unsystematically'. Rice and Brooks (2004) agree that dyslexia is not one clear thing but many, with the term serving as a conceptual clearinghouse for a variety of difficulties, deficits and causes.

COMPENSATORY DYSLEXICS

The British Psychological Society's (BPS) working party's operational definition for practioners linked accuracy with fluency:

> Dyslexia is evident when accurate and fluent word reading and/or spelling develops very incompletely or with great difficulty. This focuses on literacy learning at the word level and implies that the problem is severe and persistent despite appropriate learning opportunities. (Reason *et al.* 1999, p.64)

Thomson (2002, 2003) is critical of the BPS definition as it downplays the importance of diagnosis compared to helping to choose the most suitable personalised intervention. Cooke (2001, p.49) contests that the BPS definition would discount those who have overcome literacy/reading difficulties, thus many might lose the dyslexia diagnosis whilst still suffering from other difficulties, e.g. short-term memory deficits, disorganisation, difficulties completing forms and writing, etc. Cooke notes that these individuals are sometimes misguidedly called 'compensated dyslexics' as they lack core difficulties or, as the label might suggest, have developed advanced compensational strategies to overcome core difficulties.

STRENGTHS AND WEAKNESSES

The Miles Dyslexia Centre (2010) set up by Tim Miles (the most famous British researcher of dyslexia) defines dyslexia as:

> a combination of abilities and difficulties which affect the learning process in one or more of: reading, spelling, writing, and sometimes numeracy/language. Dyslexics have weaknesses in the following areas: memory, processing speed, short-term memory, visual perception, auditory perception, spoken language, and motor skills.

It also stresses that 'in place of weaknesses, dyslexics are gifted with creative or oral skills, and that the impairment occurs regardless of socio-economic or linguistic backgrounds'. The above definition notes strengths (that could be seen as compensatory) as well as weaknesses, and that any impairment is regardless of economical and linguistic experiences.

EDUCATIONAL AND SOCIAL NEGLECT

Tonnessen (1995) argues for better definitions of dyslexia, to embody symptoms, causality or prognosis. Hence the observable and measureable signs of underlying conditions and processes should be used for diagnosis, rather than cognitive deficits (measured through psychometric measures).

Heaton and Winterton (1996) note the many factors that could cause a child to experience difficulties when learning:

- low intelligence
- socio-economic disadvantage
- inadequate schooling
- physical disability (e.g. visual or hearing difficulties)
- visible neurological impairment going beyond reading and writing
- emotional and behavioural difficulties affecting attention concentration and responsiveness to teacher direction
- dyslexia.

(Heaton and Winterton 1996)

Dyslexics are affected by a range of the above factors, e.g. the Rose Report details the inability to respond to well-founded intervention. Whilst this is a very subjective definition, it is not beyond intellectual argument that children educated in inner-city schools or in families with socio-economic disadvantages would have worse access to good or excellent education. Evidence (Alexander-Passe 2006, 2008; Edwards 1994; Scott 2004) points to children manifesting emotional and behavioural problems owing to unsuitable/undifferentiated teaching in schools, and being misdiagnosed as having behavioural difficulties without teachers examining the core reasons for their adverse behaviour.

Tannock in Elliot and Grigorenko (2004) argues that most of Heaton and Winterton's criteria are problematic as each could be related to dyslexia:

- Low intelligence – dyslexia is commonly diagnosed in individuals with low reading IQ compared to a normal or above average general IQ level.
- Socio-economic disadvantage – as noted above, negative environmental circumstances, reduced access to resources and low levels of parental education are known to have a strong impact on a child's language and literacy development (Hartas 2011; Wolf 2007). It would be unfair to only diagnose dyslexia based on the differential expectations, perceptions and access to additional support that would result and the predicted judgements based on a child's life experiences.
- Inadequate schooling – this is a subjective statement based on the school curriculum, approaches to teaching/learning, the perceived skill of the teaching staff, quality of the learning environment and parental support to support the school's work (Taylor *et al.* 2010a).
- Physical disability (e.g. visual or hearing difficulties such as glue ear are known to correlate with dyslexia in young dyslexics).
- Visible neurological impairment going beyond reading and writing.
- Emotional and behavioural difficulties affecting attention concentration and responsiveness to teacher direction – there are correlations between dyslexia and attention deficit and hyperactivity disorder (ADHD) (Gilger, Pennington and DeFries 1992; Mayes and Calhoun 2006), with many dyslexics manifesting attentional difficulties made worse by poor/undifferentiated teaching practices.

SECONDARY EFFECTS

There is a growing argument that for too long the main focus has been on the cause or causes of dyslexia, and there has been little focus on understanding the effects of having such a long-term disorder (their experiences/secondary effects), especially in adults.

Along with managing these long-term effects (Armstrong 2011 ; Fitzgibbon and O'Connor 2002; McLoughlin, Leather and Stringer 2002; Morgan and Klein 2003), using the secondary effects as part of the diagnosis criteria would bring the following advantages:

- describing the recognisable/observable behaviours seen, thus helping dyslexics to be referred for screening/diagnosis
- acknowledging that dyslexia is more than difficulty acquiring literacy skills
- offering an emotional/affective dimension to the disorder.

MOTIVATION

The US National Research Council (US-NRC) (Snow, Burns and Griffin 1998) identifies three reasons for reading difficulties:

1. Difficulties of understanding and using the alphabetic principle in order to develop accurate and fluent reading.
2. Poor acquisition of the verbal knowledge and strategies important to comprehend written material.
3. A lack of motivation to read.

(Snow *et al.* 1998)

Morgan *et al.* (2008) argue that dyslexia falls into the first and third categories as a byproduct of the difficulties poor readers face in education. Catts and Adlof (2011) suggest a bidirectional link between reading and motivation; where high-engagement reading-related activities can be a factor in reducing reading difficulties in children.

The US-NRC definition, according to Rice and Brooks (2004, p.33) poses a critical question. Not whether dyslexics differ from 'normal' readers, but are dyslexic individuals different from 'poor readers'?

CREATIVITY/DIVERGENT ABILITIES

For more than two decades, research has been carried out to identify positive attributes of this disorder; these investigations began with biographical and neurological studies. West (1991) located famous and influential individuals who had school learning difficulties, yet had found alternative ways of learning and succeeded in life (e.g. Albert Einstein, Leonardo da Vinci), making correlations between these factors and dyslexia, and creativity. Thus, public perception of creativity amongst dyslexics has grown (e.g. 712,000 hits on Google). Since West, the use of famous names with dyslexia (e.g. Charles Schwab, Richard Branson, Tom Cruise, Richard Rogers, etc.) has become widespread (BBC News 2006; General Communication Headquarters 2006; Davis Dyslexia Association International 2015; International Dyslexia Association 2006; McLoughlin, Fitzgibbon and Young, 1994; National Literacy Trust 2015) to illustrate the career heights that dyslexics can reach.

Alexander-Passe (2012a) discusses the positive side of dyslexia. Contributing authors such as Thomas West tell of dyslexics having amazing abilities. Dyslexics can do well in business (e.g. Sir Richard Branson), in architecture (e.g. Lord Richard Rogers), as actors (e.g. Tom Cruise), in finance (e.g. Charles Schwab) and science (for example Albert Einstein, Thomas Edison). Sometimes it seems it's 'trendy' to be dyslexic, but only when you have made it. Climbing up the greasy pole, it's not cool to be dyslexic. However, in certain industries, e.g. computer gaming, companies actually prefer to employ dyslexics and will openly advertise for them as they have been known to think in 3D and can problem-solve in their heads without the need for actual construction or electrical/programming systems.

Many dyslexics are good at business and have succeeded well beyond the levels of 'normal' people. Sir Richard Branson is an excellent example of a brilliant dyslexic, who used his eccentric personality to spearhead a new way of selling music, dealing with music artists, and creating a luxury airline brand that other airlines follow. Whilst being severely dyslexic and avoiding reading and writing, he has found a team that supports him in his work. Not only is he creative in business, but creative in finding the best people to support him.

Research has tried and failed to highlight any inert creative/divergent abilities in dyslexics. However, critics argue that measures to assess such skills are paper-based and therefore put the dyslexic at a disadvantage, hence they are not good indicators of their inert abilities.

Gerber, Ginsberg and Reiff (1992) noted that 'learned creativity' was one of the characteristics of the highly successful dyslexic, using problem solving and devising compensating strategies to address their weaknesses. Other external factors in dyslexics succeeding at work are 'goodness of fit' and the seeking and use of support systems.

However, this could be misleading and could give false hopes to parents, as a high proportion of dyslexics leave full-time education with few or no qualifications (Grant 2010).

DIAGNOSIS

Moving towards a practice-based definition, common symptoms of dyslexia include:

- difficulties in phonological awareness
- poor short-term (or working) verbal memory
- poor ordering and sequencing
- weak spelling
- clumsiness
- a poor sense of rhythm
- difficulty with rapid information processing
- poor concentration
- inconsistent hand preference
- impaired verbal fluency
- poor phonic skills
- frequent letter reversals
- poor capacity for mental calculations
- difficulties with speech and language
- low self-image
- anxiety when being asked to read aloud.

Elliott and Gibbs (2008) and Rice and Brooks (2004), however, warn against using such a list of symptoms for diagnosis, as many poor readers and others with reading problems could be grouped together and misdiagnosed as dyslexic. Siegel and Lipka (2008) add that the same variables could be measured by different researchers in different ways, thus it is hard to establish they are measuring the same concept. Thus, can comparisons of such samples/studies really be meaningful?

Another factor that should be considered is that symptoms of dyslexia may differ according to an individual's age, thus difficulties at preschool would be different to those at primary/secondary school, and then again in adulthood. Each stage faces different literacy demands, adding to the complexity of diagnosis and intervention. The Rose Report identifies three core difficulties: weakness in phonological awareness; weakness in verbal memory; and weakness in verbal processing speed. Again none of these alone or together is enough for diagnosis.

Before getting to the nuts and bolts of diagnosis, it should be noted that dyslexia is seen as a dimension rather than a categorical diagnosis (Pennington and Bishop 2009; Snowling 2008). The Rose Report states:

> Until recently, a child was deemed to either have or have not dyslexia. It is now recognised that there is no sharp dividing line between having a learning difficulty such as dyslexia and not having it. (Rose 2009, p.33)

Elliot and Grigorenko (2004) argue that such a statement, along with a later one in their report 'accurate diagnosis can be made by specialists', is perplexing. The problem is: if dyslexia isn't a distinct category, then it cannot easily be diagnosed.

Compared to other disabilities, dyslexia lacks a medical means of diagnosis. Whilst magnetic resonance imaging (MRI) and computerised tomography (CT) scanning and DNA research is ongoing (Dyslexia Research Trust 2014), and has been for more a decade, there is little progress in creating a medical diagnosis route. The lack of a clear diagnosis route has meant large variants in diagnosis rates, and this will be discussed at a later point.

IQ

Until recently there was a generally agreed route of diagnosis based on IQ (Fletcher *et al.* 2007; Shaywitz 1998), normally a discrepancy between verbal IQ (verbal comprehension and working memory) and performance IQ (perceptual organisation and processing speed); based on a discrepancy model to identify if a child's reading was poorer than his cognitive ability. It was believed until quite recently that those with dyslexia differed from poor readers in terms of IQ measurement. Both groups have difficulties reading, but dyslexics have normal or higher than normal IQ levels, and poor readers have low IQs. This created the hypothesis, reported on by the media, that dyslexia was a middle class syndrome of high IQ children – thus, a child with dyslexia was bright, but struggled in some areas.

The ACID profile was popular with educational psychologists in the 1980s to 1990s. This noted that dyslexics scored low in the arithmetic, coding, information and digit span subtests of the Weschler Intelligence Scales for Children (WISC-R) (Vargo, Grosser and Spafford 1995). The WISC-R was the most commonly used diagnostic tool used by educational psychologists – the only specialists allowed to diagnose dyslexia. If the ACID profile scores were lower than those of the other subscales, then dyslexia was diagnosed. Alternatively, Kaufman (1994) supported a SCAD profile, with the symbol search subtests replacing the information measure, but the ACID profile was more accepted, and seen as the recommended standard.

It was argued that individuals with high IQs would be receptive to specialised intervention, whereas those with low IQs would not, as Sir Cyril Burt, England's first school psychologist noted:

> Capacity must obviously limit content. It is impossible for a pint jug to hold more than a pint of milk and it is equally impossible for a child's educational attainment to rise higher than his educable capacity. (Cited in Elliott and Grigorenko 2014, p.19)

Thus many poor readers of lower IQ were not diagnosed as dyslexics and subsequent help was denied. However, it is now generally accepted that IQ has little diagnostic value in identifying dyslexia (British Psychological Society in Reason *et al.* 1999; Frederickson 1999; Ward *et al.* 1995). This came about in part due to a change in understanding of dyslexia based on its phonological/word recognition core aspects rather than memory.

The National Institute of Neurological Disorders and Strokes supports such a view, defining dyslexia as:

> A brain-based type of learning disability that specifically impairs a person's ability to read. These individuals typically read at levels significantly lower than expected of them, despite having normal intelligence (IQ). (NINDS 2010, para.1)

Vellutino *et al.*'s (2004) empirical review supported this view, concluding that 'intelligence tests have little use diagnosing specific reading difficulties' and advising that practitioners should move from using cognitive/biological psychometric measures, towards assessments aiding educational and remedial activities. Thus, there has been a significant change in diagnosis methodology, which has, according to some, dented the rigour of dyslexia diagnosis – not just through using non-professional standardised measures, but by allowing diagnosis by lower qualified educational practitioners (e.g. specialised teachers).

Modern diagnostic dyslexia reports undertaken by a specialised teacher have the following features:

Advantages

- The addition of specialist teachers to assess dyslexics as well as educational psychologists could mean that more children can be assessed.
- The price of assessments could drop based on supply and demand.
- Greater examples are given of the individual's range of difficulties.
- Teachers are given concrete examples of difficulty rather than a psychometric score.
- Teachers are given intervention direction and guidance for phonological skills programmes.
- Assessment training is focused on dyslexia rather than a broad range of learning difficulties.

Disadvantages

- The assessment takes much longer as a wider range of measures is used.
- Assessments are hard to compare nationally as measures of assessment vary.
- Training for specialised teachers is shorter and is at a master's rather than a doctorate level.
- As specialised teachers are mainly trained in dyslexia, they lack the ability to test for other co-morbidly occurring conditions (e.g. language disorders, ADHD, social, emotional and behavioural difficulties (SEBD), etc.), which can have an impact on a child's learning.

UNEXPECTED DEFICITS

As noted before when looking at definitions, 'unexpected deficit... from effective classroom instruction' is a subjective term featuring in Lyon *et al.* (2003), the Rose Report (2009) and the British Psychological Society (Reason *et al.* 1999) definitions.

One could argue that such an element in the diagnosis of dyslexics rather than poor readers could be defined as environmental. As yet there is no biological assessment route for dyslexia, thus some experts are beginning to question the basis of dyslexia (Elliott and Grigorenko 2014). If educational environmental experiences differ between these two learning difficulties, how should this be measured? Tonnessen (1995) argues that maybe dyslexia should be diagnosed based on an individual's progress.

Fuchs and Fuchs (2009) suggest this would mean the diagnosis would have a reduced focus on levels of functioning in relation to an individual's strength and weaknesses, and an increased focus on a child's failure to respond to standard and validated instruction.

This approach to teaching is defined as 'response to intervention' (RTI) and is used in schools as an intervention method in both the USA and the UK. RTIs are defined as:

- WAVE 1: Intervention by the teacher in a classroom setting, e.g. extra mentoring and/or seating for normal curriculum tasks.

- WAVE 2: Small group work to assist the learner, e.g. literacy or numeracy booster sessions.
- WAVE 3: One to one remedial interventions by a specialised literacy/special educational needs (SEN) teacher.

The above is helpful in aiding understanding of how students 'perceived as at risk of dyslexia or reading difficulties' might gain help, and students would move up the WAVE pathway depending on need; however, this list does little to define the concept of 'effective instruction'. It is still within the scope of individual schools and teachers to assess the most suitable interventions for students.

Returning to the Rose Report (2009), it notes that dyslexia is a continuum and, like autism, very few individuals have the same difficulties. If reviewing the list of symptoms at the start of the chapter, one could imagine that if individuals have a little bit of this and a little bit of that, as well as a few other symptoms it would be hard for any intervention programme to remediate all difficulties. Thus the conclusion that a student is not making expected progress lies wholly within the teacher's professional judgement.

This 'guesswork' around the correct intervention methods is heavily critised by Reynolds and Shaywitz (2009), and is argued by Kavale, Spaulding and Beam (2009) to be conceptually flawed, inadequate for practice and politically, rather than scientifically, motivated. It is also argued that by using such a model, bright children who score to a commensurate level but below their potential might be overlooked.

Reynolds and Shaywitz (2009) suggest that removing scientific/psychometric measurement assessments from the diagnosis process falls into the realms of subjectivity and uses a model that requires all children assessed to fail to read for the same reasons, whereas there may be a number of educational/environmental factors that can impact on a learner. Fletcher and Vaughn (2009) amongst others are critical of the above argument as they believe cognitive profiling does little to assist in the intervention of individuals.

It is argued that using the RTI model, students would be labelled 'learning disabled' rather than 'dyslexic', giving a label of 'resistance' to traditional learning strategies without reflecting on any underlying cognitive or biological difficulties. Similarly, McKenzie

(2010) argues that there are many reasons why an individual may not respond adequately to intervention, and that labelling a child with a learning disability if they do not respond to intervention is not scientifically or clinically justifiable (Hales *et al.* 2010). One could argue that the child just failed to respond to poorly differentiated teaching, thus the teacher is at fault and it is he or she who failed rather than the child.

PREVALENCE

As we have seen, there are differing definitions of dyslexia and differing assessment criteria, and prevalence rates of dyslexia also vary. As noted before, each definition is relevant to different groups: educators, advocates, researchers. Thus, depending on the definition adopted, different prevalence rates will result.

The Rose Report (2009) supports this in their literature review, which suggests that prevalence varies according to the definition adopted, cut-off rates in samples, and whether the samples came from clinical practice, schools or the population at large.

Reported prevalence rates can vary widely:

- Orton (1937), 10 per cent of the school population
- Shaywitz (1996), 20 per cent of children
- British Dyslexia Association (Crisfield 1996), 10 per cent mild and 4 per cent severe
- Shaywitz and Shaywitz (2005), 17.5 per cent is suggested from a longitudinal study
- Dyslexia Foundation of New Zealand (2008), 10 per cent of children
- International Dyslexia Association (2012), 20 per cent of the population have some symptoms
- National Institute of Child Health and Development (2007), 15–20 per cent of the US population
- Hulme and Snowling (2009), 3–6 per cent and 3–10 per cent of children
- Mather and Wendling (2012), 5–8 per cent of children
- Butterworth and Kovacs (2013), 4–8 per cent of children.

It is interesting that whilst studies by national/international organisations have high prevalence rates, those from expert researchers in the fields have much lower prevalence rates. Elliot and Grigorenko (2014) suggest national/international organisations base assessment on an individual scoring one standard deviation (SD) below normal values, as a subjective assessment of unexpected progress from standardised teaching methods. However, researchers tended to use 1.5 to 2 SD points below normal values for identification criteria.

Such a position is argued by MacMillan and Siperstein (2002) to result in some children failing to receive additional educational support that others with similar strengths and weaknesses might receive elsewhere. Also using standard deviation scores for assessment criteria will mean that a child may be diagnosed dyslexic in one test where 1 SD is used, but in a second test in another catchment area he will not, thus losing the label. Elliott and Grigorenko (2014) argue there is little agreement about cut-off points and the permanence of a dyslexia label.

Alternatively, as an individual's reading performance is relative to others, and can fluctuate over time, could a dyslexia diagnosis go and then come back? Were they cured or was the measurement faulty? If a child gained in literacy levels through hard work and positive effective interventions, should he/would he lose the label of dyslexia? If he did, his intervention/support would be removed and regression would be likely. Such a long-term start–stop approach based on achievement levels could be detrimental to a child's academic career.

GENDER

For a long time there has been a disagreement concerning gender differences in dyslexia (Chiu and McBride-Chang 2006), with a higher boy to girl ratio. Girls have been found to be better readers (Berninger *et al.* 2008); however, such a difference has not been found in native Spanish, Chinese and German children (Chan *et al.* 2006; Jiménez *et al.* 2007; Landerl and Moll 2010). The following studies support a higher ratio of dyslexic boys to girls with literacy deficits:

- Finucci and Childs (1981), 5.90:1
- Wolff and Melngalis (1994), 4.28:1
- Flannery *et al.* (2000), 1.5:1
- Katusic *et al.* (2001), 2.00 to 3.00:1
- Rutter *et al.* (2004), 3.19:1 to 1.39:1
- Liederman, Kantrowitz and Flannery (2005), 1.74 to 2.00:1
- Fletcher *et al.* (2007), 1.3:1 to 1.6:1.

Rimkute *et al.* (2014) suggest in a Finnish study that, whilst prevalence rates were similar in both genders, literacy difficulties have a more significant deleterious impact on boys. Shaywitz's (1996) longitudinal Connecticut study found that three to four times as many boys were identified as girls, with boys also manifesting co-morbid externalising (e.g. behavioural) disorders and attention seeking, whereas girls used internalising behaviours, were less obtrusive and thus were underdiagnosed (Pennington 2009). Bramlett *et al.* (2002) note that schools tend to refer students with conduct behaviours (typically found more in boys) over internalising disorders (typically found more in girls), thus supporting the underdiagnosed hypothesis.

To summarise, before examining different theories of dyslexia: dyslexia is not one single definable condition, but a collection of symptoms that create a diagnosis. The dyslexia community (educators, teachers, etc.) has moved from an IQ-based diagnosis to one based on manifestations, which aims to provide specialist teachers with recommended interventions.

There are numerous definitions of dyslexia, which not only hampers diagnosis, but has meant hundreds of thousands of individuals may have been denied the identification they need to gain help to reach their potential. Scott (2004) notes that many dyslexics only gain diagnosis when their own children are assessed; thus, many are only identified in adulthood.

Armstrong and Squires (2014) question the term 'diagnosis' regarding dyslexia, and prefer the term 'identified'. Pollak (2009) and Cooper (2009) argue that the term 'diagnosis' comes from a medical model of dyslexia, thus medical terminology; however, as current assessment models for dyslexia are educational in nature (assessment to advise on appropriate intervention) rather than medical (the use of psychometric measures), Armstrong suggests educational terminology would be more appropriate, and would be more in line with the social model of disability supported by legislation, e.g. the UK's Equality Act (HMSO 2010).

COGNITIVE THEORIES

The next section will examine a number of theories:

- phonological deficit
- rapid naming and the double deficit
- short-term and working memory
- low-level sensory processing (visual processing/magnocellular)
- attentional factors
- psych-motor processing.

PHONOLOGICAL DEFICIT

For the past 40 years the 'phonological deficit hypothesis' has been dominant (Stanovich 1988; Stanovich and Siegel 1994; Vellutino *et al.* 2004). Researchers of cognitive processing in children with reading difficulties found that three processes are significant in learning (phonological processing, short-term/working memory and processing speed), compared to typically achieving readers (Johnson and Babel 2010; Nicholson and Fawcett 2006).

Hulme and Snowling (2009) noted that this hypothesis originates with Pringle Morgan, considered by many to be the 'father of dyslexia'. Reading entails the segmentation of texts into tiny units of language called graphemes (letter sounds). Graphemes are then converted to phonemes (syllables), which then are joined to become complete sounds of words. For this to take place, the reader needs to assemble and address the phonology of a word. Dyslexics, according to this hypothesis, have difficulty with phonemic representations and phonemic recall due to poor short-term memory and other weaknesses in brain mapping. Hulme and Snowling go further to stress that language impairment affects the way the brain encodes and decodes phonological features of spoken words. They stress that the inability is not just in reading words, but also in reading accurately, rapidly (fluency) and with expression – as incorrect expression can lead to difficulties with spelling, as one affects the other.

Looking at these skills in more detail, they require (Duff, Hayiou-Thomas and Hulme 2012; Wagner and Torgesen 1987):

- phonological awareness
- verbal short-term memory
- slow retrieval of phonological information stored in the long-term memory, as found in rapid automatic naming tasks
- measures of phoneme awareness.

It is argued that children with dyslexia are hindered in reading due to faulty representation of speech sounds, which leads to problems in precise processing of spoken words. Without typical skills they develop fuzzy logic in their reading based on rough and unprecise mapping of sounds to words (Blachman 2000). Bradley and Bryant (1985) argue that weak phonological skills cause a child to have difficulties in linking the verbal and visual elements of words. Thus, Melby-Lervåg *et al.* (2012) argue that phonemic awareness is a strong predictor of reading development. However, Share (2008) counters this, suggesting that there is an overestimation of the importance of phonological/phonemic awareness in reading development. Other researchers note its importance for young learners, but not older ones (Furnes and Samuelsson 2010; Ziegler *et al.* 2010).

Corriveau, Goswami and Thomson (2010) found that children who join school with poor/no exposure to reading instruction tend to do worse in phonemic tasks; however, they improved when exposed to print, suggesting early experiences at home and in preschool are reflected in poor phonemic awareness – nurture rather than nature (Ramus and Szenkovits 2008).

Whilst many phonological interventions bring about improved reading skills, Olson (2011) questions the long-term effectiveness of such interventions, and suggests that a significant number of struggling readers find phonological intervention ineffective.

RAPID AUTOMATIC NAMING

Rapid automatic naming (RAN) is the ability to name quickly visual stimulus already known, such as letters, words, images, colours and sounds. Kirby *et al.* (2010) argue that naming speed is related to almost all aspects of reading; however, Savage (2004) contends that assessment of such skills is not consistent enough for the diagnosis of reading ability, although others beg to differ (Denckla and Rudel 1974; Wolf and Bowers 1999). Correlations to reading fluency seem strongest when stimuli are presented in a row rather than singularly (serial rather than discrete processing) and when there is oral production of the names of the stimulus rather than a non-verbal pen and paper response, according to Georgiou *et al.* (2013).

To conclude, measures of RAN are more predictive in younger and poorer readers, it is a skill that is still deficient in many children and adults (Pennington *et al.*, 1990; Vukovic, Wilson and Nash, 2004).

THE DOUBLE DEFICIT

Wolf and Bowers (1999) argue that dyslexics can be divided into three groups:

1. Those with phonological difficulties but with average naming speed.
2. Those with a rapid naming deficit but average phonological skills.
3. Those with both phonological and rapid naming difficulties.

According to this model, those with the double deficit have the most severe form of reading difficulties, found in a range of languages (Torppa *et al.*, 2013; Wolf, Bowers and Biddle 2000). However Vaessen, Gerretsen and Blomert (2009) and Ackerman *et al.* (2001) argue there is no difference between those with single and double deficits; they also raise doubt as to the existence of a subgroup of poor readers with naming speed deficits. Kirby *et al.* (2010) suggest such conflicting results come from differences in orthographies and study samples, as some studies use developing readers, whilst others use those with reading difficulties, with different cut-off points and age groupings being evident.

Manis, Doi and Bhadha (2000) and Sunseth and Bowers (2002) note the close association between rapid naming and reading fluency, rather than single-word identification and letter-sound decoding (phonological skill), although Fletcher *et al.* (2011) question this, and their earlier study (Fletcher *et al.*, 2007) notes that rapid naming was not a core element of dyslexia, thus poor readers who demonstrate difficulties solely in reading speed (rather than accuracy) would not necessarily be labelled dyslexic. As with phonological skills, there is much debate as to the nature and role of rapid naming in reading disability (Georgiou *et al.* 2013). Snowling and Hulme (1994) and Wagner and Torgesen (1987) suggest that rapid naming deficits are best seen as reflecting the underlying phonological deficit, but others criticise this as lumping together a number of rogue elements under the phonological category (Nicolson and Fawcett 2006).

Ziegler *et al.* (2010) conclude it is misleading to see RAN as an independent non-phonological component; however, it is agreed that it has a slight phonological element to it and it is this element that allows it to be a predictor of reading performance (Vaessen *et al.*, 2009).

SUMMARY OF THEORIES

Fletcher *et al.* (2007) suggest the historical research into dyslexia and the differences between poor readers and dyslexia has failed to date to locate a simplistic hypothesis of a single cause. Whilst the presence of a phonological deficiency is agreed by many, the nature and role of its underlying elements are still debated. Research is beginning to investigate the role of underlying auditory, visual and attentional factors in reading (Wallace 2009). Ramus and Ahissar's (2012) recent empirical review noted diverse theories without a single agreed explanation for the cognitive process deficits.

Due to the varying nature of dyslexia, Menghini *et al.* (2010) found only 18.3 per cent of dyslexics had a purely phonological deficit, whereas 76.6 per cent had phonological among other deficits (e.g. visual processing, selective and sustained attention, implicit learning and executive functioning); with 41 per cent demonstrating impairment in four or five types of tasks. Wilcutt *et al.*'s (2010) review agreed that phonological awareness was a strong predictor of reading disability.

Elliott and Grigorenko (2014, p.85) conclude 'there continues to be considerable disagreement about the nature, role and relevance of underlying cognitive processes in dyslexia. It is unsurprising, therefore, that the elaboration of a widely accepted casual model that can meaningfully inform educational intervention has proven to be elusive'. They go on to question the value of phonological interventions, even in young children, for sustained long-term benefit (Kearns and Fuchs 2013; Olson *et al.* 2011). Elliott and Grigorenko (2014, p.87) also note 'with the exception of phonological/ phonemic awareness research, studies have had little impact on the development of widely employed, and empirically supported, classroom-based or clinic-based educational interventions geared to address reading disability'.

ASSESSMENT

To date, a number of high profile UK court cases have highlighted the plight of a number of unidentified dyslexics, whose parents feel schools and local educational authorities (LEAs) have failed their child. Argument has centred on whether, if correct assessment and intervention had taken place, their child would have not suffered emotional distress and experienced a poor education. The UK's Children and Families Act (2014) makes education mandatory for children under the age of 16 years old, reinforcing the 'duty of care' teachers and schools have for their students – similar to the duty of care a parent has to protect against both emotional and educational neglect.

Elliott and Grigorenko (2014, p.124) suggest the following questions need to be asked:

- How can we best identify young children at risk of word reading difficulties and use this information to prevent later problems?
- What can be done to help those who are resistant to initial interventions?
- Is there anything special about specialist dyslexia teaching that is particularly effective for poor readers?

DYSLEXIA SCREENING

There are a number of screening measures for dyslexia, which tend to include a broader range of skills than traditional academic measures. The Dyslexia Early Screening Test (DEST) (Fawcett and Nicolson 1995) has 12 subtests to screen children between the ages of four and a half and six and a half years (other versions of this measure are suitable for primary and secondary school-aged children), these include measures of rapid naming, memory, shape copying, sound order, knowledge of upper and lower case letter names, postural stability and bead threading. Fawcett and Nicolson (1995, p.15) state that their measure of 'postural stability...is one of the best predictors of resistance to remediation'.

INTERVENTIONS

Vaughn and Roberts (2007) argue that interventions must enable individuals to catch up with their peers, and that the key elements of such a literacy programme should include:

- phonemic awareness
- phonics
- spelling/writing
- reading fluency
- vocabulary
- comprehension (reading and writing).

(Vaughn and Roberts 2007)

Elliott and Grigorenko (2014) found that over the past 20 years, numerous studies have investigated structured intervention one to one approaches for positive literacy outcomes, stressing the value of phonic-based approaches (Slavin *et al.* 2011). Interventions with less emphasis on phonics, e.g. Reading Recovery, were less effective in younger children and older struggling readers, where the use of phonics is perceived to have less impact (Flynn, Zheng and Swanson 2012).

Both Scanlon *et al.* (2005) and Scanlon *et al.* (2008) examined interventions for 'at risk' kindergarten children and found that two

30-minute sessions each week throughout the school year reduced the number of poor readers in the first grade. Elliott and Grigorenko suggest that:

> a powerful means of reducing treatment resistance is to provide modest amounts of small-group intervention in kindergarten before early differences in literacy skills are exacerbated by subsequent failure to profit from classroom instruction... followed up in the first grade by an intensive intervention with a particular focus on the development of phonological skills. (2014, p.137)

Slavin *et al.* (2011) suggest that such gains in literacy may not necessarily persist for the rest of a child's academic career unless they are maintained with structured interventions to cope with increasing literacy/phonological demands.

O'Connor *et al.* (2005) make a cautionary note that educators should allow for the changing academic demands on individual students and should be constantly vigilant to assist them in their school development, e.g. a child may not need help in primary school, but does need it in secondary school. This is where some SEN commentators argue for the need for a label so that this constant monitoring is required.

DYSLEXIA SUMMARY

- A hidden impairment (Riddick 2000).
- Has a neurological basis, but in practice it is hard to distinguish between a dyslexic and a poor reader.
- '*Medical* matter in *origin* and an *educational* matter in its *treatment*' (Miles and Miles 1990).
- A lack of suitable intervention can mean they are deemed as 'resistant to intervention', even though only inappropriate intervention was offered.
- Individuals can have a high or low IQ.
- There is no cure but correct interventions can teach strategies to overcome difficulties.

- Has a genetic basis, but only a 50 per cent variance, hence it is not guaranteed to be passed from one generation to the next (Nicolson 2005).
- There is no single agreed measure for use in diagnosis, thus a number of measurements are used to define a pattern of difficulties.
- There is no single agreed definition, as each group has a definition based on their own needs (political, scientific, etc.).
- There is no single agreed intervention to treat all dyslexics, as interventions are personalised.
- Diagnosis needs to move from the use of psychometric measures to those that will aid in selecting the correct choice of interventions.
- There is a public misconception that dyslexia only affects reading and writing. It also can affect organisation, short-term memory, motor skills, etc. It is argued by some that the name 'dyslexia' is unsuitable for the deficits it includes (Elliott and Grigorenko 2014; Fletcher 2009). The DSM-V lists dyslexia under 'Specific Learning Disorder', which may be a more suitable overall name.
- The label of dyslexia is perceived as a means to gain additional resources out of schools' tight budgets, along with more sensitivity towards these children, rather than teachers seeing them as lazy, unintelligent, unmotivated, etc.
- Dyslexics can develop negative coping strategies to hide/camouflage their difficulties, thus delaying receiving the interventions they need. These strategies can result in an incorrect behavioural label rather than the diagnosis of underlying educational deficit difficulty.
- Dyslexics are often misdiagnosed, misunderstood or ignored in schools (Steinberg and Andrist 2012).
- Dyslexics experience frustration, disappointment and anger due to being misunderstood in schools (Steinberg and Andrist 2012).

CONCLUSIONS

This chapter has investigated dyslexia from its definitions and origins to its broad range of interventions. Early diagnosis is vital, along with early intervention. Whilst dyslexia has been identified for over a century, there is still much debate and argument about its definition and intervention, resulting in many generations of dyslexics suffering from the lack of consensus.

KEY MESSAGES

- Aim to understand the particular strengths and weaknesses of each person with dyslexia, as no two dyslexics are alike.
- Dyslexia should be seen as a means rather than an end – it defines a learning difference, but it is not a life sentence of disability.
- Parents should encourage school-aged dyslexics to find subjects/sports/hobbies they are good at. In many cases they are very good at a particular subject, sport or hobby, surpassing the ability of their peers, e.g. design, creativity, car mechanics, etc. This is where dyslexics can come into their own and excel, which of course raises their self-esteem and self-worth.
- Educators should plan activities that will allow dyslexics to shine and should not rely on reading, writing and spelling to define academic success.

Chapter 2

A DYSLEXIC LIFE

INTRODUCTION

The young dyslexic growing up at home with his parents and family would ideally have been nurtured in a caring environment. Where there are no other siblings there is little comparison made by parents, and other family members may not have noticed any differences in ability compared with peers.

There are many persisting factors to dyslexia that occur from an early age to adulthood; according to the British Dyslexia Association (BDA) (2015) these include: obvious 'good' and 'bad' days, for no apparent reason; confusion between directional words, for example up/down, in/out; difficulty with sequence, e.g. coloured bead sequence, later on with days of the week or numbers; and a family history of dyslexia/reading difficulties.

This chapter will look at the lives dyslexics commonly lead, from their early years all the way to adulthood.

PRESCHOOL/NURSERY

As soon as a child enters nursery he will begin to compare himself to his peers, as educational professionals begin to teach the basic stepping stones for learning language. It is at this point that dyslexia may start to have an obvious effect on a child's life. The teacher will begin to notice difficulties in using basic language and remembering the building blocks to learning. Short-term memory deficits will mean the child forgets instructions or things learnt the lesson or day before; organisational and sequential difficulties will lead to confusion when carrying out tasks, data overload and getting required steps in the wrong order. The child may be clumsy, and frequently knock things over, which can cause embarrassment.

The effect of these early difficulties will mean the outwardly happy child who went into nursery at the start of the year may become bad tempered, lose friends, withdraw and not enjoy his day at nursery. He will begin to compare himself with others and perceive himself as lacking, and his lack of language will mean he is unable to communicate his frustration and he will lash out or withdraw as a consequence.

The US government is trying with mixed success to develop nursery-based dyslexia/SEN screening/baseline assessments to early screen for dyslexia and to start initial interventions to prevent literacy deficits having a long-lasting effect on children. This positive programme to catch children before they fail at school is in sharp contrast to the failure-deficit models used in the UK, which require a child to first fail to achieve normally, before screening and intervention is offered. Research points to early screening and intervention as key to effective treatment.

BDA (2014) lists a number of common symptoms found in preschool/nursery-aged dyslexics. It builds a picture of children who have difficulty with motor skills (use of their hands) and life skills such as balance, clapping, understanding directions, being able to repeat simple instructions in the correct order, being able to dress themselves and staying focused on tasks. Imagine yourself waking up from a stroke and not being able to do these tasks – you would be frustrated, especially when others around you could – thus the frustration in young dyslexics is understandable. Following a stroke, an individual can have dyslexic-type difficulties called 'acquired dyslexia', which is defined as the loss of skills once had (Leff and Schofield 2010).

PRIMARY SCHOOL

At primary school the dyslexic child will bring with him his experiences of nursery school. If he had positive experiences, enjoying success in learning he will start primary school hopeful and with an open mind. If, like many dyslexics, he had a negative nursery experience, as he struggled to read with others easily outperforming him, then primary school is seen as another hostile environment.

If he was lucky enough to have been screened for dyslexia in nursery and, even more luckily, to have been given some early interventions, then this would have been communicated to his new primary school, especially to the special needs coordinator (SENCO), whose job it is to plan screening and interventions for students. Such children should continue with these programmes of intervention and will begin to succeed in school.

In the UK, screening is usually delayed until a child has fallen at least two years behind his chronological age in literacy. Such children would have presented with a range of learning difficulties as noted in the BDA list (see the bulleted list on pages 54–55), which teachers may have misdiagnosed as immaturity, mild learning difficulties or laziness. Each year the child would have moved up school classes and such symptoms would have been missed or misdiagnosed. Normally it is not until the SAT tests (in Year 6) that schools begin to examine their pupils and highlight those who need literacy and numeracy booster classes, but again learning difficulties are rarely diagnosed unless very pronounced. Whilst the above is a generalisation, there is substantial evidence to suggest this is commonplace (Miles and Miles 1990; Riddick 1995).

What are normally diagnosed, because of their greater prominence, are behavioural difficulties. Such children who struggle in school, and feel each year that their peers surpass them academically, lack the emotional maturity to communicate their difficulties; instead, they find alternative means to gain attention. These coping strategies can easily lead to a child being labelled with SEBD, and they will then be mentored and helped to avoid manifesting their anger. But what is missing is an analysis of why such a child would use emotional and behavioural strategies in the first place.

The list of dyslexic symptoms on pages 54–55 helps the reader to understand the far-reaching consequences of having a learning difficulty, which go beyond acquiring language. As at the preschool/ nursery age, the primary school-aged dyslexic is unlikely to have mastered life skills, but is still considered bright as long as the work is verbal. The literacy requirement has increased greatly in primary school, on top of which, the dyslexic is still struggling to acquire basic motor and language skills. It is unsurprising the BDA list of symptoms includes 'lack of confidence and a low self-image', as he is seeing his peers develop each year and surpassing his own abilities tenfold. Each year he falls further behind, and this becomes more evident to both parents and teachers. As noted earlier, with the deficit model of dyslexia identification, dyslexics will now be two or more years behind in reading, thus questions would be raised as to why the child is not achieving according to his chronological age group. The question is, will such students be diagnosed with: 'garden-variety poor reading disability','dyslexia/specific learning difficulty' or 'social, emotional and behavioural difficulties'? The last develops in reaction to frustration from falling behind in learning and being unmotivated to even try (as previous attempts have failed). This book will look at these and other manifestations of failure in later chapters.

Lackaye and Margalit (2006), Morgan *et al.* (2008) and Alexander-Passe (2006, 2008) found dyslexics and/or those with reading disabilities can suffer from low self-concept and self-efficacy, with low levels of engagement and other emotional coping strategies that can have a significant bearing on a child's motivation. As a result of this many conceal or camouflage the true nature of their reading difficulties from their teachers and underachieve as a result of this (Wadlington, Elliot and Kirylo 2008).

Sternberg and Grigorenko (2002, p.82) argue 'there is no need to distinguish between reading disability and poor reading. One need only identify problems in reading and treat them accordingly'. They ask whether the dyslexia label just gets in the way of children getting the help they need. Others argue that if comprehensive screening took place in schools, many dyslexics would not have suffered the needless negative effects of countless years of failure; thus, to save the next generation, dyslexia screening is recommended followed by suitable interventions.

The question posed in Chapter 1 was 'would dyslexic children be identified as poor readers or dyslexic?' The use of RTI or WAVE 1, 2 and 3 as found in most UK schools would mean intervention starts with classroom teachers, and then moves on to small group interventions. It is probable that, whilst dyslexic students will improve as a result of such interventions, it will be slow, ineffective and an unproductive use of the struggling student's time at school. The use of WAVE 2 and WAVE 3 will mean the dyslexic child is removed from class for more specialised interventions (group or individual) with trained or untrained staff. The removal model will mean the dyslexic can fall even more behind and will probably lose the richness of a broad national curriculum as non-core subjects are deemed more suitable for withdrawal sessions.

It would be hoped that after a number of terms in WAVE 2 and WAVE 3 the school and SENCO would request more detailed investigations. However, studies suggest that diagnosis is generally left until the student is in his last year (thus falling four or more years behind his peers) or until he starts secondary school (Cogan and Flecker 2004). In both situations the child in question has been educationally neglected for many years. The British Dyslexic Association (BDA) lists the following learning difficulties presented in children of primary school age:

- Has particular difficulty with reading and spelling
- Puts letters and figures the wrong way round
- Has difficulty remembering tables, alphabet, formulae, etc.
- Leaves letters out of words or puts them in the wrong order
- Still occasionally confuses 'b' and 'd' and words such as 'no/on'
- Still needs to use fingers or marks on paper to make simple calculations
- Has poor concentration
- Has problems understanding what he/she has read
- Takes longer than average to do written work
- Has problems processing language at speed
- Has difficulty with tying shoe laces, tie, and dressing

- Has difficulty telling left from right, order of days of the week, months of the year, etc.
- Surprises you because in other ways he/she is bright and alert
- Has a poor sense of direction and still confuses left and right
- Lacks confidence and has a poor self-image.

(BDA 2014)

SECONDARY SCHOOL

The dyslexic entering secondary school will probably by now have substantial difficulties in his learning, and the increased academic workload is likely to be too much for him to easily deal with. At the start of secondary school each student is given initial testing to assess baseline abilities in English, maths and science (commonly called cognitive ability testing (CAT)/Midys testing), to assist the school in streaming and setting students so that mixed ability classrooms are formed. It is hoped that lower ability students will be put into lower sets where teachers are specially trained in SEN; however, this is commonly not the case and the best teachers are typically given to the higher ability students to stretch them to ensure the school's progression up the national league tables.

The bulleted list below summarises the symptoms commonly seen in dyslexics of secondary school age, from which it can be seen that even basic tasks can present substantial difficulty to young dyslexics (see p.54).

It is to be hoped that primary schools would brief the child's new secondary school as to interventions tried without success, along with other important information. However, a child moving to secondary school will find support withdrawn, as the new school will want to see how they cope in a mainstream setting before WAVE 2 resources are re-allotted. It is also the case that the CAT testing will highlight large numbers of students who had slipped through the net at primary school; however, large secondary schools commonly lack the resources to support such a large number of students, which can be between 50 and 60 per cent of each school year cohort (in a six-form intake in an average secondary school this can mean 90 or more possible struggling/SEN students in a year group with 180 students). To really give the support required to such a cohort a team of five specialised teachers would be needed per year, thus 35 per school. In many UK mainstream secondary schools they have a maximum of three or four specialised teachers per school, which includes the SENCO; thus, while the need is there, the school capacity to provide interventions is substantially limited due to lack of SEN funding.

Recent UK education legislation (the Children and Family Act 2014) has required every teacher to teach a mixed ability class and for each teacher to be 'a teacher of SEN'. Thus, the focus has moved from specialised teachers to normal classroom teachers who are overstretched already. It is not unreasonable to hypothesise that many dyslexics, reading disabled and SEN students are missing out on the expert interventions they need to progress effectively in the classroom. The 'Every Child Matters' (Chief Secretary to the Treasury 2003) or ECM policy, as legislated in the UK Children's Act (2004) is an unattainable objective when class teachers lack basic SEN training to identify and teach SEN students in their classrooms, and school SEN budgets mean a shortfall in specialist teachers employed in individual schools. The following list summarises the symptoms seen in dyslexic children aged 12 or over:

- Still reads inaccurately
- Still has difficulties in spelling
- Needs to have instructions and telephone numbers repeated
- Gets 'tied up' using long words, e.g. 'preliminary','philosophical'
- Confuses places, times, dates
- Has difficulty with planning and writing essays
- Has difficulty processing complex language or long series of instructions at speed
- Has poor confidence and self-esteem
- Has areas of strength as well as weakness.

(BDA 2014)

THE DYSLEXIA DEBATE

Recent debate has focused on the effectiveness of using the term 'dyslexia' in educational settings. Elliott and Grigorenko (2014) argued in a recent controversial book 'The Dyslexia Debate' that the term is not only misleading (as it can cover more than just difficulty with reading and writing), but as intervention for dyslexics is indifferent to that for poor readers, that dyslexia is not a distinctive learning disorder and as such the term should be discontinued. They also note that using the term dyslexia can 'reduce the shame and embarrassment as a consequence of having literacy difficulties. It may help exonerate the child, parents and teachers from any perceived sense of responsibility' (Elliott and Grigorenko 2014, p.176).

Bishop (2014) tends to agree that the term is incorrect but concludes that there are other conditions such as depression and schizophrenia which are also 'massively problematic in terms of validity and reliability' (Kendell and Jablensky 2003). However Bishop suggests that whilst the terms may be incorrect and misleading, the strongest argument for retention comes not from science but public perception. That 'some of the most passionate defences of the dyslexia label come from those who have built up a sense of identity around this condition, and who feel they benefit from being part of a community that can offer information and support'. Also the term 'poor readers' leads readers to assume that such difficulties could be fixed through more effort and quality teaching, whereas 'dyslexia' suggests something different, long-term, and requiring specialist intervention. Bishop interestingly concludes that 'at present we are between a rock and a hard place. The rock is the term "dyslexia", which has inaccurate connotations of a distinct neurobiological syndrome. The hard place is a term like "poor readers" which leads people to think we are dealing with a trivial problem caused by bad teaching'.

The 2010 OFSTED review of special educational needs (SEN) and disability in UK schools found that pupils were often incorrectly identified as having SEN, and that good or outstanding teaching would remove such a barrier to learning, '...as many as half of all pupils identified for School Action would not be identified as having special educational needs if schools focused on improving teaching and learning for all, with individual goals for improvement' (p.5).

However it also noted that identification was generally inconsistent and many SEN pupils were not identified, that children with similar difficulties were treated differently; and lastly that parents' views of inconsistency were well-founded. The review also found that parents pushing for a statement of SEN (now replaced with 'Educational Health Plans') may not be enough to guarantee the high level of specialist interventions required. They noted that many schools misidentified pupils with SEN to cover up for their poor quality teaching and that by diagnosing them as having SEN they were assisted in removing their GCSE results from school result league table data, and gaining additional government funding.

The Bercow Report (2011) for the UK's Department for Education supports OFSTED's view that SEN is inconsistently supported in the UK, and that even having statement of SEN does not guarantee the specialist support needed, noting 'the current system is characterised by high variability and a lack of equity. [It] is routinely described by families as a "postcode lottery"' (Bercow 2011, p.14). It again stresses the need for early screening and intervention in schools, something that has been noted for several decades in UK schools. This lack of 'early screening and intervention' has meant millions of dyslexics in the UK have lacked the specialist intervention they need to reach their potential, and this can be argued to lead to many dyslexics ending up in prison (Hewitt-Mann 2012).

ADULT DYSLEXICS

Whilst it would be hoped that all dyslexics would be identified and helped at school, hopefully starting in nursery or in primary/secondary school, sadly it would seem to be more common that dyslexics leave school without identification and with very few if any qualifications to show for their ten years in mandatory education. Dyslexics are one of many groups of teenagers likely to have experienced educational neglect, all of whom face the challenge of developing careers that will satisfy them both economically and mentally in order to become self-sufficient adults.

They saw their higher performing peers surpass them at school and leave with both higher examination grades and having experienced a larger, broader curriculum. Such peers would be looking to go to college or university and start down the traditional path to well-paid careers.

Dyslexics as a group are commonly guided towards lower level vocational courses leading to lower paid and lower skilled careers in reliable practical industries (e.g. motor engineering, beauty, social care, retail, catering, etc.). They would see their peers moving at a much faster pace financially and this is likely to cause resentment, frustration and, in some cases, anger. Each of these is a risk factor.

'Resentment' can lead dyslexics to find illegal routes for quick financial gain (e.g. theft, mugging, drug dealing, etc.) so they can also have the material wealth of their peers. The downside to this is of course being caught and ending up in prison (BDA and HM Young Offender Institution Wetherby 2005; Mottram 2007). Research indicates that higher number of adults with low literacy levels are found in prison, compared with the general population. Projects in the UK have found large groups of mainly unidentified dyslexics in prisons, a picture replicated in Sweden and the USA (Alm and Andersson 1995; Kirk and Reid 2001; Morgan 1997).

As part of a pioneering teaching and mentoring project at Chelmsford Prison, Susan Clayton, the head of learning at HMP Chelmsford notes:

> These are people who have been failed by the education system year ago… They are now excited about this project of having a (learning) mentor, realising that they aren't stupid; that they are actually quite clever people. They just needed to have this particular learning style approach for them, so they could move forward. (Hewitt-Mann 2012, p.28)

Tony Blair, the then Prime Minister commented on the programme that 'many of those people in the prison population did not have the educational opportunities [that most of the population received] – often because they are dyslexic, had not been diagnosed properly or did not get the extra help they needed' (Hansard 2007).

'Frustration' is a huge problem in dyslexic adults caused by poor identification and intervention in schools. Large numbers of adults leave school without adult levels of English language skills; the term functional illiterate is used to describe those adults who only have enough skills to operate in a simplistic way in society

(Jama and Dugdale 2012). The frustration of living in this way can head in three directions, internally, helplessness and externally:

- Internally – this can lead to dyslexics coping with their frustration by using emotional coping mechanisms, such as self-harming, withdrawal and depression.
- Helplessness – dyslexics can feel trapped and helpless in their ability to change their situation. They feel unable to learn to improve themselves; however, they do not want to fall into negative emotional or behavioural coping paths.
- Externally – this can lead dyslexics to be angry about their situation and lash out, which might manifest in causing damage to property, e.g. slashing the tyres or damaging the paintwork of expensive cars, or hurting or mugging people who are perceived as successful in life. This of course can lead them to prison due to criminal activity.

The bulleted list below notes known symptoms of dyslexia in adults and, unlike the school-based symptom lists (see pages 54–55 and page 56), the symptoms are grouped into areas of strengths and weaknesses. Moving from school into the realm of work means that difficulties are sometimes cloaked with coping strategies, e.g. difficulties writing are now reframed as avoiding writing, protecting self-worth. Any attempt now to provide intervention will be faced with protective strategies, which will need to be tackled before the dyslexic will even attempt any development of numeracy/literacy skills. Adult educators are skilled in working with individuals with learning difficulties, first developing the individual's self-worth to motivate them into learning. The following is a list of symptoms presenting in adult dyslexics:

- Reading – slow reading, difficulty understanding what was read, may hide reading problems.
- Writing – avoid writing or are not able to write at all.
- Spelling – spell poorly or rely on others to correct spelling for them..
- Memory – poor memory skills, prone to forgetting directions. Rely on memory rather than on reading information.

- Oral language – very competent in oral language. Have good 'people' skills.
- Talents – can be entrepreneurs, although lowered reading skills may result in difficulty maintaining a successful business. Often are spatially talented, professions include, but are not limited to, engineers, architects, designers, artists and craftspeople, mathematicians, physicists, physicians and dentists. Have good spatial thinking skills, May be very good at 'reading' people (intuitive).
- Work – in jobs that are often well below their intellectual capacity.
- Personality – lack confidence and have poor self-image.
- Other – difficulty in concentrating, restlessness, time management problems, dependence on digital watches, difficulties with planning, organisation, materials and tasks.

(Interdys 2014; LearningRX 2014; WebMD 2014)

CONUNDRUM OF FAILURE

Tanner's (2009) study of adult dyslexia makes use of a 'conundrum of failure' model to explain a typical negative adult dyslexic experience and is supported by a broad literature review. The model is explained as:

- System failure – this occurs when inappropriate educational opportunities are given to dyslexics at school, resulting in 'academic or school failure' (Humphrey 2002; McNulty 2003; Wolff and Lundberg 2002). This is said to lead to low expectations, insensitive teaching, ignorance, no identification or misidentification of needs and a weak curriculum. Thus the traditional educational system has failed and this has a knock on effect in adulthood through reduced career prospects.
- Constructed failure – in the UK there is no mandatory screening of dyslexia or disabilities when a child enters school, thus a child is required to continuously fail educationally for many years before identification and interventions are considered (Poole 2003). Thus, failure is a mandatory element of the diagnosis of an invisible disorder.

- Public failure – Scott (2003) and Fink (2000) discuss and support the concept that at school and in the workplace the inability of dyslexics to perform basic tasks (literacy and numeracy) makes the dyslexic's failure public. This can lead to humiliation and teasing, and many dyslexics choose to avoid tasks rather than give additional demonstrations of their inabilities.
- Family failure – dyslexics in families with non-dyslexic siblings can feel they are unable to fit into their family norms and those of society, and that they are failing their parents due to their inability to perform at school, as 'strong literacy skills are believed to be the key to academic success' (Scott 2003).
- Personal failure – Raskind *et al.* (2002), in a 20-year longitudinal study, found that many dyslexics experienced continued failure and a fear of learning and new or unknown situations (Palombo 2001). This personal failure to achieve according to family and societal norms can be self-perpetuating causing lifelong self-doubt.

Tanner's study used Nosek's (1997) three categories of dyslexics:

1. The candid dyslexic – willingly discloses and acknowledges his dyslexia to himself and others.
2. The closet dyslexic – conceals his dyslexia from himself through denial and from others out of shame and fear.
3. The confused dyslexic – doesn't know he is dyslexic and struggles through school and life unaware of what causes his troubles with words.

Of the 70 diagnosed adult dyslexics (male and female, 17–70 years, with the majority in the 22–45-year age group) investigated in the study:

- 48 (the majority) had developed compensatory strategies to hide their difficulties (closet dyslexics)
- 25 of the above 48 acknowledged their dyslexia to themselves but were selective about disclosure to others (closet dyslexics)

- 12 had experienced lifelong frustration with their literacy but did not know why (confused dyslexics)
- five openly disclosed their dyslexia (candid dyslexics).

To conclude, adult dyslexics are complex individuals who have typically experienced educational failure and neglect, and these have a huge effect on their ability to survive and succeed in a society that holds literacy and academic attainment as having greater value than vocational skills. The pressure to attain at the same level as their peers causes many dyslexics to find alternative means to obtain the spoils of society, which could potentially lead to criminal acts.

ADULT RELATIONSHIPS

The next section examines the close relationships of dyslexics; first with family and work colleagues, and second friendships, which can lead to dating and marriage (long-term relationships). Can the dyslexic operate their secondary persona in such instances?

Different family structures offer differing levels of support: siblings would have been aware of his struggles, but in adulthood may not be aware of how much he is still affected by his dyslexia. Parents are more likely to understand their child's difficulties, especially the dominant parent (generally the mother), however, they may be blinkered as to the extent that his learning difficulties may affect relationships with others, as they are so used to their dyslexic child that they are oblivious to his differences. In the main they are relieved their child has survived school and gained employment; and to them this means he has 'overcome' his difficulties and moved on.

In the workplace the dyslexic is there to perform a task or role, and in positive environments this has meant 'reasonable adjustments' have allowed him to perform his tasks to the same level as his peers (e.g. Dictaphones, spell/grammar-checkers, other ICT). Work colleagues only see the secondary persona, as in most cases they do not have time to think further.

When it comes to friendships, it is noted by Alexander-Passe (2010, 2012a) that dyslexics avoid mixing socially with work colleagues, as they lack confidence in general discussions (e.g. discussing news events and other topics) in large groups, as they feel unable to keep track of conversations and remember what has or hasn't been said earlier. This pressure is felt to be greater in groups where they feel others are superior to themselves in intelligence and culture, in which case they tend to either make their excuses and leave early, or not go at all. Alexander-Passe (2010, 2012a, 2012b) found that dyslexics generally belittle their views compared to those of their peers, and this adds to their social exclusion.

When it comes to finding long-term partners, their prior avoidance of social situations means they lack confidence in meeting others. This lack of confidence means they are unable or unwilling to talk to others in social settings, or feel unable to hold a serious conversation long enough for another person to feel attracted to them. This is before they even mention that they are dyslexic and, if they dare, their troubled schooling.

Marriage offers the dyslexic numerous safeguards but also many new dangers. Whilst it is possible to have a secondary persona at work and with friends, when it comes to living with someone 24/7, the ability to hide being quirky or different is much harder. Partners will see the significant difficulties faced by their dyslexic partners, and how much they rely on routines to survive each day. Without understanding dyslexia (if their partner is even diagnosed) they will begin to get frustrated and angry about their partner's inability to do what they perceive to be basic tasks (e.g. taking telephone messages and buying all the items from a shopping list).

At this point it would be useful to look at dating and relationships in others with disabilities and specifically learning disabilities (both developmental and acquired).

Parker (1993a) talks about people who became carers after their partners became disabled after marriage, noting:

> married couples are left virtually unsupported, either practically or emotionally, at times when their relationship may be under considerable strain. Sexual relationships may falter or cease because of lack of knowledge, embarrassment or not knowing whom to approach for help. Other couples may be left in an empty shell of a marriage because no practical alternatives to their situation are offered. (Parker 1993a)

Care Givers (2012) suggests this is due to the 'patient–caregiver relationship', as after a while, you may find that you are no longer emotionally attached to the relationship, and this means relationships are likely to fail, unless other reasons are found to hold the relationship together.

Schulz (2008) and Berg *et al.* (2003) suggest that married couples, where one has an acquired learning disability, use a variety of approaches and patterns when collaborating in their daily lives, including the division and delegation of tasks. Schulz (2008) noted that study participants felt this strengthened the relationship rather than weakening it. Parker (1993a, 1993b) notes that power differences exist in such relationships, which can mean an unbalanced division of household chores. This can also mean that a disabled partner, who has devolved a lot of their power over, say, financial matters, can feel emasculated, and an unequal partner in the relationship. In turn, the more able partner who takes on 'more than their fair share' of choices can feel overwhelmed by the responsibility, and can develop resentment for such a heavy responsibility.

Garee and Cheever (1992) document examples of several married couples where one or both members of the couple have disabilities. Coping strategies used include: use of technology, planning of the home environment, focusing on strengths, having realistic expectations of what each other can do, doing what each can do, having a sense of humour, creating their own roles, finding time for oneself, work, awareness of self-care issues and having a strong love bond. This need for 'finding time for oneself' is also supported by Schulz (2008), who notes 'generally speaking, the more severe the disability a participant had, the less alone time they had because of the amount of care or assistance they needed'. Thus, the need for some time out 'to collect one's thoughts' was deemed important for mental health.

This concept of imbalance and weighing up the advantages and disadvantages of one's relationship is seen in 'social exchange theory' (Cropanzano and Mitchell 2005; Duck 1983; Michener 1977; DeLamater and Myers 2004; Murstein, Ceretto and MacDonald 1977). According to this theory, relationships are seen as an exchange between parties as an attempt to increase rewards and reduce costs, and people evaluate relationships with others by comparing alternatives (Dowd 1975; Murstein *et al.* 1977). This negotiated exchange between parties is seen as the following equation: OUTCOME = BENEFITS − COSTS; and, importantly, because different individuals have different expectations of relationships, an individual's satisfaction is dependent on more than just outcome. This difference in expectation is therefore seen as the following: SATISFACTION = OUTCOME − COMPARISON LEVEL. When the comparison level is different between partners, they decide whether to stay in such a relationship; however, this has much to do with the alternatives open to them – people who feel they have alternatives, e.g. the non-disabled partner; are less dependent on staying in an unhappy relationship, this is described as: DEPENDENCE = OUTCOME − COMPARISON LEVEL OF ALTERNATIVES.

Miller (2005) argues against 'social exchange theory', as it reduces human interaction to purely rational processes arising from economic factors; the theory has a linear structure, whereas some relationships might skip steps or go backwards; and finally, this theory relies on the ultimate goal of relationships being intimacy.

Comparing marriages between disabled and non-disabled people, Berg *et al.* (2003), using open-ended interviews with young and old non-disabled married couples, investigated how they used collaboration in their relationship. Most couples in the study by Berg *et al.* reported that they collaborated with each other to make decisions and problem solve about managing finances, household repairs and other major decisions such as where to live. Patterns were identified in their collaboration, such as division of labour due to traditional sex roles, interests, abilities and/or other motivations, or the use of lead roles in the collaboration. Some of the sample commented that they believed they complemented each other in their approach, and few reported difficulties in collaboration.

Much of the empirical research noted is concerned with acquired disability – whilst this is very different to dyslexia, which is a developmental disorder, the acquired element could apply in a sense to dyslexics who are diagnosed during the course of their marriage, normally after their children are diagnosed. In such cases, the newly diagnosed dyslexic partner is dealing with psychological issues of resentment and anger, which can lead to depression or other mental health issues. The non-dyslexic partner has already taken on larger shares of household duties and this diagnosis can sometimes be a relief as a label has now been placed on the difficulties of their partner. However, they can now feel embarrassed by their lack of support up to that point. The above empirical review relating to 'social exchange theory' may be helpful in explaining their mixed emotions in taking on the heavy burden of most household chores, and aid in understanding the emotional struggles of being in a relationship with someone with social, emotional and learning difficulties/differences.

Wright (2015) also suggests one of the most important ways you can maintain a healthy and long-lasting relationship between learning disabled and non-disabled partners is by practising good, clear, open communication.

CONCLUSIONS

This chapter has described how the symptoms of dyslexia present from early childhood to adulthood. Whilst dyslexia cannot be cured, the development of compensatory strategies has allowed many dyslexics to become professionals in a number of fields and to have well paid, successful careers. Are they cured? No, but they have learnt 'when in Rome do as the Romans do'. What they do is not second nature to them, well, not to begin with, but they have learnt to do things in a linear way, whether it makes sense to them or not. Playing the non-dyslexic game allows them not only to survive, but to excel in getting through the doorway of a career and rising to a level where they can show their real strength in divergent thinking and creativity to solve problems that most linear thinkers find hard.

Saying that, many dyslexics feel stuck in a rut growing up, and this continues in adulthood. Dyslexia can be suffocating, and this book explores these feelings of despair and helplessness.

KEY MESSAGES

- Dyslexia can have a significant impact on dating and relationships. Reading Alexander-Passe (2012a) is a good introduction to understanding this unique group better.
- Parents of dyslexics should not try every known strategy – it is important to let the dyslexic child see what works for them.
- Dyslexia is a life-long difference, and recognising this rather than rushing for possible cures will help individuals and their parents learn to manage this difference.
- Parents of a dyslexic child should look within their families for unidentified dyslexics: it will help the dyslexic child to feel accepted, and any positive dyslexic role model is useful.
- Parents, especially dyslexic parents, should be on the lookout for dyslexia in their children, as dyslexia can run in families. However, a dyslexic parent is not guaranteed a dyslexic child and vice versa, as it can skip generations.
- Adult dyslexia is misunderstood in the workplace, so greater awareness is needed to educate employers and employees.

Chapter 3

DIFFERENCE, DISCLOSURE, STIGMA AND LABELLING

INTRODUCTION

There is significant evidence to indicate dyslexics suffer from a number of deficits that cause difficulty when learning and/or working. The term 'suffer' has been used here rather than 'experience' or 'manifest' – it was chosen to add an emotional perspective to having a learning disability or impairment. 'Disability' and 'impairment' are negative words commonly used for individuals with any form of disability highlighting any difference. This chapter will look at these concepts. The following quotations come from the author's previous research on dyslexia and depression (Alexander-Passe 2010):

Did you feel normal growing up? Normal, no. I always felt different, not with everybody, as there were those in the class that you sort of clicked with, yeah because they were dyslexic as well [laugh].

Do you think you made more friends with children with similar problems? I don't know, there were a couple of people in juniors that I stayed friends with them from junior to senior school, but yeah, I was picked on because of my accent, I wore different clothes and coloured socks.

So it sounds like you enjoyed being different? I did like being different, as my parents brought me up that difference was good.

Therefore, you were happy to be different? Yes happy to be different, [however] I [also] kind of wanted to be the same, so I wouldn't feel different [amongst my peers].

(Emma; Alexander-Passe 2010)

How was your time at primary school? I always felt left out, on the outside.

By your teachers or peers? I felt I did not fit, I felt they were doing things I could not do. So it was like a two way process, if I felt I could join in, I would, and thus if I did not join in they just left me alone. Teachers tended to be rather supportive without really understanding what the problem was.

(George; Alexander-Passe 2010)

Growing up did you think you felt normal? [Pause] Strangely enough, I have not thought about that. I always thought I was a bit unique. I have never thought about it. I always thought I was some case study for some higher being and that they were keeping an eye on me. Again, it was the little world I escaped to. I always thought I was not 'run of the mill' [something different/special].

Did that make you feel good, being a little bit different? Yes, I would say, I used it to my advantage in my own little world. I did think I was different, not stupid – different from everybody else.

Do you think that was your shell, like a safe shell? I had never thought about it in that way, but yes maybe.

(Peter; Alexander-Passe 2010)

DIFFERENCE

Armstrong (2011, p.14) argues that it is society and not the dyslexia itself that causes any impairment or disability, and that public perceptions are powerful elements in a person's self-image and in forming an individual's personality characteristics.

A child only questions the normality of his parents and home life when he begins school and sees differences between himself and his peers. Society is powerful and so are school environments, e.g. a ginger or white-haired child only realises he is different in the company of others.

Thomson (1990) researched the self-esteem of dyslexic children starting at and attending a special school for dyslexics. Results indicated that social and academic self-esteem scores rose substantially when students attended the special dyslexia school, suggesting that amongst learners like themselves (those with literacy and numeracy deficits) they did not perceive their learning difficulties as disabling and discriminatory. This supports the hypothesis that it is society and our environment that is more disabling to dyslexics than the actual disability.

What is it in society and our environment that causes dyslexics to be considered disabled? Advocates of the medical model of disability would say that dyslexics are not perceived as normal in education and the workplace and, whilst they look normal and speak normally, they have an invisible disability that only presents itself when written communication is required. The UK Disability Discrimination Act (2005) lists dyslexia as an invisible disability along with stammering. We live in a society that views literacy as king. The ability to read in society is so important that the inability to master such skills puts individuals at a disadvantage.

When individuals travel to a foreign country in which they do not know the native tongue, e.g. China and Chinese, their inability to speak and read puts them at a distinct disadvantage and they can feel discriminated against by the natives, who know the language well and can't see why anyone wouldn't have such skills. This is a similar analogy to that used by Fawcett (1995) to describe dyslexia.

Dyslexics feel like a foreigner in their own country and environment, and what is so frustrating is that everyone around them can speak and write normally. Humans have a strong need to fit in and this is an important factor for self-esteem, therefore dyslexics can feel alienated in environments requiring reading. The second human construct we need to understand is the need to feel safe. If humans do not feel safe they will develop strategies to maintain safety, in the case of dyslexics it is through avoidance. Morgan and Klein (2001, p.53) suggest that dyslexics have strong awareness, comparing themselves with their peers, and recognise intuitively their undefined and unacknowledged learning difficulties, with many adults noting that they felt this way from an early age. Gilroy (1995) notes that, in her experience, dyslexics tend to compare themselves unfavourably with their peer group, and Griffiths (1975) found that dyslexic students saw themselves as less intelligent than their peers. In Morgan and Klein (2003), a five-year-old boy called Rob asked his mother for a new brain like the tin man in *The Wizard of Oz*, as his brain didn't work the same way as his friends' brains. This seems to be the ultimate in recognising one's difference!

Young dyslexics find their life changes as they start school, and move from a safe and friendly environment (like home) to one where they must be on edge to defend themselves not only in the classroom, but in the playground as well. In primary and early secondary school, all children wish to be the same and to conform – as teachers note, 'dyslexic children – all children – hate to fail, hate to be different, hate to be singled out as having "special needs"' (Burden 2005).

The undiagnosed dyslexic child sticks out as being different and his segregation to the slow classroom table or the remedial class will not help the situation. As unfair comparison has put him on edge, he now become hypersensitive to criticism as a logical reaction to frequent failure – more frequently experienced than his peers (as found by Edwards 1994 and Riddick 1996). Cutting and Dunn (2002, p.856) found that generally 'five year olds…were sensitive to criticism; they reacted significantly more negatively in response to criticised failure than in response to non-criticised failure'. Such a reaction causes the onset of anxiety and lower self-esteem, indicating how fast school failure affects children.

Erikson (1950) suggested that our early childhood experiences play a significant part in our attitudes towards ourselves and our place in the world. This shaping is called self-concept and is easily damaged. Rogers considers self-concept to be:

> composed of such elements of the perceptions of one's characteristics and abilities: the perceptions and concepts of the self in relation to others and to the environments; the value qualities which are perceived as associated with experiences and objects; and the goals and ideas which are perceived as having positive or negative valence. (Rogers 1959, p.138)

Or, as Burns (1982, p.7) suggests, 'self-concept is best regarded as a dynamic complex of attitudes held towards themselves by each person' and has two parts: self-image and self-evaluation. However, Hansford and Hattie (1982) point out that self-concept, self-image and self-esteem are often used interchangeably without adequate definitions and are applied without valid and reliable measurement techniques. This comes in part from the hypothesis that self-concept is based on a highly subjective set of constructed attributes and feelings which take on meaning for the individual through evaluation compared to their particular society (Burns 1982), as also found with self-efficacy.

This chapter looks at 'difference' around dyslexia. The medical model of disability would say that dyslexics are abnormal and need to be fixed before re-engagement with society. But if they can't be fixed what happens then? The social model of disability would say that we are all different, so what is the problem?

The evidence presented in this chapter from Alexander-Passe (2010) supports the hypothesis that dyslexics believe they are different, be it in a positive or negative way.

FEELING DIFFERENT: CHILDHOOD

The following excerpts, like others in this book, come from Alexander-Passe (2010), and suggest that young dyslexics have a range of experiences which indicate to them that they are different to their social group at school. In many ways the analogy of being a foreigner seems apt, as young dyslexics feel they are outsiders in places where they should feel accepted and normalised.

I never quite fitted in. I felt different. I was often on the fringe of things, of my peer group. But I suppose if I analyse that, I did not feel quite normal.

So it sounded like home life was okay, but with your peers you felt like you did not quite fit in? For example, I was about ten years of age; I do not know why it sticks in my mind. We read Treasure Island in class and we had to create some artwork from the text, about how the mountain was described. Everybody else did an almost vertical 'Nero rock', but I created a conical shaped mountain and it was different to everybody else [laugh], so it's things like that.

So really, you saw things differently to your peers? Yes, some of the time.

(Brian; Alexander-Passe 2010)

When you were at primary school, do you think you felt normal? No, I never felt normal, I have always felt 'other' really, that is from beginning to end (of my school life) and to now.

You were talking about being different to your peers, do you think you liked being different? I appreciate it much more now.

So you like being different now, but not growing up? I was happy to be different but I did not like the reactions it caused. Because I liked what I liked, I knew what I liked was important to me, and I didn't want to talk about make-up and things, I was upset that my not liking what they liked caused me to be ostracised and bullied and that sort of thing.

Were you being physically bullied? Yes, a couple of times.

You did not fight back? I am four foot, nine inches now, so no.

(Kirsty; Alexander-Passe 2010)

ABNORMALITY

Do you think growing up you knew other people your age with similar problems? Yes, I think especially in my maths class, you saw others with similar problems but there was not a label for it, we all thought we were stupid as we were together. You saw others in your year find things easy, it is as if you are the only one with those problems, like the *Little Britain* sketch 'the only gay in the village', well I felt 'the only dyslexic in the class'.

(Kirsty; Alexander-Passe 2010)

Did you feel normal amongst your peers? No. The interesting thing was I felt the difficulty was, and I knew at the time, for some subjects I was in the top ability group and I was in the top set for them; I coped well and felt comfortable there. But for the other things, I was in the bottom sets, with a different group of peers. So I had to adjust to being in two distinct social groups.

Did you feel abnormal at school, as you did not fit into the boxes? I think probably I did, you never quite fit in with all my mates doing metalwork or woodwork who were not academic, as I was and I liked reading adult books on history, so I was on a different level to them.

So you did not fit into either group then? I was too academic for all the practical stuff I was being made to do in the lower sets, but I felt I was a visitor to the top sets of subjects I was good at.

(Norman; Alexander-Passe 2010)

The above quotations indicate that young dyslexics recognise they were not alone in struggling at school. Dyslexic or not, with a label or no; no matter, all were commonly bunched together in the lowest set, commonly with the worst teacher, whose job it was to keep children quiet and away from trouble rather than actively teaching those with learning difficulties (Edwards 1994; Riddick 1995).

ENJOYING DIFFERENCE

Do you like being different? Yes. Yes I do.

Does that give you a buzz? Yes, it can do. You can do different things.

Because difference came up with your schooling, I wasn't sure if it was a common theme in your life? I think that there was a time when I was around 14 years old, and I subconsciously made my difference a positive thing, why be afraid of being different, why not celebrate it? Be a bit eccentric. It is a good thing.

Do you think all of your hobbies and being different gives you a sense of confidence? Yes, probably yes.

Do you think it could have been a way of dealing with your difficulties? It probably was. Looking back at it now, as soon as I read your email I started to think about it, there does seem to be a common theme there.

(Harry; Alexander-Passe 2010)

Whilst dyslexia can be perceived as negative and restricting one's abilities, there are those who see positives. The above quotation develops this theme, in that as a teenager he enjoyed being different, and dyslexia gave him this. However, it takes a strong character to experience the negativity that comes from dyslexia and develop resilience so that no matter what, they enjoy such differences.

Those who enjoying standing out and being eccentric can develop emotional health to help them to not only survive school but conquer childhood.

FEELING DIFFERENT: ADULTHOOD

POSITIVE DIFFERENCES

You remind me of another volunteer who is also a massive science fiction fan. He said that being dyslexic was like being Spock from *Star Trek*, as he was different and didn't quite fit in. Yes I can see that, sci-fi is full of characters who are 'other', you have 'Doctor Who' who is different from all the people around him, he goes on all these adventures but in the end he is on his own. He can deal with it; I get my confidence from others like you. I find other dyslexics who are like me, so I think in sci-fi they also do that. There is very much a sci-fi community.

Do you think, growing up, that sci-fi was your hobby, to get your self-confidence, knowing all the detail? Yes, I had very little interest in the other things [like make-up]. I was not sporty, that was not something I could identify with. I was not girly, so again I could not identify with that. But with sci-fi, when you are different you are celebrated. Spock is different and really smart, which is like me… I love learning new things. I like Stephen Fry who is bipolar; so on one side he is jokey, happy and mad, but there is a private side that is quite dark and troubled, because he can't understand why people like him, why he is so smart. I think it is the same with me: 'why can't I do this thing that everybody else can do [reading and writing]?'

(Kirsty; Alexander-Passe 2010)

If you were describing dyslexia to a friend, how would you describe it? It's like being a Martian; I've been living on this earth for a long time so I'm quite good at coping with it by now, coping with planet earth [laugh].

So is it similar to the book title Men are from Mars, Women are from Venus? Yes. Therefore, you feel you are very different. I find I don't fit very well into the modern world. It is one of the reasons why I don't have a job.

(Trixie; Alexander-Passe 2010)

You say you are an eccentric, do you enjoy being different? Oh yes, oh yes, oh yes [I love/enjoy to see the look on people's faces.]. Yes I do enjoy it...yes! I have made it [my dyslexia] a positive; you can make it a negative, and worry like crazy...but I don't do that.

(Jasper; Alexander-Passe 2010)

Whilst during the teenage years, difference can be enjoyed, as adults difference can be a double edged sword. It is not always positive, but if you turn it around and enjoy the experiences being different can bring, then it can allow the ability to flourish in society. The 'Spock from *Star Trek*' analogy is interesting as it encapsulates the idea that difference can be good but can lead to some darkness below the surface. Kirsty also talks about celebrating difference.

GOOD AND BAD

How does dyslexia affect your daily life? Does it affect it? I am an electrician and not a barrister.

Do you feel lacking daily? Yes and as I get older it gets harder, because I am not as agile now. When I met my wife, it was fantastic, I was working, I had my own place and I had as much money as I have now. Whereas that money paid for posh meals, it must now support my whole family, and that is the issue! If I was a barrister, I would be more comfortable.

So you are talking about progression? With progression would be more money. And I would imagine at my age I would be a partner, all the things my peers are doing.

Do you compare yourself to your peers a lot? I am proud of myself, and what I have achieved with what little I have. I think I am an enigma as well; I would like to think that.

That people cannot quite get you? Yep and that I can be in a van with my overalls, and then drive my wife's car, a decent car in a suit, so I can flip between the two... I quite enjoy that.

Do you enjoy not wearing a suit? The whole routine thing, I saw them this morning. Have you seen them? Every day going to the train station, the same? So maybe this is right for me. I have tried, I have had a few office jobs, but I come back to doing this.

Have you ever felt rejected due to your dyslexia? Yes I do.

It sounds like rather than you rejecting them, you became contrary instead? To be different? Yes, even when I was on building sites and the rest were reading the Sun, I would go in with *The Times* [a broadsheet newspaper], so yes.

To be contrary and different? Yes.

Is that a feature of dyslexia? Rebelling is a common trait as a reaction to failing, to be different, do you feel normal now? No, because I cannot read anything I have written down, I am not the stereotypical 46 year old, like a lawyer or accountant. But I quite like being different. I think I am a novelty act because of that.

That is a strange terminology: 'a novelty act'. If you go down the list of the people I know, the professions of those around me socially and through work, I'm very different to them. I was at a party recently and someone came up to me and said 'you're the only one in this room that can actually do something'. So yes, I thanked him for that, so I enjoy being different.

(Malcolm; Alexander-Passe 2010)

Malcolm was an interesting research participant. Whilst he had a chip on his shoulder about not being a barrister, something he dreamt of being as a child, he enjoyed being 'contrary and different' and in some ways a novelty in a world full of linear 'boring' non-dyslexics. Divergence is a strength commonly found in dyslexics: they are known to be multi-skilled, with the ability to turn their hand to more than one career, and to mix with more than one social group.

SOCIAL CONSTRUCT: IS DYSLEXIA ONLY A DISABILITY AT SCHOOL?

Many dyslexics would argue that the social construct that dyslexia is only relevant in school is wrong and misleading, as the evidence points to dyslexia being a lifelong disability/disorder. Whilst you won't see or hear about dyslexia in adult circles, it does not mean it's not there. Adult dyslexics who seem to cope well with their disability have developed coping strategies that allow them to circumvent difficulties. They have developed support structures and patterns of behaviour that make them look normal so they don't stand out. Dyslexia is understood to mean illiteracy in most workplaces, thus dyslexia is perceived as negative and a form of low intelligence.

IS DYSLEXIA A TABOO SUBJECT?

Have you ever discussed dyslexia in a social setting? How much would your friends know about it? Everyone has an opinion about homosexuality, communism, the current government, and so on, but do they have one on dyslexia? Would mothers discuss dyslexia with other mothers without the fear of their child being perceived as abnormal, lazy or stupid? Would mothers make play dates for their child with a dyslexic child, or would they avoid this for fear of them not mixing with other suitably intelligent children?

It is common for children to be inconsiderate towards other children they perceive as strange and abnormal as they lack the social skills we learn as adults and thus demonstrate their thoughts without worry of how they are perceived. Adults, on the other hand, have learnt the social skills of keeping certain thoughts to themselves, as it is the polite thing to do (or so they are taught by their parents). Does this mean they don't think in the same way as children? Are they any more flexible and adaptable? What does being polite actually mean – thinking things but not vocalising them in public?

In certain circles dyslexia is perceived as cool and an asset, for example in artists, designers, actors, etc. Many companies seek out dyslexics, as they believe they have the rare ability to visualise complex three dimensional models (e.g. those used in buildings, plumbing plans, computer programming, etc.) before they are built. This has the potential to save time and money and to see problems before they crop up. However, in other professions, many dyslexics might hide their difficulties (e.g. writers, surgeons, nurses, etc.) for fear of discrimination.

DISCLOSURE

In a study of dyslexic nurses, Dale and Aiken (2007, p.14) note 'many have gone to considerable lengths to hide their difficulties'. Morris and Turnbull's (2007) study found there was widespread concealment of student disabilities in clinical settings among dyslexic student nurses. As one student nurse said 'when they [staff] find out they withdraw from you and make out you're not on the same level…they try to rubbish you and make you feel you've got nothing in your brain' (p.38). However, without disclosure no 'reasonable adjustments' and mentoring are possible. Disclosure has risks in the workplace; however it can have its benefits. In the UK and the USA disclosure brings access to the support required to do the job well. Access to Work and the Disability Support Allowance can make all the difference to succeeding at work or in futher education.

The need for disclosure is complicated by the fact that many dyslexics do not perceive themselves as disabled (Blankfield 2001) or are not seen by others as being disabled. However, the legal and bureaucratic position of dyslexia, included in employment legislation and law, defines it as a disability. Also to gain additional support and adjustments in the workplace individuals would need to disclose their dyslexia within the first six weeks of employment.

To disclose dyslexia at work at the interview stage may mean that you will not be offered the job. Is it a risk worth taking? If you avoid disclosure until you start, your employer could argue you had withheld important information relating to your ability to fulfil the job – thus you could be fired for non-disclosure.

Nalavany, Carawan and Sauber (2013) investigated dyslexia as a hidden disability. They note that adult dyslexics face complex decisions over disclosure. Hellendoorn and Ruijssenaars (2000) found that most participants in their study felt dyslexia impacted on their daily life, and they experienced many educational and career-related problems. Nalavany, Carawan and Rennick's study (2010) used concept mapping (a mixed qualitative-quantitative methodology) to describe and understand the psychosocial experiences of 39 adults with confirmed and self-identified dyslexia.The final concept map generated nine distinct cluster themes: organisation skills for success; finding success; a good support system makes the difference; on being overwhelmed; emotional downside; why can't they see it?; pain, hurt, and embarrassment from past to present; fear of disclosure and moving forward (2010).

Barga (1996) studied the experiences of nine university students with learning disabilities (another term often used for dyslexia in the USA). Over a six-month period, students experienced labelling and stigmatisation, which they considered to be a barrier to their education. Whilst all participants were selective when disclosing information about their disability to others, six reported deliberately using avoidance behaviours and concealment to hide their disabilities, fearing ridicule and stigmatisation. They feared rejection, ridicule and stigmatisation, so adjusted their lives to avoid the likelihood of perceptions of difference. Dyslexic participants noted regular examples of clinical misunderstanding and often misinformed ignorance and hostility from staff with regard to their dyslexia. Barga argues that dyslexia continues to attract an unwarranted stigma, which in some individuals can adversely influence the development of a constructive relationship with their mentor.

Rao (2004) reported that many undergraduate students avoid reporting their disability to avoid negative social perceptions, although admit that their academic achievement may suffer as a result.

Empirical evidence suggests that dyslexia is similar to religious orientation or homosexuality, in that they are all invisible sources of potential stigma. Such invisible groups according to Beatty and Kirby (2006) have difficulty forming group awareness, because people are reluctant to publicly claim a potentially damaging identity socially and in the workplace.

Being visible means declaring one's hidden identity and 'coming out' to employers, friends and family. Such disclosure is weighed up for its advantages and disadvantages before taking the plunge to openly disclose. Thus, in some ways dyslexia and homosexuality can be grouped together, as they are both incorrectly perceived as negative traits; this is especially prevalent in the workplace, as only by 'coming out and disclosing', can protection be gained through discrimination legislation.

Gordon and Rosenblum (2001) point out that, ironically, the laws which protect people with invisible identities also create and reinforce stigma by naming and categorising groups. Certain groups lack the ability to advocate for themselves, perhaps because they are a minority (e.g. being black or a woman in the last century or being gay in this century), or because, as can be the case with dyslexics, many of them lack the skills to do so. In the UK, the main national charity protecting the rights of dyslexics (the British Dyslexia Association) was set up and run for many years by parents of dyslexics for school-aged dyslexics. Unintentionally, they supported the argument that dyslexic children were unable to voice their concerns and were incapable of fending and campaigning for themselves. However, this organisation has evolved, with dyslexics being involved, especially at the top, and with a developing focus on adult dyslexics.

In a personal relationship when should you disclose dyslexia? If you mention it on your first date, will there be a second? If you leave it until a relationship has settled, then you could be perceived as lying, e.g. not admitting that you are a drug addict or addicted to gambling. Alexander-Passe (2012a) found that some dyslexics mentioned their dyslexia on the first date as a discussion point such as wearing glasses for reading, whereas others waited several dates into the relationship, as they wanted to secure the relationship before dropping the bombshell. The author concluded it had a lot to do with how dyslexia is perceived by the individual. Is it a strength or a weakness?

STIGMA

Susman (1994) defines stigma as an adverse reaction to the perception of a negative evaluated difference. It is not the attribute of the individual who bears the difference, but rather it resides in the interactions between the person with the difference and others who evaluate the difference in negative terms (Goffman 1964). Critics of stigma argue it is too broadly conceived an idea (Cahill and Eggleston 1994).

Schulze and Angermeyer (2003) suggest that stigma adds a dimension of suffering to the primary illness – a second condition that may be more devastating, life-limiting and long-lasting than the first.

Link and Phelan (2001) define stigma as having five main components:

1. Labelling – the recognition of differences and the assignment of social factors to those differences, e.g. recognising that the individual may have different biological/neurological traits to the norm.

2. Stereotyping – the assignment of negative attributes to these social factor differences, e.g. differences that matter and are deemed by others to be undesirable.
3. Separation – occurring when the reactions to others leads to the avoidance of those with the undesired difference (felt stigma).
4. Status loss/discrimination – when the individual with differences is not allowed to fully participate in society or a community, thus the value of their place is reduced and their worth is devalued by other people's views. This is based not on their abilities but on other people's perceptions (enacted stigma).
5. Power differential – occurs when those with authority use their position to bar or reduce those with the difference from taking full roles in society, e.g. a company boss who feels negatively about disability may not shortlist a person with a disability for a vacant job.

Stigma comes from making a conscious choice to discriminate against another individual, be it at school, walking down the street, at work or socially. Within the medical model of disability, stigma can cause families to send a disabled or sick person away 'for their own good' but really it is to protect the family from social stigma.

Stigma and discrimination go hand in hand as part of the medical model of disability. This has meant that disabled individuals, such as those with dyslexia, are unable to get jobs, as there is an incorrect perception that if a person can't read or write, they are 'stupid' or 'unintelligent'. In schools children may avoid making friends with those on the slow table, or may make nasty remarks when a dyslexic child is made to read aloud in class and stumbles over their words.

WORK-BASED STIGMA IN ADULTS

Little research has been undertaken to study dyslexia and stigma. Alexander-Passe (2010) was one of the first investigative qualitative studies to look at adult dyslexics, and much of this book is based on this investigation.

Morris and Turnbull (2007) looked at a sample of 87 trainee nurses during their clinical placements in hospitals and argued that dyslexia continues to attract an unwarranted stigma and can adversely affect the learning experience. One nurse noted 'I overheard heard him [her mentor] tell another nurse that I wouldn't make it as a nurse because I'm dyslexic'. Disability awareness training in the workplace and improved education/service partnerships to support these students is considered crucial. Co-workers too, often discriminate and stigmatise by only seeing the perceived negative aspects of dyslexia (McLaughlin, Bell and Stringer 2004).

Rice and Brooks (2004) and Elliott and Place (2012) point out that using the label of dyslexia can be counter-productive as it stigmatises individuals; however, Elliott (2005) argues the lack of a label will stigmatise poor readers who lack the dyslexia label – damned if you do, damned if you don't!

In a study of dyslexia in prisons, MacDonald (2010) argues that dyslexic inmates without a label of dyslexia felt stigmatised by their literacy inabilities. In fact the stigma of restricted reading and writing ability had an indirect impact on offenders' self-confidence. MacDonald concludes (p.95) that 'the data in this study suggests it is not the label causing the stigma, but the symptoms. Removing the label only reduced the educational support and prohibits their legal rights.'

SCHOOL-AGED CHILDREN

In an interview study of 27 children and 16 adults, all dyslexic, Riddick (2000) suggested that, although labelling can lead to stigmatisation, this is not always the case. It is argued that stigmatisation can take place in the absence of formal labelling, and stigmatisation can precede labelling, thus Riddick sees a greater gain from labelling than not.

UNFAIR ADVANTAGE

Green *et al.* (2005) found that those with an invisible disability were seen by others as 'faking it' to gain special privileges or advantages, making comments such as 'what's the matter with her? She's not in a wheelchair!'

Lisle (2011) argues that there is growing evidence that a stigma exists towards those with a learning difficulty, e.g. suggesting that people with learning difficulties are intellectually inferior (Denhart 2008; Gerber, Reiff and Ginsberg 1996; McNulty 2003). Interestingly, Snyder *et al.* (2010) found those with non-physically visible disabilities reported more negative experiences than those with physical disabilities, questioning the validity of invisible disabilities in public perceptions (Are they really disabled? Are they just trying to gain an unfair advantage?).

The use of a label that identifies dyslexia has been found to affect teachers' perceptions and actions: many felt sorry for the students (Frymier and Wanzer 2003), and some perceived them as not only more difficult to teach but also less intelligent (Frymier and Wanzer 2003; Gersten, Walker and Darch 1988). Frymier and Wanzer (2003) found that many of the negative perceptions of teachers were due to the negotiation between student and teacher about reasonable accommodations, and the teacher questioning the validity of a non-visible disability. Lock and Layton (2001) found that some college professors held a belief that the label 'learning disabilities' was an excuse to get out of work and was down to laziness/not trying hard enough. In actual fact, studies suggest that dyslexics and those with learning difficulties work themselves to the point of exhaustion and illness to achieve as per their peers (Barga 1996; Denhart 2008; Reiff, Gerber and Ginsberg 1997; Rodis, Garrod and Boscardin 2001).

WHAT CAUSES THE STIGMA OF BEING DYSLEXIC?

Lisle (2011) argues that stigma towards those with dyslexia/learning disabilities persists for the following reasons:

- Lack of knowledge – Duchane, Leung and Coulter-Kern (2008) found that teachers' stigma towards those with dyslexia comes from misunderstanding or a lack of knowledge about disabilities. Lisle (2011) found educators with better knowledge of disability legislation had a more positive attitude towards those with learning disabilities.
- Invisibility of disability cues – Upton, Harper and Wadsworth (2005) found that perceptions of accommodation deservedness

were greater for disabilities that are more visible and have more obvious educational implications; thus the visibility/invisibility of disabilities is an important influence on the formation of disability perceptions. The lack of physical cues hinders non-disabled individuals from understanding any educational difficulties. It is still perceived by many that those with dyslexia or learning difficulties have lower IQ levels, so performing on a par with or better than peers and claiming extra accommodations can be misunderstood as cheating by both educators and students (Elacqua, Rapaport and Krusea, 1996; Field, Sarver and Shaw 2003; Winter 1997).

- Self-fulfilling prophecies – Jussim, Eccles and Madon (1996) and Hornstra *et al.* (2010) discuss the correlations between teachers' expectations of students with learning difficulties or dyslexia and the resulting student achievements, with those treated as having low ability believing such perceptions and acting/achieving accordingly. Evidence suggests that students with dyslexia/learning difficulties are more likely to drop out of college and university than those without learning difficulties or dyslexia and this will lead to social and economic disadvantage for these students, which is argued to lead many such individuals into criminality (Kenyon 2003; Mishna 2003; Morrison and Cosden 1997).
- Confirmation of bias – it is argued by Nickerson (1998) that educators will interpret information in a manner consistent with existing beliefs or explanations. Thus once a view of dyslexia/learning difficulties has been formed, maybe from teaching a single individual with such learning differences, they will tend to ignore individual characteristics, treating all with a single definition and giving a single type of accommodation (Higgins *et al.* 2002). However, as noted earlier, all dyslexics are different and the differences are along a continuum, thus all dyslexics need tailored accommodations.
- Out-group homogeneity – it is argued that because dyslexics and those with learning difficulties are viewed by others as being of lower intelligence than themselves, they tend to be grouped together and ignored in social settings. This

comes from convenience, rather than treating all people as individuals.

- Ableism – Hehir (2007) explains that there is an assumption in society that those without disabilities are more capable than those with disabilities, and in society groups tend to socialise with likeminded individuals. Thus, as seen in school playgrounds, those who like football socialise together, and those with disabilities socialise together. It is also argued that in schools the use of withdrawal for intervention groups will mean that some groups deemed incapable and abnormal, thus can be shunned and barred from joining certain high achievement social groups This can create an unwelcoming and inaccessible environment for individuals with disabilities.

THE EFFECT OF LABELLING WITH DYSLEXIA

Several studies in the USA and UK have investigated the impact of labelling in schools. Foster, Schmidt and Sabatino (1976) showed a film of a non-disabled child to two groups of 22 primary/elementary school teachers. One group was told the child was normal (control), the other group (experimental) was told the child had learning disabilities. The study found the experimental group rated the child more negatively, which led researchers to conclude the label generates negative expectations in teachers affecting their objective observations of behaviour and may be detrimental to a child's academic progress.

In a larger study of 88 teachers Foster and Salvia (1977) found similar results: 'teachers perceived more deviance when the child was labelled learning disabled than when he was labelled normal' (p.533). And again Gillung and Rucker (1977) found similar outcomes with 176 regular and 82 special education teachers in seven urban and suburban educational districts/authorities: 'teachers apparently perceived a child described with a label as having more severe academic or behavioural problems and requiring more intensive special services than the same child described without a label'.

More recently, a study of 247 general and special educational teachers found that teachers were more willing to refer non-labelled students to gifted and talented programs (91%) than the same student labelled with emotional/behavioural disability (70%) or labelled as having a learning disability (63%) (Bianco 2005). Some of the teachers remarked that they wanted disabled students to be in a less pressured environment.

The focus now turns to student peers: are they affected by labels? Sutherland *et al.* (1983) suggest students were not rejected by their peers based on a disability label, but were more likely to be rejected by their actions. However, those who were informed as to the positive attributes of the learning disabled students held their disabled peers in higher regard. The authors argue teachers need to inform their classes of positive-strengths rather than purely focusing on negative-weaknesses.

Bak *et al.* (1987) investigated how non-disabled peers viewed students being removed for intervention sessions without the use of labels for difficulties. Two scenarios were investigated: removal to the 'resource room for 25% of the school day' and removal to the 'special needs room for 80% of the school day'. Results indicated that students were sensitive about students who left the classrooms during the day – the authors noted 'the absence of formal labels did not prevent children from forming negative (although realistically pessimistic) expectations based on their own experiences with special class children's academic limitations' (Bak *et al.* 1987, p.154). Non-disabled students were aware of the differences when other students were being taught for long periods outside the classroom, and negatively perceived removal for intervention.

Labels seem to have both negative and positive affects in education. Knowing a child's label, especially those of mental retardation, emotional/behavioural difficulties and learning difficulties tends to affect teacher perceptions and expectations for student success (Bianco 2005; Foster and Salvia 1977), with teachers also highly influenced by student behaviour over labels (Levin *et al.* 1982).

Studies point to labelling of dyslexia having a positive effect by providing an acceptable explanation for a student's difficulties in reading, spelling or writing effectively, compared to negative concepts of laziness or having a low IQ (Reid 1996; Riddick 2000; Solvang 2007; Taylor *et al.* 2010a).

Taylor, Hume and Welsh (2010b) investigated self-esteem levels in three groups of students: with a dyslexia label, with a general special educational needs label or no label at all. The authors noted:

> being labelled as having a general need negatively affected children's self-esteem, because unlike the label dyslexia, this label offers very little in the way of an explanation for the child's academic difficulties, and because targeted interventions are not as available for those with a less specific label. (Taylor *et al.* 2010b, p.191)

Riddick (2000) also found the dyslexia label was preferred by children to a general 'special educational needs' label. In Norway Per Solvang (2007) also found that discovering they had the label 'dyslexia, many students were relieved that their difficulties were not their fault, removing the status of lacking motivation or having a low IQ'. However, it did cause more of a problem with the parents as it led to the implication that they had given the child the neurological difficulties through their genes.

CONCLUSIONS

Living with dyslexia is very hard for many, as they have learnt from a very young age that they are different, and this has an impact on their self-esteem. Undiagnosed dyslexics stand out more and this causes both confusion and frustration, but also confusion to those around them as there is a mystery as to why they struggle with the most basic of tasks.

Whilst denial and lack of disclosure are very similar in their outcome, it is in their development that they are different. Denial is the withholding of information to oneself, whilst the lack of disclosure is the withholding from others of important information that could be perceived as negative. As Dale and Aiken note (2007), many dyslexic nurses have gone to considerable lengths to hide their dyslexia for fear of discrimination, which is further complicated by some dyslexics denying they have a disability or a difference at all. The two together create a confusing mix that even dyslexics find hard to fathom.

Disclosure is hardest for adult dyslexics applying for jobs as they have no way of knowing whether disclosure of their dyslexia would put them out of the running altogether. If offered a position, fear of losing it can lead them to use concealment to camouflage their difficulties. This toxic cycle of concealment leads to a lowering of self-esteem and the individual is always on guard for fear of doing something abnormal.

Stigma comes from the lack of knowledge about dyslexia; hence others create a concept of dyslexia that comes from negative perceptions. This can create lead to negative stereotyping based on misunderstanding the true nature of the difficulties faced. As dyslexia varies greatly, individuals should explain how it affects them personally, rather than allowing incorrect generalisations to manifest.

Like disclosure, labelling can have a huge effect on a dyslexic. Not just due to the public association with a group with disabilities, but also due to being treated as a generalisation or a stereotype, rather than an individual, e.g. all black people are…, all gay people are…, all dyslexics are…, etc. In schools, teachers were found to treat children differently according to a label rather than trusting their professional judgement. However, a minority of research found the label can be helpful at a local level for the individual to understand the type of strengths and difficulties they may possess.

KEY MESSAGES

- Dyslexics are different, but these differences can be positive.
- Stigma comes from lack of knowledge and ignorance. Dyslexics should not let others' lack of knowledge affect them. Instead, educate them!
- Dyslexics should tell people about their dyslexia so it's not a secret.
- Much that people believe about dyslexia is wrong. Educate yourself, and then educate others.

- Setting the right level of challenge is very difficult for dyslexics, and, if persistently wrong, can affect their abilities to learn, with long-lasting effects.
- Schools can learn a lot from adult education, in how they rebuild a learner's self-belief in their abilities by fine-tuning the challenge set to students. The aim must always be to avoid anxiety, by never making learning situations threatening.
- Talking to learners and asking them to set their own pace in lessons can assist in moving forward in a positive way, this will also aid self-efficacy.
- Dyslexics look normal, they are! We are in a multi-cultural world, we are all different! But we are all normal. Being different is normal in society.

Chapter 4

ACCEPTING A DYSLEXIC IDENTITY

INTRODUCTION

This chapter looks at the creation of a dyslexic identity. The process that an individual goes through, from when they become aware of a difference, all the way to transformation into a balanced dyslexic individual, is highly complex.

Higgins *et al.* (2002) propose several aspects to the acceptance of a disabled (dyslexic) identity:

- awareness of a difference
- acceptance of labelling
- understanding/negotiation of the disability
- compartmentalisation
- transformation.

AWARENESS OF A DIFFERENCE

As a dyslexic starts nursery and school, he develops an understanding that he is different; however, denial of difference is first manifested until such a time that the difference begins to be significant – then it is obvious to all. He is frustrated and confused and asks why he is unlike his peers? He may be told he is, and can think of himself as 'stupid' (Burden 2005; Reiff, Gerber and Ginsberg 1997; McNulty 2003), with a knock on effect on his self-esteem. Cosden, Brown and Elliot (2002), Alexander-Passe (2010) and Scott (2004) argue that both the dyslexic and their parents need to be aware of such a difference before anything productive can take place. Denial from parents that their child has a problem, perhaps by doing his homework for him, will affect the dyslexic at school, and can delay identification, with the child coming to think of himself as useless and unworthy.

ACCEPTANCE OF LABELLING

Dyslexics and their parents commonly have issues over labelling, which come from the acceptance of difference. The perception is that a label can confirm a difference so severe that it warrants a label. Early screening and intervention is seen by many educationists to be the key to helping the dyslexic to achieve his potential at school (Johnson, Peer and Lee, 2001; Lyon *et al.*, 2001), as leaving screening/identification until late in primary school or early secondary school will mean negative concepts of difference will be established, with possible secondary emotional manifestations as a consequence.

Riddick (1996) and Zetterqvist-Nelson (2003) discuss the use of labelling and also whether such a label is a suitable definition of a person made up of combinations of strengths and weaknesses. Alexander-Passe (2010) mentions a research participant labelled as a young child, who found the label a negative badge or 'noose around her neck'. It limited her ability to attempt subjects as they were known to be difficult for dyslexics. Her curriculum was reduced and she concluded the label was a negative factor in her life, especially at school. Zetterqvist-Nelson (2003) had similar findings, in that dyslexics preferred non-labelling as they did not want to stick out amongst their peers. However, participants did find the label useful on a personal level as an explanation for their difficulties, along with providing a sense of moral relief that their difficulties were not their fault; but not on a public level, as it could be a cause of bullying or weakness in the eyes of others (as also found by Singer 2005). Both Zetterqvist-Nelson and McNulty (2003) agree that the positivity of the labelling comes from an individual's understanding of his diagnosis.

UNDERSTANDING/NEGOTIATION OF THE DISABILITY

Self-conceptualisation is important for the development of a self-image. If the dyslexic is going to create a realistic self-concept, then he needs to develop first an understanding of his difficulties, but just as important is an understanding of his strengths. This way he will see both the positives and the negatives in himself, and begin to see that others around him, not just dyslexics, also have strength and weaknesses – allowing the dyslexic to negotiate a more balanced view of himself. Cosden *et al.* (2002) suggest in adolescence, when strengths and weaknesses are better understood, self-acceptance begins to be possible. They advocate that dyslexics, like others with differences, require the availability of significant others (parents, teachers, etc.) to aid their understanding and acceptance of any disability. Davenport (1991) found that high acceptance allowed the positive receipt of help in academic studies and to value that support in the classroom.

COMPARTMENTALISATION

Dyslexics, like others with differences, not only need to develop a sense of their difference, but to accept that a label is not the sum total of an individual. All dyslexics are different as dyslexia is a spectrum disorder, thus no two dyslexics will have the same difficulties. The ability to understand this is the start of compartmentalising their difference – 'they have a disability but they are not the disability' (Peterson, Ekensteen and Rydén 2006; Reiff *et al.*, 1997). This process also comes from the realisation that there are strengths and weaknesses in everyone and that each person is a complex combination of the two.

Cosden *et al.* (2002) suggest that a certain level of cognitive development is required for compartmentalisation:

> As the child's cognitive complexity increases, including their meta-cognitive abilities, they are more able to see themselves from multiple perspectives. That is, they are able to hold on to a self-perception that includes strength and weaknesses without denying their disability, exaggerating their skills, or becoming overwhelmed by the academic problems. (Cosden et al. 2002, p.44)

TRANSFORMATION

Transformation begins with the acceptance of all the above processes: awareness of dyslexia/difference, understanding it and what it brings, the realisation of strengths and weaknesses, compartmentalisation and realisation that dyslexia is not only negative but brings many positives with it too, e.g. divergent problem-solving skills, oral skills, creativity, sporting ability, etc.

Transformation comes from turning negative perceptions of dyslexia to positive ones. In a study of dyslexic adults, Alexander-Passe (2010) found that when offered a theoretical pill to cure their dyslexia, they did not choose to be cured as, first, they enjoyed their difference, and second, they would miss their unique abilities. However, many noted that as a child they would have jumped at the chance, as they recognised that having dyslexia at school is a painful experience, battling against discrimination and misunderstanding.

In studying successful dyslexics, Logan (2009), Higgins *et al.* (2002) and Maughan (1995) found that such individuals had emphasised their positive attributes to create successful careers, and had recognised that support is needed at times for their weaknesses; Sir Richard Branson is a good example of such a strategy, as a highly skilled marketer and entrepreneur who relies on an excellent support team to deal with literacy tasks.

It is argued that awareness, understanding and acceptance of one's disability are crucial for the development of a positive self-concept.

CONCLUSIONS

The Higgins model is interesting as it nicely conceptualises how an individual accepts the identity of a dyslexic, or not as the case maybe. Any who reject their difficulties and labelling will tend to develop emotional defence strategies as denial will cause internal conflict. This chapter points to individualising and compartmentalising their dyslexia as a blend of strengths and weaknesses, to transform their difficulty into a difference; something that the social model of disability would argue is positive and allows positive self-esteem to develop.

KEY MESSAGES

- Denial features highly in many undiagnosed dyslexics, and this can be psychologically damaging, as not facing up to the truth can lead to feelings of shame, and always being on one's guard can be emotionally tiring.
- Acknowledging their differences and difficulties is the first stage to accessing help. Owning up to being dyslexic allows the individual to express how it personally affects them, rather than being defined by a broad blanket term that is incorrect.
- Understanding that dyslexia is only part of the whole person can be a positive step towards compartmentalising it. Creating a list of strengths and weaknesses is a proactive means to understanding how dyslexia can be an asset as well as a difficulty.
- Seeing that dyslexia can be a positive attribute is the way that successful dyslexics see themselves. They delegate the things they find hard, and celebrate their strengths.

Chapter 5

SELF-BELIEF

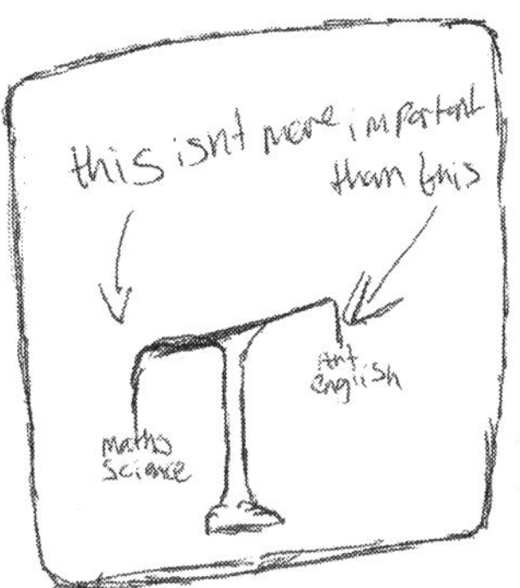

INTRODUCTION

This chapter investigates self-esteem, self-efficacy and shame. One could see each as three parts of the same concept, which is the investigation of the self. Previous chapters have looked at the perceptions of the individual of situations encountered and whether they are considered a threat. This chapter investigates self-perception, i.e. the beliefs about himself,an individual bases his self-worth on: his confidence, his worthiness for a prize; and his ability to achieve his potential.

'Self-efficacy' and 'locus of control' (LOC)[1] are other sorts of judgement, the judgement of not only our abilities, but whether our abilities are sufficient alone to achieve set goals. Do we require the help of others? Are we self-sufficient?

Lastly we have shame. Shame and self-esteem are linked in that one plays off the other: the development of self-esteem comes from one's self-judgement of another person's perceptions. If one is embarrassed about the judgement of others, then shame develops and is something to be avoided, shame becomes a taboo and an embarrassment.

---

1 Locus of Control (LOC) is an aspect of personality psychology that refers to the extent to which individuals believe they can control events that happen to them. People considered to have an internal LOC believe they can internally control events happening around them, whereas an external LOC refers to the perception that others around them have control over their lives (e.g. who controls a child's learning, is it the teacher or the child taking ownership of their own learning?).

WHAT IS SELF-ESTEEM?

Self-esteem, like self-concept and other similar concepts starting with 'self', is concerned with overall personal evaluation of a person's worth, thus self-worth. 'Self-esteem' encompasses beliefs about a person, e.g. I am confident, I am worthy.

James (1890) defined self-esteem as being the sum of our successes (what we have achieved) divided by our pretentions (what we think we ought to have achieved). He argues that in order to increase self-esteem one needs to: gain successes, avoid failure and to maintain self-esteem, so one could adopt less ambitious goals (or realistic goals) that would increase the frequency of success. He concludes that self-esteem is competence-orientated, but with the ability to change or develop.

'Worthiness' was brought into the debate by Rosenberg (1965), who defined self-esteem as the ability of the individual to judge themselves. However, this requires a value judgement comparing oneself to others and is social or culturally based. Coopersmith (1967) defined self-esteem as 'the extent to which the individual believes himself to be capable, significant, successful and worthy' (p.59), which combines the theories of James and Rosenberg. Coopersmith goes on to add that self-esteem is important to a person's identity and awareness, and that having high or low levels will influence a person's attitude to life. Mruk (1999) adds that 'self-esteem is the lived status of one's competence in dealing with the challenges of living in a worthy way over time' (p.26). Thus, self-esteem is a dynamic lived phenomenon, therefore, ongoing and open to change as we make comparisons based on our values and project these conclusions onto our feelings. Mruk suggests self-esteem can fluctuate more than stable characteristics such as personality and intelligence.

Branden (1996) asserts that there are three components to self-esteem:

1. Self-esteem is an essential human need that is vital for survival and normal healthy development.

2. Self-esteem arises automatically from within, based upon a person's beliefs and consciousness.

3. Self-esteem occurs in conjunction with a person's thoughts, behaviours, feelings and actions.

Branden (1994) adds that:

> it [self-esteem] is directly affected by how we act. Causation flows in both directions. There is a continuous feedback loop between our actions in the world and our self-esteem. The level of our self-esteem influences how we act, and how we act influences the level of ours self-esteem. (Branden 1994, p.15)

Marsh (1990), amongst other researchers, has conceptualised self-esteem as being an important predictor of academic and other achievement. Thus belief in oneself will affect one's abilities, as a self-fulfilling prophecy (Bandura 1986): if you believe you will do well, there is a good chance you will. Studies with teachers have found that if the teacher believes you will do well, you probably will, and vice-versa: students will fail or struggle if the teacher believes that will happen (Jerald 2007).

Several researchers have established an understanding that scholastic achievement and academic self-esteem are linked (Bandura 1990; Harter 1983; Swalander 2006), with the relationship being reciprocal, e.g. poor attainment can lower self-esteem and low self-esteem can lead to poor achievements. Marsh and Yeung (1997) argue that academic attainment is the more important factor, whilst Swalander (2006) and Guay, Larose and Boivin (2004) suggest that age is another important factor affecting the relationship.

White (2002) stated that 'If a problem is not biological in origin, then it will almost always be traceable to poor self-esteem'. James (2002) goes on to 'link low self-esteem to alcohol and drug abuse, teenage pregnancy, child abuse, chronic welfare, dependency and poor educational performance'.

In 1996, the State of California (James 2002) set up a task force to raise the level of self-esteem in its population. They saw having high self-esteem as a 'social vaccine'. However, not all agreed with this perspective. Critics of self-esteem, such as Seligman (1995), argue 'is it just coincidence that during the era when America made feeling good and boosting self-esteem in children a primary aim, the incidence of depression has sky-rocketed and feeling of self-esteem have plummeted?' He also argues that America has developed into a 'feel-good society' at the expense of a 'doing-well society' and this is causing problems. He argues that 'doing well' requires gaining mastery and overcoming difficulty, failure and adversity, the necessary building blocks to developing stable and positive self-esteem. Furthermore, 'feeling good' requires failure and difficulty, thus there is no short cut to building a stable and positive society.

Drives towards a 'feel-good society' in the UK have led to reducing failure in school through the removal of competition, e.g. at sports days (Faubert and Blacklock 2012), with all students being praised for taking part rather than for being the best. Barber (1997) argues in his critique of the UK educational system that 'schools ought consciously to promote young people's confidence and self-esteem'. He argues that low expectations lead to low self-esteem and failure, whereas high expectations lead to high self-esteem and success. Parker (2002) notes realistic perceptions of ability are important, with American children perceiving their ability in maths to be high, despite scores that are consistently low in international tables.

Branden (1994, p.15) noted:

> the fostering of self-esteem must be integrated into school curricula for at least two reasons. One is to support young people in persevering with their studies, staying off drugs, preventing teenage pregnancy, abstaining from vandalism and gaining the education they need. The other is to help prepare them psychologically for a world in which the mind is everyone's chief capital asset.

Interestingly, like Davis, Branden makes correlations between fostering self-esteem and use of drugs, as drug use and abuse, like the use of alcohol, begins as a recreational activity. It can give individuals a heightened sense of self-esteem/self-concept (Baumeister, Smart and Boden 1996; Godsall *et al.* 2004) and is very much based on the 'feel-good society', gaining pleasure and the sense of feeling good by whatever possible means, rather than through hard work and effort. Branden links the natural high to high self-esteem, and the artificial high to low self-esteem. Drug addiction comes from craving the unworthy artificial high self-esteem on a more frequent basis. If high self-esteem is a vaccine to society's woes, then teaching the ability to gain mastery of it must be an aim.

THEORIES

Psychologists such as Abraham Maslow (1987) conceptualised 'self-esteem' as a basic human need and important for motivation. He describes two types of esteem: the need for respect from others (recognition, acceptance, status, appreciation), and the needed for self-respect, or inner self-esteem (self-love, self-confidence, skill, aptitude). These two forms are included in his 'hierarchy of human need' (see Figure 5.1) and both are needed for self-actualisation, defined as 'the need to be good, to be fully alive and to find meaning in life' (Schacter, Gilbert and Wegner 2011, pp.486–487). Maslow thought that the healthiest form of self-esteem came through the genuine respect of others, rather than from fame and flattery.

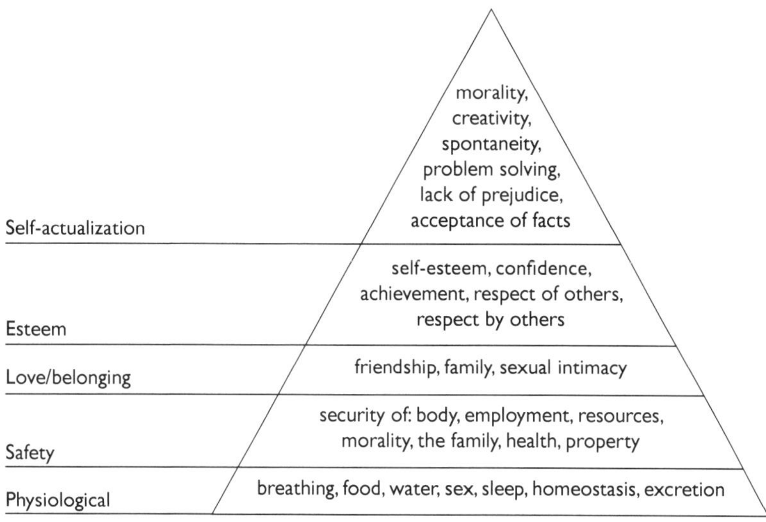

Figure 5.1 Hierarchy of human need (Maslow 2014)

Carl Rogers (1959), the greatest exponent of humanistic psychology self-esteem, noted that many people despise themselves and consider themselves to be of low value and unworthy. To improve self-esteem, unconditional acceptance and self-acceptance need to be developed.

Another related theory is that of 'self-efficacy' (Bandura 1986). This is a situation-specific self-confidence, a belief in one's competence to handle the task faced. People with high self-efficacy – that is, those who believe they can perform well – are more likely to view difficult tasks as something to be mastered rather than something to be avoided. According to the theory, self-efficacy is enhanced by four factors: inactive attainment (successful performances), vicarious experiences, verbal persuasion and psychological state (emotional arousal). This means that:

- Successful past experiences lead to higher mastery expectations, while failures lower them.
- Observing other people performing activities successfully can lead observers into believing that they can also improve their own performance as they learn from watching others.
- People can be persuaded through suggestion into believing that they can cope successfully with specific tasks.
- The individual's emotional states influence self-efficacy judgements with respect to specific tasks. An emotional state such as anxiety can lead to negative judgements of one's ability to complete a task.

HIGH AND LOW SELF-ESTEEM

Each experience, positive or negative, is likely to affect self-esteem in one way or another; a positive experience will enhance self-esteem and a negative one will reduce self-esteem. As a child grows he will initially gain an image of himself through his parents' eyes – this will include positive and negative experiences but his self-concept will be built in a caring and supportive environment. The more unconditional love and respect is given, the greater his self-esteem. The question is how stable or fragile is self-esteem?

A child'a time at school, from nursery, through to primary and secondary school, will have a significant impact on the development of his self-esteem and by proxy his self-concept. Consistent success in tasks will improve an individual's self-esteem and, likewise, consistent failure will lower it. But does it matter whether one has high or low self-esteem? Young children are less influenced by the perceptions of peers, but adolescents are very much influenced by them. The human need for acceptance is important when it comes to self-esteem, as Maslow (1954) recognised: 'the need for respect from others: recognition, acceptance, status, appreciation' is important for the generation of high self-esteem; likewise social acceptance brings about confidence and high self-esteem, whereas rejection by peers leads to isolation, self-doubt and low self-esteem (Leary and Baumeister 2000).

The first list below indicates the effects of positive or high self-esteem and lists attributes that we recognise as being good to have – personality characteristics that we would like for ourselves, our children and our students. The second list indicates the attributes that develop from low or negative self-esteem, recognised as unhelpful in trying to gain the most from life and situations, and to fulfil life's potential. A person with low self-esteem feels unworthy, incapable and incompetent. Whilst having a positive outlook on life can be self-perpetuating, so too can a negative one that affects an individual's motivation for life and activities.

Outward signs of positive self-esteem include:

- confidence
- self-direction
- non-blaming behaviour
- an awareness of personal strengths
- an ability to make mistakes and learn from them
- an ability to accept mistakes from others
- optimism
- an ability to solve problems
- an independent and cooperative attitude
- feeling comfortable with a wide range of emotions
- an ability to trust others
- a good sense of personal limitations
- good self-care
- the ability to say no.

Signs of low self-esteem include:

- a negative view of life
- a perfectionist attitude
- mistrusting others – even those who show signs of affection
- blaming behaviour
- fear of taking risks
- feelings of being unloved and unlovable
- dependence – letting others make decisions
- fear of being ridiculed.

Emler (2001) adds that those with low self-esteem are likely to:

- show symptoms of depression and be unhappy more often
- become pregnant as teenagers (females)
- have suicidal thoughts and make suicide attempts
- experience longer periods of unemployment and earn less in their 20s (males)
- suffer from eating disorders (females)
- be victimised
- fail to respond to social influence
- have more difficulty forming and sustaining successful close relationships.

SELF-EFFICACY AND LOCUS OF CONTROL

Another aspect of the 'self' movement is 'self-efficacy' – the extent to which individuals see themselves as being in control of the forces affecting their life (Bandura 1997; Hammond 2002). Self-belief in the capacity to produce given attainments is based on a person's judgement of their ability to perform academic tasks or succeed in academic activities (Pajares and Graham 1999). The importance of self-belief to maintain the motivation to continue tasks in the face of barriers or hostilities cannot be underestimated (Bandura et al. 1996).

Individuals need to feel they have the ability to control their fate in life (e.g. at school, in the home, etc.) and need to know how they can effect change for better or worse. The greater the self-esteem, the more an individual is able to understand and predict their own future. The absence of self-efficacy is defined by Peterson, Maier and Seligman (1993) as 'learned helplessness', a perceived inability to control the factors that affect one's life (discussed in more depth later in this book).

Maxted (1999) considers there to be three main barriers to learning: cultural, structural and personal. Lack of motivation is a personal barrier, and lack of self-confidence and self-esteem can have a casual effect on motivation – this being the difference between those who feel they 'can't' do something and those who 'won't' do something. Crowder and Pupynin (1995) and Maxted argue that negative perceptions, based on past failure, need to be tackled and overcome before new learning can be attempted. This is similar to the learning that takes place in adult education, where success is built based on developing new positive learning experiences before new challenging learning is attempted in a learning environment that is seen as refreshingly different, and more positive than their previous schools. Bell (2009) states 'It all comes back to confidence and belief in yourself' (p.33), and the DfEE (2000) notes adult dyslexic students commenting that 'only classes exclusively for dyslexic adults are worthwhile' (p.23). Humphrey (2003) also emphasises the crucial value of support systems (peer tutoring and mentoring) in adult education, in that all learners have a shared history of educational failure so support each other to gain success.

The idea of a 'looking glass' self-concept was put forward by Cooley ([1922] 1992) to explain how opinions of self build one's self-image. Comparisons between the self and others are developed when children start school, and concepts of self created early on are hard to modify, as they start a chain of self-efficacy.

Another interesting concept is that of the 'locus of control' (LOC), developed by Rotter (1966) to investigate and understand the activity that affects the self-efficacy of individuals, the self-perception of abilities and how this affects future performance. Two forms of LOC are suggested to exist: internal and external. An individual who possesses an internal LOC perceives that his ability to perform in future tasks is based on his own abilities and skills (internal responsibility), whereas an individual with an external LOC perceives that future performance in tasks is based on the assistance of others (environmental). Studies of LOC in dyslexics found higher incidences of external LOC, whereby individuals blame external factors (e.g. bad luck or a poor teacher) for their lack of academic success.

SHAME, SELF-ESTEEM AND DYSLEXIA

Shame, according to Nathanson (1992) is one of the most powerful negative emotions, and the very idea of shame is so embarrassing that most people do not even want to talk about it. Ingesson (2007) argues that illiteracy is 'very much related to shame' (p.24) and that shame in illiteracy has been observed in those who struggle to read and write (Burden 2005; Hellendoorn and Ruijssenaars 2000). It is this shame that Burden found in young dyslexics caused humiliation and embarrassment, thus Ingesson argues that shame and low self-esteem are linked, and dyslexics commonly experience both.

'Despite a barrage of anecdotal evidence from teachers and practitioners, there is a paucity of published research in self-concept and self-esteem in children with dyslexia' (Humpreys and Mullins 2002, p.13).

Lawrence (1996, p.1) argues that 'one of the most exciting discoveries in educational psychology in recent times has been the finding that people's levels of achievement are influenced by how they feel about themselves (and vice-versa)'.

The following have been common themes in papers about the dyslexia experience at school:

- teasing, bullying and feelings of exclusion (Edwards 1994; Humphrey 2003; Riddick 1995, 1996)
- unfair treatment by teachers (Edwards 1994; Humphrey 2003; Humphrey and Mullins 2002b; Osmond 1996)
- teacher resistance to the idea of the existence of dyslexia (Riddick 1996).

Osmond (1996, p.21) notes 'the worst problem any dyslexic has to face is not reading, writing or even spelling, but a lack of understanding [in those around them]'. He found that students were asked to read aloud to the rest of the class against their will, along with dyslexic students being sent out of regular lessons to receive special lessons.

Edwards (1994) reported that dyslexic students were commonly humiliated by teachers, and made to do activities that they knew would show the dyslexic in a bad light to their peers, resulting in peer teasing and persecution.

Humphrey and Mullins (2002a), using a self-esteem manifestation inventory with two groups of dyslexics of 8–15 years old (attending special and mainstream schools) and a similar aged control group (without any learning difficulties), found:

- Both dyslexic groups were likely to continuously ask for help and reassurance in tasks, compared to controls.
- Both dyslexic groups were more likely to display timid behaviour and avoid situations of possible educational stress, compared to controls.
- The dyslexic mainstream group has significantly lower self-esteem levels than the other two groups based on reading ability and writing ability.
- The dyslexic mainstream group has significantly lower self-esteem levels than the controls based on spelling, perceptions of intelligence and popularity.
- There are no self-esteem differences between the special school and controls on self-esteem ratings of reading, spelling, writing, perceptions of intelligence and popularity.

Humphrey and Mullins conclude that the self-esteem of dyslexics in mainstream schools is much lower than those taught permanently in special schools. This suggests mainstream settings allow greater negative comparisons of worthiness affecting both motivation and self-concept.

Similarly, Humphrey and Mullins (2002b) interviewed dyslexics in both mainstream and special school settings along with controls.

They found 33 per cent of mainstream dyslexic children believed they were 'stupid, lazy or thick' (p.8), with 25 per cent of dyslexics in mainstream schools and 33 per cent of dyslexics in special schools perceiving themselves as less intelligent than their peers. The authors argued that mainstream schools were unsupportive of difference causing 'emotional baggage' or 'scars' (Edwards 1994). Humphrey and Mullins (2002b) also found the sample tended to attribute their success to external factors (e.g. quality of the teacher) rather than their own abilities (e.g. their intelligence). It was concluded that both dyslexic groups had a low LOC, and lacked control of their destiny/success in regard to learning (perceived inadequacies), whereas the control group blamed failure on internal factors such as lack of effort or lack of interest in a subject, but not lack of ability. The authors found non-dyslexic controls had stronger LOCs and were more realistic about their ability to affect change. The lack of control over their destiny/future in the dyslexic group correlates with attribution theory and 'learned helplessness' (Peterson *et al.* 1993), and several authors have also correlated dyslexia with 'learned helplessness' (Alexander-Passe 2010; Burden and Burdett 2005; Glazzard 2010, 2012).

Both Bosworth and Murray (1983) and Chapman (1988) found that dyslexic children and those with learning difficulties displayed less internal LOCs in academic contexts, compared to children without learning difficulties, thus such groups lack self-belief in their abilities and see others (e.g. a teaching assistant) as having a greater effect on their achievements.

Glazzard (2010, 2012) argues that peers are an important source of self-esteem (Kirchner and Vondraek 1975) and dyslexics perceive themselves negatively measured against their peers, this affecting their self-image in mainstream classroom settings. Like Humphrey and Mullins (2002b), Burden and Burdett (2005) found students had a more positive self-image and had 'a positive attitude towards learning' (p.103) in a special school setting.

There is strong evidence suggesting dyslexics suffer from low self-esteem when they fail consistently at school and that deviant behaviour is a common byproduct (Hales 1994; Humphrey and Mullins 2002a; Kirk and Reid 2001; Morgan 1997; Riddick 1996; Scott 2004). Riddick *et al.* (1999) and Peer and Reid (2001, p.5) agree that 'frustration leads very often to antisocial or deviant behaviour' amongst dyslexics, especially those with low self-esteem.

Some pupils might disrupt a class because they interpret the class work as threatening, and use attention seeking to protect self-esteem, according to Molnar and Lindquist (1989). They suggest that if the teacher (in the class with pupils), can re-interpret the nature and purpose of class work (maintaining the child's self-esteem), the child's long-term behaviour will change. But most teachers, as Molnar and Lindquist found, hand out reprimands, as this is the only way they know to quickly influence a child's present behaviour – a fire-fighting technique. Low self-esteem will also mean the development of a poor or negative self-image.

Such beliefs become self-fulfilling prophecies due to the expectation of failure (Riddick 1996). Morgan and Klein (2001) note that childhood experiences of being labelled as 'thick' and public humiliation caused by continual failure often result in choices that reinforce low self-esteem.

Specialist schools for dyslexics can improve self-esteem, especially social and academic self-esteem (Thomson and Hartley 1980), and Scott (2004) suggests the best improvements in self-esteem comes from literacy, as literacy improvements reduce the difference between dyslexics and their peers, and that 'difference' is the core problem.

Empirical studies note correlations between low self-esteem/anxiety and academic failure (Burns 1979) – more so with dyslexics, as Humphrey and Mullins (2002b, p.199) note: 'the experience of dyslexics at school has clear and demonstrable negative effects on the self-concept and self-esteem of children'. Riddick *et al.* (1999, p.241) indicate 'the powerful meditating effect of literacy performance on how individuals perceive themselves and are perceived by others', suggesting literacy failure can distort the dyslexic's self-perception.

Brinckerhoff, Shaw and McGuire (1993) identify the lack of positive self-concept as being the one consistent counselling issue that presents itself in people with learning difficulties, with Morgan and Klein (2003) suggesting this is also the case amongst dyslexics. Battle (1992) claims that once an individual's level of self-esteem is well established, it becomes difficult to alter and remains relatively stable over time.

Mark, diagnosed at 22, a research subject in Morgan and Klein (2003), was diagnosed as having low self-esteem from the failure to identify and address his dyslexia. As a child he read a comic book about World War II, and thought 'if the Germans invaded England, they won't waste a bullet on me'. Jackie, another subject in the same study, diagnosed at 29, provided an explanation for her frustration and anger. As an adult she is still bitter about the lack of support from her family, school and peers. She was very aggressive at school, and used to throw chairs at people in anger; as her peers knew she could easily be provoked, so they provoked her a lot:

> They called me thick, stupid, hit me etc.... I was bullied 'big time' by my peers [all the time] and bullied by my teachers. My teachers used to tell me I was mental and that men in white coats would take me away. My mum would always take the side of the teachers, which didn't help the situation. (Morgan and Klein 2003, p.51)

CONCLUSIONS

Belief in our abilities and the concept we create for ourselves is vitally important for each and every one of us. It frames our ability to function in society and our relationships with others.

Self-esteem is a complex set of views about ourselves, and is part of a continuous feedback loop that affects how we interact with those around us. If we believe we have positive attributes (e.g. being intelligent, beautiful and liked), then we will be emotionally healthy and interact with others with high regard for people's views. However, if we believe we have negative attributes (e.g. we are ugly and stupid) then we will act accordingly and withdraw from others.

Self-efficacy is based on the concept that if others believe that we are stupid or clever, then we are likely to fulfil these prophecies, as others will act according to these views. The difficulty is that we are likely to believe the views of others, even if they are contrary to our own views. This, unfortunately, when played out in the school classroom by teachers believing one set of pupils is clever and the other is lazy or of low intelligence, will mean that the teacher will act accordingly:

- believing in the clever child and motivating them to achieve
- ignoring lazy/attention seeking children causing them to feel unloved/uncared for
- giving those children believed to be of low intelligence easier or less demanding work that will not stretch them, causing them to believe they are stupid.

Perceptions of the self are important, but so is recognising that self-perceptions stem from the views of others. Research on dyslexics shows that many believed their teachers and peers when they told them that they were stupid, would be unable to attain in school, and were less intelligent than their peers.

In the case of dyslexics, if such individuals do not explain their learning differences, noting their strength and weaknesses, then the views around them are likely to be incorrect, which can lead to discrimination.

Research points to the development of strong positive self-esteem as a 'social vaccine' that can only work when self-esteem is developed without the dumbing down of school curriculums and the removal of competition at school. If allowing more children to achieve is at the cost of dumbing down all qualifications, then qualifications will become useless. Accordingly, if all children are awarded at prize day or sports day just for taking part, then it follows that the prize is nearly worthless.

Dyslexics have the ability to excel in many fields (e.g. science, art, design, engineering, computing, etc.), whilst it is true that they may struggle in English, maths and science. If you dumb down the qualifications they aim for, then have they really gained as per their peers?

Self-esteem in dyslexics is argued to come from renewed focus on their abilities, especially non-academic ones, as these are areas they can succeed in, commonly surpassing the achievements of their peers. Thus they can create a balanced self-perception and see that dyslexia is not wholly negative and punitive.

Self-efficacy and the locus of control are described in this chapter, in the context of the development of self-belief: the belief that they can affect their own lives, that they are the factor that controls their successes and failures. This is called an internal locus of control, as internally they believe they can affect change. In contrast, an external locus of control is the belief that others around them, e.g. a teacher, parent or just luck, are responsible for their successes at school or in life. This is dangerous, as if individuals lack the belief that they are in control of their own destiny, they will develop learned helplessness as noted by Seligman (1991). Research unfortunately finds that an external locus of control is common in dyslexics, and this affects their ability to effect change in their lives.

KEY MESSAGES

- Dyslexics should do their best to develop self-belief, in order to effect change in their own lives.
- Parents should teach dyslexics to challenge misconceptions about their own dyslexia, as there is no such thing as one size fits all!
- Educators should try to help dyslexics to recognise their talents, which are commonly found in non-academic subjects.
- We need to foster and celebrate all 'real' achievements and avoid 'synthetic false' achievements as they destroy the effort they take to attain.

Chapter 6

STRESS AND ANXIETY

INTRODUCTION

This chapters looks at stress and anxiety, two conditions that affect the emotional health of individuals. Stress and anxiety are formed by self-perceptions of the situations that surround individuals. Individuals may judge a situation *in situ* as threatening, or, based on past experience, they may pre-judge a situation as a threat. This chapter looks at the dyslexic experience and how threats are judged, with theories to support the concepts discussed.

STRESS

WHAT IS STRESS?

Stress is the reaction of the body and brain to situations that are perceived to be a threat, in that the stressor is too great for our coping abilities, causing an appraisal of stress. The stressor can be an event, experience or environmental stimulus (*Collins English Dictionary* 2012). Aldwin (2000) suggests it refers to negative life events that may turn into positive ones after the intervention of stress, e.g. to show what is possible if an individual is pushed a little out of their comfort zone.

The stressor could be physical (a ball being kicked towards us or the room around us being on fire) or psychological (being afraid of saying the wrong thing). Stress, or our reaction (stress response) to stress is our body trying to protect itself from the stressor. This reaction triggers a chemical response in our body that can assist us in coping with the stressor (alarm stage), e.g. adrenaline/epinephrine is pumped into our blood supply to give us an energy boost (alertness) to either run away from a fierce-looking barking dog, or face it head on. The result of such a chemical response will stimulate heart action, and increase blood pressure, metabolic rate and blood glucose concentration. It is hoped that our natural resources will be enough to overcome the threat; however, if not, the body is charged to supply additional chemicals to empower the body. However, once adrenaline is depleted, exhaustion sets in and the body is unable to cope with the threat and must withdraw and take 'flight'. Adrenaline and other chemical resources help the body to adapt quickly in order to survive and rid itself of stressful stimuli – a nervous system activation. However an over-release of adrenaline can also cause over-stimulation resulting in confusion and panic.

STRESS AND COPING MODELS

The Lazarus (1968, 1991) model of coping is important for understanding the field of coping research, noting three key aspects: (1) coping is context-bound rather than primarily driven by stable personality characteristics; (2) coping strategies are defined by effort; and (3) coping is seen as a process that changes over time during a particular encounter. The model emphasises cognitive appraisal as an intrinsic component of the coping process, with continuous appraisal taking place, starting with 'primary appraisal' (what is at stake to me, harm or benefit?) then 'secondary appraisal' (what can I do about it, what are my options?). Secondary appraisal looks at the possible options available and this is based in part on the organismic/variation as part of the S–O–R model (Stress–Organismic–Response). Personal variation will give a battery of possible responses for the individual to choose from. For example, which weapon should a soldier use in a particular situation? Grenade, rifle, tank, talking, etc., some choices will be too extreme for the situation, some will be unsuitable or ineffective and others will be ideal. Past experience (self-efficacy) will guide the option or options chosen.

Frydenberg (1999, p.48) gives a definition from a 15-year-old girl: 'coping means different things to different people. It means adapting, dealing with problems, arriving at solutions, getting knowledge and trying out things. Some people can do it better than others'. There are a range of options available to all, which may include: seeking social support; focusing on solving the problem; working hard; worrying; investing in close friendships; seeking to belong; wishful thinking; not coping; tension reduction; social action; ignoring the problem; self-blame; keeping feelings to oneself; seeking spiritual support; focusing on the positive; seeking professional help; seeking a relaxation diversion; or physical recreation. Individuals may use a number of options together or one at a time and continual appraisal will mean the options, variations and stressors may change or vary.

Pastorino and Doyle-Portillo (2009) discuss daily hassles as sources of stress, in that psychological conflicts are experienced and choices need to be made. Three main types of conflicts are detailed:

- Approach–approach conflict – occurs when a person chooses between two equally attractive options (e.g. to see a film or go out for a meal).
- Avoidance–avoidance conflict – occurs when a person chooses between two equally unattractive options (e.g. eating an ant or a beetle).
- Approach–avoidance conflict – occurs when a person must choose between two situations with both good and bad attributes (e.g. going to a good school, which will help them educationally but it will be hard, or an easier school, which will have lower educational benefits).

WHAT ARE NORMAL LEVELS OF STRESS?

At school or nursery, children learn about the world around them and more about what is socially acceptable behaviour. The question posed is what is a normal amount of stress? The answer may lie with the environment one exists in – society sets the tone of what is 'normal'.

Children learn at different rates, so what might be stressful to one child may not be to another. It is only by integration with one's peers that we can judge what is normal.

From these environments children learn about differences and expectations, and this impacts on their cognitive development. With the development of the abilities to verbalise and differentiate their feelings comes a dramatic increase in emotion-focused strategies (Band and Weisz 1988; Altschuler and Ruble 1989) and their ability to regulate their own emotions until they become overwhelming (Aldwin 2000). Through childhood to adolescence and then to adulthood they develop a range of coping strategies to deal with the thousands of stressors they encounter (e.g. schoolwork pressures, puberty, dating, examinations, socialising, marriage, children and home/work balance, getting old, etc.).

If society deems your learning to be abnormal (not normal), then stressors increase (pressure to learn as one's peers). Thus, an individual's appraisal system will choose whether such pressure is a threat or not. From such an appraisal the body puts into action a number of strategies to progress from point A to point B.

Current thinking suggests that it is best to try and protect children from all harm; however, Aldwin (2000) suggests that it is really not possible to remove all stress from a child's life and it may not be desirable anyway as stress drives emotional development. If it were removed, it would be an even greater shock when individuals are removed from the protective shell as adults.

Measures such as the 'Social Readjustment Rating Scales' (Holmes and Rahe 1967) rate stressful life events – a score of 300 points equals a risk for illness, 150–299 equals moderate risk, below 150 has a slight risk, for example:

- death of a spouse – 150 points
- death of a parent, unwed pregnancy – 100 points
- getting married – 95 points
- divorce of parents – 90 points
- suspension from school, being involved with drugs, birth of a sibling – 50 points.

Nosek (1997, p.41) notes the following neurological/chemical reactions to stress, which can become more and more extreme leading to 'muscle tension, intestinal disturbances, headaches, and rise in blood pressure signalling the "fight or flight" reaction, which can trigger extreme episodes of fear, leading to a loss of self-control'.

The two types of stress can be defined as:

- Acute stress – caused by stressors that occur for a very short amount of time. Mostly individuals can resolve the stressful situation and return to a normal mental/physiological state. Acute stress can be positive to overcome hurdles, however extreme high levels can lead to exhaustion.
- Chronic stress – caused by constant streams of demands, risks, pressures and threats that go on for a significantly long period of time. If these are prolonged this can have serious health implications, e.g. onset of strokes, heart disease or a heart attack. It can also lead to attempted suicide. Prolonged stress can become normalised, however, this can mean individuals are unaware of the health implications.

SYMPTOMS OF STRESS

Physiological

- cardiovascular: increased pulse rate, high blood pressure, chest pains
- respiratory: shortness of breath, hyperventilation, dizziness
- gastro-intestinal: loss of appetite, gas pains, indigestion, diarrhoea, nausea
- other: headaches, muscular tension, sleep disturbances, general weakness, sweating.

Psychological

- emotional: anger, guilt, mood swings, low self-esteem, depression
- anger
- pessimism
- irritable temper
- loss of interest
- loss of control.

Physical or mental performance

- difficulty concentrating and reduced vigilance – easily distracted
- errors, omissions, mistakes, incorrect actions, poor judgement and memory
- tendency to cut corners, skip items and look for the easiest way out
- slowness or hyperactivity
- focusing on manageable detail rather than serious threats
- tendency to pass responsibility onto others
- indecision or decisions postponed
- increased risk taking
- hurried and illogical actions.

GOOD AND BAD STRESS

All humans have a built in capability to deal with or protect ourselves from stress, allowing us to either run away from it (flight) or face it head on, overcoming any fears or threat (fight), as proposed by Selye (1976). The key to understanding stress is that each individual makes a primary appraisal of the situation as to whether it is stressful or not; then, if they find that it is a stressful situation, they carry out a second appraisal to determine whether to face it head on, or run away from it.

Good stress

During good stress we feel empowered and are able to deal with the stress or have the capability to overcome it. Our body triggers adrenaline to assist us in dealing with the threat, allowing us to overcome hostility. We are motivated to overcome perceived hostilities.

Bad stress

Bad stress happens when we lack the feeling of empowerment and feel the opposite. We perceive a situation or stressor as being too much and our bodies get confused. Often the body can be so confused that it freezes from indecision about the best way to proceed, which can lead to its own problems.

Cohen, Janicki-Deverts and Miller (2007) discuss the dangers of chronic psychological stress from long-term stressors, e.g. a partner or parent with dementia or from sexual assault. Health and stress have been correlated (Herbert and Cohen 1993; Ogden 2007; Schneiderman, Ironson and Siegel 2005), with stress leading to increased levels of unhealthy behaviours (e.g. smoking, poor eating habits) and susceptibility to illness (colds, insomnia, depression, anxiety, heart disease, cancers).

STRESS AND DYSLEXIA

Dyslexics face many stressful situations in their lives, and on a very regular basis. In school they are faced on an hourly basis by situations such as having to read and especially having to read aloud to others. Tests and assessments are stressful for all children; however, for the dyslexic it is a greater challenge to remember facts and information that most children can easily recall. In such cases the dyslexic may perceive the stressor as too much and choose to run away from it, either physically by avoiding the test, or emotionally by making themselves sick in class so there is a legitimate reason for their absence. Those dyslexics that stay and try to do their best can be best related to a child in a fight with one hand tied behind their back. They may proceed with the task, but on an unfair basis, likely to fail.

Ryden (1989) observes the fatigue that many dyslexics suffer as they try and push themselves to achieve as per their peers, which has an adverse effect on tiredness, irritability and susceptibility to illness. Biggar and Barr (1996), researching 20 dyslexic schoolchildren, found their first response to a stressor was to conceal their inabilities and this traps them in an emotional state that can delay their learning and impacts on their motivation to attempt tasks.

Concerning good stress, Fawcett (1995) argues concerning successful dyslexics: 'it may well be that these children started off with a constant struggle in acquiring literacy, and then simply carried on fighting throughout their adult lives to reach heights to which others cannot aspire'. This suggests that stress can be positive for dyslexics, as they can develop a constant drive to aspire.

Thomson (1996) suggests there are two reactions that result from stress in school-aged dyslexics. First 'under-reactions', where the child withdraws and manifests extreme anxiety, e.g. trembling and sweating when asked to read. This results in low self-opinion, with the child generalising failure to all aspects of their lives. The second is 'over-reaction' to stress, e.g. being seen as successful in other, mainly non-academic, areas, playing the class clown, hiding failure under a 'couldn't care less' attitude and manifesting silly behaviour. The 'couldn't care less' attitude can lead to aggression and anger towards peers (Edwards 1994; Alexander-Passe 2006).

Alexander-Passe (2008) found the following profiles were created from the dyslexic teenage samples investigated through a standardised quantitative and qualitative methodology:

- Dyslexic females are likely to have negative perceptions of their teachers' and peers' feelings towards them and experience stress as a result, resulting in negative peer comparisons leading to poor academic self-concept of their abilities. This will result in them using behavioural manifestations to misbehave or act out in class.
- Dyslexic males are likely to experience stress relative to their grades, to test taking and to their general academic performance, resulting in mainly emotional, but also physiological manifestations.
- Compared to their control siblings, dyslexics perceive negative peer feelings towards them, which results in a poor self-concept of their abilities.
- Unfair sibling comparisons in three families resulted in emotional manifestations of stress (shyness, loneliness), whereas dyslexics in two other families tended to manifest through behaviour, maybe to gain parental attention.
- Birth order investigations note that dyslexics are not commonly first born in their families, and this can add to unfair sibling comparison, with dyslexia being initially dismissed due to the first born being dyslexia-free.

ANXIETY

WHAT IS ANXIETY?

Anxiety can be ether specific to a single situation or task, or global, and related to a number of tasks. It is based on an individual's perception of tasks or stressors before they occur. Barlow (2000) defines anxiety as 'a future-orientated mood state in which one is ready or prepared to attempt to cope with upcoming negative events'. It is the difference between perceived and present stressors that differentiates anxiety from fear. Alternative words to describe anxiety are dread or apprehension. Csikszentmihalyi (1997) alternatively perceives anxiety as having insufficient coping skills.

Barker (2003) focuses on the behavioural effects of anxiety:

- mild cases can manifest in nail biting, nervous habits, poor sleeping patterns, irritability, restlessness
- moderate cases can cause avoidance of situations, watching for the feared stimulus, nightmares
- severe cases can manifest as phobias and mental health trauma as in post-traumatic stress disorder.

Test anxiety is understood to include fear of failure causing apprehension about taking tests. This can manifest in sweating, dizziness, headaches, racing heartbeats, nausea, fidgeting, uncontrollable crying or laughing and drumming on desks. The fear of negative public evaluation from parents, peers, teachers and others can cause significant anxiety in such pressured environments. There is some discussion as to whether test anxiety is anxiety or, as the DSM-IV sees it, a type of social phobia (Beidel and Turner 1988; Liebert and Morris 1967; Rapee and Heimberg 1997).

Social anxiety can be seen in individuals with stammers, in that a single stimulus or multiple feared stimuli regarding speech have caused such a trauma, that it causes them to be fearful of any situation in which speaking is required (Blumgart, Tran and Craig 2010). Whilst 70 per cent of such children grow out of a stammer, 30 per cent retain it into adulthood as a lifetime affliction. Those who develop social phobia can avoid interactions with others outside a small family circle, and avoid embracing or shaking hands, leading to a condition called 'avoidant personality disorder' (Settipani and Kendall 2013).

Anxiety is commonly defined as either a ‘state’, which is short-term, or a ‘trait’, which is a long-term condition. As a ‘state’ condition a person with anxiety could be fearful of making the wrong decision due to too many choices being given, with possible outcomes being unknown; or indecision could be affected by alcohol, drugs or caffeine, causing a racing heart and shakiness (Hartley and Phelps 2012). When anxiety is a ‘trait’, the fear is long term as is sometimes found in the case of phobias or post-traumatic stress disorder, the fear of environments or objects (e.g. spiders, tight spaces, heights).

CAUSES

There are many possible causes of anxiety in individuals; these can include:

- genetic factors
- parental rejection
- lack of parental warmth
- high hostility towards them as children
- harsh disciplinary parent or teacher
- anxious child-rearing
- modelling of dysfunctional/drug-abusing behaviours
- child abuse (emotional, physical or sexual).

(Bienvenu and Ginsberg 2007)

GOOD AND BAD ANXIETY

Whilst all individuals have doubts at time about their ability, they tend to use this to be extra cautious and better their performance. Where anxiety become all-consuming and all tasks, which may lead to ridicule from their peers are feared (e.g. test anxiety), then such anxiety can become toxic and unhealthy for individuals.

ANXIETY AND DYSLEXIA

Dyslexics can feel anxiety in a range of situations where they run the risk of being seen by others as being stupid or incompetent. Many typical school activities can induce anxiety, e.g. reading aloud, taking tests, spelling tests, writing tasks, group activities and discussions. The anxiety carries out to non-academic subjects like sports, where they may drop balls or be overly clumsy. Outside school they may avoid social activities, they may turn up at the wrong time, get on the wrong bus or misread social clues. As adults they may avoid career paths or jobs that might highlight their literacy or numeracy difficulties, and unfortunately their anxiety at the thought of being seen as stupid or unworthy can cause them to avoid dating and long-term relationships due to their low self-worth and perceptions of unworthiness. Gilroy (1995) notes the majority of dyslexics she meets conceal the true nature of their difficulty, with Maughan (1995, p.362) stating that dyslexic adults 'appear to set self-imposed boundaries on their occupational choices', which is viewed as a coping strategy. McLoughlin *et al.* (1994), like Hales (1995), observed that dyslexic adults employed a number of 'subterfuges to avoid detection' as they were anxious about their capabilities to perform in literacy-based environments, with one subject having had 27 jobs since leaving school in order to constantly conceal the true nature of his intellect, and to cover up his difficulties with basic tasks. Hales (1995, pp.182–183) notes this can require a 'substantial mental juggling act and can easily lead to anxiety levels far in excess of what would otherwise be expected'.

Aldridge (1995, p.110) remarks that as adults receiving comments on their performance in the workplace or at university, dyslexics commonly have 'flash-backs to particularly painful and fearful classroom experiences'.

The DfEE report 'Freedom to learn' (2000) investigating adult learners commented:

> the main additional barrier for learners with dyslexia acquiring basic skills stems from their previous learning experiences. Many adults with dyslexia feel that they have had humiliating and damaging experiences of school education and many report unsuccessful attempts to acquire basic skills through adult basic education classes. (DfEE 2000, pp.22–23).

CONCLUSIONS

This chapter looks at stress and anxiety, argued to be two sides of the same coin.

Both occur due to an individual's perceptions of a situation he faces. Stress is caused by the perception that a current situation is too challenging. It is a value judgement that each person makes based on their own abilities. To some, stress is a challenge to overcome, whereas to others it is too much of a challenge leading to an emotional overload of distress/panic. Thus, it is personally constructed and hard to measure.

Anxiety is based on the fear of a stressful situation that an individual has in the past found emotionally distressing. Thus anticipating a second or third experience of that stressful situation can cause an individual to develop anxiety to protect themselves from further emotional harm. However, others might argue that anxiety prevents fear of a particular situation from being overcome.

In the case of dyslexics, stress is caused by literacy and numeracy demands that force them to try and attain as per their peers, and as per society's perception of 'normal' abilities. Both at school and in the workplace, dyslexics are challenged to attain but lack the skills and abilities to do so. This causes a learning task to become feared and anxiety is developed as a self-protecting strategy. This anxiety can have long-lasting effects, starting with a small child struggling with reading in primary school, and leading to a father not reading to their own child at bedtime.

KEY MESSAGES

- Dyslexics should try and be realistic about what they can achieve at each stage of their lives. As soon as they gain mastery of one goal, they should move onto the next. Not everything can be achieved at once!
- Dyslexics come home from school exhausted and they need help to unwind before starting on homework. They are likely to be frustrated from failure at school, so should be given space and encouragement.
- A teacher's aim must always be to avoid anxiety, by never making learning situations threatening.

Chapter 7

DYSLEXIC COPING PROFILES

INTRODUCTION

This chapter looks at empirical profiles of dyslexics to understand how they cope and function in modern society. This is important for educators and policy makers alike, as it can shape policy decisions and assist in understanding this complex set of learners.

Studies of school-aged children, teenagers, college/university students and adults assist educators in understanding that the coping strategies used by dyslexics have common elements that would not necessarily be found in the general population.

Risk avoidance to protect self-esteem as discussed in previous chapters is common and features in these profiles.

RELEVANT STUDIES

Several researchers have attempted to understand the dyslexic profile in order to inform educational policies and give non-dyslexics a better understanding of the condition.

Ingesson (2007) suggests there are four main groups of dyslexics from his quantitative and qualitative study on 75 teenagers with dyslexia: relaxed, strugglers, best adjusted and resigned. Table 7.1 (on page 127) depicts the profile of each group and describes a number of areas that can inform educational policy:

- The relaxed group members have a good support network and have found positivity at school through non-academic endeavours. Whilst they know they perform poorly at school, they also know that life post-school will not be purely down to academic results.
- The struggler group members understand that academic success comes through hard work and they seem prepared to do what is required to keep their necks above the water. They have good support at home and this has allowed them to remain positive about life after school.
- The best adjusted group members seemed to utilise support networks both at school and at home and this has brought them success in various environments supporting their self-esteem, which motivates them to continue with their studies and look beyond to college.
- The resigned group members struggle to cope at school and this had a knock on effect on both their self-esteem and their relationships with peers and their parents. Their lack of success in non-academic hobbies can mean they experience failure in most settings and this is affecting their emotional well-being.

To conclude, these profiles are fairly descriptive of how many dyslexics cope at school and are supported by research featured in the previous chapters.

TABLE 7.1 INGESSON'S (2007) COPING PROFILES FOR SCHOOL-AGED DYSLEXICS

GROUP	ATTRIBUTES
Relaxed	Optimism, acceptance of disability
	High sense of global self-worth (through deprecation of school achievements, e.g. reading/writing)
	Felt had done poorly at school
	Academic competence was perceived as less important than being social, good at sport or practical
	Their parents were more accepting of child's abilities/difficulties, and optimistic that they would do well despite academic difficulties
	They had found a niche at school/out of school in a subject they did well, e.g. sport/art/drama to make them more positive/give them higher self-esteem
	Average IQ
Strugglers	Optimism, acceptance of disability, strong sense of global self-worth, coherence
	Average IQ
	High belief in self (self-efficacy) – had come to terms with their struggles at school
	Felt their self-esteem had decreased over time
	Worked very hard to maintain schoolwork
	Received extensive help from parents (mainly mothers)
	Had struggled with feelings of inferiority but were now adjusted in school and with peers
	Persisted at school despite adversity
	Internal locus of control (felt responsibility to do well)

GROUP	ATTRIBUTES
Best adjusted	Mothers supported with reading, writing and homework
	Did not want to let mothers down with poor schoolwork
	Internal locus of control
	Persisted at school despite adversity
	Had experienced success at school and seen their persistence had paid off
	High motivation to do well
	Plans to go to college
	High belief in self (self-efficacy) – had come to terms with their struggles at school
	Low academic self-esteem
	They had found a niche at school/out of school in a subject they did well, e.g. sport/art/drama to make them more positive/give them higher self-esteem
	Good relationship with parents
	Mothers had belief in their child's potential
	Family attitude that difficulties are there to overcome (positive frame of mind)
Resigned	Low global self-worth, felt had done poorly at school
	Mothers concerned about their child post-school
	Lower IQ, which may be reflected in other difficulties at school
	Poor relations with peers
	Poor relations with parents
	Poor support from parents and teachers
	Vulnerable to stressful experiences
	Low psychological well-being
	Lack of hobbies at school
	Low perceived competence in academic and social domains

From a qualitative study of 142 college students with dyslexia and their parents, Kurnoff (2001) created the following four coping profiles: conventionalists, low profilers, independents and pragmatists. Table 7.2 depicts these profiles, which like those of Ingesson denote dyslexics who experience both success and failure in academic settings. Kurnoff's sample was from a college in the USA, and the study emphasises the need for support systems, both at school/college and at home. It describes how many years of failure in school settings have left individuals wary of disclosure in academic settings; however, if support is avoided then the dyslexic will be unfairly discriminated against when their work is marked. Both studies suggest that survival is the aim rather than flourishing in such settings.

TABLE 7.2 KURNOFF'S (2001) PROFILES OF DYSLEXIC STUDENTS AT COLLEGE

Conventionalists	Are identified with dyslexia and are happy with the label Known as having dyslexia Known to SEN unit, so get support from academic counsellors and tutors Depend heavily on support to cope with the workload Get extra time for assignments Work less to create personal strategies as these are given to them Have little time to look beyond provided strategies to create their own, even if those provided are unsuitable Prefer structure and stability when learning
Low profilers	Want to lie low Happy to be average and survive their course Deny their dyslexia/difficulties Refuse to ask for extra time for assignments Light on coping strategies (they go with the flow) Do not disclose difficulties Unknown to SEN unit (avoid it), so do not get support Rely heavily on work being proof-read at home by parents Have been hurt in the past by identifying themselves as dyslexic Scared to disclose dyslexia, fear discrimination Often leave it too late to ask for extra time for tasks and can burn out
Independents	Create lots of their own personal strategies Good at problem solving, creative thinkers Do not generally get extra time for assignments Known unofficially to SEN unit, see what is on offer and then do their own thing Create their own peer support network Will ask professors personally for extra time for tasks without disclosing their dyslexia Heavy computer users for support software Tend to be individualistic Prefer flexibility Visionary about college attendance Prefer to do things their own way

Pragmatists	Are identified with dyslexia and are happy with the label Known as having dyslexia Known to SEN unit, so get support from academic counsellors and tutors Get extra time for assignments Top up support through personal strategies (and these are successful) Work closely with counsellors, proof-readers, note takers

Alexander-Passe (2004, 2009a) investigated 26 teenagers with dyslexia; three profiles were formed by triangulating the results of measures of self-esteem, coping and depression with an interview study. Three profiles (see Table 7.3) were created from analysis of the three standardised quantitative measures:

- avoiding
- trying
- feeling good.

These describe three ways dyslexics cope at school, namely:

- 'avoiding' tasks that cause anxiety and stress (reading, writing, assessments) and blaming others for their failure in tasks
- 'trying hard' at school and gaining a belief in their own skills to overcome challenges at school, as they had experienced success in such settings
- 'feeling good' about themselves because of popularity at school and a good relationship with their parents.

TABLE 7.3 THREE PROFILES FOUND IN THE QUANTITATIVE STUDY: AVOIDING, TRYING AND FEELING GOOD

Avoiding	High use of avoidance coping High use of distraction to cope with schoolwork (avoid work) High use of emotion coping (external locus of control)
Trying	High use of task-based coping (internal locus of control) High academic self-esteem (belief in their own abilities and have experienced success at school/in tasks) Low use of social diversion to cope with peers Low depression
Feeling good	High social self-esteem (popular with peers) High general self-esteem (feel good about themselves) High parental self-esteem (their parents believe in them and they get on well with them)

The qualitative aspect of the study enlarged the three groups into four (striving, dodging, disrupting and withdrawing) and Table 7.4 fleshes out their profiles based on the quantitative data, so that they better describe children coping in educational settings, aiding educationalists for identification purposes. Table 7.5 identifies disrupting (negative coping) as the largest overall coping strategy used by students in the study (39.9%), followed by dodging (negative coping) with (36.4%), with only a fifth (19.6%) using a positive strategy in their schooling. This suggests teenage dyslexics tend to survive school by any means possible rather than achieving as per their potential.

TABLE 7.4 FOUR STRATEGIES AS FOUND IN THE QUALITATIVE STUDY: STRIVING, DODGING, DISRUPTING AND WITHDRAWING

	STRATEGY 1: STRIVING	STRATEGY 2: DODGING	STRATEGY 3: DISRUPTING	STRATEGY 4: WITHDRAWING
General personality	Will try new tasks and have a positive outlook on life Never secretive	Will frequently try new tasks with a generally positive outlook on life Sometimes secretive		Will never try new tasks, depressive and very negative about life Very secretive
How they react to success	Will always expect success and are willing to take risks to gain success	Will frequently expect success and will frequently take risks to gain success	Will sometimes expect success and will only sometimes take risks to gain success	Will never expect success and will never take risks to gain success
How they react to failure	Will never expect to fail and will always attempt the task again Will always handle failure well		Will frequently expect to fail and will frequently be put off attempting the task again Will sometimes handle failure well	Will always expect to fail and will always be put off attempting the task again Will never handle failure well
What support do they get?	Can attract support from their parents, peers and teachers	Can't attract support from their teachers, since they cover up their dyslexia	Negate all chance of support as their disruptive behaviour is seen as the main problem	Support from anyone is refused
Attitude towards school	Worthwhile	Sometimes worthwhile	Not worthwhile	Not at all worthwhile
How they deal with school	Always realistic about their abilities at school Always react well to school tests Many (5+) friends at school	Frequently realistic about their abilities at school Frequently react well to school tests Few (3–5) friends at school	Sometimes realistic about their abilities at school Sometimes react well to school tests Some (2–3) friends at school	Never realistic about their abilities at school Never react well to school tests No (0–1) friends at school
How teachers perceive them in school	Always confident and/or ambitious Always have a positive outlook on schoolwork No behavioural problems in class	Frequently confident and/or ambitious Frequently have a positive outlook on schoolwork Some behavioural problems in class	Sometimes confident and/or ambitious Sometimes have a positive outlook on schoolwork Frequent behavioural problems in class	Never confident and/or ambitious Never have a positive outlook to schoolwork Consistent behavioural problems in class

TABLE 7.5 MEAN PERCENTAGE DATA (AND STANDARD DEVIATIONS) FOR THE FOUR HYPOTHETICAL STRATEGIES

MEANS (SD)	STRATEGY 1: STRIVING	STRATEGY 2: DODGING	STRATEGY 3: DISRUPTING	STRATEGY 4: WITHDRAWING
Pilot study (n = 7)	19.2 (13.8)	42.5 (10.1)	30.2 (9.8)	7.8 (4.7)
Main study (n = 19)	19.7 (14.5)	34.2 (12.5)	39.4 (11.7)	6.5 (5)
Overall (n = 26)	19.6 (14)	36.4 (12.3)	39.9 (11.8)	6.8 (1.9)

Alexander-Passe (2009b) investigated low, medium and high trait dyslexics, compared to a control group. The study investigated the personality profiles of different severities of dyslexics, using Vinegrad's (1994) dyslexic trait measurement checklist, along with an experimental version of Eysenck and Eysenck's (1975) Personality Inventory (Extroversion–Introversion and Neuroticism–Emotional Stability scales).

The sample of 87 adults contained 50 per cent self-diagnosed dyslexics and 50 per cent controls. Four groups were created according to the number of traits scored: 0–4 traits (n = 18, 20.4%), 5–9 traits (n = 23, 26.1%), 10–14 traits (n = 30, 34.1%) and 15–19 traits (n = 16, 18.4%).

Overall, males were more confident, more independent, more optimistic, more highly disciplined, more resistant to fears/anxieties, less frequently ill and more impulsive compared to females.

The second part of the study investigated academic success, defined as gaining a university degree. Of the 30 with moderate (10–14) dyslexic traits (11 males and 19 females), 23 took O levels (76.7%), 3 only took CSEs at school and 5 (18%) left school with no qualifications.

Those with moderate dyslexia traits (10–14) were found to be more likely to attain academic success on a par with their peers, than those with high (15–19) numbers of dyslexic traits, and 46 per cent of the whole sample had gained a degree (44% among those in the 10–19 dyslexic trait group), and again personality was found to be a differential in the 10–19 trait group, along with gender and trait severity. The moderate (10–14) trait group was perceived as having the most likely success personality profile according to empirical studies.

From these results, profiles indicating gender and success differentials were created to better inform both educators and parents of the personality traits required for success with a learning difference/difficulty (Table 7.6).

TABLE 7.6 DYSLEXIC ADULT PERSONALITY PROFILES (ACADEMICALLY SUCCESSFUL AND UNSUCCESSFUL)

ACADEMICALLY SUCCESSFUL DYSLEXIC MALES	ACADEMICALLY SUCCESSFUL DYSLEXIC FEMALES
Physically inactive and lethargic Casual, easygoing and have less need for order Resistant to irrational fears or anxieties Confident in themselves/abilities Enjoy freedom, independent and are realistic about abilities Do not regret past actions/behaviour Cheerful, optimistic and mentally healthy Careless, late and unpredictable Enjoy socialising and meet people easily Live dangerously, can be gamblers and enjoy taking risks Like ideas, discussions and speculation	Do not regret past actions/behaviour Cheerful, optimistic and mentally healthy Resistant to irrational fears or anxieties Systematic, orderly and can be cautious
ACADEMICALLY UNSUCCESSFUL DYSLEXIC MALES	**ACADEMICALLY UNSUCCESSFUL DYSLEXIC FEMALES**
Careful, highly disciplined and finicky Easily upset by things that go wrong Active and energetic Have low self-opinion and feel like unattractive failures Lack self-reliance and can easily be pushed around Self-blaming and can be self-questioning of life Pessimistic, gloomy and depressed Reliable, trustworthy and a bit compulsive Few special friends and enjoy solo activities Prefer familiarity, safety and needs security	Self-blaming and self-questioning of life Pessimistic, gloomy and can be depressed Are easily upset by things that go wrong Can make hurried and premature decisions

CONCLUSIONS

A number of studies were detailed in this chapter, investigating school-aged, teenage, university/college students and adult dyslexics.

There seems to be a consensus that dyslexics are affected by previous learning situations and this affects their abilities in present and future educational environments.

Three main coping methods were found:

- those who cope by various means (normally utilising support systems)
- those who manage to cope by focusing on non-academic subjects to retain positive self-esteem, which can at times mean disrupting to camouflage their inabilities
- those who do not cope, and suffer as a result from low self-esteem and lack of self-belief.

It is important to recognise that dyslexics commonly use a range of strategies to cope, and that whilst one may be dominant, they can use more than one to deal with a range of situations, e.g. an individual may be happy to be labelled as dyslexic and to receive help at primary school, but in secondary school may avoid this and try to cope by themselves.

KEY MESSAGES

- Dyslexics who recognise their learning/coping style amongst those listed, should know that they are not alone, and that others survive the minefield of education as will they.
- Dyslexics are not normal learners, in that they see learning situations as stressful and full of anxiety. Educators should use these profiles to plan provision, and to recognise why dyslexics choose certain paths for survival, then guide them into alternative provisions that protect their anonymity with their peers.

Chapter 8

DEFENCE MECHANISMS AND COPING STRATEGIES

INTRODUCTION

As noted in Chapter 6, there are different reactions to stress and what is stressful for one may not be for another: some may shrug off being reprimanded, whilst others may take it personally, withdrawing to cry; some might get angry and lash out, and others might take on board the comments and try and improve themselves. Lazarus and Folkman (1984) and Aldwin (2000) argue there are four main approaches to coping:

- person-based approaches
- situation-based approaches
- interactionist approaches
- transactionist approaches.

Defence mechanisms are a type of coping that results in automatic psychological responses exhibited as a means of protecting the individual against anxiety (Dziegielewski 2010). Valliant (1977) argues that defences have six important properties:

- They mitigate the distressing effects of both emotion and cognitive dissonance.
- They are unconscious (or, otherwise stated, involuntary).

- They are discrete from one another.
- Although often the hallmarks of major psychiatric syndromes, they are dynamic and, unlike the brain disease they mimic, are reversible.
- They can be adaptive, even creative, as well as pathological.
- If to the user defences are invisible, to the observer defences appear odd, even annoying.

This chapter will look at different theories of ego-defences.

COPING STRATEGIES VS DEFENCE MECHANISMS

The study of coping strategies has its roots in psychoanalytic descriptions of ego-defence mechanisms, which are concerned with dealing with internal conflict. Whilst Freud (1961) began work on studying defence mechanisms in 1924, his daughter A. Freud (1966) completed the majority of the work that is the basis on which they are now understood. Specifically, how the ego is the moderator between the id (devil on one shoulder) and the superego (angel on the other shoulder). It is explained that when the ego has a difficult time making the id and superego happy, it employs one or more defence mechanisms as a coping strategy.

Vaillant (1977) identifies five major functions of defence mechanisms:

1. to keep affects within bearable limits during sudden life crises (e.g. following a death)
2. to restore emotional balance by postponing or channelling sudden increases in biological drives (e.g. at puberty)
3. to obtain a time-out to master changes in self-image (e.g. following major surgery or unexpected promotion)
4. to handle irresolvable conflicts with people, living or dead, whom one cannot bear to leave
5. to survive major conflicts with conscience (e.g. killing in wartime, putting a parent in a nursing home).

(Vaillant 1977, p.10)

Overall, Valliant's notion of defence is far more broad than that of Freud since it includes conscious defences.

Holmes (1984) puts it more succinctly, listing three central features of defence mechanisms: (1) avoidance or reduction of negative emotional states; (2) distortion of reality to various degrees, from mild to blatant; and (3) lack of conscious awareness in using defence mechanisms. As noted in the DSM-IV:

> Defence mechanisms (or coping styles) are automatic psychological processes that protect the individual against anxiety and from the awareness of internal or external stressors. Individuals are often unaware of these processes as they operate. Defence mechanisms mediate the individual's reaction to emotional conflicts and internal and external stressors. (American Psychiatric Association 1994, p.751)

A recent review by Whitbourne (2010) defines defence mechanisms as including:

1. *Denial* – You can consider this the 'generic' defence mechanism because it underlies many of the others. When you use denial, you simply refuse to accept the truth or reality of a fact or experience.

2. *Repression* – One step above denial in the generic classification scheme, repression involves simply forgetting something bad. You might forget an unpleasant experience from the past, such as a car accident in which you were found to be at fault. You might also use repression when you 'forget' to do something unpleasant such as seeing the dentist.

3. *Regression* – From repression to regression – one little 'g' makes all the difference. In regression, you revert back to a childlike emotional state in which your unconscious fears, anxieties and general 'angst' reappear.

4. *Displacement* – In displacement you transfer your original feelings that would get you in trouble (usually anger) away from the person who is the target of your rage to a more hapless and harmless victim. Here's the classic example: You've had a very unpleasant interaction with your boss or teacher, but you can't show your anger towards him or her. Instead, you come home and, so to speak, 'kick the cat' (or dog).

5. *Projection* – The first four defence mechanisms were relatively easy to understand, I think. Projection is more challenging. First, you have to start with the assumption that to recognise a particular quality in yourself would cause you psychic pain. Let's say you're worried that you're not really very smart. You make a dumb mistake that no one says anything about at all, and accuse others of saying that you're dumb, inferior or just plain stupid. You are 'projecting' your insecurities onto others and in the process, alienating them (and probably looking somewhat foolish as well).
6. *Reaction formation* – Now we're getting into advanced defence mechanism territory. Most people have difficulty understanding reaction formation, but it's really quite straightforward. Let's say that you secretly harbour lustful feelings towards someone you should probably stay away from. You don't want to admit to these feelings, so you instead express the very opposite of those feelings.
7. *Intellectualisation* – You might also neutralise your feelings of anxiety, anger or insecurity in a way that is less likely to lead to embarrassing moments than some of the above defence mechanisms. In intellectualisation, you think away an emotion or reaction that you don't enjoy feeling.
8. *Rationalisation* – When you rationalise something, you try to explain it away. As a defence mechanism, rationalisation is somewhat like intellectualisation, but it involves dealing with a piece of bad behaviour on your part rather than converting a painful or negative emotion into a more neutral set of thoughts. It's easier to blame someone else than to take the heat yourself, particularly if you would otherwise feel shame or embarrassment.
9. *Sublimation* – We've just seen that people can use their emotions to fire up a cognitively oriented response. Intellectualisation tends to occur over the short run, but sublimation develops over a long period of time. Sublimation occurs when people transform their conflicted emotions into productive outlets.

(Whitbourne 2010, paras 3–11)

In short, Whitbourne argues defence mechanisms are one of our commonest ways to cope with unpleasant emotions. Although Freud and many of his followers believed that we use them to combat sexual or aggressive feelings, defence mechanisms apply to a wide range of reactions from anxiety to insecurity.

Kreitler and Kreitler (2004, p.203) suggest that coping strategies differ from defence mechanisms in four ways: (1) they are performance programmes rather than conflict resolution programmes; (2) they may be, and often are, enacted overtly rather than internally; (3) they may be applied consciously; and (4) they deal with major defined threat or stress that endangers the individual's physical or psychological survival or both. Similar aspects of the two are denial, displacement and rationalisation. Cramer (1998, 2000) adds that defence and coping can be differentiated based on psychological processes, but not based on outcome.

A. Freud (1966) identified several major defence mechanisms: suppression, denial, projection, reaction formation, hysteria, obsessive-compulsive behaviours and sublimation:

- Suppression and denial are similar but in varying forms, in that the individual will refuse to acknowledge an event or feeling.
- Those using suppression will not think about the event, whilst those using denial won't even acknowledge there was ever such an event.
- The hysterical person will inappropriately focus on the event and may spend all day crying about it.
- The obsessive-compulsive will spend so long checking and rechecking for the event that he/she may miss it.
- Those using projection and reaction formation are similar in that they both externalise the problem.
- Those using projection will see the event as wrong and project their anger at others. With reaction formation they will invert their own feelings or anger into admiration and think how great the people running the event are.
- Those using sublimation will learn from the event for the future.

(A. Freud 1966)

With these models, the environmental stimulus has very little or nothing to do with the coping strategy chosen, rather the defence strategy chosen aims to reduce anxiety by whatever means possible. Freud argues the behaviours, feelings and cognitions evoked by the stressful event situation are determined by the individual's personality structure and developed in early childhood and are not easily modified.

Aldwin (2000) suggests that defence mechanisms can either be used fleetingly, only under great stress, or can be habitual, whilst Shapiro (1965) argues that people can be characterised by their predominate use of a particular mechanism, e.g. the obsessive-compulsive is characterised by being rigid, distorting the experience, or losing sight of reality.

Strategies discussed to date have tended to be negative; Vaillant (1977) and Haan (1977) discuss both positive and negative mechanisms.

Vaillant's study tracked 100 men from 1930 to the 1970s indicating a range of unconscious adaptive styles at different stages of these men's lives. He notes that even strategies involving planning and anticipation are unconscious and are concentrated on the regulation of emotion and the preservation of ego integrity, and these strategies were termed as projective, immature, neurotic and mature.

Vaillant (1977) explains them as:

- projective mechanisms (denial, distortion and delusional projection)
- immature mechanisms (fantasy, projection, hypochondriasis, passive aggression and acting out)
- neurotic mechanisms (intellectualisation, isolation, obsessive behaviour, undoing, rationalisation, repression, reaction formation, displacement and dissociation)
- mature mechanisms (sublimination, altruism, suppression, anticipation and humour).

The adaptative styles that Vaillant suggests can be seen in everyday life dealing with both everyday events and trends from childhood. Vaillant demonstrated over a period of time that: defences are stable over time; largely independent of the person's environment; and associated with a host of meaningful social, personal and biological characteristics.

Conte, Plutchik and Draguns (2004) question what constitutes a defence, as the number of defences considered to exist varies widely among researchers (Brenner 1994; Plutchick, Kellerman and Conte 1979; Vaillant 1977; Wong 1998). There are ten defences according to A. Freud (1966); eight defences according to Vaillant (1971); 11 defences according to Brenner (1973); and 31 defences included in the DSM-IV (APA 1994). Critics of Vaillant not only point to the lack of females in his study, but also to the lack of investigation of problem-solving techniques over the life course, however, the latter were included in later parts of his work. Vaillant's study does, however, document how learning, heredity, love and social support play major roles in the defences chosen unconsciously by individuals over time.

In contrast to the work of Vaillant, Haan (1977) attempts to create a more straightforward approach to understanding how conscious and unconscious defences are chosen and used, maintaining that defence mechanisms are inherently pathological and constructed via a hierarchy of adaptation based upon the extent to which the strategies used reflect conscious or unconscious processes. Haan identifies ten basic or generic ego processes that can be expressed in three modes (coping, defence and fragmentary processes):

- coping (conscious, flexible, purposive and permits moderate expression of emotion)
- defensive (compelled, negating, rigid and is directed towards anxiety rather than the problem)
- fragmentation or ego failure (distorts 'intersubjective reality' and is automated, ritualistic and irrational).

The ten generic processes are then divided into four functions: cognitive, reflexive–intraceptive, attention seeking and attention–impulsive regulation. The processes are not only used to reduce anxiety, but also to regulate cognitive processing, provide self-reflective capacity and focus attention.

Haan (1977, p.49) notes that coping processes happen when assimilation and accommodation are evenly matched or unpressured, defensive processes happen when there are marked imbalances between assimilation and accommodations, and fragmentation happens when the imbalances between the assimilation and accommodation are so great that the individual retreats as the requirements are not only beyond the person's capability, but irrefutably contradict and confuse their self-constructions and make a retreat to another reality preferable.

Haan argues that generally a mixture of coping and defensive strategies are used in healthy development, moving from defensive to coping modes, described as gaining progressive control over behaviour. Critics of Haan question her assertion that rational coping can only happen when individuals are under normal stress, as those at war and fighting a fire can make rational and good judgements (Aldwin 2000; Horowitz 1986). Hann's study at Berkeley with men and women and Vaillant's study with men at Harvard are supportive of each other and suggest that defence and coping are both adaptive.

Cramer (1991), taking an alternative view, identifies three main defence mechanisms: denial, projection and identification. She explains these in the following way:

- 'Denial' inhibits thought or emotion by the attachment of a negative marker to the idea or affect.
- 'Projection' as a defence is complex, involving three steps: differentiating between internal and external; comparing the thought or feeling with internal standards; and attributing unacceptable thoughts/feeling to an external source. This displacement onto another avoids the shame or guilt of owning the emotions.
- 'Identification' being the most complex of the three, requires the capacity to differentiate self from others, to differentiate among others, to form inner representations of others and to adopt some qualities of important person (whilst rejecting others) in the process of identification. Thoughts and feelings are not inhibited, but taken over from others and incorporated into the self, protecting the self through affiliation.

(Cramer 1991)

Cramer (2004) suggests that defence mechanism use varies with age and that younger children use denial the most. In a study of three main defences (denial, projection and identification), 'denial' was construed as a developmentally early defence, reaching an early peak. 'Projection' rises to its highest level in late childhood and pre-adolescence, and declines thereafter. The developmental progression for 'identification' exhibits a progressive ascent all the way to late adolescence. Roecker, Dubow and Donaldson (1996, p.351), like Cramer; found that junior high school children report distancing/denial mechanisms to deal with interpersonal conflicts. These studies were corroborated in part by Smith and Danielsson (1982) with Swedish samples and Dias (1976) with Swiss samples. However, Wertlieb *et al.* (1987) and Donaldson *et al.* (2000) suggest that school-aged children use more wishful thinking to deal with school and sibling difficulties. Their study found that whilst the level of use of a particular strategy may vary across situations (school, peers, siblings, family), it did not alter the overall pattern of strategies chosen. Wishful thinking topped all other strategies (followed by emotional regulation, problem solving, cognitive restructuring and distraction) and was stable over gender, type of stressor reported or age (early or middle adolescence). Older adolescents used a much wider range of strategies but these were related to those chosen in early and middle adolescence. Stark *et al.* (1989, p.351) noticed that adolescents use more self-criticism with school problems than with parent or friend problems.

Whilst Donaldson *et al.* found these mechanisms were stable across stressors, Band and Weisz (1988) found they were not, thus such a conclusion needs further investigation.

Cramer and Gaul (1988) also found that children who experience failure tend to rely on maladaptive and immature defences, whilst children who experience success tend to utilise more mature defences. Accordingly, given that perfectionists are generally intolerant of failure and have an elevated fear of failure (Flett *et al.* 1991), changing a child's defences will be easier when they experience successful outcomes and develop a heightened sense of self-efficacy (the ability to control ones destiny), rather than when they are fully developed and strategies are reinforced and rigid in adulthood.

Another alternative model is found in Meissner (1980), who suggests a greater range of defence mechanisms, about double those of Vaillant (1992), with a greater concentration of immature mechanisms, including regression.

White (1974) aims to clarify the differences between coping and defences, in that coping has three important functions:

- securing adequate information about the environment
- maintaining satisfactory internal conditions for both action and for processing information
- maintaining the organism's autonomy or freedom of movement, freedom to use its repertoire in a flexible fashion.

White 'recognises the importance of obtaining information about the environment and defence processes are necessary prerequisites for gathering information and acting upon the environment' (1974, p.55). They are also seen as supporting problem-solving activities. Thus defence mechanisms are a necessity rather than a pathological component to coping/adaptation, and are developmental for the higher goal of autonomy and freedom.

To conclude, there are various empirical theories and models in the area of defence mechanisms and coping strategies. Once the use of defence mechanisms is clarified, it allows greater understanding of suitable remedial options available. In the case of dyslexics, if coping or defence mechanisms are understood by teachers, it will allow adverse secondary manifestations to be understood for what they are – cries for help and a means of dealing with the stressful tasks or environments faced in daily life, e.g. at school, university, home, socially and in the workplace.

DYSLEXIC DEFENCE MECHANISMS

Fear of failure is a powerful psychological concept and can be extremely potent in changing an individual's whole basis of pre-judging new learning situations, or any situation that may risk public ridicule. Once the appraisal is of fear, the body aims to avoid or escape from such a threat in various ways; however, parental example and the reaction of parents to their own and their child's difficulties have a strong impact on how they act themselves. If the parenting style is understanding and supportive, then the child may be encouraged to try and risk again; if the parenting style is strict, repressive and unsupportive, then the child will develop mechanisms to reduce their exposure to any feared stimulus.

First, in the case of dyslexics, they will try basic word avoidance (e.g. writing less and using simple words); however, this commonly is not sufficient to deal with school demands or threats in learning situations.

Mature defensive mechanisms are likely to be developed first, and are classed as either emotional or behaviourial (Meissner 1980; Vaillant 1977) – with the former being social withdrawal, self-blame, perfectionism, hiding in class and feeling sad. Behavioural defence mechanisms are likely to include task avoidance, truancy, frustration, bad temper, bullying, pessimism and sublimination. Scott (2004, p.257) notes from clinical experience that dyslexics are outstanding at defence mechanisms and 'the subtext is that you get lost in the smoke screen of the dyslexic's behaviours [defence mechanisms] and do not notice the failure and vulnerability beneath'. Scott notes that counsellors commonly report that one never forgets a dyslexic client as they are very cunning, 'refined and slippery' and that commonly their defences can isolate them from others, noting 'in short, we have to notice when the iron defences turns into iron cages'. Alexander-Passe (2006, 2009a, 2009b, 2010) suggests that clear emotional or behaviourial differences exist among dyslexics, and gender splits can also be evident.

The key is understanding why some children choose emotional and others behavioural defensive strategies. Experience suggests that children with strict and repressive parents choose emotional strategies, whilst those with parents displaying aggression replicate such aggression at school (aggression begets aggression). Such children learn that it's okay to display anger and a bullied child is more likely to bully others, or even younger siblings. However, in primary school, immature emotional strategies may be evident. These include bed-wetting, delayed or regressive language skills, sulking, thumb sucking and crying, hypochondria, passive aggression and blocking out. These regressive strategies are direct responses to difficulties at school and reflect a wish to return to infancy and the safety of their mother. Regressive strategies are less common in late primary school, however, regressive language skills such as stammering are habit forming and can be life-long complaints. Other immature behavioural strategies may also be evident during primary school years, with shouting, acting out, temper tantrums, biting and attention seeking used as a means to ward away feared stimuli (e.g. reading aloud in class).

Whilst it is unclear how much is too much fear, children and adolescents with dyslexia experience high levels of stress as their dyslexic difficulties evolve from the classroom to the playground, and to socialising outside of school (the whole school experience). Any defence strategies used are cries for help; however, these secondary manifestations are commonly treated without looking at primary causes.

When the fear gets too much and mature and immature mechanisms are ineffective (e.g. fail to protect the individual from threats), the individual will look for more complex escape mechanisms, either extreme emotional or behavioural defensive mechanisms, with isolation, intellectualisation, depression, projection, escapism, drug abuse and self-harm being some of the strategies of those using emotional mechanisms. Such responses are perceived by them as the only means left to them to escape or control the risk in their hostile world, but can lead to suicidal tendencies. Those who use extreme behavioural mechanisms to cope are likely to turn to revenge on teachers leading to violence, displacement or possibly criminal activities – not only to repay the hostility they themselves have experienced from a society they feel excluded from, but also as a means to gain self-esteem from material gain. When a child starts to use defence mechanisms, they are saying to themselves and others 'I can't cope, help me.' Whilst some defences are shouted, others are whispered, and, if they are not heard and responded to, the feelings of failure are reinforced. Factors such as the degree and longevity of the trauma (e.g. a bad supply teacher may only be there for a day or a week) are important – if the trauma is continuous (e.g. bullying or unfair teacher/tutor), then extreme responses may be used to escape the threat.

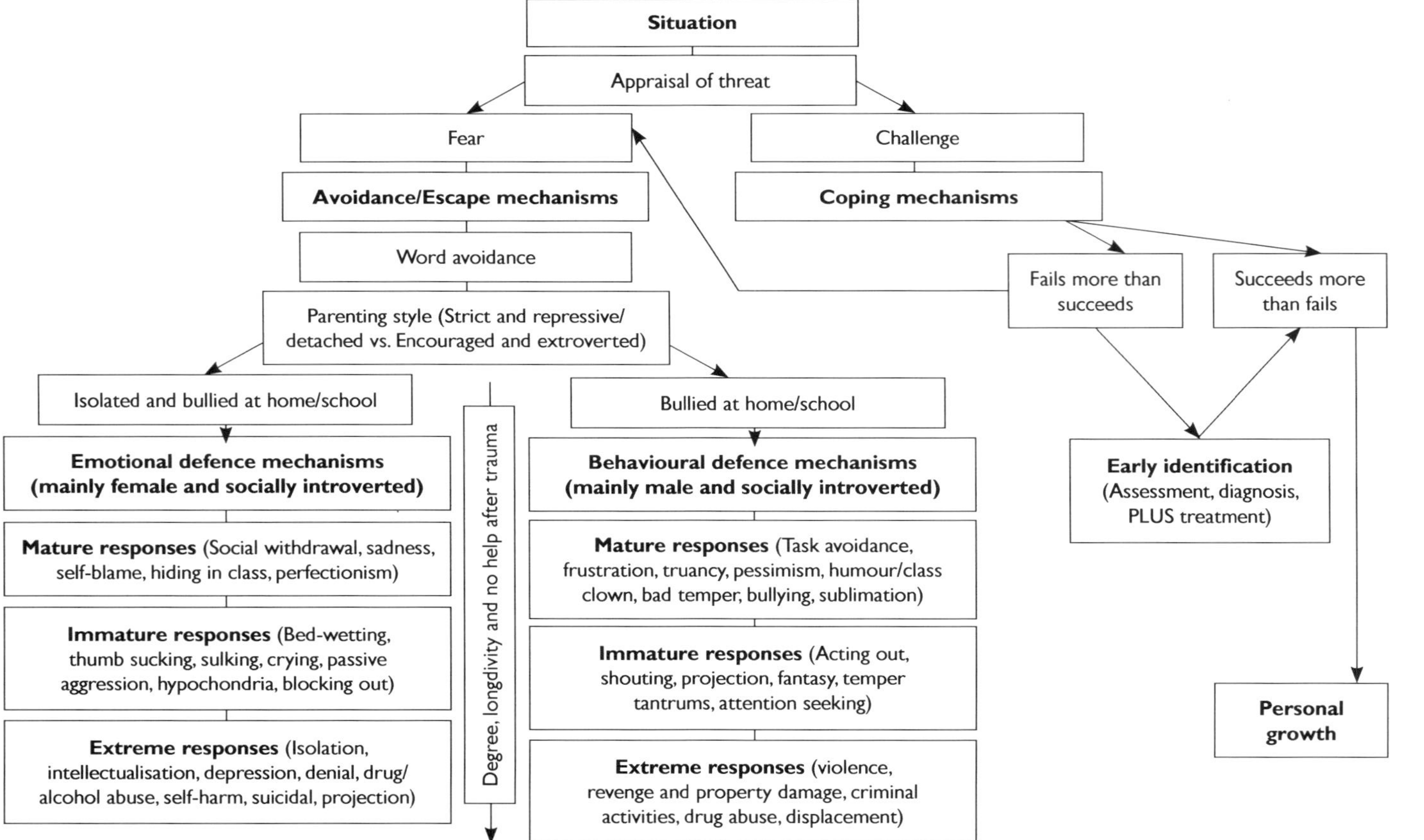

Figure 8.1 Hypothetical model of 'dyslexia defence mechanisms' (Alexander-Passe 2010)

Figure 8.1 details hypothesised 'dyslexia defence mechanisms' (DDM) (Alexander-Passe 2010) to assist educators in understanding how school-aged dyslexics cope at school. School-aged dyslexics are a unique group due to the reactions of educators and peers to their invisible learning difficulties and the resulting emotional reactions to maintain their self-esteem, and it is hypothesised they require a different framework in understanding how such individuals deal with constant stressors compared to the work of Vaillant (1977) and Meissner (1980), where adult males were investigated. The DDM framework begins by noting the importance of early identification and how important it is for teachers to identify children who are failing more than they are succeeding in the classroom.

The framework importantly recognises the importance of parents in a young dyslexic's life. If the parents are supportive, understanding and empathetic, then the child will learn resilience, but if this is missing, then the child will aim to avoid and withdraw into a safety shell.

CONCLUSIONS

This chapter began by investigating the differences between coping and defence mechanisms: one being positive, moving individuals forward, and the other being a negative technique used as a means to deal with negative environments.

Starting with Freud and moving to Valliant, the work of various researchers has increased our understanding of how individuals deal with stress and anxiety with a range of techniques such as denial, repression, regression to projection and sublimination.

The development of the hypothetical DDMs means that both educators and dyslexics themselves can better understand how dyslexics cope with challenging situations, and what triggers them to use avoidance as a core defence in activities that challenge their literacy skills. DDMs are hypothesised to be split into emotional and behavioural (each with mature, immature and extreme) defence mechanisms, and are affected by the coping models used by their peers and parents. Home is an important environment commonly overlooked; however, in the case of dyslexics, supportive and non-threatening parents are an important key to the young dyslexic's mental health.

KEY MESSAGES

- Dyslexics should try to recognise their own coping strategies and defence mechanisms, and then ask themselves whether they are helping or hindering them?
- Dyslexics should try to move towards coping strategies by being proactive to plan intervention before a situation becomes a threat that may require/demand defensive stances (defence mechanisms).
- Much of what a dyslexic does to cope at school comes from self-protection of their self-esteem.
- Educators should look beyond bad behaviour in class to the source of pupil frustration. One might find a dyslexic who is lost and trying to cope the best they can. Treat the cause, not the manifestation.

Chapter 9

PRE-DEFENCE MECHANISM: AVOIDANCE

INTRODUCTION

The concept of avoidance plays a central role in general psychology theory (psychotherapy, concepts of normality and abnormality, and personality development). From a psychological viewpoint, humans are reactive beings, and past conditioning (experiences), will determine (pre-judge) how they will deal with future experiences, as humans are creatures of habit and predictable. Avoidance comes from psychological protection of the self.

This chapter looks at the most common coping strategy used by dyslexics, and details how this can affect daily lives, and can restrict the dyslexic from reaching their potential in life (at school and in the workplace).

THEORIES

Theories by Beck, Steer and Brown (1996), Meichenbaum (1977) and Mahoney and Thoresen (1974) include terms such as reinforcement, conditioning, drive reduction, stimulus and environmental determinism; all based on individuals avoiding a feared stimulus (object, event, thought, situation or feeling) to prevent future unpleasant experiences (feelings of fear and anxiety). Avoidance is seen as a learned maladaptive response, quickly learned and reinforced when stress and anxiety are successfully avoided. However, Bednar and Peterson (1999, p.72) note it is a self-defeating behaviour pattern, because it prevents the individual from re-approaching any feared stimulus and learning that such fears are exaggerated and irrational, that 'avoidance is a psychological attribute that one would not wish to possess to any significant degree'.

Freud (1961) alternatively suggests that avoidance of anxiety plays a key part in neurosis, as the individual attempts to avoid feared stimuli using varied and elaborate defence mechanisms to protect the ego and distance them from dealing with unpleasant psychological events. He uses terms such as deny, distort, repress, displace, sublimate and disguise to describe the phenomenon.

McCall suggests 'the moment we choose avoidance over coping, we openly and undeniably announce to ourselves (and to any others who care to observe) that we have detected impulses within that are so unacceptable that they cannot be faced realistically' and 'obviously, the prospects for personal growth are virtually non-existent when the individual's response to threat is' to avoid it and deny it existed (1975, p.81).

Use of avoidance influences an individual's self-perceptions, and avoidance is an escape from unpleasant psychological events, and an escape from a conflict between how they see the world (in a bubble) and the one that really exists, thus denial. The opposite of avoidance would be coping, and, as avoidance is the essence of abnormality, coping must therefore represent normality and the ability to deal with psychological threat successfully. However, coping is not just the ability to deal successfully with psychological threats, but the ability to tolerate more anxiety-laden conflicts in difficult situations without evasive (avoidance) actions being required.

DYSLEXIA AND WORD AVOIDANCE

Pollock and Waller (1994) found that dyslexic children were perceived as immature (in their vocabulary choice and mode of expression) by school teachers and examination board markers, as they preferred using words they knew how to spell. But if they did use words where the spelling was uncertain, they felt that they were accused of being careless and risked lowering their self-esteem for their effort. Thus word avoidance has attractive advantages to young dyslexics – they think it is better to be perceived as immature than to risk embarrassment.

Do you think you used short words in essays more than longer expressive words? Yes, I still do really. I think it is the confidence issue still with words. It is about confidence in getting the spelling right.

(Rachel; Alexander-Passe 2010a)

CONCLUSIONS

Avoidance is a powerful and subtle strategy that aims to protect one's self-esteem. Only we know when we are doing it, as in the majority of cases we camouflage its use. Avoidance can range from a subtle change in an activity that one doesn't like, to avoiding due to a phobia causing severe anxiety.

In dyslexics, avoidance begins by choosing to use smaller words that they know how to spell, in preference to words that they are unsure of spelling correctly. Dyslexics ask themselves is it better to look unintelligent than stupid? The former is more normal than the latter, and so dyslexics begin to choose only to use smaller and more basic words; however, this can lead to task avoidance (avoiding reading or writing).

KEY MESSAGES

- Avoidance is the start of a slippery slope and can lead to dyslexics avoiding demonstrating their true abilities to others.
- Showing their difficulties is the first step to improvement in spelling and writing for dyslexics; however, camouflaging such difficulties will mean the absence of help, and being incorrectly labelled as 'okay' and 'ordinary'.
- Parents should look it whether their child is avoiding reading and writing and ask themselves why? What is it covering up?
- Educators should question a child's avoidance in the classroom. A child using word avoidance could be an unidentified dyslexic.

Chapter 10

EMOTIONAL DEFENCES

INTRODUCTION

This chapter looks at emotional defence mechanisms as a reaction to threats to the self. It is broken down into: mature mechanisms (e.g. social withdrawal, self-blame, hiding in class and perfectionism), immature mechanisms (bed-wetting, stammering, crying, hypochondria and passive aggression leading to depression) and extreme mechanisms (isolation, depression, denial, drug abuse, self-harm and attempted suicide).

All are cries for help, but manifested in different ways. Children, teenagers and adults are not always good at communicating stress, and educators need to be skilled in identifying the root cause of a manifestation. In the case of a dyslexic, the manifestation of emotional coping is a cry for help; however, others may misread the manifestation in isolation. Therefore, they treat self-harming without asking why the self-harm began.

Quotations are used to demonstrate the sense of helplessness and the pain that many dyslexics experience whilst coping with a learning difference in a hostile society that misunderstands their difficulties/learning differences. The quotations used in this chapter come from Alexander-Passe (2010).

MATURE MECHANISMS

TABLE 10.1 MATURE MECHANISMS (EMOTIONAL)

Socially withdrawn	Avoiding situations that require remembering, reading, writing and spelling, e.g. avoiding visits to cinemas as they are unable to read bus numbers or read lists of films shown
Sadness	Feeling sad when getting things wrong
Self-blame	Self-blaming and internalising when getting bad marks
Hiding in class	Sitting at the back of the class and not putting their hands up, to avoid their learning difficulties being highlighted, e.g. when asked to read aloud in class or to answer a question from the books given
Perfectionism	Working painstakingly long on an assignment to avoid getting bad marks and losing face by failing in tasks

SOCIAL WITHDRAWAL

Dealing with these problems growing up, how did you cope? Withdrawing or angry? I withdrew.

How did you withdraw? I think I tended to work on my own a lot, reading alone. I had more motivation to learn things I was interested in.

You were talking about your twin sister being a lot more outgoing, would she be the one with all the friends and you were more of the loner? Yes. But I did have friends but not all the close friends she had, the social network she had.

Growing up you were talking about sitting in your room and reading rather than being social, do you think you were doing that as a protective bubble? Yes. You find sometimes I put a protection there, a bubble to keep people away…[growing up] I think I was quite solitary, withdrawn and not comfortable in social situations, and stuff like that growing up. You get to 40 years old and I feel I have missed out on a lot of stuff. My defence mechanisms were once protecting me but are doing me no good as an adult and have damaged my ability to function and do other important things, like relationships. I seem to be protecting myself constantly, protecting myself from things that I should be doing – a bit risk-adverse.

So your bubble was once good but now it is harming you? Yes. It has made my self-esteem fragile; I have this fear of rejection, not being worthy if I do something, people will turn round and say 'you must be pretty stupid to not be able to do that'.

(Norman; Alexander-Passe 2010)

Before you were talking about going into your bubble, because it was the safest place. Yes it is, because I feel understood and more confident there, I do not have to deal with other people and for it to be safe. I guess I am turning into more of a hermit I suppose.

(Rachel; Alexander-Passe 2010)

Hales (1994) and Thomson and Hartley (1980) argue that dyslexics often react to their difficulties by withdrawing emotionally, and Gardner (1994) notes that dyslexics are prone to withdraw from situations in which they perceive they cannot cope.

Alexander-Passe (2010) asked participants 'Do you now/or have you felt isolated and gone into a bubble for self-protection?' Overall 77 per cent felt they did as adults and 70 per cent felt they did as children. Interestingly, the figures suggest that, although there is a difference between those dyslexics who were depressed and those who were not, many dyslexics in this study used this as a strategy. A total of 73 per cent of the depressives went into a bubble as a child, whereas 57 per cent of non-depressives used the bubble as a safety strategy, with non-depressive males using it more than females (75% compared to 33%) as a child. In adulthood there was a similar difference between depressives and non-depressives using the bubble strategy (68% compared to 55%), again with non-depressive males using this more than similar females (50% compared to 33%). The frequencies suggest that exclusion or self-exclusion and isolation are protection strategies that many dyslexics use to cope with the perceived hostile environment and society that surrounds them.

The interview evidence suggests that going into 'their own world' or into a science fiction virtual world allows dyslexics to protect their self-esteem. This was done in several ways, from daydreaming of a better place to withdrawal to libraries or bedrooms as children. In adulthood this can mean avoiding socialising with peers and becoming a hermit to protect themselves from others who might not understand them. As one participant noted, his bubble protected him as a child and was advantageous, but as an adult it does him harm by making him into a hermit and phobic of situations that might develop him.

SELF-BLAME

When you get things wrong, how does it make you feel? I beat myself up about it and when I was in a mental health hospital they sort of put it to me [told me] that half the time my self-blame was due to my need to be perfect. I think it's a big issue for dyslexics being perfectionists, as what they are doing is constantly ridiculed and that [reading and writing] is a sign of intelligence, especially in education. You know you beat yourself up and call yourself stupid as you have done something wrong, because you are constantly battling all the time. I am not as bad as I used to be, I let it go now and say its people's ignorance.

(Maureen; Alexander-Passe 2010)

When you get things wrong, how does it make you feel? I get annoyed with myself, but, as I said, 'by hook or by crook,' I will get things done in the end, so, yeah I do not think it affects me that much.

Do you beat yourself up about things? Self-blame? Yeah, I am very self-critical. That is my thing, and I am very rarely happy and contented with something I had done. Very, very rarely. If I lay a driveway I won't be happy with it, but I'm not saying I'm a perfectionist, I just would…there's always something that I think I could have done better, but unless it is really bad I won't go and change it, so that does not 'in my book' make me a perfectionist, as it doesn't have to be perfect, it just needs to be 98 per cent and there's always something with every project I've done. I tell myself 'I could have done that better.'

(Peter; Alexander-Passe 2010)

The interview evidence and Riddick (1996) speculate that the levels of self-blame are high amongst dyslexics, in that they internalise their problems and punish themselves for their lack of progress at school. They see themselves as being faulty and broken, and, compared to their non-dyslexic siblings and peers, they believe they are like a broken machine that is never fixed.

HIDING IN THE CLASS

Sasse (1995) noted the best way to avoid class input in subjects that he found difficult or impossible as a dyslexic:

> the best place [to sit in class] was out to the side near the back where I was not in the teacher's direct line of sight. As so many

> dyslexics find, after a point, the harder you try, the worse it seems to get. I often ended up in tears! While trying to correct errors I just spelt differently but still not correctly. It wasn't only the teacher who became frustrated! (Sasse 1995, p.113)

Did you hide in your school classroom? Yes. I would choose to put myself at the back of the class, never in the front of the class.

So you chose to be invisible then. Yes

(Jean; Alexander Passe 2010)

So you tried to be invisible? Yes, I tried to avoid being seen, to blend in but also not to be seen making mistakes.

(George; Alexander Passe 2010)

How old were you when the learning problems first began to show up? I was aware of it, to me my handwriting and spelling is perfect because I can read it. It didn't occur to me that others couldn't read it, so I didn't get ten out of ten at spelling in primary school and I was missing out chunks of words when I was writing sentences and things. I would forget how to do things, so fairly early on, but no one had a name for it. As I was so quiet, I would hide myself so no one would notice.

So you avoided being on the teacher's radar then? Yes.

(Kirsty; Alexander Passe 2010)

Many dyslexics I have spoken to about this would hide in class, in the back row. Yes, I certainly would duck down a few inches behind the person in front of you, if they would ask for volunteers, I would never volunteer.

(Norman; Alexander Passe 2010)

Do you think you would try to avoid being picked on to read in class? Yes.

How? I think I used to be quiet and sit in the back row, and hope that no one noticed me.

Playing up to be sent out? No, that was not me.

So you were quiet and hiding more? Yes. If I got into trouble at school, it would be even worse at home. Hiding in the classroom is a common strategy amongst dyslexics.

(Rachel; Alexander Passe 2010)

As Rachel notes, hiding is a common strategy in dyslexics at school. Self-preservation was key to surviving each day or hour at school. Avoiding the teacher's radar was seen as important to many in the study. Unfortunately this is the worst thing a dyslexic can do at school, as such avoidance means struggling students are camouflaged to teachers. Sadly, over the past decade, the majority of dyslexics have not been identified at school, thus haven't been able to gain the intervention they need to learn basic skills, which has a knock on effect on their self-esteem and potential. So to gain the help and identification badly needed, dyslexics need to come out of hiding, risk loss of face and highlight their difficulties, otherwise the help will not be forthcoming.

PERFECTIONISM

Edwards (1994, p.61) also noticed that some dyslexics suffer from competitiveness disorders, with many withdrawing both academically and socially: 'Gareth only tries hard if he thinks he can win. If not he merely gives up… Nevertheless, he had to be very sure of his good standard before making himself vulnerable again'.

Do you think you were a perfectionist at school? Yes. I suspect like me, many dyslexics can be pedantic at times. That having learnt to do it right, you want try and get other people to do it right, spelling and punctuation and things. I struggled hard to get punctuation right, so I want others to do the same.

Could being a perfectionist be a coping strategy to control things? Um, I suspect it was a way of simplifying things – that having a very simple view of something was a delaying tactic, even if you didn't understand what is going on, e.g. the frustration of learning how to read, write or spell.

(Harry; Alexander Passe 2010).

Going back to your school years, how did you cope, did you avoid reading? I panic, as soon as I got an essay I would get straight on to it. I'm not a quick person, if I do it under pressure I would crack even more, I panic. I do what I can, then I take it to the teachers who support me and my friends at university, I never avoided it, but it would worry me.

(Phoebe; Alexander Passe 2010)

The quotations suggest that dyslexics cope in different ways. Those who have a strong work ethic will spend hours and hours on homework to submit a passable piece of work that their peers would produce in 30 minutes. Whilst this attention to detail would suggest to a teacher that the child 'isn't dyslexic', it is the knock on effect on other subjects that will trip up the dyslexic. Whilst perfectionism may be possible in primary school, at secondary school the workload increases substantially and the ability to produce perfect work reduces, causing anxiety and other emotional manifestations.

Each dyslexic copes in their own unique way, and some choose perfectionism as a means to not only protect themselves from classroom humiliation, but also from teacher humiliation in the form of work being handed back full of red scribbles and negative notes from teachers.

Harry's quote suggests that perfectionism is a means of simplifying things, but in essence it means working much harder than your peers and this cannot be anything but stressful. The evidence from Phoebe suggests that some dyslexics panic as soon as they get work – this is a form of perfectionism as it means they will drive themselves to despair to get the work done.

In adulthood, perfectionism can manifest as multiple photocopying of application forms, then starting in pencil to allow drafting and redrafting processes until the application form is perfect in their eyes. After drafting and redrafting it several times and then checking with a partner, the perfectionist commits to using a pen. What is propagating the perfectionisms? From discussions, it is about controlling their interaction with the environment and not allowing their weaknesses to be picked up. Norma notes that perfectionism is a means to safeguard self-esteem, as any failure is taken personally and can result in long-term helplessness and feelings of inferiority.

A total of 62 per cent of the overall sample felt that perfectionism was a strategy they used to control the world, with higher frequencies amongst males than females (73% compared to 44%); the frequency was higher amongst depressive males (71% compared to 53%) than similar females; and substantially higher amongst non-depressive males compared to similar females (75% compared to 0%). Perfectionism was used by more depressives than non-depressives

(59% compared to 43%) and interestingly more by depressives with a degree than without (73% compared to 46%).

Scott (2004) and Reiff *et al.* (1997) look into the use of perfectionism in successful dyslexics and surmise that it is this strategy that allows them to produce the best work possible without regard for time or personal health.

IMMATURE MECHANISMS

TABLE 10.2 IMMATURE MECHANISMS (EMOTIONAL)

Bed-wetting	Regressive manifestations from stress that show helplessness
Stammering	This is another regressive defense mechanism where speech patterns return to infant states. This can be temporary or a long-term habit. It is sometimes used to look weak and gain sympathy
Thumb sucking (pen sucking)	Regressive manifestation that returns individual to womb or infantile emotional and comfort states
Sulking	Regressive manifestations that says 'it's not fair' and is a toddler stage response to the world as being unfair
Crying	Regressive manifestation that shows complete helplessness and a return to a state of infant and toddlerhood where they need someone else to fix things for them
Passive aggression	Internalising feelings. An early form of depression
Hypochondria	Physical manifestations of emotional stress and trauma, e.g. phantom pains in legs as soon as tests approach, or vomiting. This is an extreme cry for help and attention
Blocking out	Trying not to think about the feared stimulus. Thinking that it will go away if it is not thought about, without realising it won't

REGRESSION

Vaillant (1992) suggests that immature defence strategies are used from birth to approximately 9–11 years old. As Riddick (1996, p.103) records from an interview with the mother of a dyslexic child: 'She was like a different child once she started school. There were tears and tantrums, she used to beg me to not send her, and it was hell really. I didn't know what to do for the best'.

Riddick comments that tantrums are common features of general early childhood and do not necessarily relate to a symptom of dyslexia; however, they are a sign of frustration. Scott (2004, p.258) found in dyslexics: 'sucking of fingers and clothing, curling into balls under desks, bed-wetting and soiling, rocking, holding of genitals and the constant company of furry toys. When these infantile behaviours appear in an older child, they represent a signal that he is no longer coping and are symptoms of real distress'.

BED-WETTING

Nocturnal enuresis is a condition in which a person who has bladder control while awake urinates whilst asleep, as a form of regression to an infantile state of helplessness. The condition is commonly called bed-wetting, and it often has a psychological impact on children and their families. Children with the condition often have low self-esteem and weak interpersonal relationships, poor quality of life and poor performance at school (Van Hoecke *et al.* 2004; Von Gontard 2004). Von Gontard (1998) linked enuresis with delayed speech, motor and speech milestones (each correlate to dyslexia). Miles (1994, p.144) noted a case of an eight-year-old dyslexic child who was 'still bed-wetting and full of nervous twitches'. Scott (2004, p.171) postulates that '30% of dyslexic children suffer from enuresis, some of it very severe including total soaking of the bed, every night, for months on end'.

If parents are aware that a bed-wetter has no medical problems, but the child is having difficulty with paying attention in school, concentrating on academic material, impulsive behaviour, fidgetiness, intermittent explosive tantrums or conduct disorder, then dyslexia maybe the underlying problem. Therapeutic Resources (2004) note that, in a study of 1822 children with attention-deficit hyperactivity disorder (a condition with co-morbidity/links to dyslexia, see Fawcett and Peer 2004; Gilger *et al.* 1992; Ramus, Pidgeon and Frith 2003), 48 per cent were bed-wetters.

Watkins (2004) believes:

> sometimes enuresis (bed-wetting) may be due to anxiety, a change in the home situation (such as the birth of a sibling) or an emotional trauma. We particularly look for emotional factors in children who were previously dry and start to wet again. A child with shaky bladder control may be more likely to revert to wetting when under stress.

Scott (2004, p.171) suggests that bed-wetting in dyslexic children is common (approximately 30% of all dyslexic children), usually starts when they begin to have problems at school and can go on for months at a time. Miles (1993) notes two cases of bed-wetting, along with Thomson (1995) and Von Gothard (1998). There is a double stress from the bed-wetting, first from the act itself, and second from the reactions of others, including peer and sibling teasing affecting self-esteem and causing anxiety.

Riddick (1996, p.136) records a teacher giving one of her pupils 20 hard spellings a week as a form of bullying: the child's mother commented that 'he was worrying himself sick before the spelling test. In fact, he started bed-wetting because of the pressure of the spelling test, she destroyed his confidence'.

Congdon (1995, p.93) notes other manifestations in dyslexics: 'emotional disturbance arising from the problem are: enuresis (bed-wetting); stammer; sleep-waking; asthma; and various physical symptoms, such as vomiting and recurrent abdominal pains for which no physical cause can be found'.

Riddick (1996, p.48) also examines the instance of a seven-year-old boy who had a new teacher unsympathetic to his dyslexic difficulties. He became distressed and his behaviour at school deteriorated, his mother noted he cried himself to sleep each night, he started to wet the bed and came home shaking (with fear) if he had a spelling test to revise for the next day. His mother was frequently contacted about his bad behaviour at school, but by then his behavioural problems were seen as the main cause for concern. When asking his teacher whether his behaviour could be down to a learning difficulty, the response received was 'rubbish he's just very immature, when he learns to behave properly and knuckles down to the work he'll be ok'. The next year his teacher was more sympathetic and identified him as dyslexic, helped him and his behaviour improved again.

HYPOCHONDRIA

Another aspect of school refusal is shown by individuals who develop psychosomatic disorders or other illnesses to avoid school: 'I used to pretend I was sick, make myself puke, and say I don't wanna go today', said one dyslexic teenager (Edwards 1994, p.110). Edwards gives a powerful example of psychosomatic pain in the following story of a 12-year-old dyslexic: Trevor developed a pain in his right leg requiring crutches. To him it felt like a rare disease. The hospital doctor concluded that he was dyslexic but intelligent, was therefore frustrated, and that the frustration was expressed as pain in the right thigh, which occurred about once every six months and could last ten days at a time. Strangely enough, she found this same teenager was reluctant to truant, as he felt there would be 'repercussions and [that it] was pointless anyway' (p.39).

This suggests a main difference between normal truants and dyslexics avoiding school (social conscience).

The other immature mechanisms described in Table 10.2 are discussed in more detail in Alexander-Passe (2007).

EXTREME MECHANISMS

TABLE 10.3 EXTREME MECHANISMS (EMOTIONAL)

Isolation	A self-protecting mechanism to withdraw to an environment that is safe and non-threatening
Intellectualisation	Logically thinking about the threat and taking a superior attitude to the feared stimulus: I'm not wrong, he/she is
Depression	An extreme state of helplessness indicating that all strategies have failed and need to be rebuilt to progress
Denial	A self-protecting state that refuses to believe or accept actions that conflict with internal values. Altering facts to fit into belief systems
Projection	Taking an extreme emotional stance that the feared stimulus is out to get them
Drug or alcohol abuse	An extreme reaction to stress where the individual abuses drugs or alcohol to escape painful realism by altering his mental state to access safe haven. Life-threatening addiction may follow
Self-harm	An extreme reaction to anxiety that aims to control his own body in a world where he is unable to control any other aspects of his life. It can involve controlling food intake as in bulimia, causing bodily harm as a means to inflict pain on the self as punishment or a means to control the body's reactions to stress, e.g. cutting oneself can be a tension release
Suicide or attempted suicide	Used when the individual feels completely helpless and decides that the burden he creates is too great for others

ISOLATION (SELF-PROTECTING WITHDRAWAL)

Gardner (1994) found that dyslexics are prone to withdraw from situations in which they perceive they cannot cope (e.g. spelling tests). This withdrawal can be both from specific lessons and for whole days. Withdrawal for long or frequent periods can also be caused by a reaction to certain teachers who humiliate them in front of their peers.

Scott (2004) also suggests that, whilst externalising (aggression) strategies are common in dyslexic males, internalising strategies such as depression and withdrawal are most commonly found in dyslexic females.

Alexander-Passe (2010) found withdrawal leading to depression was commonly seen as the best way of protecting themselves from further harm, along with reducing the likelihood of exclusion by those around them.

DEPRESSION

Do you think depression and dyslexia could be related? About the time I was studying at Oxford Brookes, there were issues at work to do with the NHS reforms and a question over the future of the unit. I do remember when that tutor gave me back a poor assignment, it took me back to when I was at school and that really caused me at the time a lot of anguish. It was not that long after that that the GP [doctor] gave me the anti-depressants. That is when I had the clinical depression.

(Anita; Alexander-Passe 2010)

Do you think dyslexia and depression are linked? Oh, yes definitely. With the children, I work with and the people I work with, I definitely think it is.

Do you see depressed dyslexic children a lot? Yes, I do, I see the effects dyslexia has on them and how they are down on themselves and how they think they are stupid or thick or they are not proper because they are not the same as everybody else. One of the kids I work with has self-harmed, a couple of them have problems eating and I look at my dyslexic son and think how lucky I am, he actually copes very well.

(Emma; Alexander-Passe 2010)

Do you think dyslexia and depression could be linked? Yes. I think it is as a result of us not fitting into the perfect world created by the media made up of perfect people. We [dyslexics] don't have the [perfect] stereotypical image. We can't ever live up to that, we can aspire to be that but we can never be that. In my personal experience through school, it was the most difficult time of life, then leaving school and going out to work. In my last job, I was bullied because of my dyslexia, due to the fact I can't remember things, store things and process things as well as the next person, all of that caused my depression.

(Jean; Alexander-Passe 2010)

The system is just not prepared for us, there isn't anything in place, you can't just turn round and say, I've got depression and I need help and there's dyslexia there too, because specialists dealing with depression and those dealing with dyslexia are usually different. I don't know about you but I see it as very different balls to catch, it's a different ball game you know we are playing hockey...they are playing netball. Those dealing with the depression will find an abnormal type of depression, ours is very much a build-up of negative experiences backlogging to the year dot [since the age of two or three years old], misinterpretation of what people say, and so on, there's loads more to it, it's not all standard [depression], I don't know if that helps, there's more to it.

(Natasha; Alexander-Passe 2010)

There is very little research that actually supports a correlation of depression with dyslexia; the majority of empirical references are based on observations (Rutter 1983; Duane 1991; Ryan 2004; Scott 2004) rather than actual studies. Two such studies exist that investigate depression in dyslexic children and teenagers. Boetsch, Green and Pennington (1996) found that the reports of depression by parents and teachers of primary school children were not confirmed by the children's own self-reports of depressive symptomatology. The second study, by Alexander-Passe (2006), used the Beck Depression Inventory (Beck, Steer and Brown 1996), the Coping Inventory for Stressful Situations (Endler and Parker 1999) and the Culture-Free Self-Esteem Inventory (Battle 1992) measures with 19 teenage dyslexics. Results strongly suggested gender differences, with females using more emotional and avoidance-based coping, resulting in lower percentile scores in general and academic self-esteem with moderate depression. Males tend to use more task-based coping, resulting in normal percentile self-esteem levels and minimal depression.

However, Grigorenko (2001) observed depressive disorders are elevated in young adults with learning disabilities, with a 14–32 per cent frequency, meaning that 68–86 per cent are not depressed. Scott (2004) asks what variable is missing in understanding such a correlation; she suggests that social isolation is the missing variable. As Kennedy, Spence and Hensley (1989, p.562) note, depressed children often have 'deficits in social skills and interpersonal relationships' due to being rejected or isolated by their peers. Thus, it is the dyslexics who are isolated and rejected by their peers who will be the most vulnerable to depression.

Alexander-Passe (2010) found interview evidence strongly suggests that being different and negative interactions with society were the triggers that led to depression and other negative manifestations in dyslexic individuals. One participant (Jean) explains that she felt unable to fit into 'normal' stereotypical images and the pressure to fit into such images was highly damaging. As discussed earlier, participants felt different to their peers and dealing with this on a long-term basis was emotionally damaging. Depression in dyslexics comes from that realisation that they are different, inferior, and that they are helpless to change their situation.

Scott (2004) hypothesises that dyslexics either internalise or externalise the psychological effect of having dyslexia, with the former more likely. Support comes from Grigorenko (2001, p.112) suggesting 'internalizing, effects include stress, depression and anxiety and, on balance, are those most widely associated with learning disabilities'. Support comes from Alexander-Passe (2006) and Wilcutt and Pennington (2000), with Hales (1994) finding that dyslexic females scored higher than controls on anxiety and depression. Riddick (1996) speculated that the levels of self-blame, sensitivity to others and over the perceived perfection of others amongst dyslexic females made them particularly vulnerable to adjustment problems.

Duane (1991) and Fawcett (1995, p.14) note 'in terms of emotional stability, her study suggests a threefold increase in psychiatric diagnosis in children with dyslexia, in particular of conduct disorders and depression'. Fawcett suggests that such problems are a natural consequence of years of school failure.

Depression is a frequent complication in dyslexia, according to Ryan (2004), Burden (2005) and Scott (2004). Although most dyslexics are not clinically depressed, children with this type of learning difficulty are at higher risk of intense emotional feelings of pain and sorrow.

DENIAL

McNulty's (2003) empirical review investigated the lack of personality research in the field of dyslexia, noting the work of Palombo (2001), which found that many individuals with learning disabilities (such as dyslexia) develop 'self-narratives' – stories that they tell themselves to make sense of their emotional lives and subjective experiences. These self-narratives are concerned with the level of acceptance or denial the individual feels about their disability and these play a part in whether they view themselves positively or negatively. In McNulty's study, denial referred to a conscious rejection of diagnosis even whilst realising a problem exists. Disavowal was also noted in more serious cases of denial, which occurs when individuals do not even realise there is a problem (Siegal 1996).

Alexander-Passe (2010) recorded cases of parents never reading books or newspapers, telling those around them (family, work colleagues, etc.) and even their children that they 'forgot their reading glasses' to avoiding helping their children with their homework. Cases of dyslexic parents trying to read their child's reading book and relying on the photos to create the story are commonplace. Also there have been cases of bright dyslexics turning down promotions and staying in menial low paid jobs to avoid paperwork (reading and writing). In one case, it was remarked that an uncle kept a book of all the words he needed in his daily job, so they were all spelt correctly. The denial of the individuals in these cases meant they ignored obvious signs of a difficulty and carried on regardless, rather than admitting there was a problem that needed to be investigated further, possibly out of embarrassment.

The Daily Telegraph (2010) reported on an incident where a UK post/mail man was charged with theft for not delivering 400 letters. He dumped them in a field rather than telling his supervisors he was unable to read the addressees or a road map to find out where they should have been delivered to.

DRUG OR ALCOHOL ABUSE

There are few empirical studies investigating drug abuse amongst dyslexics. However Scott (2004, p.169) suggests that in general 60 per cent of dyslexic alcoholics, mainly men, start drinking due to anxiety. As a counsellor, she found high frequencies of drug- and alcohol-related anxieties amongst dyslexic child and adult clients, and postulates that dyslexics are more likely than non-dyslexics to use drink and drugs to cope with anxiety. She found a significant proportion of dyslexic children, as young as 13 years old, wishing to beat their addiction to tobacco, cocaine, marijuana, ecstasy, drink and anti-depressants. Drug, alcohol and food abuse was found to be a means to reduce anxiety amongst children and adolescents with dyslexia. Dyslexics who use drugs as an emotional defence mechanism look to escape their daily hell or feelings of being abnormal, but their drug use sabotages their means to gain help.

SELF-HARM: INTRODUCTION

Self-harm is an area of dyslexia that is rarely investigated and thus research in this area is scarce. The latest DSM-V (American Psychiatric Association 2013) has now created a new category: non-suicidal self-injury (NSSI), which includes cutting or burning oneself without suicidal intent. Other types of NSSI include hitting, pinching, banging or punching walls and other objects to induce pain, breaking bones, ingesting toxic substances and interfering with healing of wounds. NSSI typically begins in mid-adolescence, with adolescents injuring themselves impulsively, engaging in self-harm with less than an hour of planning and commonly reporting feeling minimal or no pain. Once started, self-injury seems to acquire addictive characteristics and can be quite difficult for a person to discontinue. While some studies indicate that NSSI is more frequent in girls than boys, other studies indicate that there are no consistent gender differences (Peterson *et al.* 2008).

SELF-HARM: CHILDREN/YOUNG PEOPLE

Poustie and Neville (2004) postulate that paracetamol overdosing and cutting are the two most common forms of self-harm reported for children and young people, and self-harm is often not a singular occurrence: it is commonly repeated, and can go on for many years (Harrington *et al.* 1998).

According to Bywaters and Rolfe (2005), although some young people want help to find alternative means of coping with emotional pain and distress, they use self-harm as a means of communicating the severity of their anguish, trauma and pain to others. They add that children and adolescents who self-harm may not see their actions as a problem, due in part to perceptions that their actions were non-fatal and affected no-one but themselves.

In a UK community sample, Hawton *et al.* (2002) found 6.9 per cent of a 4000 school pupil sample (15–16 year olds) had engaged in acts of deliberate self-harm in the previous year, with only 12.6 per cent of such episodes leading to hospital treatment.

Edwards (1994) recorded instances of children who got into fights to avoid going to school, as a few days off with a hurt/broken arm was worth it to avoid having to take tests, complete writing tasks or submit homework. The need to avoid reading aloud in class meant they took extreme measures of avoidance. Based on her experiences as a counsellor to dyslexics, Scott (2004) noted that dyslexics (young and old) use self-harming strategies to cope with the emotional effects of constant failure in educational settings, and the direct and indirect bullying they experienced from both teachers and their peers. Alexander-Passe (2010) in a study of 29 dyslexic adults found high levels of self-harm, which ranged from alcohol abuse or cutting to over-eating..

SELF-HARM: FOOD

Like alcohol, food is a legal substance. Food-based self-harm (Haw *et al.* 2001) has many dimensions. It can take the form of comfort eating as a result of a stressful situation, e.g. a poor mark in an examination or getting things wrong. If taken to an extreme, comfort eating can lead to binge eating – a means to reduce stress, as food is commonly seen as a reward for children and sweet foods like chocolate raise the body's blood sugar and trigger chemical reactions to calm the body. Binge eating is a faulty and uncontrollable means to rebalance self-esteem and treats the symptoms rather than the cause. Sugar (methylanthines) cravings can be as powerful as drug addiction cravings, with sugar being more easily available and legal.

A secondary element of binge eating is that it can be a conscious attempt to change body size, to put people off from getting close to them, along with a conscious attempt to reject society and society's values. Finally, food-based self-harm can take the form of exercising extreme control over food intake in the form of anorexia.

Scott (2004) found that anorexia and bulimia were commonly used by dyslexic girls, representing a need to exert personal control for the sufferer, in a world where they are unable to control other elements (e.g. school and home life). They may also be used as a cry for help, as having such disorders gains the attention of parents and health officials; however, as with truancy and behavioural manifestations, health and educational professionals will commonly treat the manifestation without looking for the root cause.

SELF-HARM: BODY INJURY

Swales (2010) suggests that the intense pain from cutting can lead to the release of endorphins and so deliberate self-harm may become a means of pleasure seeking, although in many cases self-injury abuse becomes a means to manage pain. This is in contrast to the pain that may have been experienced earlier in the sufferer's life, over which they had no control according to Cutter, Jaffe and Seagal (2008).

SUICIDE OR ATTEMPTED SUICIDE

Correlations between bullying, school failure, pressure to achieve academically, peer rejection, feelings of frustration, depression, guilt and hostility have been made with childhood suicide (Harrington *et al.* 1994; Thompson and Rudolph 1996). Thompson and Rudolph (1996, p.446) note that children with 'learning disabilities or other learning difficulties that cause constant frustration are more likely to attempt suicide...gifted children may attempt suicide because their advanced intellectual ability makes relating to children their own age difficult'. Suicide attempts are said to increase during the school term and decrease during school holidays (Winkley 1996), and that attempts also increase in May and June to correspond with GCSE examinations.

Peer (2002, p.32) observes that the six cases presented to him from a dyslexic forum suggest that such children are fragile, vulnerable and feel the ramifications for failure are enormous. Riddick (1996, p.107) describes how the problems encountered because of dyslexia are enough for dyslexic children to want to kill themselves, with one mother saying 'he wanted to be dead, there was nothing for him. He wanted his tie so that he could hang himself'. Scott (2004) states that many cases of dyslexia-led suicide are not recorded as such children are unable to write suicide notes (Dyslexia and Youth Suicide 2010; Fox 2010; *Scottish Daily Record* 2002; Spencer-Thomas 2013).

When children begin to withdraw, they are extremely quiet, or highly active and agitated. Suicide may be seen as an option by dyslexic children as a result of excessive bullying and rejection according to Winkley (1996). Scott (2004) suggests that problems related to dyslexia may cause suicide, and the real numbers of cases are unknown. However, as little research has been conducted in this area, numerous newspaper reports and anecdotes are the only real data to go on (*Birmingham News* 2010; Dyslexia and Youth Suicide 2010; Fox 2010; Kosman 2010).

When a dyslexic attempts suicide, they are saying 'enough is enough, I can't take it anymore'. Whilst other indirect factors are involved, the effect of dyslexia on relationships and the pressure that dyslexics feel as outsiders, should not be underestimated. Many do not fit even into their own families and, unless they find a sympathetic life partner, their suffering continues in trying to fit into a world that many dyslexics find inhospitable.

RESEARCH INTRODUCTION

As part of a wider study into dyslexia and depression, this chapter looks at feedback from research participants concerning dyslexia and self-harming, and related topics. See the Appendix for more details about the sample of dyslexic men and women, some of whom have been diagnosed with depression, with many who have self-harmed (Alexander-Passe, 2010).

RESULTS: PROFILES

Overall, the vast majority (85%) of this group (n = 29) self-harmed to cope with their difficulties, with more than half feeling worthless (65%) and helpless at times (61.5%). Whilst 30.8 per cent used alcohol to self-harm/cope with stress, coping using food was the most popular strategy (34.6%), followed by bodily harm. A total of 50 per cent of this group had thought about suicide, with 42.3 per cent having attempted such a strategy.

Breaking down the data by gender, it showed more females (n = 18) than males (n = 11) self-harmed (83.3 compared to 63.6%). Females had significantly higher scores for feeling unworthy (72.7%) and helpless (66.7%). Whilst males predominately self-harmed with alcohol (45.5%), females used food (38.9%). Interestingly, whilst 36.4 per cent of the men thought about suicide, only 9.1 per cent had attempted it. This was compared to the females, where 55.6 per cent had thought about suicide and 50 per cent had actually attempted it.

Of the depressed male sample (n = 7), 71.4 per cent self-harmed and alcohol was the most popular method of self-harming (42.9%). Feelings of unworthiness were more common than those of helplessness (42.9% compared to 28.6%). Whilst 42.9 per cent of the depressed males had thought about suicide, only 14.3 per cent had actually attempted it.

In the larger depressed female sample (n = 15), the vast majority (86.7%) self-harmed, with food and bodily harm being the main forms. A large total of 66.7 per cent felt worthless and 60 per cent felt helpless. Some 60 per cent had thought about suicide and 53.7 per cent had attempted it at some point.

Interestingly, looking at degree and non-degree educated participants, more with a degree self-harmed than those without (90.9% compared to 72.7%). Whilst a higher number of participants with a degree felt worthless (63.6%), more without a degree felt helpless (63.6%). Interestingly, those with a degree tended to self-harm with food, those without a degree self-harmed with bodily harm and with alcohol.

These profiles aim to aid the reader in understanding how this sample group of adult dyslexics coped with the difficulties in their lives caused by their dyslexia (e.g. social stigma and feelings of abnormality). See Alexander-Passe 2010 for the wider study.

SELF-HARM: ALCOHOL

Have you ever self-harmed due to the frustrations that dyslexia brings? Taking drugs? I do drink too much.

Do you drink to drown the pain? Yes, it gets me out of, out of it all really. It is like…it helps you sleep so you are not up all night worrying, going over things 60 times. So it slows down your brain so it allows you to sleep, it numbs out the fears and self-anger. Yes.

(Rachel; Alexander-Passe 2010).

Have you ever self-harmed due to the frustrations that dyslexia brings? Yes. It certainly seems like that in the last six months. I left myself to die when I was 25 years old.

Did you drink then? Yes.

Was it serious drinking then? Yes.

Could it have been because you didn't feel you fitted in? No. I just didn't want to exist.

So it was a form of self-harm then? Yes. I guess I drunk too much as I felt I didn't fit in and didn't want to exist.

(Philip; Alexander-Passe 2010)

Like cigarettes, alcohol is a legal drug for anyone over the age of 18 years old. Interview evidence suggests that drinking alcohol begins as a social activity, but can turn into a coping strategy to deal with work stress and, in excess, can form a vehicle for attempting suicide. Rachel notes that it can slow down her brain and Philip said that when he drinks he doesn't feel dyslexic anymore. Are the two things related? Participants commonly mentioned that they thought much faster than their ability to communicate and write down their thoughts. Does alcohol slow down the brain or relax the individual to such a degree that they lose their inhibitions or cares about the world around them? Alcohol serves as a central nervous system depressant, which can cause relaxation and cheerfulness effects. Gorenstein (1987) suggests that alcohol affects the frontal lobes, which is where dyslexics are known to have unique neuron architecture, thus the ability of alcohol to numb the effects of dyslexia cannot be ruled out; however, no research has been carried out to date in this area.

SELF-HARM: FOOD

Have you ever self-harmed because of your dyslexia? Not deliberately self-harmed, but I'm overweight and I have been all my life, and I wonder if firstly it is related to my unwillingness to participate in sport and secondly that comfort eating played a part in it.

So you think the stress of dyslexia made you self-harm with food? I do wonder if that is part of it, associated with growing up with it. It is about triggers to such self-harm. I guess one could gauge how it affects you, from the odd biscuit or chocolate bar to binge eating. It is about having a need; it is about getting away from what you have been doing.

So does it take you away from your stress? Yes. It is not classical self-harm but it is harmful behaviour.

(Anita; Alexander-Passe 2010)

How about with food, self-harm can be comfort eating? Yes, I over-eat [laugh].

Do you think as a child you used food as a comfort? Yes, I always have.

Do you think it is form of control? [Pause] Yes, I think I have put on quite a lot of weight as I did not want to get into another relationship. It was my control that way.

So it was a protection of putting people off then? Yes.

(Rachel; Alexander-Passe 2010)

Have you ever self-harmed from your frustrations? Yes, if you feel crap you might want to go for the chocolate. I'm unsure if that is a dyslexic thing or a stress thing.

(Phoebe; Alexander-Passe 2010)

According to the evidence, food can be a means to control body shape/appearance. Do dyslexics use food to punish their body, as many of them view their brains as having faulty wiring? One participant used to bang his head against walls. Could this have been to try and get his brain to work properly, in the same way you would bang a toy to get it to work, or was it frustration and self-harm as a sort of revenge? Another participant with anorexia said she did not use her anorexia to get attention as she would wear layers to disguise her weight loss; so was it therefore self-punishment and bodily control that were her motivations? She admitted that she avoided being noticed in class to avoid reading out aloud, to be invisible, so an alternative hypothesis could be that she was trying to reduce her size to be even more invisible. Lastly, self-harm with food can be used as an excuse to avoid sport and social interactions.

Toby began by using food as a comfort, but later it became an excuse to not interact with others. Being large was also a reason to cover up his lack of coordination and ability on the playing field, as he had very active and sporty siblings. His continued use of food as a means to avoid can be translated as a self-harming strategy.

SELF-HARM: BODILY HARM (CUTTING)

Have you ever self-harmed yourself because of your difficulties? Yes. I used to self-harm, I slashed my wrists open and stuff. I used to eat loads of food and [do] all sorts [of things] really.

Did you ever attempt suicide? Not as such.

So when you slashed your wrists, how old were you? About 13 years old.

Do you know what the triggers were for that? It was depression.

Could it be linked to anything related to the school, like tests? No.

Bullying? I suppose you could link it with the bullying.

Do you still have those thoughts? Yes.

Do you know what triggers these thoughts? Just a lot of stress, which is pretty much my really big trigger.

(Jean; Alexander-Passe 2010)

Do/Did you self-harm? Why? What are the triggers? Yes. I still self-harm and have done since about the age of four. My triggers are anger and frustration. I cut my arms and belly. As a kid I would scratch my hands or bang parts of my body like my head. I am currently having therapy which is addressing this issue.

Have you ever thought about or tried to commit suicide? Yes.

What were the triggers? I get very low sometimes and this is what triggers my negative thoughts.

(Susan; Alexander-Passe 2010)

I used to slap my head if I got really frustrated with life, I would hit my head very hard, and I would hit my head against a wall.

(Trixie; Alexander-Passe 2010)

Interview evidence suggests bodily harm can include hitting oneself in frustration (e.g. fists), banging oneself (e.g. hitting your head against walls) and cutting oneself. Whereas the hitting and banging oneself could be related to frustration at the self-perception of one's body being faulty, cutting is a different matter. Cutting seems to come from the need to damage one's own body as revenge for it causing pain and aggression, and is likely to also come from the need to control. Cutting can also be called self-mutilation based on hyperstress or dissociation, as noted in Figure 10.1.

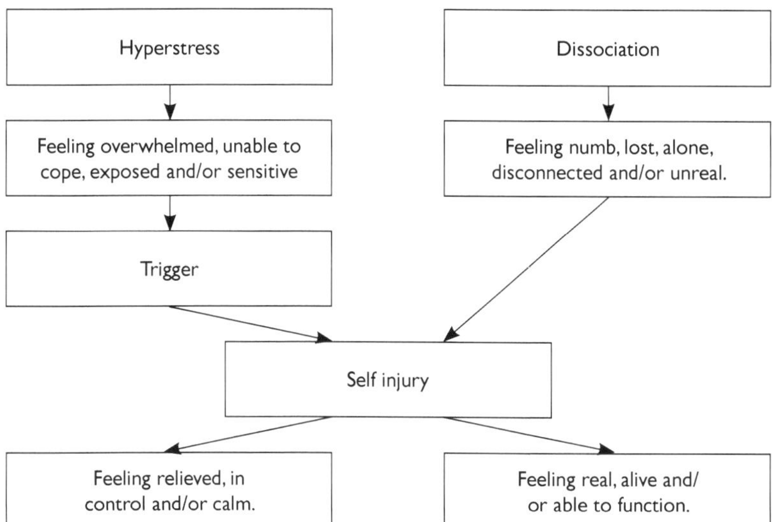

Figure 10.1 Precursors to self-injury

Figure is adapted from LifeSIGNS (2005). Available at www.lifesigns.org.uk/precursors-to-self-injury.

Interview evidence suggests that causing self-bodily harm is related to depression and occurs as part of a dyslexic feeling helpless and frustrated with his inability to control his situation. Bodily harm or self-mutilation is a means to regain control, in a world in which the dyslexic feels he has no control – to bleed is a release of the hyper-stresses caused by daily life, especially school.

THINKING ABOUT SUICIDE

Have you ever thought about or tried to commit suicide? Yes, but I don't like blood. I am really, really, really not brave…so I do not know if I could have gone through with it. There are loads of times when you think about it, when you plan it, but I do not know if I could go through with it.

How young do you think you were when these thoughts first came into your mind? Probably quite young, although I wouldn't see death as a way out, because I didn't have that concept, I just wanted this to stop, the inability to do everyday things and you just think 'I want to be like everybody else.' I wanted to be normal, so you wanted it to stop, to fall into a hole and not be there. I felt that as I was unproductive and I was worthless.

(Kirsty; Alexander-Passe 2010)

During my school years, I would quite often wish I had never been born, but actually I do remember as an early teenager kind of not wanting to wait till I could drive, because I couldn't wait to get into a car and just drive it into a brick wall.

Why the car? Unsure but I wanted to do that so it would all be over, not dealing with it all.

(Emma; Alexander-Passe 2010)

Have you ever thought about or tried to commit suicide? Yes.

How early was that, the first time? The thoughts were…about 14 or 15 years old when I was going through depression and things.

(Rachel; Alexander-Passe 2010).

These quotations are powerful messages that dyslexics can feel worthless in society: that as a byproduct of society's perception of them, they felt they had nothing to offer society, either in a voluntary or working path. Such pain and anguish leads many to see suicide as a valid way out of their suffering and to relieve their families of the burden of their existence.

ATTEMPTING SUICIDE

Please describe your time at school? Was it enjoyable? I quite enjoyed school until I went to secondary school, then I found it really difficult, I wasn't diagnosed dyslexic till I was 17 years old. I used to hate school because I couldn't understand why I couldn't do things that others could do. My primary school was fine, it was just secondary school that things weren't good, I took an overdose when I was 14 years I just couldn't cope with it. I just felt there was too much pressure; I just can't work under so much pressure. There was always too much to do and it takes so much longer to do it as well [due to the unidentified dyslexia]. They expected me to go in during my holiday to catch up! My overdose was due to school, I didn't know what to do. I couldn't tell anyone I couldn't cope with the work [load]. They never sent me for a dyslexia assessment. I was only diagnosed at college, they first tested for it and I finally got it done [an assessment]. They never picked up on it at school, in fact rather than put me into remedial classes for my learning difficulties, I was put into higher classes because, I don't know, it was mainly the coursework I struggled with, apparently I was above average intelligence or average intelligence.

At school, because I didn't know I was dyslexic I just felt stupid and I got accused of attention seeking and being difficult because I just couldn't do the work, obviously I now know I'm dyslexic but at the time it felt everyone was out to get me. Back then to cope I self-harmed, I just didn't know how to cope with it.

I suffered a bit from bullying at school, it was everywhere really [playground and socially] but it was really linked into my depression, I just didn't interact with anybody and then someone found out I had been in hospital [for my suicide attempt] and then it was tough, it became public knowledge. I think they saw me as easy prey/easy target.

(Kirsty; Alexander-Passe 2010)

Do/did you self-harm? Why? What were the triggers? When I was a child, and again as a teenager. I was depressed and confused/ uncommunicative in a social setting, I still do now, getting really depressed and it brings back all those issues of growing up and not feeling like I can communicate with people but part of me has come to accept who I am now.

I attempted suicide a few times [long silence]. I went through a stage when I thought enough was enough and I will rid the world of me. I ended up in mental health [care] at 25 years old because I just had enough, I needed someone to tell me that I was okay, it was okay and what I was experiencing wasn't nice – what people were doing to me [wasn't nice] and I got a lot of reassurance in the mental health [care]. Looking outwards and how to look outwards – basically that it was [other] people who have the problem and not me, and I didn't have to go inside myself and that I could brush these things off and that it's [other] people's issue. Because I came to that point when like I would end up being suicidal. I was too suicidal in my head and it was happening too many times. I was pushed too far.

(Maureen; Alexander-Passe 2010)

Have you ever thought about or tried to commit suicide? Why? What were the triggers? Yes. I took an overdose this summer and more recently drank so much I ended up tearing my oesophagus. These were both very scary occasions. I get very low sometimes and this is what triggers my negative thoughts.

(Susan; Alexander-Passe 2010)

How early do you think you did this sort of thing? I think quite young. Not smoking or drinking, but hitting myself, yes.

Have you ever attempted suicide? Yes.

How young were you? I was, I'm just trying to remember when the first time was, I thought about it when I was at school, the first time I sort of got the equipment out to do it, was when I was at university.

Do you know what the triggers were for that? I was very suddenly depressed.

Did you feel abnormal there, struggling? Was it from problems learning? Yes in that there were frustrations when I was at university, when I first got there.

(Trixie; Alexander-Passe 2010)

Have you ever thought about or tried to commit suicide? Yes. It's like the feeling when you go abroad and you don't really feel comfortable there, none of the signs make sense, none of the places make sense, but you just want to feel comfortable, you can't really settle in there.

You sound like you feel you don't fit in? Yes [it's that], I also don't feel that I should exist.

(Philip; Alexander-Passe 2010)

The interview evidence includes different suicide concepts. Some thought 'wouldn't it have been easier if I had not been born?', with others thinking 'I wish I could fall into a black hole'. Many school-aged dyslexics are naive to all the implications of suicide, but just want all their pain and suffering to end.

Attempting suicide is not only a cry for help, but an admission that someone is unable to cope and that suicide is the only option they see open to them. Suicide is seen by some not only as a means to escape from this earth, but to relieve others of the burden of their existence.

CONCLUSIONS

The true nature of emotional suffering is shown in words not numbers. Qualitative methodologies bring a richness that quantitative data cannot match. The interview data make the suffering real and place it within our own contexts.

The main focus of this chapter was to investigate self-harming as a reaction to difficulties and as a byproduct of depression, with particular reference to the results of a 2010 study (Alexander-Passe 2010). Overall, self-harm in its many forms was used by the majority of the sample, with food and alcohol abuse more common than bodily harm. Self-harm was used by individuals to regain control in their life – when they felt they had little or no control over other aspects (e.g. school, relationships).

Food is an interesting form of self-harm, particularly in the form of binge eating as it could often lead to obesity, which is another means of distancing the dyslexic from society (there is an illogical perception in society that fat people are abnormal and off-putting). Many self-harmers mentioned feelings of unworthiness to explain why they resorted to punishing their bodies for causing them emotional pain.

With bodily harm, it was interesting to note that for those who hit their heads in frustration – it was to hurt themselves to gain a stimulus from feeling pain (a natural high), rather than an expression of anger. Many in the study perceived dyslexia caused them to have a faulty brain, so there may be something in the idea that they hit their 'broken' body in order to to get it to work. In the case of cutting, again, there was a chemical and psychological release from spilling blood and this was used as a way of regaining control.

Not surprisingly self-harm was greater in the depressive compared to the non-depressive sample; however, the type of self-harm varied. Males and non-depressives tended to predominantly self-harm with alcohol, followed by food and then rarely with bodily harm, whereas females in general, tended to predominantly self-harm with food, then bodily harm and lastly alcohol. Overall, depressives self-harmed predominantly with food and then equally with alcohol and bodily harm. Each group had their own profile and this suggests that self-harm is a complex issue, with self-harm activities happening both in childhood and adulthood. In this study, children self-harmed when they were as young as five to ten years old in reaction to schoolwork pressures, as well as feeling different to their peers.

In a world where dyslexics are unable to control many aspects of their lives (especially young dyslexics), self-harm by anorexia, bulimia or cutting are common ways to regain control over their bodies, as also noted in Alexander-Passe (2009b, 2009c, 2010) and Scott (2004).

The interview evidence points to attempted suicide as a way of coping with not fitting in to society; it comes about as a result of frustration and anxiety about their difficulties (Alexander-Passe 2010).

Half the sample thought about suicide and less than half went on to actually attempt suicide. These thoughts, along with the high frequency of feelings of helplessness in the sample, suggest that suicide was viewed by many as one option to end their helplessness. Reported cases of suicide attempts as children were common in this study, as many felt there was no other option open to them to deal with the pressures from schoolwork and the perception that their parents did not understand what they were going through. What this suggests is that parents and schools need to look out for children at risk and put policies in place to manage the workload of children. Drug overdoses, cutting wrists and alcohol poisoning (on purpose) were found in this study to occur in both depressive and non-depressives. These occurred due to feelings of helplessness and are an important aspect to highlight, as dyslexia should not just be seen as a problem affecting a person's ability to read and write. The long-term emotional effects of feeling alienated by your peers and frustrated by your difficulties, even in carrying out simple basic tasks, should not be underestimated.

In summary, the study looked at how dyslexic adults are still affected by their difficulties and their childhood experiences of school. The longevity of school trauma and its effect on adult happiness and career progression means that school is an important period in a dyslexic's life and educators need to focus on preventing further generations from experiencing negative and emotionally damaging school experiences, which can trigger lifelong mental illness.

KEY MESSAGES

- They say it's good to talk, and it is. Dyslexics need to understand that they are not alone and that their problems are not unique. It is important for them to find other dyslexics to talk to.
- Dyslexics, especially young dyslexics, need access to counselling services, along with social groups for dyslexics. This way they will learn they are not alone, and that many others feel the same way, and struggle to make sense of it all.
- Educators should examine the root cause of emotional defences, as this will allow understanding of the triggers and give direction for treatment.
- Counselling help will assist dyslexics to find balance, and recognise their own skills and abilities, so that they can see a positive way forward in their lives.
- Counsellors without experience of dyslexia can easily underestimate the impact dyslexia has on a child's life. Thus dyslexia training should be recommended for counsellors, along with the creation of a national list of suitably qualified dyslexia-trained counsellors/psychotherapists, etc.
- Counselling will allow dyslexics to recognise that their emotional coping may have helped them as children in school, but as adults these strategies are counter-productive as they get in the way of forming meaningful adult relationships.

Chapter 11

BEHAVIOURAL DEFENCES

INTRODUCTION

This chapter investigates behavioural defence mechanisms, which have been developed as a result of threats to the individual. They include: mature mechanisms (task avoidance, frustration, truancy, distraction, sublimination and bullying); immature mechanisms (acting out, anger, shouting, biting, attention seeking and fantasy); and, lastly, extreme mechanisms (violence, revenge, property damage, criminal activities, drug abuse and displacement).

Like emotional defence mechanisms, behavioural mechanisms are calls for help but using externalising rather than internalising actions. These are developed from a range of sources, starting with the parenting style they see at home (aggressive) to peer idolisation (copying peers who gain popularity by criminal activities or drug abuse). It is important to recognise that behavioural mechanisms are learnt or copied from those around them. The quotations used in this chapter come from Alexander-Passe (2010).

MATURE MECHANISMS

TABLE 11.1 MATURE MECHANISMS (BEHAVIOURAL)

Task avoidance	Avoiding homework or work assignments that would highlight their inabilities and render them open to public ridicule, e.g. losing homework on purpose or forgetting to bring books to school
Frustration	Getting frustrated by failure or being unable to understand tasks due to dyslexia, e.g. unable to read or understand homework
Truancy	A more extreme form of task avoidance. Avoiding classes or school when there are tests or stressors, e.g. teacher that bullies them
Distraction: bad behaviour, humour and being the class clown	Using humour to deflect the adverse effects of dyslexia, e.g. being the class clown to divert peers' attention from their inability to read or playing drunk to avoid misreading bus numbers
Bad temper	This is an advanced form of frustration and is a lesser form of anger. The individual diverts attention from their difficulties by blaming others, e.g. bad teacher or bad luck
Pessimism	Rather than risk failing at tasks, the individual will pre-judge the task and protect themselves by pre-judging that they will do badly or fail at a test. This, however, stops the individual from trying their best
Bullying	A form of anger. The individual will choose a weaker target and project their hostility onto them. This is another expression of frustration. Commonly people who use bullying or are bullied themselves by others, e.g. parents, teachers, peers. Now they continue the cycle of hostility
Sublimination	Using their intelligence means to gain revenge on the feared stimulus e.g making sure no one is around to incriminate them.

TASK AVOIDANCE: INTRODUCTION

If academic success cannot give dyslexics self-worth, then they begin to withdraw from classroom activities (negative environments), according to Morgan (1997). There is a growing body of evidence to suggest that children with dyslexia avoid tasks that highlight their difficulties. High on the list of causes of this avoidance are the ways in which teachers and schools deal with failure (Fontana 1995):

> Too often the teacher instils in children a fear of making mistakes and of showing their failure to understand, and this leads to conservative and stereotyped patterns of learning which inhibit reflective thinking and a genuine grasp of the principles upon which knowledge is based. (p.158)

Alexander-Passe (2004) found that within large schools avoidance of competing generally goes unnoticed, compared to smaller schools. This extreme non-participation through lack of confidence is a recurring characteristic of dyslexics (Scott 2004). Avoidance strategies deflect attention from the dyslexic's low academic ability and underperformance; however, teachers see these avoidance strategies very differently, perceiving students as lazy with lack of parental support (Alexander-Passe 2004)

'She told me he sometimes deliberately broke the point of his pencil 10 times a day', the mother of a dyslexic noted to Van der Stoel (1990, p.92). Such techniques are aimed at spending the maximum time off-task and consequently less time at the desk doing work, although dyslexics (especially females) tend to prefer less obtrusive ways to avoid academic work, such as rarely putting up their hands or sitting at the back of classes to be invisible (i.e. not picked on by teachers to take part in the class).

Riddick (1996, p.130) found pupils commenting that they 'daily avoided using difficult words to spell, wrote less [avoiding making mistakes] and put off starting work as coping strategies', as also observed by Alexander-Passe (2004, 2009a, 2009b).

Out of 45 noted strategies of dyslexic children found by Riddick, avoidance was featured in 35 of them. The other ten were characterised by asking classmates to help. These findings were similar to Mosely's (1989) study concerning adults and children with general spelling difficulties.

Anxiety causes humans to avoid whatever frightens them, and anxiety related to dyslexia is no exception. However Ryan (2004) notes that teachers misinterpret this avoidance as laziness. In fact he notes that the avoidance is more related to anxiety and confusion than apathy. Reid (1988) found when pupils felt unwanted, rejected, uncared for and disillusioned, they start to manifest their disaffection by staying away, disrupting lessons, or underachieving, thus avoiding the feared stimulus.

Negative experiences of school, as experienced by the dyslexic teenagers in Edwards (1994), have associated reactions of: lack of confidence; self-doubt/denigration; sensitivity to criticism; behavioural problems; truancy/school refusal; and competitiveness disorders.

Dyslexics often react to their difficulties by withdrawing emotionally, or conversely becoming aggressive, and compensating by obtaining negative attention from others (Thomson and Hartley 1980, p.19). Supporting Butkowsky and Willows (1990), Hales (1994) suggests there is strong evidence to imply that dyslexics are more disturbed by criticism, leading to future avoidance, and also that dyslexics experience considerable amounts of criticism at school, especially before their condition is diagnosed. Alexander-Passe (2006) found that, compared to males, females used more emotional and avoidance-based coping, resulting in lower percentile scores in general and academic self-esteem, and moderate depression.

TASK AVOIDANCE: AVOIDING WRITING

Do you think you were ever trying to avoiding schoolwork, like reading aloud? Yes, at all costs.

What work did you try to avoid? My mother got me an English tutor to help with my English and the tutor basically wrote all my essays for me. We wrote such detailed notes that in the end my mother was paying her to do my work for GCSE, she [the tutor] knew what she was doing and I knew what she was doing, she was being paid to do it. I also copied my science work, so really I did not do much in the end. But I did the subjects I enjoyed like craft and technology.

(Izzy; Alexander-Passe 2010)

I would avoid doing the written side of stuff by being the teacher's helper, helping people.

Really? Yes, I got out of a lot of work that way.

Do you think it was a form of avoidance? Yes, definitely.

What else did you do to avoid schoolwork? I would help people, I would chatter, I would go and take messages and books, and do things, sharpen pencils, anything I could do really.

Everything to avoid writing? Yes, if I could do the positives. I would never misbehave or get into trouble as I would not want to disappoint my parents, but I would do, whatever strategies I could to kind of avoid doing [written] work.

(Emma; Alexander-Passe 2010)

The previous quotations add weight to the argument that school-aged dyslexics will avoid writing tasks in peer-group settings. Dyslexics can be very creative when they look to save their self-image and self-respect amongst their peers. A helpful and quiet dyslexic has more chance of staying under the teacher's radar than a loud pupil who is crying out for attention, even if it is negative attention.

TASK AVOIDANCE: AVOIDING READING ALOUD IN CLASS

How early on did your learning difficulties begin to show up? Reading difficulties? I think it took me longer to learn to read. I think also, well I had some very good strategies; you know I could avoid stuff. I would say 'oh I've just done that' or I just closed the book to lose my place.

How were you at reading aloud in class? Not very good. I still am not very good unless I know the text.

Do you think you used short words in essays more than longer expressive words? Yes, I still do really. I think it is the confidence issue still with words. It is about confidence in getting the spelling right.

Do you think you lost homework on purpose, back then? Yes, plus I also had a very good friend that would allow me to copy off her [laugh].

That is good and helpful. Yes.

(Rachel; Alexander-Passe 2010)

Did you avoid certain tasks at school? Like reading? Yes, like the plague.

So what sort of things did you do to avoid reading and writing? If there weren't enough text books I would get the other person to read it aloud, you know. I traced quite a lot with my finger.

Did you offer to do errands, sharpening pencils all the time? Yes.

(Jean; Alexander-Passe 2010)

Did you get frustrated with your learning difficulties at school? No, only on certain occasions with certain things. I hated reading aloud and that was very embarrassing and so I would have tactics to avoid having to reading aloud [in class].

(Harry; Alexander-Passe 2010)

Do you think you avoided things at school like reading aloud? Oh yes, I avoided it. I would do anything to not read aloud.

So what sort of things did you do to avoid reading aloud? I do not know, faking falling asleep, anything really. When you are put on the spot, you sort of mumble your way through it. I think the teachers realised there was a problem so they tended to avoid me after a while. So they left me out, my turn always seemed to happen at the end of the lesson and that sort of thing. They knew there was a problem, rather than make it an issue they said I would read next time around, then someone else started and I was thus forgotten about.

(George; Alexander-Passe 2010)

Do you think you were avoiding things inside of the classroom? How were you with reading aloud? Oh gosh, yes, I would never have wanted to read aloud, I very much tried to keep or hide, into the background with things like that.

Do you remember any strategies to avoid stuff in the classroom? Not particularly, I just tried to make myself as inconspicuous as possible.

(Anita; Alexander-Passe 2010)

What were the issues in the classroom? Were they about reading aloud? My self-doubts about myself and not wanting to look foolish in front of the group. The fear of looking foolish in front of the group, coming out with something inappropriate or wrong. I can rationalise it, it is almost totally illogical but that was the fear. I once had to read a passage in an assembly for the whole school and I got some words mixed up, I found that hard.

(Brian; Alexander-Passe 2010)

The whole sample was very vocal about avoiding reading in front of their peers, for fear of embarrassment and ridicule, not just in the classroom but in the playground. Fear breeds anxiety, and dyslexics experience huge fears in school. Again the dyslexic's ability to find divergent coping strategies meant they saw school as a place to survive and not to flourish.

TASK AVOIDANCE: AVOIDING DIFFICULT SUBJECTS

Do you think you choose subjects that required less writing? Oh, yes. I dropped foreign languages as soon as I could, I most certainly was a belligerent child by that stage, thinking 'why are they trying to teach me a foreign language when I'm having enough problems with my own?' I was trying to get extra help in English, trying to look around to see what could be done, as I just knew I was not keeping up with the other people. I chose sciences and things like that, that were easier than those that were classed as 'the arts'.

(Anita; Alexander-Passe 2010)

Do you think you chose subjects requiring less writing? Yes. I went for the practical ones.

(Rachel; Alexander-Passe 2010)

Would it be fair to say that you chose to avoid subjects that would show up your difficulties? Looking back at it, I did.

Even subjects you thought you would enjoy? Yes, quite possibly, at one stage I was quite creative in writing but I wouldn't have chosen to take that into A level, I chose the sciences, as you didn't have to read things out, you used practical skills rather than reading and writing skills. Looking back some of my choices may have been because of the dyslexia.

(Harry; Alexander-Passe 2010)

Many noted they made examination decisions, and thus career choices, based on how much writing was required in a particular subject, rather than their actual enjoyment or the intellectual stimulus the subject brought. However such choices did allow dropping languages, an area that most dyslexics struggle in, as Anita stresses: 'Why are they trying to teach me a foreign language when I'm having enough problems with my own?'

DISTRACTION: BAD BEHAVIOUR

It was a school where spelling was important and if you got it incorrectly, you had to write it again three times, if you still got it wrong, you had to write it out ten times… I did a lot of that [laugh].

So do you think back then you avoided things to cover up for your difficulties? I think I did, yes, I would do things in the classroom, so I would be sent outside.

Therefore, you played up to avoid work. Yes. I spent a lot, the last three years of primary school standing outside the classroom [laugh]. I got very good at occupying myself in my head.

(Trixie; Alexander-Passe 2010)

Whilst not a common strategy, there were those who used any means possible to avoid the classroom and a resulting written test. They saw it better to be labelled disruptive than stupid by both teachers and peers. With a class of up to 30 students, it is hard (not impossible) for a teacher to recognise underlying difficulties masked by disruptive behaviour.

DISTRACTION: HUMOUR AND BEING THE CLASS CLOWN

Morgan and Klein (2003, p.72) noted that some dyslexics used a range of strategies to avoid tasks and disguise and distract their inabilities at school, e.g. being the class clown. Edwards (1994) and Riddick (1996) also noted the use of humour or cheekiness is used in adulthood to cover the embarrassment caused by misreading words and other dyslexic errors. Morgan and Klein suggest that using humour in this way results in reducing anxiety by using existing strengths; however, it meant the dyslexic is always guarding against making socially inexcusable errors.

Do you use humour to cover up? Oh yes, yeah. It probably was my defence against bullying [at school], people aren't going to bully you if you are laughing [at your own difficulties, but is this self-denigration?]. I suspect, if someone is sitting on you, you just laugh it off; they go away and pick on someone else.

So you used humour fairly early on to cover up? I probably did, yeah, maybe without realising.

(Harry; Alexander-Passe 2010)

So say that you couldn't do things, you would try to make people laugh to cover up the fact? I suppose in the beginning, but after a while…[that was my personality].

(Izzy; Alexander-Passe 2010)

So it sounds like you were trying to gain approval from your peers by acting up? Yes, that is what it was really about. I think most people do. I think people always want to be liked and if people think you are funny, you will do things to get that: you would rather people laugh at you for doing stupid things than laugh at you because you are stupid.

(Izzy; Alexander-Passe 2010)

The quotations suggest it is better to be seen as funny than stupid, but again this masks the dyslexic's ability to get the help they badly need – it is common for dyslexics to pass through many years of school without detection.

TRUANCY: SCHOOL PHOBIA/REFUSAL

Edwards (1994) notes a 12-year-old boy who used to get into fights with larger or other (dyslexic) kids to get off school. The injuries were for mutual avoidance reasons, not anger, and usually meant two to three days off school. Palti (2010) also observes school phobia in dyslexics due to the stress of school and school failure.

Anxiety causes humans to avoid whatever frightens them, and dyslexia is no exception. However, Ryan (2004) notes that teachers misinterpret this avoidance as laziness. In fact he notes that the avoidance is more related to anxiety and confusion than apathy. Reid (1988) found when pupils feel 'unwanted, rejected, uncared for and disillusioned…they start to manifest their disaffection by staying away, disrupting lessons, or underachieving'.

Łodygowska and Czepita (2012) investigated school phobia amongst dyslexics to determine the impact of a type of therapy on school phobia on this sample. A total of 165 dyslexic children were investigated from three groups: (1) children receiving regular therapy; (2) children receiving occasional therapy; (3) children not receiving therapy. Results indicated that children receiving occasional therapy demonstrated higher levels of school phobia. These children exhibited a higher level of fear in situations when their knowledge was tested. Girls revealed a higher level of school phobia and knowledge testing fear, regardless of their therapeutic experience.

RUNNING AWAY FROM HOME

Home is an important environment for a dyslexic, as parents play a crucial part in a child's upbringing, to nurture and support. But if home life is unsupportive then the child will feel totally isolated. This area of dyslexia is under-researched and is a taboo topic; however, the participants in Alexander-Passe (2010) strongly support such a concept.

Growing up, did you ever truant or run away from home? No, I never ran away from home, but I did think about it.

Why did you think about it? Because I was about 13 or 14 years old, my life was not brilliant, my mum was getting at me and I was struggling at school, I think I was oppositional, and I thought 'they don't care about me.'

(Andrea; Alexander-Passe 2010)

Did you run away from home? Oh, yes [laugh].

How old were you when that first started? Well…I was young; I used to pack a little red vanity case.

The same thing with me. I had a packed bag under my bed, for when things were too much and I remember my mum making fun of it, as she could not quite get it. Yes I used to go and get my teddy and sit on the third step up, when I was really sad when little. And then it progressed to the vanity case and I did go once to the corner of the street. And it scared me, as I did not know what to do then.

It really is similar to attempting suicide, it's the feelings of not being wanted? Yes. I used to write help signs and stick them on the window, for people to come and rescue me.

(Rachel; Alexander-Passe 2010).

Growing up were there any occasions of running away, truanting from school or self-harming as a child? I used to truant from school, yes, on several occasions in secondary school, from like being 11 years old to 16 years. I [also] ran away from home on two occasions in between those years, I did that because everything was getting on top of me with school and the bullying, struggling [with schoolwork]. I was trying to escape.

(Samuel; Alexander-Passe 2010)

Growing up do you ever remember truanting or running away from home? I never truanted from school but I would run away from home, there really wasn't anywhere to run to in our village, but I would often pack my little bag with five sets of knickers, socks and take my dog with me.

It sounded like you did not feel you fitted there. Feeling adopted, that has certain feelings with me — I just felt I was not part of the family, I did not fit in. I suppose when we had our bag packed we felt safer. I used to always take the dog with me; the dog and I were very close. If someone who knew me spotted me, I knew I had to go home straight away. There was no logic to it except for I felt I was packing my bags; I was getting out of here.

(Shelley; Alexander-Passe 2010)

Did you ever try to run away from home? Yes.

How old were you then? Eight years old.

How far did you get? Not very far, it was pathetic really [laugh]. I got round the block, stayed away for about 45 minutes, and then decided to return home.

I also did that, I also always kept a packed bag under my bed. My parents always made fun of it. Yes, I had a little case, I used to have a few clean knickers in there, I used to change the things I put it in, but basically it was there so I could go and had the things I wanted.

Did you feel you didn't fit into your family? Yes, particularly with my mother.

(Trixie; Alexander-Passe 2010)

You were talking about running away from home. Was it often? I planned to do it more than I did. I only went down the street.

I remember having a packed bag under my bed, just in case I couldn't cope and needed to leave fast, how about you? I also did that, but I was aware that I had nowhere to go. I was aware that it was a dangerous world out there. Where I was running to might have been just as dangerous as where I was running from, and at least if I was at home I was under my mum and dad's protection. I knew they loved me, so it was quite fleeting ideas about running away from home.

(Kirsty; Alexander-Passe 2010)

There seems to be a difference between running away from home and truanting from school, which differentiates the dyslexic from the low ability delinquent child. The quotes suggest that they feared their parents enough to not avoid school, and saw the moral and academic benefit of being there. However, at home they experienced stress and anxiety.

Alexander-Passe (2006) found in researching dyslexics (n = 78) and their non-dyslexic siblings (n = 77), that there were huge stressors in the home for dyslexics with parents who were unsupportive and lacked understanding of the challenges they faced at school, and this could be seen as a trigger to run away and truant. Home is meant to be a safe haven for dyslexics after a stressful day at school feeling alienated and educationally neglected. If home life is similar, with the same feelings given from the important adults in their lives, then the dyslexic can feel totally rejected and may run away from home, or develop mental health manifestations as a result, e.g. withdrawal, etc.

IMMATURE MECHANISMS

TABLE 11.2 IMMATURE MECHANISMS (BEHAVIOURAL)

Acting out	An advanced form of bad temper. The individual seeks to either divert attention from their difficulties by picking on someone else (projection), or it is an expression of their frustration
Shouting	Another expression of frustration. This is related to bullying in that it is either directed at a weaker individual or as a response to hostility towards them, e.g. a parent shouting at the child that they aren't trying hard enough
Biting	Regressive manifestations relating to helplessness and infancy occurring as a result of the inability to express one's hostility in words
Temper tantrums	Regressive manifestations also relating to helplessness and infancy occurring as a result of the inability to express frustration
Attention seeking	This manifestation aims to gain the attention of others by any means possible, e.g. shock, crying, anger
Fantasy	Imagining causing harm an the individual, e.g. in a daydream. This can help to relieve the pressure to injure

FANTASY: DAYDREAMING

Daydreaming and use of a fantasy strategy can allow an individual to progress through life more easily. However, there is no research that would support the idea that such a strategy is commonly used by dyslexics. The closest would be Richardson and Stein (1993) and Richardson (1994) investigating psychological and personality traits of successful dyslexics. Findings indicate that these individuals used unusually perceptual experiences and a strong sense of intuition or belief in paranormal experiences, with 73 per cent of their successful dyslexic sample saying yes to the following question: 'Do things sometimes feel as if they are not real?', compared to 49 per cent of the controls. They also found that there were significant indications that successful dyslexics were eccentric, extroverted and used unusual perceptual experiences (hunches, gut reactions and delusions) for decision making. It is believed that Einstein (believed to be dyslexic) daydreamed a lot and this was how he was allowed the mental freedom to find the solution to countless problems. He says in one famous quotation: 'when I examine myself and my methods of thought, I come close to the conclusion that the gift of fantasy has meant more to me than my talent for absorbing positive knowledge' (Quotes.net 2014).

I was always a bit of a daydreamer, taking myself away to the back of the school playing fields.

Do you think you were a daydreamer to survive school? Yes.

Do you know where you went in your daydreams? No, just out of school, in my junior school, it was over the school fence to the fields, which joined onto river leading to the main part of town and the industrial estates.

So really, you were dreaming of a river path leading away from the school. Yes.

(Jean; Alexander-Passe 2010)

Would you daydream a lot at school? Yes, it's really weird, I found one of my old reports from school and every one says 'Kirsty is a daydreamer', I must have done it all the time, I wasn't aware of it. They would talk to me, the teachers, and I would spring out of it and I would say 'oh, I'm sorry.'

(Kirsty; Alexander-Passe 2010)

Do you think you daydreamed in class? Yes, all the time. It was probably one of my biggest problems. There were numerous times when the teacher would wake me, 'Peter, Peter', as I was in my own world, and it was normally a much nicer place to be in [laugh].

(Peter; Alexander-Passe 2010)

Avoidance in school takes several forms, e.g. daydreaming comes from zoning out in lessons, going to a place that is more relaxing and peaceful. Constant daydreaming, as the above quotations suggest, indicates an inability to cope and helplessness; looking to a place of safety. However Einstein suggests that zoning out and daydreaming gives the brain the space to create and find novel solutions to common problems.

EXTREME MECHANISMS

TABLE 11.3 EXTREME MECHANISMS (BEHAVIOURAL)

Violence	An extreme form of frustration where the individual chooses a target weaker than them to express their frustration and anger. This is a form of projection causing bodily harm
Revenge and property damage/ Displacement	Another extreme form of frustration and can mean projection of anger from suffering at the hands of others. It can be directed at property damage or individuals, e.g. setting fire to a school or a library or letting down the tyres on teachers' cars to get revenge on teachers who bullied them
Criminal activities	Another extreme expression of frustration. This is a means to improve self-esteem by gaining in monetary terms by stealing or mugging. This may be their only way to earn money if they are unable to gain employment
Drug abuse	Drug abuse is a means to taking high risks in order to gain self-esteem; this can include high drug doses or being an adrenaline junkie. Addiction may follow that is life threatening

VIOLENCE AS A FORM OF BULLYING

Did your peers bully you? Yes that did happen, because basically I could not process what they were saying to me, so they were always able to win the argument as they could process things faster, I felt I was always one step behind them. Things would start out friendly but become stressful when they realised I couldn't keep up with them. They would bully me with words, to make me feel stupid, making out that they were okay and that I was a bit weird.

(George; Alexander-Passe 2010)

You said earlier that you did feel bullied at school? Yes, I was bullied at school by my school peers and my dyslexia was one of things they would bully me about. I think I was bullied because I was a very introverted child that found it hard to relate to other children and I feel that my dyslexia made me introverted.

(Milly; Alexander-Passe 2010)

Evidence points to dyslexics being bullied at school, and the anger that can build up in dyslexics can lead them to bully others as a consequence, first to increase their own self-esteem, and second, to continue the cycle by picking on someone weaker than themselves.

VIOLENCE, REVENGE, PROPERTY DAMAGE, CRIMINAL ACTIVITIES

Schools tend to group low achieving students together, whether they have a higher intelligence or not. They just see low achievement and label accordingly. In addition, students who misbehave in class due to frustration or boredom are easily labelled as 'trouble' and likely to have behavioural problems without teachers looking deeper into possible causes.

Dyslexics in low ability groups tend to experience the worst teaching in schools, as many schools will give the best teachers the higher ability pupils in order to raise the school's academic level for school league tables. Hence in the case of dyslexics, they will experience teaching that is aimed at engagement and in a vocational style, rather than challenging them to achieve more.

Dyslexics and, especially, unidentified dyslexics will easily fit into delinquent groups in school, as they are turned off from education and have experienced educational neglect. This camaraderie can continue out of the school gates and the dyslexic may be drawn into socialising with these groups. This is may include gang membership, likely to involve criminal activity as an initiation, initially, and then to increase their standing in the group.

In addition it has been suggested that many dyslexics leave mainstream education unable to find gainful employment and can be forced to use illegal means to support themselves and their families. They see their peers leave school and get well paid jobs or go off to university, but they may be unable to get a basic job due to low school leaving qualifications, hence to survive and also gain the same standard of living, criminal activity is an attractive option.

A last reason for manifesting behaviour of this type could be that dyslexics are angry at school and society for not helping them in school, for allowing them to fail in their examinations and for treating them poorly. The anger can easily translate to damaging property in revenge, e.g. slashing teachers' car tyres (property damage), burning schools (arson) and attacking authority figures (grievous bodily harm) – this can be classed as displacement of their anger.

The 'Raising your Game' project (Mencap 2014) for 14–19-year-old offenders, found that many dyslexics were drawn into gangs and when caught, due to confusion, were unable to defend themselves properly (e.g. unable to explain their actions or give a reasonable alibi). They found the whole criminal justice system mystifying and were unfairly treated by the system. The project aimed to support unidentified dyslexics with training and social skills, so when they re-entered society they would have the skills to gain employment with a renewed self-confidence.

As referred to in Chapter 2, a project by Hewitt-Mann (2012) found that in one UK prison (HMP Chelmsford) 53 per cent of the inmates (2029) were dyslexic, compared with approximately 10 per cent of the general population. Similar projects in the UK, USA and Sweden have found similar frequencies, and also note high numbers of prisoners with learning disabilities found in prisons (Alm and Andersson 1995; Antonoff 1998; Davis *et al.* 1997; Kirk and Reid 2001; Morgan 1996, 1997).

Assessing the basic literacy skills of the whole HMP Chelmsford prison population, the following was found:

- 10 per cent had preschool literacy levels
- 9 per cent had the literacy levels of a five-year-old
- 21 per cent had the literacy levels of a seven-year-old
- 32 per cent had the literacy levels of a nine-year-old
- 21 per cent had the literacy levels of a 12+-year-old.

Other statistics help to understand the sample:

- 48 per cent left school with no qualifications
- 56 per cent had been expelled/excluded from school
- 22 per cent had been to a SEN school or had SEN support at school (although 53% were dyslexic)
- 62 per cent had not passed the driving theory test
- 0.5 per cent had passed the construction skills certification scheme (CSCS) to work on a building site.

Hewitt-Mann taught literacy skills to identified groups; which resulted in the governor commenting: 'Since Jackie has been working with the prisoners, you can see a huge difference in them – much calmer and frustration levels are less, resulting in a happier prison with less problems on the wing' (Hewitt-Mann 2012, p.8).

To conclude, Rice and Brooks (2004, p.2) suggest literacy interventions in prisons have the 'potential for restoring to society those people who are excluded from full citizenship because they have yet to attain functional literacy'.

CONCLUSIONS

This chapter has focused on the task avoidance typically found in dyslexics at school – a very common defence mechanism.

Avoidance of writing tasks by forgetting pens, textbooks, etc., along with the skilful avoidance of reading using numerous excuses (e.g. forgetting glasses, going on errands for teachers, acting the class clown, getting sent out for bad behaviour, not volunteering in class, etc.) mean that dyslexics are able to survive school without an attack on their self-esteem. Task avoidance is self-preservation from bullying (from teachers and students), humiliation (from teachers and students) and from admitting they have a learning difficulty (the dyslexic themselves). This latter point is important as it again highlights how dyslexics camouflage their difficulties, can be in denial that there is a problem, and how all of this prevents them from getting the help they need to achieve their academic potential.

Thus, it is important to recognise the manipulation dyslexics use in school to survive on an hourly basis, and educationalists need to put in place policies that aim to sabotage such strategies, e.g. early screening and early intervention so that dyslexics are recognised for their intellectual abilities and placed in sets according to ability/ potential rather than academic production.

Placing dyslexics in low ability classrooms in mainstream education according to their written performance rather than their verbal intellect will possibly place them with teenagers who are more likely to have behavioural problems, thus more impressionable dyslexics are likely to follow such peers to gain favour or popularity.

Children and teenagers are highly impressionable and thus are susceptible to the influences of others. If they are refused entry to more academic social groups at school, they are likely to mix with other groups who are generally less intellectual. Therefore, awareness of their exclusion from school social groups should inform educational policy makers.

The interview evidence points to a difference between those who play truant from school and those who run away from home. Dyslexics tend to be the latter and delinquents the former. Dyslexics do not run away from home just to avoid school, where they perceive they are unlike their academic achieving peers, but also home life, and the pressure from parents to attain according to societal norms.

The very high percentage of dyslexics (mostly undiagnosed) and others with low literacy in prison indicates the lack of career choices available to those with low academic qualifications. Many of those in prison with unidentified dyslexia are there due to lack of educational opportunities, as schools have been shown to have low identification rates of those with reading and writing difficulties. However, prisons have the potential to restore to society those who have been excluded through low literacy levels, as suggested by Rice and Brooks (2004) (see Chapter 2).

Lastly, it should be noted that dyslexics who turn to criminal damage are commonly motivated to gain revenge against the people who excluded and bullied them due to their difficulties. Many adult dyslexics when they finally gain diagnosis are commonly full of hatred towards their old teachers who missed the vital clues suggesting learning difficulties. Their cries of 'what I could have been if I'd known I was dyslexic earlier' are heart-felt, so the resentment that some dyslexics feel towards an educational system that let them down, and allowed them to believe they were worthless and stupid, is understandable.

KEY MESSAGES

- Some dyslexics harbour great resentment against society and the educational system that let them down. They should try and release such anger and frustration before it becomes a behaviour defence mechanism.
- Dyslexics need an outlet for their anger and resentment, and counselling is just one avenue open to parents to assist their child. Others are channelling such anger into sports and letting it defuse without harming others.
- The emotional pain that dyslexics feel due to unidentified dyslexia can be akin to being imprisoned for 30 years for a crime that they had not committed, then finally being released and told they are innocent.
- Dyslexia is commonly only diagnosed after children score at least two chronological years behind peers at school. However, for a bright child this means failing for many years until their peers overtake them. Thus, to be commonly told by teachers and peers that they are stupid can cause huge amounts of resentment, which need an outlet.
- Teachers need to recognise that dyslexics can use a whole host of advanced strategies to avoid feared academic activities (reading and writing). It is important not to label children with social, emotional and behavioural difficulties (SEBD) or ADHD too quickly, as the root causes of the child's behaviour need to be determined. What are such behaviours masking?

Chapter 12

VULNERABILITY TO DEPRESSION

INTRODUCTION

The concepts of risk and resilience are often seen as two sides of the same coin. According to Haeffel and Grigorenko (2007, p.435) risk refers to the heightened probability of negative outcome among individuals possessing certain vulnerabilities or sharing exposure to certain conditions. Resilience is a dynamic process encompassing the manifestation of positive functioning, despite possessing vulnerabilities or the presence of high risk.

Thus, risk factors increase the likelihood of developing a particular outcome, whereas resilience factors decrease the risk of developing that outcome. Unfortunately, it is impossible to create intervention that eliminates all life stressors and to create total resilience, and this would be seen by many as unproductive. Stressful life events can be perceived by two individuals differently, one may develop psychopathology (negative effects leading to mental health issues), whilst another may perceive them as important for positive long-term changes. Haeffel and Grigorenko note that, without understanding the relationship between stressful life events, it is difficult to determine how one should intervene to develop resilience and reduce risk.

NATURE AND NURTURE

By 2020 it is projected that depression (including depressive disorder) will be the second leading cause of disability worldwide (Murray and Lopez 1996), with Greenberg *et al.* (2003) suggesting that depression is a great, and will be an even greater, financial burden on world economies, with US$83 billion a year in the USA suggested as the potential cost. Thus, understanding the risk and resilience leading to depression is important for our society.

According to cognitive theories of depression (Abramson, Metalsky and Alloy 1989; Beck 1967) cognitive vulnerability reacts with stress to produce depression. Thus, both nature and nurture are to blame for depression. These theories suggest that those at risk of depression tend to generate negative interpretations of stressful life events which have adverse results for their health and self-worth. 'People who generate these negative interpretations develop hopelessness, which is a proximal and sufficient cause of depression', (Haeffel and Grigorenko 2007, p.437).

Goodman and Gotlib (1999) and Gibb (2002) note that children may acquire cognitive vulnerability by receiving direct inferential feedback from negative parental practices and other significant adults. This link has been seen by others as particularly robust, according to Cole, Jacquez and Maschman (2001) and Turk and Bry (1992).

Other researchers suggest that childhood maltreatment (not related to physical or sexual abuse) was related to cognitive vulnerability to depression (Gibb *et al.* 2001). Rose and Abramson (1992) suggest that emotional abuse is an especially potent contributor to cognitive vulnerability to depression because, unlike in cases of physical or sexual abuse, the abuser, by definition, supplies negative cognitions to the victim. Thus, as Haeffel and Grigorenko (2007) note, early social environments may be an important determinant of whether children develop cognitive vulnerability. They also suggest that research could identify parents who tend to generate negative interpretations for their children's behaviours and then intervene with cognitive training to assist them in developing more positive interpretations for their children.

Nolen-Hoeksema, Girgus and Seligman (1986) and Turner and Cole (1994) suggest that children should be targeted for treatment before the age of 11 years old, to change their interpretations and thus vulnerability to depression, as their vulnerability has yet to stabilise; however, Abela (2001) disagrees with this, as children develop cognitive vulnerability at 11 years old, and so intervention should wait until this age to develop resilience (Haeffel and Grigorenko 2007, p.440). Nolen-Hoeksema (1990) also suggests that precognitive vulnerability interventions should focus on girls, as there are significant gender differences in levels of depression among adults, with twice as many women experiencing depression compared with men. As Kessler (2002) suggests, once a person has had depression, they are at higher risk of subsequent episodes, thus it is seen as critical to prevent the initial first onset of depression.

HOPELESSNESS

Haeffel and Grigorenko (2007) state that:

> if hopelessness causes depression, then creating hopefulness should treat depression. Consistent with this hypothesis, research on hopefulness and research on placebo effects suggests that positive expectations for improvement can lead to improvements in depressed mood. Similar to a self-fulfilling prophecy, generating hopefulness for improvement seems to lead to real improvement. (p.442)

Cognitive behavioural therapy (CBT) is perceived as one of the most effective treatments for depression, based on the concept of helping individuals to reinterpret their life events, which falls within the concept of hopefulness.

Rudolph (2009) suggests that:

> one of the most powerful determinants of children's course of development is the social context in which they live. In particular, experiencing a stable and supportive environment during childhood is likely to foster healthy cognitive, social, and emotional development, whereas experiencing a disruptive or stressful environment has been linked to a wide range of adverse mental health outcomes, including depression. Stress and the accompanying emotional distress may then interfere with some of the major tasks of childhood, such as academic

> achievement and fulfilment of educational goals. Thus, a child's early supportive and stable experiences at home and at school are vital for healthy emotional development. (p.1)

Stress may take many forms in a dyslexic child's life, from an accumulation of minor daily hassles (Scott 2004) to more severe chronic strains or specific negative life events. Each of these stressors is related to depression. Rudolph *et al.*'s (2001) study suggested that school-related stress (such as poor academic performance, negative feedback from parents and teachers about schoolwork, and daily hassles in the school environment) can lead to an increase in depression. They also note that unpredictable or disruptive environments (e.g. school) may undermine children's sense of control and mastery, leading to a sense of helplessness or hopelessness that acts as a precursor to depression. Family disruption, as well as exposure to chronic stressful circumstances within the family, with peers and in school settings, predicted decreases in perceptions of control, and increases in helpless behaviour in academic and social situations. These maladaptive beliefs and behaviour were in turn associated with depression. Thus, exposure to stress and failure are also likely to influence adversely children's perceptions of their competence.

Cole (1991) found that negative environmental feedback can be internalised by children in the form of negative self-perceptions and low self-esteem, which then heightens depressive symptoms. Thus, stress within the school environment may exert specific influences on children's academic-related beliefs, self-perceptions and goals, and consequently, on emotional well-being at school. Such views were also supported by Roeser and Eccles (1998). Rudolph (2009) concludes that:

> depression has been linked to a range of negative school-related outcomes, including poor grades, a lack of persistence in the face of academic challenges, and decreased classroom participation. These effects may range from short-term declines in academic performance to long-term problematic school outcomes. (para. 6)

She also notes that:

> whether it is most common for academic difficulties to precede depression or for depression to precede academic difficulties has not yet been clearly determined. It is also possible, of course, that the presence of significant academic difficulties in depressed children reflects a common third influence...[and that] research has suggested that depression may be most strongly associated with academic stress, failure, and school conduct problems when it co-occurs with acting-out behaviour or attentional deficits. (Rudolph 2009, p.3)

CONCLUSIONS

This book is nearing its end. A journey has taken place that leads the reader to understand that dyslexics are highly vulnerable to depression and other emotional manifestations due to the absence of mass identification and the lack of interventions to assist those who finally gain diagnosis.

Hopelessness is a good description of the feeling that many dyslexics have, when faced with life without understanding their potential, and being 'stuck' in circumstances that prevent them from moving out of low-paid and low-stimulation employment. For those who feel trapped in a society without the tools to take an active part in it, it is like living abroad in a foreign country without the language skills to get a job, buy food and make friends. As a child, hopelessness can lead to a downward spiral that can decrease self-worth to such a level that self-harming and attempted suicide are options worth considering, as the child asks himself: 'what is there to live for?'

Dyslexics need both educational and psychological interventions to avoid a downward path towards depression and self-harm. Treating one and not the other will just build resentment towards a society they feel excluded from.

KEY MESSAGES

- Dyslexics should try to stay positive and see any difficulties as temporary not permanent. Help is available to them through local dyslexia groups, e.g. British Dyslexia Association helplines.
- Parents of dyslexics should look out for withdrawing strategies in their child, e.g. avoiding, sleeping too much and having few/no friends. Why are they withdrawing? Their self-confidence needs to be rebuilt to allow them to re-enter the world.
- Educators should develop policies to recognise 'at risk' children, so they don't spiral into depression, and recognise that constant learning failure is a trigger for withdrawal and depression.

Chapter 13

LEARNED HELPLESSNESS TO OPTIMISM

INTRODUCTION

This chapter offers a possible strategy to challenge hopelessness and move towards a positive route to challenge emotional and behavioural defence mechanisms.

Learned helplessness is a theoretical basis to understand hopelessness, in that individuals attribute the world around them and their activities to lack of self-control. This moves beyond the study of locus of control (LOC) into an arena that challenges the perceptions that others have more control over them than themselves.

Seligman (1991) takes a Montessori approach (see below) that attaining mastery of any activity (academic or non-academic) takes time and that real mastery only comes from first overcoming failure.

Challenging learned helplessness and pessimism is important through attribution theories[1], so that realistic and accurate self-feedback is created. Only when realistic and specific feedback is given can specific skills be tackled. Taking a global view of inabilities is a dyslexic's downfall as it holds them like a prison cell in learned helplessness.

1 Fiske and Taylor (1991) argue that attribution theories describe how ordinary people use information to arrive at causal explanations for events. We try to make sense of the world by adding meaning and explanations, whether they are correct or not.

LEARNED HELPLESSNESS

Seligman (1975a, 1975b, 1991), the esteemed professor of psychology at the University of Pennsylvania, USA, is seen by many as the originator of the optimism movement. Researching the power of learned optimism and hopefulness as a treatment for pessimism and helplessness, he states that masterful action is the crucible in which preschool optimism is forged. It is the parents' role to help the child to make a habit of persisting in the face of challenges and to overcome obstacles. Once the child enters school, such mastery is needed to help deal with failure and to help him form good theories about how he succeeds, why he fails and, importantly, what he can do to change failure into success. These theories, according to Seligman, underpin a child's optimism or pessimism.

Parents want their children to achieve tasks first time round, and to be the best in their class. But according to Montessori (1965) to gain real mastery, one needs to first experience failure, and then overcome it after several attempts. If mastery is gained first time round, then the necessary and vital building blocks are missed out.

Seligman believes that parents who cushion their children from failure are doing them a disservice and holding them back from normal development – weakening them 'just as certainly as if we had belittled, humiliated and physically threatened them at every turn'. Seligman goes on to note that the feel-good self-esteem movement, which avoids children failing in tasks by simplifying curriculum or tests, cheapens success and will 'produce a generation of very expensive failures' (Seligman 1998, p.45).

PESSIMISM

On the treatment for pessimism and helplessness, Seligman comments that whilst optimism is seen as a treatment for depression, if parents and teachers use optimism to change the attributions of children (how they perceive and explain events to themselves) to more positive ones and the attributions are not realistic or true (e.g. you are special, it doesn't really matter if you didn't do well in that test), then the effects will be empty and will fall apart. However, if the lessons to the child are more realistic, specific and a challenge to their perceptions of the world (e.g. challenging 'I am dumb'), to form realistic attributions, then the effect will be worthwhile and long term. Seligman calls this 'accurate optimism' (Seligman 1998, p.298).

In school, and other learning situations, individuals who are optimistic will recover quickly from defeat, as they will see defeat as a challenge to overcome, and that such defeat is temporary, specific and not pervasive. However, those who are pessimistic will wallow in defeat, as they see the defeat (failure) as permanent and pervasive. They will become depressed and stay helpless for a long time, as they see any setback as defeat, and one defeat is like losing a war. They will not easily challenge defeat, will shy away from trying such tasks again and any new failure in similar tasks will confirm their helplessness (Seligman 1998, p.137).

Seligman concludes, after several research projects investigating optimistic versus pessimistic samples (in schools, universities, West Point military academy and the workplace), that those who succeed in life and school are not always those who are the most talented, but those with the most optimistic frame of mind (optimistic attributions).

Treatments to turn pessimistic attributions to optimistic ones start with investigating how individuals perceive negative events and trying to recognise the emotional connection that results (e.g. failing in a task makes them feel sad and useless). Using an ABC (adversity, belief and consequence) technique, this can be investigated even with young children, from the age of eight years old. One example of this is:

> Adversity: My teacher, Mr Minner, yelled at me in front of the whole class, and everybody laughed.
>
> Belief: He hates me and now the whole class thinks I'm a jerk (an idiot).
>
> Consequences: I felt really sad and I wished I could just disappear under my desk.
>
> (Seligman 1998, p.237)

Treatment starts by investigating other meanings to events and trying to find realistic but possible ways forward to energise individuals.

With an ABCDE technique (adversity, belief, consequence, disputation, energisation), the above example is expanded:

> Adversity: My teacher, Mr Minner, yelled at me in front of the whole class, and everybody laughed.
>
> Belief: He hates me and now the whole class thinks I'm a jerk.
>
> Consequences: I felt really sad and I wished I could just disappear under my desk.
>
> Disputation: Just because Mr Minner yelled at me, it doesn't mean he hates me. Mr Minner yells at just about everybody, and he told our class we were his favourite class. I guess I was goofing around a little, so I don't blame him for getting mad. Everyone in the class, well everyone except for maybe Linda but she's a goody-goody, but everybody else has been yelled at by Mr Minner at least once, so I doubt they think I'm a jerk.
>
> Energisation: I still felt a little sad about being yelled at, but not nearly as much, and I didn't feel like disappearing under my desk anymore.

The aim is to change important attributions from pessimistic (e.g. I'm thick), permanent (e.g. I will always be thick), pervasive/global (e.g. I will always be thick in everything) and impersonal (e.g. I will always be thick in everything, and it isn't my fault, I had bad teachers at school), to optimistic and personal (e.g. I could have tried harder), temporary (e.g. I will try harder next time) and non-pervasive/specific (e.g. I will try harder next time in tests). Thus, allowing a chance to improve and try again, along with seeing oneself as the key to changing the situation and improving. If one blames others (e.g. I had bad teachers at school) rather than seeing oneself as the key to change (e.g. I need to spend personal time learning some new skills), then situations will not improve.

The following is an explanation of the terms used in this technique (Seligman 1996, 1998, p.163):

- Permanent: the cause is something that will persist.
- Temporary: the cause is changeable or transient.
- Pervasive: the cause will affect many situations.

- Specific: the cause will only affect a few situations.
- Personal: I am the cause.
- Impersonal: the cause is something to do with other people or circumstances.

The key is to change negative views of events, by being specific rather than global in feedback/attribution of events, e.g. changing 'I am useless at school' (global) to 'I have problems in maths, specifically algebra' (specific).

DYSLEXICS AND RESILIENCE TO FAILURE

In the case of dyslexic students and adults, it is very hard to develop resilience to failure, as constant and repeated failure is common in school-aged dyslexics, especially amongst unidentified dyslexics at school. However, this book has highlighted that dyslexics tend at some point to give up, and choose to avoid difficult-to-spell words, to hide in class and avoid the most difficult/challenging tasks. This is highly negative and comes from their belief that to survive the day and avoid humiliation is their main daily aim. Such avoidance is denial and hides the problem from teachers. Many teachers in mainstream education have large numbers of students, and teachers are relieved to have quiet students – but quiet students in most cases are those avoiding the teachers' radar. Intelligent students are the ones who challenge the teacher and ask questions. Only the students who stay on the teacher's radar will get the help they need.

In Alexander-Passe (2010), parents were also seen to be to blame, as they used similar avoidance themselves. Parents wanted their children to do well, and to do well in homework tasks. Answering your child's questions is positive, but completing their homework for them is negative. If they got it wrong but completed it themselves, then the teacher would know the child needs extra help. If the homework is returned with everything correct, then the teacher thinks everything is okay and they have done their job properly. This being the case, if the homework is correct, but the child is unable to do the tasks themselves in school, the teacher would conclude the child is lazy and isn't paying attention, as there is a mismatch from the homework to the classroom work. Thus, parents should allow their children to fail in homework tasks, as only this will inform their teachers that extra help is needed.

As Seligman notes, mastery is the ability to gain knowledge after failure, and it is common to find dyslexics who have done well despite their difficulties (e.g. Richard Branson, Albert Einstein, etc.): they have found strategies to turn events around and focus on their strengths and talents, rather than their weaknesses. Parents should feel hopeful about their child's education and future, as they have a substantial part to play in developing their child's mastery and resilience, turning their helplessness into hopefulness.

To conclude, much can be done to assist dyslexic parents and dyslexics in schools/universities to change their attribution explanations from pessimistic to optimistic (and realistic), and to avoid helplessness and depression.

KEY MESSAGES

- It is important to reprogram dyslexics so they are not trapped by misconceptions about their own abilities and how much dyslexia affects their lives.
- The ABCDE technique (adversity, belief, consequence, disputation, energisation) has the potential to remove the need for defence mechanisms, so that avoidance is not needed, and dyslexics can gain the skills and mastery they need to achieve their potential.
- Parents have a vital part to play in developing resilience amongst dyslexics, so that they gain the ability to bounce back from adversity and failure in tasks, and so that dyslexics see that failure is a vital cog in the development of mastery and that they are a mixture of areas of strength and weaknesses, as are their friends, family and peers.
- Challenge misconceptions regarding learning and career barriers. There are no limits to what a dyslexic can achieve; it just may not be through traditional routes, e.g. going to university after a vocational course rather than A levels or going to university as a mature student rather than straight from school.

Chapter 14

DISCUSSION AND CONCLUSION

The study of dyslexia rarely focuses on the manifestations that occur as a result of having a learning difficulty or difference (secondary effects). In the main, research and publications have been focused on understanding the core difficulties presented, and how such difficulties (reading and writing) can be remediated in school settings.

Dyslexia as a term is fraught with difficulties, with close to a dozen different names used to try to better define its difficulties. Educators such as Elliott and Grigorenko (2014) argue against the use of the term, and many have been up in arms saying they wish to dismiss 'dyslexia'; however, they are not arguing that children and adults do not experience difficulties, but are only saying the term is incorrect, and dyslexic-friendly teaching methods are good for all. I agree that the term is incorrect, as dyslexia affects more than just words, but it would be hard to change a term that is as generic as 'hoover' is for vacuum cleaners. Maybe the focus should be on helping dyslexics to learn rather than trying unsuccessfully to define the indefinable.

Reading empirical reviews and encountering public perceptions, it could be assumed that dyslexia only affects children, and once dyslexic children learn to read and write, the dyslexia is cured, and they are no longer dyslexic. Those with dyslexia will tell a different story. They will detail personal journeys of both discovery, and coping with the difficulties they experience, starting at school and continuing throughout their lives.

Commonly you will hear from dyslexics that they felt they were stupid at school and no one really understood them – not their teachers and often not even their parents or siblings. They will tell you they thought they were stupid because everyone told them so. Experiences of bullying are commonplace and come from the dyslexic's inability to achieve at school, and this inability can affect the social dimension of school. Children can be cruel and tend to avoid children with difference, as they mainly want to mix with children like themselves. So clever children are unlikely to mix with those they perceive as abnormal, as it can reflect badly on them.

In such a challenging and hostile environment, the dyslexic knows they can either sink or swim. 'Sinking' comes from believing what everyone else is saying – that they are worthless – and withdrawing as a form of protection. 'Swimming' is finding another means to gain popularity, e.g. being the class clown, physically attacking anyone who tries to humiliate them or developing other skills of note (sports, drama, craft and alternative hobbies).

This book details the defence mechanisms commonly found in dyslexics, starting with the pre-defence mechanism of avoidance of words, and then moving on to emotional or behavioural defence mechanisms as a means of coping and protecting themselves from stress and anxiety.

At the heart of these mechanisms is the need for self-protection – from harm and unfair treatment, protection from humiliation, and unfair comparison to siblings and peers by parents and teachers. But in an ideal world these protections would not be needed.

In an ideal world, all young children would be assessed for both their strengths and weaknesses as they enter primary school, and then reassessed again at the start of secondary school. As part of this assessment, each child would be screened for reading, writing and mathematical skills, so that suitable interventions could be put in place before a child experiences repeated and continuous failure of tasks. It is the repeated and continuous failure that causes the stress that then leads to the anxiety that can triggers defences for self-preservation.

The basic need for identification is a complex issue, as parents, educators and policy makers argue about the merits of identification, and the injustice that, once identification is made, intervention does not always automatically follow. UK schools are slow to identify dyslexia, and work on a deficit model whereby a child must fail for many years at school before identification is considered. This compares unfavourably to the USA, who are pioneering early screening, so any child with learning difficulties can be identified and intervention can lead to educational gains, before educational helplessness is developed. All educators advocate early intervention and this can only help to reduce the mental health manifestations which this book discusses in detail.

As noted in prison studies, the lack of identification all through school causes great frustration, and dyslexics (mostly identified) are humiliated by their highlighted difficulties (e.g. being unable to read aloud in class, or work being handed back by teachers with red marks all over it and an F grade, etc.). No wonder extreme defences are manifested. However, such manifestations then overtake the source of their difficulties. Hence aggression towards teachers is treated by punishment and an SEBD label rather than looking at the cause – being continuously humiliated in class and their learning needs being discounted and ignored. Humiliation from one lesson has a cascade affect on others, even when the teacher is helpful, the dyslexic child is still reeling and calming down from their last humiliating lesson.

Boosting self-esteem is seen by some researchers as the 'social vaccine' to create a better society, where all are treated fairly, justly and with respect. However, boosting self-esteem by removing competition so no one fails, or praising when no praise is warranted, is not going to help. What is going to make a difference is a change in society, and especially in schools, so that failure or struggling to achieve is seen as a vital cog of mastery, and that all children need to experience failure in tasks at some point to develop resilience. The key is how much failure is healthy?

This relies on the teacher's professionalism to tailor/differentiate tasks so that the correct level of challenge is achieved without denting a child's self-worth. If a child comes out of school and feels a failure, then the teacher has pitched the task incorrectly and needs in the next lesson to rebuild that low academic self-worth, so the child is again prepared to risk in the lesson to gain new knowledge.

Parents have a key role in helping a dyslexic to cope at school. First by demonstrating resilience and showing positive means of coping with stress. The balance between aggression and withdrawal is key here. Too much aggression will teach a child that behavioural defences are acceptable strategies to use, whereas too much withdrawal and self-deprecation will teach that emotional defences are the way to go. Peers and siblings are also important here, and a dyslexic struggling to survive will look to other important individuals in their lives for guidance.

Second, parents need to allow their child to send in incomplete homework if this is a true reflection of their effort and abilities. A parent doing the homework for their child is just creating more problems, as the teacher will conclude their child is lazy in class, as his parent is able to motivate them to produce carefully crafted work. If the homework and classwork match and are poor, then the teacher knows there must be a problem requiring investigation.

The aim of this book has been to highlight the emotional and behavioural strategies leading to depression that dyslexics use as a reaction to adverse educational experiences. School policies are changing, but too slowly. Schools need to provide three to five hours a week of specialist intervention for dyslexics, but they need to be identified first, and even then SEN school budgets rarely stretch to one hour a week for the students most in need. School SEN departments should be in most cases ten times their current size to really support such students in their learning, so they can reach their potential. From my experience of UK schools, I would suggest that a ratio of 1:350 specialist teachers to mainstream secondary school-aged students is common, even though research indicates that one in five students struggles at some point in their educational school life, hence such a ratio is unable to provide the interventions required – a more reasonable ratio would be 1:150. Whilst there are no available data in the UK for the actual specialist teacher ratios, the most pertinent evidence comes from Australia from Independent Schools Queensland (2013) investigating schools in that region. It found a 1:233 ratio in independent schools, a 1:270 ratio in government schools and a 1:440 ratio in religious Catholic schools.

Teachers need to take SEN seriously and differentiate effectively in lessons (e.g. targeted tasks, multi-sensory strategies and resources, effective use of teaching assistants and extra time for tasks). Soundbites from UK SEN educational policies argue that 'all teachers are teachers of Special Educational Needs' (DfEE 2001, 2014); however, without SEN training and resources, this is unrealistic. It just means SEN students will be taught by non-specialist staff, SEN departments will lose funding and skilled staff will be lost.

I would also suggest that schools should employ SEN/dyslexia-trained counsellors, so they can tackle the long-lasting effect of educational failure, and the humiliation resulting from long delays in diagnosis and intervention. Mental health is likely to be the biggest health risk to the population by the next decade, and educational failure must be regarded as a 'risk factor' for the next generation.

Dyslexics must be recognised for both their strengths and weaknesses, along with recognition that many years of educational discrimination may have had an adverse effect on them, though many have used such anger as a driving force to attain beyond the level of their peers and develop resilience against life's knocks. Most, however, are affected adversely, and this leads them to unfulfilling careers and mental health difficulties.

Commentators (Armstrong and Squires 2014) ask 'why assess for dyslexia?' and, whilst at first it seems a silly question as it would lead to help and intervention, the majority of dyslexics are not diagnosed, funding for assessment is a political football that nobody wants to run with, and teachers lack the time and skills to identify and help all dyslexics in their classrooms. The 'what if' question could be posed if all dyslexics had been identified and gained interventions:

- Would schools be more focused on learning rather than dealing with behaviour misdemeanours?
- Would dyslexics be turned on by learning, rather than turned off and disillusioned?
- Would fewer dyslexics end up in prisons and would prisons still be full to capacity?
- Would dyslexics reach their potential in life and, like Albert Einstein, solve many of life's big questions?
- Would this lead to fewer mental health difficulties in society?

Dyslexics are beginning to be recognised for what they can bring to society, and are being sought out for their problem-solving and divergent thinking abilities, e.g. in computer programming, code-breaking and design. With the provision of funding for early identification and successful interventions, the UK could in future produce a workforce who may propel the UK to the forefront of the world in terms of innovation with leaders in many fields. Surely this must be something to aim for?

Appendix

DYSLEXIA AND DEPRESSION

THE HIDDEN SORROW

INTRODUCTION

This biographical study of 29 dyslexic adults was created to investigate dyslexia, depression and gender, examining a number of variables including university education, gender, depression and self-harm. The aim was to recruit 15 males and 15 females, with at least ten to be depression free and ten to be depressive.

The majority of participants were only diagnosed as dyslexic after leaving school and this I found to be typical of most dyslexics. Whilst initially I set out to investigate depression as a subfactor, it turned out to be the main focus of the study, as the majority of those who took part were depressed at some point in their lives. Gender also turned out to be an important differential in understanding how male and female dyslexics cope with educational experiences encountered.

The study used a qualitative methodology (Interpretative Phenomenological Analysis – IPA) to investigate through a semi-structured investigative interview script the participants' emotional journeys from childhood to adulthood. Themes were then moved into quantitative data to investigate trends amongst the sample.

The study found many depressive symptoms in the non-depressive sample, detailing cases of self-harm, attempted suicide and post-traumatic stress disorder (PTSD) triggered by returning to school in the role of parents.

METHODOLOGY

SAMPLE

Participants were recruited three ways: (1) emails to UK dyslexia newsgroups; (2) adverts on dyslexic web-forums; and (3) inclusion on dyslexia associations' websites. Four dyslexic sample groups were requested (with/without depression, degree/non-degree educated), with dyslexic adults with depression being the largest group to reply.

All participants were required to provide evidence of: (1) formal diagnosis of dyslexia (e.g. educational psychologist reports); and (2) depression (e.g. a clinical depression diagnosis or at least one course of physician/GP prescribed anti-depressants). Whilst mild depression is common in society, only severe cases tend to be referred for clinical diagnosis.

See Tables A1.1–A1.3 for sample details. The mean age upon dyslexia diagnosis was 28.09 years (SD 11.83) within the depressive sample and 22.28 years (SD 14.77) in the non-depressive sample, indicating that the non-depressives tended to be diagnosed earlier; however, in both groups they were mainly diagnosed post-school and after leaving university.

In the study's original design, I felt that several sample groups were needed. Depressives compared to non-depressives became the main focus of the study due to my prior research into the emotional effects of dyslexia (Alexander-Passe 2004, 2006, 2008, 2009a, 2009b, 2009c, 2009d, 2009e).

Samples were sourced from several locations and I hoped to obtain five participants for each group (e.g. depressive males). However, the more participants enrolled, especially non-depressives, the more they turned out to fit into the depressive group better. This was due in part to them not recognising themselves as depressives (even though they exhibited the criteria defined by this study), or to the fact that their depression had occurred in childhood and they had discounted or blocked out such memories. Thus, the final sample was 29 participants, with 22 being depressive and seven non-depressive, from a five-month recruitment process. Interestingly in the depressive group, there were equal numbers of degree and non-degree educated participants, suggesting dyslexia and high emotional suffering may not limit academic opportunity.

TABLE A1.1 SAMPLE DATA: SAMPLE SIZE, MEAN AGE AND STANDARD DEVIATIONS

SAMPLE	*N*	MEAN AGE (YEARS)	STANDARD DEVIATION
All	29	40.56	12.67
Depression diagnosis	22	42.32	13.0
No depression diagnosis	7	35,14	10.89
Depressed – females	15	38.8	11.71
Depressed – males	7	49.86	11.32
Non-depressed – females	3	24	1.63
Non-depressed – males	4	43.5	6.54
Depressed – dyslexia diagnosis	22	28.09	11.83
Non-depressed dyslexia diagnosis	7	22.28	14.77

TABLE A1.2 DEPRESSED PARTICIPANTS

DEPRESSED	AGE	DIAGNOSED AGE OF DYSLEXIA	MALE	FEMALE	DEGREE EDUCATED	NON-DEGREE EDUCATED	DEPRESSED AT SCHOOL
Adrian	45	32	X		X		
Brian	70	35	X		X		X
Jasper	59	45	X		X		
Norman	40	33	X		X		X
Anita	47	45		X	X		
Emma	36	25		X	X		X
Maureen	34	27		X	X		
Rachel	40	32		X	X		X
Shelley	61	50		X	X		X
Susan	27	20		X	X		X
Trixie	58	11		X	X		X
George	54	40	X			X	
Philip	33	15	X			X	X
Samuel	48	19	X			X	
Andrea	41	39		X		X	
Karen	56	40		X		X	
Kirsty	23	16		X		X	X
Lara	25	20		X		X	X
Milly	37	7		X		X	
Natasha	40	25		X		X	
Norma	29	23		X		X	X
Phoebe	28	19		X		X	X

TABLE A1.3 NON-DEPRESSED PARTICIPANTS

NON-DEPRESSED	AGE	DIAGNOSED AGE OF DYSLEXIA	MALE	FEMALE	DEGREE EDUCATED	NON-DEGREE EDUCATED	DEPRESSED AT SCHOOL
Zara	26	8		X	X		
Harry	52	45	X			X	
Toby	34	33	X			X	
Malcolm	46	36	X			X	
Peter	42	8	X			X	
Izzy	24	5		X		X	
Jean	22	21		X		X	

MEASURES

The study began life as a semi-structured script of 24 items used for the pilot study (Alexander-Passe 2009b) with a sample of seven dyslexic adults with depression (four females and three males). This formed the basis for the main study's semi-structured interview script, which grew to over 100 items at times, lasting from one hour to nearly three hours, whilst trying to chip away at a participant's defence mechanisms to gain vital answers.

THE INTERVIEW PROCESS, CONFIDENTIALITY AND INFORMED CONSENT

All participants were sent details of the study before the interview, and all verbally confirmed participation before the start of each recorded interview. Participants were advised that they could avoid any questions that were too emotional to answer and that they could halt the interview and their participation in the study without giving any reason; fortunately, no participants took this option. As avoidance was noted in several interviews, further investigative questions were required.

Confidentiality was assured at several points: (1) in the original study advert; (2) in email confirmation/requests for basic details (name, age, education, etc.); (3) at the start of each interview; (4) participants were advised that pseudonyms would be used; and (5) they were given assurance that their records would be keep in a password locked storage facility. Each participant was also reassured that they would receive a copy of their transcript, which they would have the opportunity to check and modify.

I used self-disclosure to put participants at ease and to gain enough trust to investigate emotionally sensitive subjects.

ANALYSIS

Each interview was recorded on audio tape, transcribed, spell-checked with minimal grammar changes and, lastly, a check was made for readability. The transcript was then emailed to each volunteer for them to check and amend if required, with the opportunity for them to add additional notes or post-interview revelations, as interviews can commonly trigger post-interview thoughts. Interviews were then subjected to IPA analysis.

INTERPRETATIVE PHENOMENOLOGICAL ANALYSIS (IPA)

IPA is a relatively recent analysis model but has its historical origins in phenomenology (Husserl 1931, 1970), and the idea that 'to return to the things themselves is to return to that world which precedes knowledge, of which knowledge always speaks' (Merleau-Ponty 1962, p.ix-x). Husserl was very interested in the life-world, which comprises the objects around us as we perceive them and our experience of our self, body and relationships.

Whilst there are many forms of phenomenology in use (idiographic, eidetic and transcendental), IPA using idiographic ideals is used in this study. Smith developed IPA (Smith 2004, 2007; Smith, Harré and Van Langenhove 1995) to analyse elements of the reflected personal experience – the subjective experience of the social world. Giorgi (1994) argues that phenomenology avoids the reductionist tendencies of other research methodologies, and uses the researcher's assumptions/divergent links to inform new insights from the data, rather than forcing data to fit predefined categories – such intuition allows divergent thinking.

The researcher uses an element of interpretation to understand themes and body language, compared to Discourse Analysis (Potter 1996), which relies on precise analysis of the words used. IPA has been used successfully in many research studies (Biggerstaff 2003; Clare 2003; Duncan *et al.* 2001; French, Maissi and Marteau 2005; Thompson, Kent and Smith 2002).

IPA is suitable for this sample as it: (1) is inclusion friendly, aiding understanding in special needs samples; (2) allows flexibility and for themes from initial participants to inform the investigative interview script; and (3) is dyslexic friendly as it does not rely solely on discourse alone.

ANALYSIS METHODOLOGY USED IN THIS STUDY

This study predominately uses IPA methodology for analysis of data; however, the results from the transformations (themes) were used to create quantitative data, thus mixing qualitative and quantitative methodologies. Nineteen main themes were identified and 200 feelings or aspects were identified for these 19 themes, displayed in quantitative percentages.

This study used several forms of analysis to investigate the interview data. Initially, IPA was used (Heron 1996) to investigate the life experiences of the participants. From this two types of results were developed, the first being quotations or summaries of how participants experienced situations. These were then sorted and compiled to form the interview evidence. The majority of the quotes used in this book are taken from this project. Fuller details can be found in Alexander-Passe (2010).

REFERENCES

Abela, J.R.Z. (2001) The hopelessness theory of depression: A test of the diathesis-stress and causal mediation components in third and seventh grade children. *Journal of Abnormal Child Psychology*, 29, 241–254.

Abramson, L.Y., Metalsky, G.I. and Alloy, L.B. (1989) Hopelessness depression: A theory-based subtype of depression. *Psychology Review*, 96, 358–372.

Ackerman, P.L., Bowen, K.R., Beier, M.E. and Kanfer, R. (2001) Determinants of individual differences and gender differences in knowledge. *Journal of Educational Psychology*, 93, 797–825.

Aldridge, J. (1995) The Dyslexics Speak for Themselves. In Miles, T.R. and Varma, V. (eds) *Dyslexia and Stress* (pp.107, 110, 112) London: Whurr Publications.,

Aldwin, C.M. (2000) *Stress, Coping and Development: An Integrative Perspective.* London: Guilford Press.

Alexander-Passe, N. (2004) How children with dyslexia experience school: Developing an instrument to measure coping, self-esteem and depression. Unpublished MPhil Thesis. Milton Keynes: The Open University.

Alexander-Passe, N. (2006) How dyslexic teenagers cope: An investigation of self-esteem, coping and depression. *Dyslexia*, 12(4), 256–275.

Alexander-Passe, N. (2007) Pre-school unidentified Dyslexics: Progression, Suppression, Aggression, Depression and Repression. Retrieved 14 April 2015, www.dyslexia.co.il/en/articles/pre_school_unidentified_dyslexics.

Alexander-Passe, N. (2008) The sources and manifestations of stress amongst school aged dyslexics, compared to sibling controls. *Dyslexia*, 14(4), 291–313.

Alexander-Passe, N. (2009a) Dyslexic Teenagers: How They Cope at School and Could a New Measure be Helpful in Screening Those in Difficulty? In Larson, J.E. (ed.) *Educational Psychology: Cognition and Learning, Individual Differences and Motivation* (pp.1–80) New York, NY: Nova Science Publishers.

Alexander-Passe, N. (2009b) Dyslexia, Gender and Depression: Research Studies. In Hernandez, P. and Alonso, S. (eds) *Women and Depression* (pp.15–74) New York, NY: Nova Science Publishers.

Alexander-Passe, N. (2009c) Dyslexia, Gender and Depression: Dyslexia Defence Mechanisms (DDMs) In Hernandez, P. and Alonso, S. (eds) *Women and Depression* (pp.75–140) New York, NY: Nova Science Publishers.

Alexander-Passe, N. (2009d) Dyslexia, Children and Depression: Empirical Evidence. In Taylor, B.T. (ed.) *Children and Depression.* New York, NY: Nova Science Publishers.

Alexander-Passe, N. (2009e) Dyslexia, Children and Depression: Research Evidence. In Taylor, B.T. (ed.) *Children and Depression.* New York, NY: Nova Science Publishers.

Alexander-Passe, N. (2010) *Dyslexia and Depression: The Hidden Sorrow.* New York, NY: Nova Science Publishers.

Alexander-Passe, N. (2012) *Dyslexia: Dating, Marriage and Parenthood.* New York, NY: Nova Science Publishers.

Alexander-Passe, N. (ed.) (2012b) Dyslexia and Mental Health: *Investigations from Differing Perspectives.* New York, NY: Nova Science Publishers.

Alm, J. and Andersson, J. (1995) Reading and writing difficulties in prisons in the county of Usala. The Dyslexia Project. Uppsala: National Labour Market Board of Sweden at the Employability Institute.

Altschuler, J.A. and Ruble, D.N. (1989) Developmental changes in children's awareness of strategies for coping with uncontrollable stress. *Child Development,* 60, 1337–1349.

American Psychiatric Association (APA) (1994) *Diagnostic and Statistical Manual of Mental Disorders. DSM-IV (4th edn)* Washington, DC: APA.

American Psychiatric Association (APA) (2013) *Diagnostic and Statistical Manual of Mental Disorders. DSM-V (5th edn)* Washington, DC: APA.

American Psychiatric Association (APA) (2013) Specific Learning Disorder: Fact Sheet on the *Diagnostic and Statistical Manual of MentalDisorders. DSM-V (5th edn).* Washington, DC: APA. Retrieved 15th June 2015, www.psychiatry.org/File%20Library/Practice/DSM/DSM-5/DSM-5-Specific-Learning-Disorder-Fact-Sheet.pdf.

Antonoff, J. (1998) The Second Conference on Juvenile Justice, Dyslexia and Other Learning Disabilities. 25 March. New York, NY:.

Armstrong, D. and Squires, G. (2014) *Key Perspectives on Dyslexia: An Essential Text for Educators.* London: Routledge.

Armstrong, T. (2010) *Neurodiversity: Discovering the Extraordinary Gifts of Autism, ADHD, Dyslexia, and Other Brain Differences.* Boston, MA: Da Capo Lifelong Books.

Armstrong, T. (2011) *The Power of Neurodiversity: Unleashing the Advantages of Your Differently Wired Brain.* Cambridge, MA: DaCapo Lifelong/Perseus Books.

Bak, J.J., Cooper, E.M., Dobroth, K.M. and Siperstein, G.N. (1987) Special class placements as labels: Effects on children's attitudes toward learning handicapped peers. *Exceptional Children,* 54, 151–155.

Band, E.B. and Weisz, J.R. (1988) How to feel better when it feels bad: Children's perspectives on coping and everyday stress. *Developmental Psychology,* 24, 247–253.

Bandura, A. (1986) *Social Foundations of Thought and Action: A Social Cognitive Theory.* Englewood Cliffs, NJ: Prentice Hall.

Bandura, A. (1990) Perceived self-efficacy in the exercise of personal agency. *Journal of Applied Sport Psychology,* 2, 128–163.

Bandura, A. (1997) Self-efficacy and Health Behaviour. In Baum, A., Newman, S., Wienman, J., West, R. and McManus, C. (eds) *Cambridge Handbook of Psychology, Health and Medicine* (pp.160–162) Cambridge: Cambridge University Press.

Bandura, A., Barbaranelli, C., Caprara, G.V. and Pastorelli, C. (1996) Multifaceted impact of self-efficacy beliefs on academic functioning. *Child Development,* 67, 1206–1222.

Barber, M. (1997) *The Learning Game. Arguments for an Education Revolution.* London: Indigo.

Barga, N.K. (1996) Students with learning disabilities in education: Managing a disability. *Journal of Learning Disabilities,* 29, 413–421.

Barker, P. (2003) *Psychiatric and Mental Health Nursing: The Craft of Caring.* London: Arnold.

Barlow, D.H. (2000) Unraveling the mysteries of anxiety and its disorders from the perspective of emotion theory. *American Psychologist,* 55, 1247–1263.

Battle, J. (1992) *Culture-Free Self-Esteem Inventories.* Austin, TX: Pro-Ed.

Baumeister, R.F., Smart, L. and Boden, J.M. (1996) Relation of threatened egotism to violence and aggression: The dark side of high self-esteem. *Psychological Review*, 103(1), 5.

BBC News (2006) Famous people with Dyslexia. Retrieved 30th June 2015, http://news.bbc.co.uk/cbbcnews/hi/newsid_1770000/1775842-stm.

Beatty, J.E. and Kirby, S.L. (2006) Beyond the legal environment: How stigma influences invisible identity groups in the workplace. *Employee Responsibilities and Rights Journal*, 18(1), 29–44.

Beber, E. and Biswas, A.B. (2009) Marriage and family life in people with developmental disability. *International Journal of Culture and Mental Health*, 2, 102–108.

Beck, A.T. (1967) *Depression*. New York, NY: Harper and Row.

Beck, A.T., Steer, R.A. and Brown, G.K. (1996) *Beck Depression Inventory (2nd edn)*. San Antonio, TX: The Psychological Corp.

Bednar, R.L. and Peterson, S.R. (1999) *Self-esteem: Paradoxes and Innovations in Clinical Theory and Practice (2nd edn)* Washington, DC: APA.

Beidel, D.C. and Turner, S.M. (1988) Comorbidity of test anxiety and other anxiety disorders in children. *Journal of Abnormal Child Psychology*, 16, 275–287.

Bercow, J. (2011) The Bercow Report: A Review of Services for Children and Young People (0–19) with Speech, Language and Communication Needs. Department for Education. Retrieved 18 January 2014, http://webarchive.nationalarchives.gov.uk/20080728100011/dcsf.gov.uk/bercowreview/docs/7771-dcsf-bercow%20summary.pdf.

Berg, C.A., Johnson, M.M.S., Meegan, S.P., and Strough, J. (2003) Collaborative problem-solving interaction in young and old married couples. *Discourse Processes*, 35, 33–58.

Berninger, V.W., Nielsen, K.H., Abbott, R.D., Wijsman, E. and Raskind, W. (2008) Writing problems in developmental dyslexia: Under-recognized and under-treated. *Journal of School Psychology*, 46, 1–21.

Bianco, M. (2005) The effects of disability labels on special education and general education teachers' referrals for gifted programs. *Learning Disability Quarterly*, 28(4), 285–293.

Bienvenu, O.J. and Ginsburg, G.S. (2007) Prevention of anxiety disorders. *International Review of Psychiatry*, 19(6), 647–654.

Biggar, S. and Barr, J. (1996) The Emotional World of Specific Learning Difficulties. In Reid, G. (ed.) *Dimensions of Dyslexia. Volume 2. Literacy*. Edinburgh: Murray House.

Biggerstaff, D.L. (2003) Empowerment and Self-Help: A Phenomenological Methodology in Research in the First Year After Childbirth. In Henry, J. (ed.) *European Positive Psychology Proceedings 2002* (pp.15–24) Leicester: British Psychological Society.

Birmingham News (2010) Birmingham dyslexia charity faces closure. 13 September. Retrieved 4 January 2010. www.birminghammail.net/news/birmingham-news/2010/09/13/birmingham-dyslexia-charity-faces-closure-97319-27254326/.

Bishop, D. (2014) My thoughts on the dyslexia debate. Retrieved 18th January 2014. www.deevybee.blogspot.co.uk/2014/03/my-thoughts-on-dyslexia-debate.html

Blachman, B.A. (2000) Phonological Awareness. In Kamil, M. L. P., Mosental, P.B., Pearson, P.D. and Barr, R. (eds) *Handbook of Reading Research* (pp.483-502). Mahwah, NJ: Lawrence Erlbaum Associates.

Blankfield, S. (ed.) (2001) Think, problematic and costly? The dyslexic student on work placement. *SKILL Journal*, 70, 23–26.

Blumgart, E., Tran, Y. and Craig, A. (2010) Social anxiety disorder in adults who stutter. *Depression and Anxiety*, 27, 687–692.

Boetsch, E.A., Green, P.A. and Pennington, B.F. (1996) Psychosocial correlates of dyslexia across the life span. *Development and Psychopathology*, 8, 539–562.

Bosworth, H.T. and Murray, M.E. (1983) Locus of control and achievement motivation in dyslexic children. *Journal of Behaviour Pediatrician*, 4(4), 253–256.

Braden, R. (1996) Visual literacy. *Journal of Visual Literacy*, 16(2), 1–83.

Bradley, I. and Bryant, P.E. (1985) *Rhyme and Reason in Reading and Spelling*. Ann Arbor, MI: University of Michigan Press.

Bramlett, R.K., Murphy, J.J., Johnson, J. and Wallingsford, L. (2002) Contemporary practices in school psychology: A national F. [Bramlett *et al.* 2002] survey of roles and referral problems. Psychology in the Schools, 39, 327-335.

Branden, N. (1994) *Six Pillars of Self-Esteem*. New York, NY: Bantam Books.

Brenner C. (1994) The mind as conflict and compromise formation. *Journal of Clinical Psychoanalysis*, 3, 473–488.

Brenner, C. (1973) *An Elementary Textbook of Psychoanalysis (rev. edn)* New York, NY: Anchor Books.

Brinckerhoff, L., Shaw, S. and McGuire, J. (1993) *Promoting Postsecondary Education for Students with Learning Disabilities: A Handbook for Practitioners*. Austin, TX: Pro-Ed.

British Dyslexia Association (2015) Dyslexia and Specific Difficulties: Overview. Retrieved 15th June 2015, www.bdadyslexia.org.uk/dyslexic/dyslexia-and-specific-difficulties-overview.

British Dyslexia Association and HM Young Offender Institution Wetherby (2005) Practical solutions to identifying dyslexia in juvenile offenders: Report of a joint project of the British Dyslexia Association and HM Young Offender Institution Wetherby, 2004–05. Reading: British Dyslexia Association.

Brown Waesche, J.S., Schatschneider, C., Maner, J.K., Ahmed, Y., Wagner, R.K. (2011). Examining agreement and longitudinal stability among traditional and RTI-based definitions of reading disability using the affected-status agreement statistic. *Journal of Learning Disabilities*, 44(3), 296–307.

British Dyslexia Association (2014) Indicators of dyslexia. Retrieved 25 December 2014, www.bdadyslexia.org.uk/parent/indication-of-dyslexia.

Burden, R. (2005) *Dyslexia and Self-Concept: Seeking a Dyslexic Identity*. London: Whurr Publishers.

Burden, R. and Burdett, J. (2005) Factors associated with successful learning in pupils with dyslexia: A motivational analysis. *British Journal of Special Education*, 32(2), 100–104.

Burns, R. (1979) *The Self Concept*. New York, NY: Longman Group Limited.

Burns, R.B. (1982) *Self-concept Development and Education*. London: Holt, Rinehart, and Winston.

Butkowsky, T.S. and Willows, D.M. (1980) Cognitive-motivation and characteristics of children varying in reading ability: Evidence of learned helplessness in poor readers. *Journal of Educational Psychology*, 72(3), 408–422.

Butterworth, B. and Kovacs, Y. (2013) Understanding neurocognitive developmental disorders can improve education for all. *Science*, 340, 300–305.

Bywaters, P. and Rolfe, A. (2002) Look beyond the scars. Understanding and responding to self-injury and self-harm. London: NCH.

Cahill, S.E. and Eggleston, R. (1994) Managing emotions in public: The case of wheelchair users. *Social Psychology Quarterly*, 57, 300–312.

Care Givers (2012) Being Caregiver to Your Spouse. Caregivers Blog: Senior Care Support. Retrieved 6th July 2015, www.caregivers.com/caregiving/caregiver-to-your-spouse.

Catts, H.W. and Adlof, S.M. (2011) Phonological and Other Deficits Associated with Dyslexia. In Brady, S., Blaze, D. and Fowler, A. (eds) *Explaining Individual Differences in Reading: Theory and Evidence*. New York, NY: Taylor and Francis.

Chan, D.W., Ho, C.S.-H., Tsang, S., Lee, S. and Chung, K.K.H. (2006) Exploring the reading– writing connection in Chinese children with dyslexia in Hong Kong. Reading and Writing, 19, 543–561.

Chapman, J.W. (1988) Cognitive-motivational characteristics and academic achievement of learning disabled children: A longitudinal study. *Journal of Educational Psychology*, 80(3), 337–365.

Chief Secretary to the Treasury (2003) Every child matters. Retrieved 5 December 2014, https://www.education.gov.uk/consultations/downloadableDocs/EveryChild Matters.pdf.

Children and Family Act (2014) Retrieved 10 November 2014, www.legislation.gov.uk/ukpga/2014/6/pdfs/ukpga_20140006_en.pdf.

Children's Act (2004) Retrieved 10 November 2014. www.legislation.gov.uk/ukpga/2004/31/contents.

Chiu, M.M. and McBride-Chang, C. (2006) Gender, context, and reading: A comparison of students in 41 countries. *Scientific Studies of Reading*, 10, 331–362.

Clare, L. (2003) Managing threats to self: Awareness in early stage Alzheimer's disease. *Social Science and Medicine*, 57, 1017–1029.

Cogan, J. and Flecker, M. (2004) *Dyslexia in Secondary School. A Practical Handbook for Teachers, Parents and Students*. London: Whurr Publishers.

Cohen, S., Janicki-Deverts, D. and Miller, G. (2007) Psychological stress and disease. *JAMA*, 298, 1685–1687.

Cole, D.A. (1991) Preliminary support for a competency-based model of depression in children. *Journal of Abnormal Psychology*, 100, 181–190.

Cole, D.A., Jacquez, F.M. and Maschman, T.L. (2001) Social origins of depressive cognitions: A longitudinal study of self-perceived competence in children. *Cognitive Therapy and Research*, 25, 377–395.

Collins English Dictionary (2012) Definition of stress. Retrieved 25 December 2014; www.collinsdictionary.com/dictionary/english/stress.

Congdon, P. (1995) Stress Factors in Gifted Dyslexics. In Miles, T. and Varma, V. (eds) *Dyslexia and Stress*. London: Whurr Publishers.

Conte, H.R., Plutchik, R. and Draguns, J.G. (2004) The measurement of ego defences in clinical research. In Hentschel, U., Smith, G., Draguns, J.G. and Ehlers, W. (eds) *Defence Mechanisms: Theoretical, Research and Clinical Perspectives* (pp.393–414) New York, NY: Elsevier.

Cooke, A. (2001) Critical response to 'Dyslexia, Literacy and Psychological Assessment (Report by the Working Party of the Division of Educational and Child Psychology of the British Psychological Society)', A view from the chalk face. *Dyslexia*, 7, 47–52.

Cooley, C.H. [1922] (1992) *Human Nature and the Social Order*. New Brunswick, NJ: Transaction.

Cooper, R. (2009) Dyslexia. In Pollak, D. (ed.) *Neurodiversity in HE, Positive Responses to Learning Differences*. Oxford: Wiley-Blackwell.

Coopersmith, S. (1967) *The Antecedents of Self-esteem*. San Francisco, CA: Freeman Press.

Corriveau, K., Goswami, U. and Thomson, J.M. (2010) Auditory processing and early literacy skills in a preschool and kindergarten population. *Journal of Learning Disabilities*, 43(4), 369–382.

Cosden, M., Brown, C. and Elliot, K. (2002) *The Development of Self-esteem and Self-understanding in Children and Adults with Learning Disabilities*. London: Elbaum.

Cramer, P. (1991) *The Development of Defence Mechanisms: Theory, Research and Assessment*. New York, NY: Springer-Verlag.

Cramer, P. (1998) Threat to gender representation: Identity and identification. *Journal of Personality*, 59, 335–357.

Cramer, P. (2000) Defence mechanisms in psychology today: Further processes for adaptation. *American Psychologist*, 55, 637–646.

Cramer, P. (2004) Stress, Autonomic Nervous System Reactivity, and Defence Mechanisms. In Hentschel, U., Smith, G., Draguns, J.G. and Ehlers, W. (eds) *Defence Mechanisms: Theoretical, Research and Clinical Perspectives* (pp.325–352) New York, NY: Elsevier.

Cramer, P. and Gaul, R. (1988) The effects of success and failure on children's use of defence mechanisms. *Journal of Personality*, 56, 729–742.

Crisfield, J. (1996) *The Dyslexia Handbook*. London: British Dyslexia Association.

Cropanzano, R. and Mitchell, M. (2005) Social exchange theory: An interdisciplinary review. *Journal of Management*, 31(6), 874.

Crowder, M. and Pupynin, K. (1995) *Understanding Learner Motivation*. Nottingham: Department for Education and Employment.

Csikszentmihalyi, M. (1997) *Finding Flow: The Psychology of Engagement with Everyday Life*. New York, NY: Basic Books.

Cutter, D., Jaffe, J. and Segal, J. (2008) Self-injury: types, causes and treatment. Retrieved 4 January 2010, www.helpguide.org/mental/self_injury.htm.

Cutting, A.L. and Dunn, J. (2002) The cost of understanding other people: Social cognition predicts young children's sensitivity to criticism. *Journal of Child Psychology and Psychiatry*, 43, 849–860.

Dale, C. and Aiken, F. (2007) A review of the literature into dyslexia in nursing practice. Royal College of Nursing. Retrieved 11 December 2014, www.uhs.nhs.uk/Media/suhtideal/NursesAndMidwives/PreQualifyingNursing/RCNreportdyslexiaandpractice.pdf.

Davenport, L. (1991) Adaptation to dyslexia: Acceptance of the diagnosis in relation to coping efforts and educational plans. Dissertation Abstracts International, 52(3-B), ISSN 0419-4217.

Davis, G., Caddick, B., Lyon, K., Doling, L., Hasler, J., Webster, A., Reed, M. and Ford, K. (1997) Addressing the literacy needs of offenders under probation supervision. London: Home Office Research and Statistics Directorate.

Davis Dyslexia Association International (2015) Famous People with the Gift of Dyslexia. Retrieved 26th June 2015, www.dyslexia.com/famous.htm.

Denckla, M.B. and Rudel, R. (1974) Rapid automatized naming of pictured objects, colours, letters and numbers by normal children. *Cortex*, 10, 186–202.,

Denhart, H. (2008) Deconstructing barriers: Perceptions of students labeled with learning disabilities in higher education. *Journal of Learning Disabilities*, 41(6), 483-497

Department for Education and Employment (DfEE) (2000) Freedom to learn. The report of the working group looking into the basic skills needed for adults with learning difficulties and disabilities. London: DfEE Publications.

Dias, B. (1976) Les mechanisms de defence dans la genese des norms de conduite. Etude experimentale basee sur le TAT (Measurement of defence in the course of development of norms of conduct. An experiment study based on the TAT) Fribourg, Switzerland: Editions Universitaires.

Dienstbier, R.A. (1989) Arousal and physiological toughness: Implications for mental and physical health. *Psychological Bulletin*, 96, 84–100.

Donaldson, D., Prinstein, M.J., Danovsky, M. and Spirito, A. (2000) Patterns of children's coping with life stress: Implications for clinicians. *American Journal of Orthopsychiatry*, 70(3), 351–359.

Dowd, J. (1975) Aging as exchange: A preface to theory. *Journal of Gerontology*, 30, 584–594.

Draguns, J.G. (2004) Defence Mechanisms in the Clinic, the Laboratory, and the Social World: Towards Closing the Gaps. In Hentschel, U., Smith, G., Draguns, J.G. and Ehlers, W. (eds) *Defence Mechanisms: Theoretical, Research and Clinical Perspectives* (pp.55–76) New York, NY: Elsevier.

Duane, D. (1991) Dyslexia: Neurobiological and behavioural correlates. *Psychiatric Annals*, 21, 703–708.

Duchane, K., Leung, R. and Coulter-Kern, R. (2008) Preservice physical educator attitude toward teaching students with disabilities. *Clinical Kinesiology (Online)*, 62(3), 16–20.

Duck, S. (1983) *Friends, for Life: The Psychology of Close Relationships*. New York, NY: St. Martin's Press.

Duff, F.J., Hayiou-Thomas, M.E. and Hulme, C. (2012) Evaluating the effectiveness of a phonologically based reading intervention for struggling readers with varying language profiles. *Reading and Writing*, 25(3), 621–640.

Duncan, B., Hart, G., Scoular, A. and Brigg, A. (2001) Qualitative analysis of psychosocial impact of diagnosis of *Chlamydia trachomatis*: Implications for screening. *British Medical Journal*, 322, 195–199.

Dyslexia Action (2013) About dyslexia. Retrieved 25 December 2014, www.dyslexiaaction.org.uk/about-dyslexia.

Dyslexia and Youth Suicide (2010) Dying to read. In Alexander-Passe, N. (2010) *Dyslexia and Depression: The Hidden Sorrow*. New York, NY: Nova Science Publishers..

Dyslexia Foundation of New Zealand (2008) Dealing with dyslexia: The way forward for New Zealand educators. Christchurch, New Zealand: Dyslexia Foundation of New Zealand.

Dyslexia Research Trust (2014) Genetics of dyslexia. Retrieved 14 April 2014, www.dyslexic.org.uk/research/genetics-dyslexia.

Dziegielewski, S.F. (2010) *DSM-IV-TR™ in Action (2nd edn)* New York, NY: Wiley.

Edwards, J. (1994) *The Scars of Dyslexia: Eight Case Studies in Emotional Reactions*. London: Cassell.

Elacqua, T., Rapaport, R. and Kruse, B. (1996) Perceptions of class-room accommodations among college students with disabilities. Mount Pleasant, MI: Central Michigan University

Elliott, J.G. (2005) The dyslexia debate continues. *The Psychologist*, 18, 728–729.

Elliott, J.G. and Gibbs, S. (2008) Does dyslexia exist? *Journal of Philosophy of Education*, 42(3–4), 475–491.

Elliott, J. and Grigorenko, E.L. (2014) *The Dyslexia Debate*. Cambridge: Cambridge University Press.

Elliott, J.G. and Place, M. (2012) *Children in Difficulty*. London: Routledge.

Emler, N. (2001) *Self-esteem – The Costs and Causes of Low Self-worth*. York: Joseph Rowntree Foundation.

Endler, N.S. and Parker, J.D.A. (1999) *Coping Inventory for Stressful Situations: CISS Manual (2nd edn)* New York, NY: Multi-Health Systems.

Erikson, E. (1950) *Childhood and Society*. New York, NY: Norton.

Eysenck, H.J. and Eysenck, S.B.G. (1975) *Manual of the Eysenck Personality Questionnaire*. London: Hodder and Stoughton.

Faubert, B. and Blacklock, C. (2012) Review of evaluation studies on reducing failure in schools and improving equity. Project analytical paper. Paris: OECD.

Fawcett, A. (1995) Case Studies and Some Recent Research. In Miles, T.R. and Varma, V. (eds) *Dyslexia and Stress* (pp.5–32) London: Whurr Publishers.

Fawcett, A.J. and Nicolson, R.I. (1995) The dyslexia early screening test. *Irish Journal of Psychology*, 16(3), 248–259.

Fawcett, A.J. and Nicolson, R. I. (2004) The dyslexia screening test-Junior. London: Harcourt Assessment.

Field, S., Sarver, M. and Shaw, S. (2003) Self-determination: A key to success in postsecondary education for students with learning disabilities. *Remedial and Special Education*, 24, 339–349.

Fink, R.P. (2000) Gender, self-concept and reading disabilities. *Thalamus*, 8(1), 3–21.

Finucci, J.M., and Childs, B. (1981) Are There Really More Dyslexic Boys Than Girls? In Ansora, A., Geschwind, A., Galaburda, A., Albert, M. and Gartrell, N. (eds) *Sex Differences in Dyslexia* (pp.1–9) Towson, MD: Orton Dyslexia Society.

Fiske, S.T. and Taylor, S.E. (1991) Social Cognition (2nd edn). New York, NY: McGraw-Hill.

Fitzgibbon, G. and O'Connor, B. (2002) *Adult Dyslexia – A Guide for the Workplace.* Chichester: Wiley.

Flannery, K.A., Liederman, J., Daly, L. and Schultz, J. (2000) Male prevalence for reading disability is found in a large sample of black and white children free from ascertainment bias. *Journal of the International Neuropsychological Society,* 6(4), 433–442.

Fletcher, J.M. (2009) Dyslexia: The evolution of a scientific concept. *Journal of the International Neuropsychological Society,* 15, 501–508.

Fletcher, J.M. and Lyon, G.R. (2010) Dyslexia: Why precise definitions are important. *Perspectives on Language and Literacy,* 34, 27–34.

Fletcher, J.M. and Vaughn, S. (2009) Response to intervention: Preventing and remediating academic difficulties. *Child Development Perspectives,* 3, 30–37.

Fletcher, J.M., Lyon, G.R., Fuchs, L.S. and Barnes, M.A. (2007) *Learning Disabilities: From Identification to Intervention.* New York, NY: Guilford.

Fletcher, J.M., Stuebing, K.K., Barth, A.E., Denton, C.A., Cirino, P.T., Francis, D.J. and Vaughn, S. (2011) Cognitive correlates of inadequate response to intervention. *School Psychology Review,* 40, 2–22.

Flett, G.L., Hewitt, P.L., Blankstein, K.R. and Mosher, S.W. (1991) Perfectionism, self-actualization, and personal adjustment. *Journal of Social Behaviour and Personality,* 6, 147–160.

Flynn, L.J., Zheng, X. and Swanson, H.L. (2012) Instructing struggling upper elementary and middle school readers: A selective meta-analysis of intervention research. *Learning Disabilities Research and Practice,* 27(1), 21–32.

Fontana, D. (1995) *Psychology for Teachers (Psychology for Professional Groups)* London: Palgrave Macmillan.

Forman, S. (1982) Stress management for teachers: A cognitive-behavioral program. *Journal of School Psychology,* 20, 180–187.

Foster, G.G. and Salvia, J. (1977) Teacher response to label of learning disabled as a function of demand characteristics. *Exceptional Children,* 43(8), 533–534.

Foster, G.G., Schmidt, C.R. and Sabatino, D. (1976) Teacher expectancies and the label 'learning disabilities'. *Journal of Learning Disabilities,* 9(2), retrieved from EBSCOhost.

Fox (2010) 8 year old dyslexic attempts suicide. In Alexander-Passe, N. (2010) *Dyslexia and Depression: The Hidden Sorrow.* New York, NY: Nova Science Publishers.

Frederickson, N. (1999) The ACID test: Or is it? *Educational Psychology in Practice,* 15(1), 3–9.

French, D.P., Maissi, E. and Marteau, T.M. (2005) The purpose of attributing cause: Beliefs about the causes of myocardial infarction. *Social Science and Medicine,* 60, 1411–1421.

Freud, A. (1966) *The Ego and the Mechanisms of Defence (rev edn)* New York, NY: International Universities Press.

Freud, S. (1961) The Ego and the Id. In Strachey, J. (ed.) *The Standard Edition of the Complete Psychological Works of S. Freud* (vol. 19, pp.3–66) London: Hogarth Press (originally published in 1923)

Frydenberg, E. (1999) *Adolescent Coping: Theoretical and Research Perspectives.* London: Routledge.

Frydenberg, E. and Lewis, R. (1994) Coping with different concerns: Consistency and variation in coping strategies used by children and adolescents. *Australian Psychologist,* 29, 45–48.

Frymier, A.B. and Wanzer M.B. (2003) Examining differences in perceptions of students' communication with professors: A comparison of students with and without disabilities. *Communication Quarterly*, 51(2), 174–191.

Fuchs, L.S. and Fuchs, D. (2009) On the importance of a unified model of responsiveness to intervention. *Child Development Perspectives*, 3(1), 41–43.

Furnes, B. and Samuelsson, S. (2010) Phonological awareness and rapid automatized naming predicting early development in reading and spelling: Results from a cross-linguistic longitudinal study. *Learning and Individual Differences*, 21(1), 85–95.

Gardner, P. (1994) Diagnosing Dyslexia in the Classroom: A Three-stage Model. In Hales, G. (ed.) *Dyslexia Matters*. London: Whurr Publishers.

Garee, B. and Cheever, R. (eds) (1992) *Marriage and Disability: An Accent Guide*. Bloomington, IL: Cheever Publishing.

Georgiou, G., Parrila, R., Cui, Y. and Papadopoulos, T. (2013) Why is rapid naming related to reading? *Journal of Experimental Child Psychology*, 115, 218–225.

Gerber, P.J., Ginsberg, R. and Reiff, H.B. (1992) Identifying alterable patterns in employment success for highly successful adults with learning disabilities. *Journal of Learning Disabilities*, 25, 475–487.

Gerber, P.J., Reiff, H.B. and Ginsberg, R. (1996) Reframing the learning disabilities experience. *Journal of Learning Disabilities*, 29(1), 98–101.

Gersten, R., Walker, H. and Darch C. (1988) Relationship between teacher's effectiveness and their tolerance of handicapped students. *Exceptional Children*, 54, 433–438.

Gibb, B.E. (2002) Childhood maltreatment and negative cognitive styles: A quantitative and qualitative review. *Clinical Psychology Review*, 22, 223–246.

Gibb, B.E., Alloy, L.B., Abramson, L.Y., Rose, D.T., Whitehouse, W.G., Donovan, P., Hogan, M.E., Cronholm, J., Tierney, S. *et al.* (2001) History of childhood maltreatment, negative cognitive styles, and episodes of depression in adulthood. *Cognitive Therapy Research*, 25, 425–446.

Gilger, J.W., Pennington, B.F. and DeFries, J.C. (1992) A twin study of the etiology of comorbidity: Attention-deficit hyperactivity disorder and dyslexia. *Journal of the American Academy of Child and Adolescent Psychiatry*, 31(2), 343–348.

Gillung, T.B. and Rucker, C.N. (1977) Labels and teacher expectations. *Exceptional Children*, 43(7), 464–465. Retrieved from EBSCOhost.

Gilroy, D. (1995) Stress Factors in the College Student. In Miles, T.R. and Varma, V. (eds) *Dyslexia and Stress*. London: Whurr Publications.

Giorgi, A. (1994) A phenomenological perspective on certain qualitative research methods. *Journal of Phenomenological Psychology*, 25, 190–220.

Glazzard, J. (2010) The impact of dyslexia on pupils' self-esteem. *Support for Learning*, 25(2), 63–69.

Glazzard, J. (2012) Dyslexia and self-esteem: stories of resilience. In *Dyslexia – A Comprehensive and International Approach* (pp.163–186) Rijeka, Croatia: INTECH.

Godsall, R.E., Jurkovic, G.J., Emshoff, J., Anderson, L. and Douglas Stanwyck, D. (2004) Why some kids do well in bad situations: Relation of parental alcohol misuse and parentification to children's self-concept. *Substance Use and Misuse*, 39(5), 789–809.

Goffman, E. (1964) *Stigma: Notes on the Management of Spoiled Identity*. Englewood Cliffs, NJ: Prentice-Hall.

Goodman, S.H. and Gotlib, I.H. (1999) Risk for psychopathology in the children of depressed mothers: A developmental model for understanding mechanisms of transmission. *Psychology Review*, 106, 458–490.

Gordon, B.O. and Rosenblum, K.E. (2001) Bringing disability into the sociological frame: A comparison of disability with race, sex and sexual orientation statuses. *Disability and Society*, 16(1), 5–19.

Gorenstein, E.E. (1987) Cognitive-perceptual deficit in an alcoholism spectrum disorder. *Journal of Studies on Alcohol and Drugs*, 48, 310–318.

Grant, D. (2010) *That's the Way I Think: Dyslexia, Dyspraxia and ADHD Explained.* London: Routledge, Taylor and Francis Group.

Green, S., Davis, C., Karshmer, E., Marsh, P. and Straight, B. (2005) Living stigma: The impact of labeling, stereotyping, separation, status loss, and discrimination in the lives of individuals with disabilities and their families. *Sociological Inquiry*, 75, 197–215.

Greenberg, P.E., Kessler, R.C., Birnbaum, H.G., Leong, S.A., Lowe, S.W., Berglund, P.A. and Corey-Lisle, P.K. (2003) The economic burden of depression in the United States: How did it change between 1990 and 2000? *Journal of Clinical Psychiatry*, 62, 1465–1475.

Griffiths, A.N. (1975) Self-concepts of dyslexic children. *Academic Therapy*, 11, 83–93.

Grigorenko, E. (2001) Developmental dyslexia: An update on genes, brains and environments. *Journal of Child Psychology and Psychiatry*, 42(1), 91–125.

Guay, F., Larose, S. and Boivin, M. (2004) Academic self-concept and educational attainment level: A ten-year longitudinal study. *Self and Identity*, 3(1), 53–68.

Haan, N. (1977) *Coping and Defending*. New York, NY: Academic Press

Haeffel, G.J. and Grigorenko, E.L. (2007) Cognitive vulnerability to depression: Exploring risk and resilience. *Child and Adolescent Psychiatric Clinics of North America*, 16, 435–448.

Hales, G. (1994) *Dyslexia Matters*. London: Whurr Publications.

Hales, G. (1995) The Human Aspects of Dyslexia. In Hales, G. (ed.) *Dyslexia Matters* (pp.184–198) London: Whurr Publications.

Hales, S., Blakely, T., Foster, R.H., Baker, M.G. and Howden-Chapman, P. (2010) Seasonal patterns of mortality in relation to social factors. *Journal of Epidemiology and Community Health*, doi: 10.1136/jech.2010.111864.

Hammond, C. (2002) Learning to be healthy. The wider benefits of learning. Paper No. 3. London: Institute of Education.

Hansard (2007) Tony Blair. Hansard text of 23 May 2007, column 1270. Retrieved 25 December 2014, www.publications.parliament.uk/pa/cm200607/cmhansrd/cm070523/debtext/70523-0002.htm#07052360000111.

Hansford, B.S. and Hattie, J.A. (1982) The relationship between self and achievement/performance measures. Review of Educational Research, 52, 123-142

Harrington, R., Bredenkamp, D., Groothues, C., Rutter, M., Fudge, H. and Pickles, A. (1994) Adult outcomes of childhood and adolescent depression. III Links with suicidal behaviors. *Journal of Child Psychology and Psychiatry*, 35(7), 1309–1319.

Harrington, R., Kerfoot, M., Dyer, E., McGiven, F., Gill, J., Harrington, V., Woodham, A. and Byford, S. (1998) Randomized trial of a home-based family intervention for children who have deliberately poisoned themselves. *Journal of the American Academy of Child and Adolescent Psychiatry*, 37(5), 512–518.

Hartas, D. (2011) Families' social backgrounds matter: Socio-economic factors, home learning and young children's language, literacy and social outcomes. *British Educational Research Journal*, 37(6), 893–914.

Harter, S. (1983) Developmental Perspectives of the Selfsystem. In Mussen, P.H. (ed.) *Handbook of Child Pyschology. Volume IV Socialization, Personality, and Social Development* (pp.275–385) Chichester: Wiley.

Hartley, C.A. and Phelps, E.A. (2012) Anxiety and decision-making. *Biological Psychiatry*, 72, 113–118.

Haw, C., Hawton, K., Houston, K. and Townsend, E. (2001) Psychiatric and personality disorders in deliberate self-harm patients. *British Journal of Psychiatry*, 178, 48–54.

Hawton, K., Rodham, K., Evans, E. and Weatherall, R. (2002) Deliberate self harm in adolescents: Self report survey in schools in England. *British Medical Journal*, 325, 1207–1211.

Heaton, P. and Winterton, P. (1996) *Dealing With Dyslexia (2nd edn)* Bath: Better Books.

Hehir, T. (2007) Confronting ableism. *Educational Leadership*, 64(5), 8–14.

Hellendoorn, J. and Ruijssenaars, W. (2000) Personal experiences and adjustment of Dutch adults with dyslexia. *Remedial and Special Education*, July 21, 227–239.

Herbert, T.B., and Cohen, S. (1993) Stress and immunity in humans: A meta-analytic review. *Psychosomatic Medicine*, 55, 364–379.

Heron, J. (1996) *Cooperative Inquiry: Research into the Human Condition*. London: Sage.

Hewitt-Mann, J. (2012) *Dyslexia Behind Bars Final Report of a Pioneering Teaching and Mentoring Project at Chelmsford Prison – 4 years on*. Benfleet: Mentoring 4 U.

Higgins, E.L., Raskind, M.H., Goldberg, R.J., and Herman, K.L. (2002) Stages of acceptance of a learning disability: The impact of labelling. *Learning Disability Quarterly*, 25, 3–18.

HMSO (2010) Equality Act. Retrieved 25 December 2014, www.legislation.gov.uk/ukpga/2010/15/pdfs/ukpga_20100015_en.pdf.

Holmes, D. (1984) Meditation and somatic arousal reduction: A review of the experimental evidence. *American Psychologist*, 39(1), 1–10.

Holmes, T.H. and Rahe, R.H. (1967) The social readjustment rating scale. *Journal of Psychosomatic Research*, 11, 213–218.

Hornstra, L., Denessen, E., Voeten, M., van den Bergh, L. and Bakker, J. (2010) Teacher attitudes toward dyslexia: Effects on teacher expectations and the academic achievement of students with dyslexia. *Journal of Learning Disabilities*, 43(6), 515–529.

Horowitz, M.J. (1986) *Stress Response Syndromes*. Northvale, NJ: J. Aronson.

House of Commons (2009) Evidence check 1: Early literacy interventions second report of Session 2009–10. Retrieved 15 December 2014, www.publications.parliament.uk/pa/cm200910/cmselect/cmsctech/44/44.pdf.

Hulme, C. and Snowling, M. (2009) *Developmental Disorders of Language Learning and Cognition*. Chichester: Wiley-Blackwell.

Humphrey, N. (2003) Facilitating a positive sense of self in pupils with dyslexia: The role of teachers and peers. *Support for Learning* 18(3), 130–136.

Humphrey, N. and Mullins, P. (2002a) Self-concept and self-esteem in developmental dyslexia. Journal of Research in Special Educational Needs, 2 (2), 1-13.

Humphrey, N. and Mullins, P. (2002b) Personal constructs and attribution for academic success and failure in dyslexics. *British Journal of Special Education*, 29(4), 196–203.

Husserl, E. (1931) *Ideas: General Introduction to Pure Phenomenology* (Boyce Gibson, W.R. Trans.) London: George Allen and Unwin (originally published 1913)

Husserl, E. (1900, trans. 1970) *Logical Investigations, I and II*. New York, NY: Humanities Press.

Independent Schools Queensland (2013) Staffing trends in Queensland schools. Page 2. Retrieved 20 November 2014, www.isq.qld.edu.au/files/file/News%20and%20Media/Publications/StaffingTrendsinQueenslandSchoolsandISQReport.pdf.

Ingesson, S.G. (2007) Growing up with dyslexia. Interviews with teenagers and young adults. *School Psychology International*, 28(5), 574–591.

Interdys (2014) What are the signs of dyslexia? Retrieved 25 December 2014, www.interdys.org/SignsofDyslexiaCombined.htm.

International Dyslexia Association (2006) Other well-known people thought to have dyslexia or other learning disabilities. Retrieved 26 December 2006, www.interdys.org/well-known.html.

International Dyslexia Association (2012) How common are language based difficulties? Retrieved 25 December 2014, www.interdys.org/FAQHowCommon.htm.

Jama, D. and Dugdale, G. (2012) *Literacy: State of the Nation. A Picture of Literacy in the UK Today.* London: National Literacy Trust.

James, K. (2002) Report and literature review into the role of self-esteem as a barrier to learning and as an outcome. Department of Education and Skill, Niace. Retrieved 15th June 2015, www.developbromley.com/public/Learning/Evidence/Self-esteem.pdf.

James, W. (1890) *Principles of Psychology, Vol. 1.* New York, NY: Henry Holt

Jerald, C.D. (2007) Believing and achieving (Issue Brief) Washington, DC: Center for Comprehensive School Reform and Improvement.

Jiménez, J.E., Antón, L., Díaz, A., Estévez, A., García, A.I. *et al.* (2007) Sicole-R-Primaria: Un sistema de evaluación de los procesos cognitivos en la dislexia mediante ayuda asistida a través del ordenador. Spain: Universidad de La Laguna.

Johnson, K. and Babel, M. (2010) On the perceptual basis of distinctive features: Evidence from the perception of fricatives by Dutch and English speakers. *Journal of Phonetics,* 38, 127–136.

Johnson, M., Peer, L. and Lee, R. (2001) Identification and Intervention in Pre-school Children. In Fawcett, A. (ed.) *Dyslexia: Theory and Good Practice.* London: Whurr Publishers.

Jussim, L., Eccles, J. and Madon, S. (1996) Social Perception, Social Stereotypes, and Teacher Expectations: Accuracy and the Quest for the Powerful Self-fulfilling prophecy. In Zanna, M.P. (ed.) *Advances in Experimental Social Psychology* (pp.281–388) Amsterdam: Elsiever Inc.

Katusic, S.K., Colligan, R.C., Barbaresi, W.J., Schaid, D.J. and Jacobsen, S.J. (2001) Incidence of reading disability in a population-based birth cohort, 1976–1982 Rochester. *Mayo Clinic Proceedings, 76*(11), 1081–1092.

Kauffman, J.M., Hallahan, D.P. and Lloyd, J.W. (1998) Politics, science, and the future of learning disabilities. *Learning Disability Quarterly, 21,* 276–280.

Kavale, K.A., Spaulding, L.S. and Beam, A.P. (2009) A time to define: Making the SLD definition prescribe specific learning disability. *Learning Disability Quarterly, 32*(1), 39–48.

Kearns, D.M. and Fuchs, D. (2013) Does cognitively focused instruction improve the academic performance of low-achieving students? *Exceptional Children,* 79, 263–290.

Kendell, R. and Jablensky, A. (2003) Distinguishing between the validity and utility of psychiatric diagnoses. *American Journal of Psychiatry, 160* (1), 4-12.

Kennedy, E., Spence, S. and Hensley, R. (1989) An examination of the relationship between childhood depression and social competence amongst primary school children. *Journal of Child Psychology and Psychiatry, 30*(4), 561–573.

Kenyon, R. (2003) Bridges To Practice [Brochure]. Retrieved 2 October 2010, www.floridatechnet.org/bridges/factsandstats.pdf

Kessler, R.C. (2002) Epidemiology of Depression. In Gotlib, I.H. and Hammen, C.L. (eds) *Handbook of Depression* (pp.22–37) New York, NY: Guilford.

Kirby, J.R., Georgiou, G.K., Martinussen, R. and Parrila, R. (2010) Naming speed and reading: From prediction to instruction. *Reading Research Quarterly,* 45, 341–362.

Kirchner, P. and Vondraek, S. (1975) Perceived sources of self-esteem in early childhood. *Journal of Genetic Psychology,* 126, 169–176.

Kirk, J. and Reid, G. (2001) An examination of the relationship between dyslexia and offending in young people and the implications for the training system. *Dyslexia*, 7(2), 77–84.

Kosman, K. (2010) Suicide of a child – a parent's grief. Retrieved 4 January 2010, www.allaboutlifechallenges.org/suicide-of-a-child.htm.

Kreitler, S. and Kreitler, H. (2004) The Motivational and Cognitive Determinants of Defence Mechanisms. In Hentschel, U., Smith, G., Draguns, J.G. and Ehlers, W. (eds) *Defence Mechanisms: Theoretical, Research and Clinical Perspectives* (pp.195–238) New York, NY: Elsevier.

Lackaye, T. and Margalit, M. (2006) Comparisons of achievement, effort, and self-perceptions among students with learning disabilities and their peers from different achievement group. *Journal of Learning Disabilities*, 39(5) 432–446.

Landerl, K. and Moll, K. (2010) Comorbidity of specific learning disorders: Prevalence and familial transmission. *Journal of Child Psychology and Psychiatry*, 51, 287–294.

Lawrence, D. (1996) *Enhancing Self-esteem in the Classroom (2nd edn)* London: PCP Ltd.

Lazarus, R.S. (1968) Emotions and Adaptation: Conceptual and Empirical Relations. In Arnold, W.J. (ed.) *Nebraska Symposium on Motivation* (pp.175–266) Lincoln, NB: University of Nebraska Press.

Lazarus, R.S. (1991) *Emotion and Adaption.* New York, NY: Oxford University Press.

Lazarus, R.S. and Folkman, S. (1984) *Stress, Appraisal, and Coping.* New York, NY: Springer-Verlag.

LearningRX (2014) Dyslexia symptoms on adults. Retrieved 25 December 2014, www.learningrx.com/dyslexia-symptoms-in-adults-faq.htm.

Leary, M.R. and Baumeister, R.F. (2000) The Nature and Function of Self-esteem: Sociometer Theory. In Zanna, M.P. (ed.) *Advances in Experimental Social Psychology* (pp.1–62) San Diego, CA: Academic Press.

Leff, A.P. and Schofield, T. (2010) Rehabilitation of Acquired Alexia. In Stone, J.H. and Blouin, M. (eds) *International Encyclopedia of Rehabilitation.* Retrieved 10 February 2015, http://cirrie.buffalo.edu/encyclopedia/en/article/267/.

Levin, J.R., McCormick, C.B., Miller, G.E., Berry, J.K. and Pressley, M. (1982) Mnemonic versus nonmnemonic vocabulary-learning strategies for children. *American Educational Research Journal*, 19(1), 121–136.

Liebert, R.M. and Morris, L.W. (1967) Cognitive and emotional components of test anxiety: A distinction and some initial data. *Psychological Reports*, 20, 975–978.

Liederman, J., Kantrowitz, L. and Flannery, K. (2005) Male vulnerability to reading disability is not likely to be a myth: A call for new data. *Journal of Learning Disabilities*, 38, 109–129.

Link, B.G. and Phelan, J.C. (2001) Conceptualizing stigma. *Annual Review of Sociology*, 27, 363–385.

Lisle, K. (2011) Identifying the negative stigma associated with having a learning disability. Thesis. Bucknell University.

Lock, R.H. and Layton, C.A. (2001) Succeeding in postsecondary ed through self-advocacy. *Teaching Exceptional Children*, 34, 66–71.

Łodygowska, E. and Czepita, D.A. (2012) School phobia in children with dyslexia. *Annales Academiae Medicae Stetinensis*, 58(1), 66–70.

Logan, J. (2009) *Dyslexic Entrepreneurs: The Incidence, Their Coping Strategies and Their Business Skills.* New York, NY: John Wiley and Sons.

Lyon, G., Fletcher, J., Shaywitz, S., Shaywitz, B., Torgesen, J. *et al.* (2001) *Rethinking Learning Disabilities.* Washington, DC: Fordham Foundation Progress. Policy Institute.

Lyon, G., Shaywitz, S. and Shaywitz, B. (2003) A definition of dyslexia. *Annals of Dyslexia*, 53, 1–14.

McCall, R.J. (1975) *The Varieties of Abnormality*. Springfield, IL: Charles C. Thomas.

Macdonald, S.J. (2010) *Dyslexia and Crime: a Social Model Approach*. Saarbrücken: VDM Publishing House Ltd.

McKenzie, R.G. (2010) The insufficiency of response to intervention in identifying gifted students with learning disabilities. *Learning Disabilities Research and Practice*, 25, 160–167.

McLaughlin, M.E., Bell, M.P. and Stringer, D.Y. (2004) Stigma and acceptance of persons with disabilities: Understudies aspects of workforce diversity. *Group and Organisation Management*, 29(3), 302–333.

McLoughlin, D., Fitzgibbon, G. and Young, V. (1994) *Adult Dyslexia: Assessment, Counseling and Training*. London: Whurr Publications.

McLoughlin, D., Leather, C. and Stringer, P. (2002) *The Adult Dyslexic: Interventions and Outcomes*. London: Whurr Publications.

MacMillan, D.L. and Siperstein, G.N. (2002) Learning Disabilities as Operationally Defined by Schools. In Bradley, R., Danielson, L. and Hallahan, D. (eds) *Identification of Learning Disabilities: Research to Practice*. Mahwah, NJ: Lawrence Erlbaum.

McNulty, M.A. (2003) Dyslexia and the life course. *Journal of Learning Disabilities*, 36(4), 363–381

Mahoney, M.J. and Thoresen, C.E. (1974) *Self-control: Power to the Person*. New York, NY: Wadsworth.

Manis, F., Doi, L. and Bhadha, B. (2000) *Naming Speed, Phonological Awareness, and Orthographic Knowledge in Second Graders*. Mahwah, NJ: Lawrence Erlbaum Associates.

Marsh, H.W. (1990) A multidimensional, hierarchical model of self-concept: Theoretical and empirical justification. *Educational Psychology Review*, 2, 77–172.

Marsh, H.W. and Yeung, A.S. (1997) Causal effects of academic self-concept on academic achievement: Structural equation models of longitudinal data. *Journal of Educational Psychology*, 89(1), 41–54.

Maslow, A. (1954) *Motivation and Personality*. New York, NY: Harper and Row.

Maslow, A. (1987) *Motivation and Personality (3rd edn)* New York, NY: Harper and Row.

Maslow, A. (2014) Hierarchy of human need. Retrieved 10 November 2014, www.abraham-maslow.com/m_motivation/Hierarchy_of_Needs.asp.

Mason, J.W. (1975) A historical view of the stress field. *Journal of Human Stress*, 1, 6–27.

Mather, N. and Wendling, B.J. (2012) *Essentials of Dyslexia Assessment and Intervention*. Hoboken, NJ: John Wiley and Sons.

Maughan, B. (1995) Annotation: Long-term outcomes of developmental reading problems. *Journal of Child Psychology and Psychiatry*, 36(3), 362–363.

Maxted, P. (1999) *Understanding Barriers to Learning*. London: Campaign for Learning.

Mayes. S.D. and Calhoun, S.L. (2006) Frequency of reading, math and writing disabilities in children with clinical disorders. *Learning and Individual Differences*, 16, 145–157.

Meichenbaum, M. (1977) *Cognitive Behaviour Modification: An Integrative Approach*. New York, NY: Plenum.

Meissner, W.W. (1980) Theories of Personality and Psychopathology: Classical Psychoanalysis. In Kaplan, H.I., Freedman, A.M. and Sadock, B.J. (eds) *Comprehensive Textbook of Psychiatry (3rd edn) vol. 1.* (pp.212–230) Baltimore, MD: William and Wilkins.

Melby-Lervåg, M., Lervåg, A. *et al.* (2012) Nonword-repetition ability does not appear to be a causal influence on children's vocabulary development. *Psychological Science*, 20, 1040–1048.

Mencap (2014) Raising your game. Retrieved 25 December 2014, https://www.mencap.org.uk/raising-your-game/about.

Menghini, D., Finzi, A., Benassi, M., Bolzani, R., Facoetti, A., Giovagnoli, S. *et al.* (2010) Different underlying neurocognitive deficits in developmental dyslexia: A comparative study. *Neuropsychologia*, 48(4), 863–872.

Merleau-Ponty, M. (1962) *Phenomenology of Perception* (trans. C. Smith). London: Routledge.

Michener, A.H., DeLamater, J.D. and Myers, D.J. (2004) *Social Psychology (5th edn)* Belmont, CA: Wadsworth/Thompson Learning.

Miles, T.R. (1993) *Dyslexia: The Pattern of Difficulties (2nd edn)* London: Whurr Publications.

Miles, T.R. (1994) *Dyslexia: The Pattern of Difficulties (3rd edn)*. London: Whurr Publications.

Miles, T.R. and Miles, E. (1990) *Dyslexia: A Hundred Years On.* Milton Keynes: Open University Press.

Miller, K. (2005) *Communication Theories.* Boston, MA: McGraw Hill Publishers.

Mishna, F. (2003) Learning disabilities and bullying: Double jeopardy. *Journal of Learning Disabilities*, 36, 1–15.

Molnar, A. and Lindquist, B. (1989) *Changing Problem Behaviour in School.* San Francisco, CA: Jossey Bass.

Montessori, M. (1965) *Dr Montessori's Own Handbook.* New York, NY: Schocken Books.

Morgan, E. and Klein, C. (2001) *The Dyslexic Adult in a Non-dyslexic World.* London: Whurr Publications.

Morgan, E. and Klein, C. (2003) *The Dyslexic Adult in a Non-dyslexic World.* (2nd edn) London: Whurr Publications.

Morgan, P.L., Fuchs, D., Compton, D.L., Cordray, D.S. and Fuchs, L.S. (2008) Does early reading failure decrease children's reading motivation? *Journal of Learning Disabilities*, 41(5), 387–404.

Morgan, W. (1996) Dyslexic offender. *The Magistrate Magazine*, 52(4), 84–86.

Morgan, W. (1997) Criminals! Why are so many offenders dyslexic? Unpublished paper.

Morris, D. and Turnbull, P. (2007) A survey based exploration of the impact of dyslexia on the career progression of registered nurses in the UK. *Journal of Nursing Management*, 15, 97–106.

Morrison, G. and Cosden, M. (1997) Risk, resilience, and adjustment of individuals with learning disabilities. *Learning Disability Quarterly*, 20, 43–60.

Mosely, D. (1989) How lack of confidence in spelling affects children's written expressionism. *Educational Psychology in Practice*, April, 5–6.

Mottram, P.G. (2007) HMP Liverpool, Styal and Hindley Study Report. Liverpool: University of Liverpool.

Mruk, C. (1999) *Self-Esteem: Research, Theory, and Practice (2nd edn)* New York, NY: Springer.

Murray, C.J.L. and Lopez, A.D. (1996) *The Global Burden of Disease.* Cambridge, MA: Harvard University Press.

Murstein, B.I., Cerreto, M. and MacDonald, M.G. (1977) A theory and investigation of the effect of exchange-orientation on marriage and friendship. *Journal of Marriage and the Family*, 39, 543–548.

Nalavany, B.A., Carawan, L.W. and Rennick, R.A. (2010) Psychosocial experiences associated with confirmed and self-identified dyslexia: A participant-driven concept map of adult perspectives. *Journal of Learning Disabilities*, 44(1), 63–79.

Nalavany, B.A, Carawan, L.W. and Sauber, S. (2013) Adults with dyslexia, an invisible disability: The mediational role of concealment on perceived family support and self-esteem. British Journal of Social Work, 152v1–bct152.

Nathanson, D.L. (1992) *Shame and Pride: Affect, Sex, and the Birth of the Self.* New York, NY: W.W. Norton.

National Literacy Trust (2015) Dyslexia: A summary from the British Dyslexia Association. Retrieved 30th June 2015, www.literacytrust.org.uk/resources/practical_resources_info/691_dyslexia#strengths.

National Institute of Neurological Disorders and Strokes (NINDS) (2010) Dyslexia information page. Retrieved 1 July 2015, www.ninds.nih.gov/disorders/dyslexia/dyslexia.htm.

Nickerson, R. S. (1998) Confirmation bias: A ubiquitous phenomenon in many guises. *Review of General Psychology*, 2(2), 175-220.

Nicolson, R. (2005) Dyslexia: Beyond the myth. *The Psychologist*, 41, 658–659.

Nicolson, R.I. and Fawcett, A.J. (2006) Do cerebellar deficits underlie phonological problems in dyslexia? *Developmental Science*, 9(3), 259–262.

Nolen-Hoeksema, S. (1990) *Sex Differences in Depression.* Stanford, CA: Stanford University Press.

Nolen-Hoeksema, S., Girgus, J.S. and Seligman, M.E.P. (1986) Learned helplessness in children: A longitudinal study of depression, achievement, and explanatory style. *Journal of Personality and Social Psychology*, 51, 435–442.

Nosek, K. (1997) *Dyslexia in Adults: Taking Charge of Your Life.* Dallas, TX: Taylor.

O'Connor, R.E., Fulmer, D., Harty, K.R. and Bell, K.M. (2005) Layers of reading intervention in kindergarten through third grade: Changes in teaching and student outcomes. *Journal of Learning Disabilities*, 38(5), 440–455.

OFSTED (2010) The special educational needs and disability review: A statement is not enough. Retrieved 18 January 2014, http://dera.ioe.ac.uk/1145/1/Special%20education%20needs%20and%20disability%20review.pdf.

Ogden, J. (2012) *Health Psychology: A Textbook (5th edn)* Maidenhead: Open University Press.

Olson, R.K., Keenan, J.M., Byrne, B., Samuelsson, S., *et al.* (2011) Genetic and environmental influences on vocabulary and reading development. *Scientific Studies of Reading*, 15(1), 26-46.

Orton, S.T. (1937) *Reading, Writing and Speech Problems of Children.* New York, NY: Norton.

Osmond, J. (1996) *The Reality of Dyslexia.* London: Cassell.

Pajares, F. and Graham, L. (1999) SE, motivation constructs, and mathematics performance of entering middle school students. *Contemporary Educational Psychology*, 24, 124–139.

Palombo, J. (2001) *Learning Disorders and Disorders of the Self in Children and Adolescents.* New York, NY: Norton.

Palti, G. (2010) Specific learning difficulties and mental health. Retrieved 22 October 2014, www.spld-matters.com/article11.html.

Parker, G. (1993a) Disability, caring and marriage: The experience of younger couples when a partner is disabled after marriage. *British Journal of Social Work*, 23, 565-580.

Parker, G. (1993b) *With this Body: Caring and Disability in Marriage.* Philadelphia, PA: Open University.

Pastorino, E. and Doyle-Portillo, S.M. (2009) *What is Psychology? (2nd edn)* Pacific Grove, CA: Wadsworth.

Peer, L. and Reid, G. (eds) (2001) *Dyslexia: Successful Inclusion in the Secondary School.* London: David Fulton.

Peer, L. (2002) Dyslexia – Not a condition to die for. *Special children*, September, 31–33.

Pennington, B.F. (2009) *Diagnosing Learning Disorders: A Neuropsychological Framework (2nd edn)* New York, NY: Guilford Press.

Pennington, B.F. and Bishop, D.V. (2009) Relations among speech, language, and reading disorders. *Annual Review of Psychology*, 60, 283–306.

Pennington, B.F., Van Orden, G.C., Smith, S.H.D., Green, P.A. and Haith, M.M. (1990) Phonological processing skills and deficits in adult dyslexics. *Child Development*, 61, 1.753–1.778.

Peterson, C., Maier, S.F. and Seligman, M.E.P. (1993) *Learned Helplessness: A Theory for the Age of Personal Control.* New York, NY: Oxford.

Peterson, G., Ekensteen, W. and Rydén, O. (2006) *Funktionshinder och strategival. Om att hantera sig själv och sin omvärld [Disability and choice of strategy. About managing oneself and one's surroundings].* Lund: Studentlitteratur.

Peterson, J., Freedenthal, S., Sheldon, C., and Andersen, R. (2008) Non-suicidal self injury in adolescents. *Psychiatry (Edgmont),* 5(11), 20–26.

Plutchik, R., Kellerman, H. and Conte, H.R. (1979) A Structural Theory of Ego Defenses and Emotions. In Izard, C.E. (ed.) *Emotions on Personality and Psychopathology* (pp.229–257) New York, NY: Plenum Press.

Pollak, D. (ed.) (2009) *Neurodiversity in HE, Positive Responses to Learning Differences.* Oxford: Blackwell-Wiley.

Pollock, J. and Waller, E. (1994) *Day to Day Dyslexia in the Classroom.* London, Routledge.

Poole, J. (2003) Dyslexia: A wider view. The contribution of an ecological paradigm to current issues. *Educational Research,* 45(2), 167–180.

Potter, J. (1996) Discourse Analysis and Constructionist Approaches: Theoretical Background. In Richardson, J.E. (ed.) *Handbook of Qualitative Research Methods for Psychology and the Social Sciences.* Leicester: British Psychological Society.

Poustie, A. and Neville, R.G. (2004) Deliberate self-harm cases: A primary care perspective. *Nursing Standard,* 18(48), 33–36.

Quotes.net (2014) Albert Einstein quotes. Retrieved 30 October 2014. www.quotes.net/quote/9338.

Ramus, F. and Ahissar, M. (2012) Developmental dyslexia: The difficulties of interpreting poor performance, and the importance of normal performance. *Cognitive Neuropsychology,* 29(1–2), 104–122.

Ramus, F. and Szenkovits, G. (2008) What phonological deficit? *Quarterly Journal of Experimental Psychology,* 61(1), 129–141.

Ramus, F., Pidgeon, E. and Frith, U. (2003) The relationship between motor control and phonology in dyslexic children. *Journal of Child Psychology and Psychiatry,* 44(5), 712–722.

Rao, S. (2004) Faculty attitudes and students with disabilities in higher education: A literature review. *College Student Journal,* 38(2), 191–198.

Rapee, R.M. and Heimberg, R.G. (1997) A cognitive-behavioral model of anxiety in social phobia. *Behavior Research and Therapy,* 35(8), 741–756.

Raskind, M.H., Goldberg, R.J., Higgins, E.L. and Herman, K.L. (2002) Teaching 'life success' to students with LD: Lessons learned from a 20 year study. *Intervention in School and Clinic,* 37(4), 201–208.

Reason, R., Woods, K., Frederickson, N., Heffernan, M. and Martin, C. (1999) *Dyslexia, Literacy and Psychological Assessment: A Report of a Working Party of the British Psychological Society Division of Educational and Child Psychology.* Leicester: British Psychological Society.

Reid, G. (1988) *Dyslexia and Learning Style: A Practitioner's Handbook.* Chichester: Wiley.

Reid, G. (1996) *Dimensions of Dyslexia. Vol 1.* Edinburgh: Moray House Publications.

Reiff, H.B., Gerber, P. and Ginsberg, R. (1997) *Exceeding Expectations: Successful Adults with Learning Disabilities.* Austin, TX: Pro-Ed.

Reynolds, C.R. and Shaywitz, S.E. (2009) Response to intervention: Prevention and remediation, perhaps diagnosis. *Child Development Perspectives,* 3, 44–47.

Rice, M. and Brooks, G. (2004) *Developmental Dyslexia in Adults: A Research Review.* London: NRDC.

Richardson, A.J. and Stein, J.F. (1993) Personality Characteristics of Adult Dyslexics. In Wright, S.F. and Groner, R. (eds) *Facets of Dyslexia and Remediation.* Amsterdam: Elsevier.

Richardson, J.T.E. (1994) Mature students in higher education: Academic performance and intellectual ability. *Higher Education*, 28, 373–386.

Riddick, B. (1995) Dyslexia: Dispelling the myths. *Disability and Society*, 10(4), 457–473.

Riddick, B. (1996) *Living with Dyslexia: The Social and Emotional Consequences of Specific Learning Difficulties*. London: Routledge.

Riddick, B. (2000) An examination of the stigmatisation of the relationship between labelling and the stigmatisation with special reference to dyslexia. *Disability and Society*, 15(4), 653–667.

Riddick, B., Sterling, C., Farmer, M. and Morgan, S. (1999) Self-esteem and anxiety in the educational histories of adult dyslexic students. *Dyslexia*, 5, 227–248.

Rimkute, L., Torppa, M., Eklund, K., Nurmi, J.-E. and Lyytinen, H. (2014) The impact of adolescents' dyslexia on parents and their own educational expectations. *Reading and Writing*, 27(7), 1231–1253.

Rodis, P., Garrod, A., and Boscardin, M.L. (eds) (2001) *Learning Disabilities and Life Stories*. Boston, MA: Allyn and Bacon.

Roecker, C.E., Dubow, E.F. and Donaldson, D.L. (1996) Cross-situational patterns in children's coping with observed interpersonal conflict. *Journal of Clinical Child Psychology*, 25, 288–299.

Roeser, R.W. and Eccles, J.S. (1998) Adolescents' perceptions of middle school: Relation to longitudinal changes in academic and psychological adjustment. *Journal of Research on Adolescence*, 8, 123–158.

Rogers, C.R. (1959) A Theory of Therapy, Personality and Interpersonal Relationships, as Developed in the Client-centered Framework. In Koch, S. (ed.) *Psychology: A Study of Science* (pp.184–256) New York, NY: McGraw Hill.

Rose, D.T. and Abramson, L.Y. (1992) Developmental predictors of depressive cognitive style: Research and theory. In Toth, D.C.S.L. (ed.) *Rochester Symposium on Developmental Psychopathology, Vol. 4* (pp.323–349) Hillsdale, NJ: Erlbaum.

Rose, J. (2009) Identifying and teaching children and young people with dyslexia and literacy difficulties. London: HMSO. Retrieved 20 October 2013,www.education.gov.uk/publications/standard/publicationdetail/page1/DCSF-00659-2009.

Rosenberg, M. (1965) Quoted in Cross, K.P. (1981) *Adults As Learners*. London: Jossey Bass.

Rotter, J.B. (1966) Generalized expectancies for internal versus external control of reinforcement. *Psychological Monographs: General and Applied*, 80(1), 1–28.

Rudolph, K. (2009) Stress and depression – The role of stress in depression, the impact on academic functioning and educational progress. Retrieved 10 August 2009, http://education.stateuniversity.com/pages/2457/Stress-Depression.html.

Rudolph, K.D., Kurlakowsky, K.D. and Conley, C.S. (2001) Developmental and social-contextual origins of depressive control-related beliefs and behavior. *Cognitive Therapy and Research*, 25, 447–475.

Rutter, M. (1983) Stress, Coping and Development: Some Issues and Some Questions. In Garmezy, N. and Rutter, M. (eds) *Stress, Coping and Development in Children* (pp.1–41) New York, NY:, McGraw-Hill.

Rutter, M., Caspi, A., Fergusson, D.M., Horwood, L.J., Goodman, R., Maughan, B. *et al.* (2004) Gender differences in reading difficulties: Findings from four epidemiology studies. *Journal of the American Medical Association*, 291, 2007–2012.

Ryan, M. (2004) Social and emotional problems related to dyslexia. International Dyslexia Association. Retrieved 19 October 2006, www.IDonline.org/article/19296.

Ryden, M. (1989) *Dyslexia – How Would I Cope?* London: Jessica Kingsley Publishers.

Sasse, M. (1995) The Positive and the Negative. In Miles, T.R. and Varma, V. (eds) *Dyslexia and Stress* (pp.112–115) London, Whurr Publications.

Savage, R. (2004) Motor skills, automaticity, and developmental dyslexia: A review of the research literature. *Reading and Writing: An Interdisciplinary Journal*, 17, 301–324.

Scanlon, D.M., Gelzheiser, L.M., Vellutino, F.R., Schatschneider, C. and Sweeney, J.M. (2008) Reducing the incidence of early reading difficulties: Professional development for classroom teachers vs. direct interventions for children. *Learning and Individual Differences*, 18, 346–359.

Scanlon, D.M., Vellutino, F.R., Small, S.G., Fanuele, D.P. and Sweeney, J. (2005) Severe reading difficulties: Can they be prevented? A comparison of prevention and intervention approaches. *Exceptionality*, 13, 209–227.

Schacter, D.L., Gilbert, D.T. and Wegner, D.M. (2011) *Human Needs and Self-Actualization. Psychology (2nd edn)* New York, NY: Worth, Incorporated.

Schneiderman, N., Ironson, G. and Siegel, S.D. (2005) Stress and health: Psychological, behavioral, and biological determinants. *Annual Review of Clinical Psychology*, 1(1), 607–628.

Schulz, C.H. (2008) Collaboration in the marriage relationship among persons with disabilities. *Disability Studies Quarterly*, 28(1).

Schulze, B. and Angermeyer, M.C. (2003) Subjective experiences of stigma: A focus group study of schizophrenic patients, their relatives and mental health professionals. *Social Sciences and Medicine*, 56, 299–312.

Scott, R. (2003) A Counsellor's Perspective on Dyslexia. In Thomson, M (ed.) *Dyslexia Included: A Whole School Approach* (pp.82–92). London: David Fulton Publishers Ltd.

Scott, R. (2004) *Dyslexia and Counselling*. London: Whurr Publications.

Scottish Daily Record (2002) Dyslexic boy suicide. 20 April, *Daily Record (Glasgow, Scotland)* Retrieved 4 January 2010, www.thefreelibrary.com/DYSLEXIC+BOY+SUICIDE.-a084950535.

Seligman, M.E.P. (1975a) Helplessness. In Singer, J.L. (ed.) *Repression and Dissociation*. Chicago, IL: University of Chicago Press.

Seligman, M.E.P. (1975b) *Helplessness: On Depression, Development and Death*. San Francisco, CA: Freeman.

Seligman, M.E.P. (1991) *Learned Optimism*. New York, NY: Knopf.

Seligman, M.E.P. (1995) The effectiveness of psychotherapy: The Consumer Reports Study. *American Psychologist*, 50(12), 965–974.

Seligman, M.E.P. (1996) Science as an ally of practice. *American Psychologist*, 51, 1072–1079.

Seligman, M.E.P. (1998) The prediction and prevention of depression. In Routh, D.K. and DeRubeis, R.J. (eds) *The Science of Clinical Psychology: Accomplishments and Future Directions* (pp.201–214) Washington, DC: American Psychological Association.

Selye, H. (1956) *The Stress of Life*. New York, NY: McGraw-Hill.

Selye, H. (1976) *The Stress of Life (rev. edn)* New York, NY: McGraw-Hill.

Selye, H. (1991) History and Present Status of the Stress Concept. In Monat, A. and Lazarus, R.S. (eds) *Stress and Coping* (3rd edn) (pp.21–35) New York, NY: Columbia University Press.

Settipani, C. and Kendall, P.C. (2013) Social functioning in youth with anxiety disorders: Association with anxiety severity and outcomes from cognitive-behavioral therapy. *Child Psychiatry and Human Development*, 44, 1–18.

Shapiro, D. (1965) *Neurotic Styles*. New York, NY: Basic Books.

Share, D.L. (2008) Orthographic Learning, Phonology and the Self-teaching Hypothesis. In Kail, R. (ed.) *Advances in Child Development and Behavior* (pp.31–82) Amsterdam: Elsevier.

Shaywitz, S.E. (1996) Dyslexia. *Scientific American*, 275, 98–104.

Shaywitz, S.E. (1998) Current concepts: Dyslexia. *The New England Journal of Medicine*, 338, 307–312.

Shaywitz, S. and Shaywitz, B. (2005) Dyslexia (specific reading disability) *Biological Psychiatry*, 57, 1301–1309.

Siegal, A.M. (1996) *Heninz Kohut and the Psychology of the Self.* New York, NY: Routledge.

Siegel, L. and Lipka, O. (2008) The Definition of Learning Disabilities: Who is the Individual with Learning Disabilities? In Reid, G., Fawcett, A., Manis, F. and Siegel, L. (eds) *The Sage Handbook of Dyslexia.* London: Sage Publications.

Singer, E. (2005) The strategies adopted by Dutch children with dyslexia to maintain their self-esteem when teased at school. *Journal of Learning Disabilities*, 38(5), 411–423.

Slavin, R.E., Lake, C., Davis, S. and Madden, N. (2011) Effective programs for struggling readers: A best-evidence synthesis. *Educational Research Review*, 6, 1–26.

Smith, C.N. and Squire, L.R. (2009) Medial temporal lobe activity during retrieval of semantic memory is related to the age of the memory. *Journal of Neuroscience*, 29, 930–938.

Smith, G. and Danielsson, A. (1979) Anxiety and defensive strategies in childhood and adolescence. *Psychology Issues*, 12 (Monograph 3) International University Press.

Smith, J.A. (2004) Reflecting on the development of Interpretative Phenomenological Analysis and its contribution to qualitative research in psychology. *Qualitative Research in Psychology*, 1, 39–54.

Smith, J.A. (2007) Hermeneutics, human sciences and health: Linking theory with practice. *International Journal of Qualititative Studies on Health and Well-being*, 2, 3–11.

Smith, J.A., Harré, R. and Van Langenhove, L. (1995) Idiography and the case study. In Smith, J.A., Harre, R. and Van Langenhove, L. (eds) *Rethinking Psychology.* London: Sage.

Snow, C.E., Burns, M.S. and Griffin, P. (eds) (1998) *Preventing Reading Difficulties in Young Children.* Washington, DC: National Academy Press.

Snowling, M. (1996) Dyslexia, a hundred years on. *British Medical Journal*, 313, 1096–1097.

Snowling, M.J. (2008) Specific disorders and broader phenotypes: The case of dyslexia. The Quarterly Journal of Experimental Psychology, 61(1), 142–156.

Snowling, M. and Hulme, C. (1994) The development of phonological skills in children. *Philosophical Transactions of the Royal Society of London*, B346, 21–27.

Snyder, L.A., Carmichael, J.S., Blackwell, L.V., Cleveland, J.N. and Thornton, G.C. III. (2010) Perceptions of discrimination and justice among employees with disabilities. *Employee Responsibilities and Rights Journal*, 22, 5–19.

Solvang, P. (2007) Developing an ambivalence perspective on medical labelling in education: Case dyslexia. *International Studies in Sociology of Education*, 17(1–2), 79–94.

Spencer-Thomas, S. (2013) *Suicide Risk and Children with Disabilities.* Retrieved 15th June 2015, http://sallyspencerthomas.blogspot.co.uk/2013/04/suicide-risk-and-children-with.html.

Spielberger, C.D. (1979) Preliminary Manual for the State-Trait Personality Inventory (STPI).Unpublished manuscript, University of South Florida, Tampa.

Stanovich, K.E. (1988) Explaining the differences between the dyslexic and the garden variety poor reader: The phonological-core variable-difference model. *Journal of Learning Disabilities*, 21, 590–612.

Stanovich, K.E. (1992) Speculation on the causes and consequences of individual differences in early reading acquisition. In Gough, P., Ehri, L. and Treiman, R. (eds) *Reading Acquisition* (pp.307–342) Hillsdale, NJ: Laurence Erlbaum.

Stanovich, K.E. and Siegel, L.S. (1994) Phenotypic performance profile of children with reading disabilities: A regression-based test of the phonological-core variable-difference model. *Journal of Educational Psychology*, 86, 24–53.

Stark, L., Spirito, A., Williams, C. and Guevremont, D. (1989) Common problems and coping strategies. I: Findings with normal adolescents. *Journal of Abnormal Child Psychology*, 17, 203–212.

Stein, J. (2001) The magnocellular theory of developmental dyslexia. *Dyslexia*, 7(1), 12–36.

Steinberg, E. and Andrist, C.G. (2012) Dyslexia comes to congress: A call to action. Retrieved 17 April 2012, www.interdys.org/DyslexiaComesToCongress.htm.

Sternberg, R.J. and Grigorenko, E.L. (2002) *Dynamic Testing*. New York, NY: Cambridge University Press.

Sunseth, K. and Bowers, P.G. (2002) Rapid naming and phonemic awareness: Contributions to reading, spelling, and orthographic knowledge. *Scientific Studies of Reading*, 6(4), 401–429.

Susman, J. (1994) Disability, stigma and deviance. *Social Science and Medicine*, 38(1), 15–22.

Sutherland, J.H., Algozzine, B., Ysseldyke, J.E. and Freeman, S. (1983) Changing peer perceptions: Effects of labels and assigned attributes. *Journal of Learning Disabilities*, 16(4), 217–220.

Swalander, L. (2006) Reading achievement: Its relation to home literacy, self-regulation, academic self-concept, and goal oreintation in children and adolescents. Doctoral Thesis. Lund University.

Swales, M. (2010) Pain and deliberate self-harm. Invited article, The Wellcome Trust. Retrieved 4 January 2010, www.wellcome.ac.uk/en/pain/microsite/culture4.html.

Tanner, K. (2009) Adult dyslexia and the 'conundrum of failure'. *Disability and Society*, 24 (6), 785-797.

Taylor, J., Roehrig, A.D., Soden-Hensler, B., Connor, C.M. and Schatschneider, C. (2010a) Teacher quality moderates the genetic effects on early reading. *Science*, 328, 512–514.

Taylor, L., Hume, I. and Welsh, N. (2010b) Labelling and self-esteem: The impact of using specific vs. generic labels. *Educational Psychology*, 30(2), 191–202.

The Daily Telegraph (2010) Dyslexic postman dumped letters as he struggled to read addresses. Retrieved 19 October 2014, www.telegraph.co.uk/news/uknews/crime/7887513/Dyslexic-postman-dumped-letters-as-he-struggled-to-read-addresses.html.

The Miles Dyslexia Centre (2010) What is dyslexia? Retrieved 25 December 2014, www.dyslexia.bangor.ac.uk/whatisdyslexia.php.en?menu=3andcatid=5265andsubid=5266.

Therapeutic Resources (2004) A history of bedwetting (primary nocturnal enuresis) is a very strong clue to the diagnosis of ADD/ADHD. Retrieved 26 March 2015, www.therapeuticresources.com/bedwetting.html.

Thompson, A.R., Kent, G. and Smith, J.A. (2002) Living with vitiligo: Dealing with difference. *British Journal of Health Psychology*, 7, 213–225.

Thompson, C.L. and Rudolph, L.B. (1996) *Counselling Children (4th edn)* Pacific Grove, CA: Brooks/Cole.

Thomson, M.E. (1990) *Developmental Dyslexia: Its Nature, Assessment and Remediation*. London: Wiley-Blackwell.

Thomson, M. (1996) *Developmental Dyslexia: Studies in Disorders of Communication*. London: Whurr Publications.

Thomson, M. (2002) Dyslexia and diagnosis. *The Psychologist*, 15, 151.

Thomson, M. (2003) Monitoring dyslexic's intelligence and attainments: A follow-up study. *Dyslexia*, 9, 3–17.

Thomson, M. and Hartley, G.M. (1980) Self-esteem in dyslexic children. *Academic Therapy*, 16, 19–36.

Thomson, P. (1995) Stress factors in early education. In Miles, T.R. and Varma, V. (eds) *Dyslexia and Stress* (pp.5–32) London: Whurr Publications.

Tonnessen, F.E. (1995) On defining 'dyslexia'. *Scandinavian Journal of Educational Research*, 39, 139–156.

Torppa, M., Parrila, R., Niemi, P., Lerkkanen, M.-K., Poikkeus, A.-M. and Nurmi, J.-E. (2013) The double deficit hypothesis in the transparent Finnish orthography: A longitudinal study from kindergarten to grade 2. *Reading and Writing*, 26(8), 1353–1380.

Turk, E. and Bry, B. (1992) Adolescents' and parents' explanatory styles and parents' causal explanations about their adolescents. *Cognitive Therapy and Research*, 16, 349–357.

Turner, J. and Cole, D.A. (1994) Developmental differences in cognitive diatheses for child depression. *Journal of Abnormal Child Psychology*, 22, 15–32.

Upton, T.D., Harper, D.C. and Wadsworth, J.S. (2005) Postsecondary attitudes towards persons with disabilities: A comparison of college students with and without disabilities. *Journal of Applied Rehabilitation Counselling*, 36(3), 24–31.

Vaessen, A., Gerretsen, P. and Blomert, L. (2009) Naming problems do not reflect a second independent core deficit in dyslexia: Double deficits explored. *Journal of Experimental Child Psychology*, 103(2), 202–221.

Vaillant, G.E. (1971) Theoretical hierarchy of adaptive ego mechanisms. *Archives of General Psychiatry*, 24, 107–118.

Vaillant, G.E. (1977) *Adaptation to Life*. Boston, MA: Little, Brown.

Vaillant, G.E. (1992) *Ego Mechanism of Defence: A Guide for Clinicians and Researchers*. London: American Psychiatric Press Inc.

Van der Stoel, S. (1990) *Parents on Dyslexia*. Clevedon: Multilingual Matters.

Van Hoecke, E., Hoebeke, P., Braet, C. and Walle, J.V. (2004) An assessment of internalizing problems in children with enuresis. *Journal of Urolology*, 171(2 of 6), 2580–2583.

Vargo, F.E., Grosser, G. and Spafford, C.S. (1995) Digit span and other WISC-R scores in the diagnosis of dyslexia in children. *Perceptual and Motor Skills*, 80, 1219–1229.

Vaughn, S. and Roberts, G. (2007) Secondary interventions in reading: Providing additional instruction for students at risk. *Teaching Exceptional Children*, 39, 40–46.

Vellutino, F.R., Fletcher, J.M., Snowling, M.J. and Scanlon, D.M. (2004) Specific reading disability (dyslexia): What have we learned in the past four decades? *Journal of Child Psychology and Psychiatry*, 45(1), 2–40.

Vinegrad, M. (1994) A revised adult dyslexia checklist. *Educare*, 48, 21–4.

Von Gontard, A. (1998) Annotation: Day and night wetting in children – A paediatric and child psychiatric perspective. *Journal of Child Psychology and Psychiatry*, 39(4), 439–451.

Von Gontard, A. (2004) Psychological and psychiatric aspects of nocturnal enuresis and functional urinary incontinence. *Urologe A*, 43(7), 787–794

Vukovic, R.K., Wilson, A.M. and Nash, K.K. (2004) Naming speed deficits in adults with reading disabilities: A test of the double-deficit hypothesis. *Journal of Learning Disabilities*, 37, 440–450.

Wadlington, E., Elliot, C. and Kirylo, J. (2008) The dyslexia simulation: Impact and implications. *Literacy Research and Instruction*, 47(4), 264–272.

Wagner, R. (1973) Rudolf Berlin: Originator of the term dyslexia. *Annals of Dyslexia*, 23(1), 57–63.

Wagner, R.K. and Torgesen, J.K. (1987) The nature of phonological processing and its causal role in the acquisition of reading skills. *Psychological Bulletin*, 101, 192–212.

Wallace, M.T. (2009) Dyslexia: Bridging the gap between hearing and reading. Current Biology, 19, R260–R262.

Ward, S., Ward, T., Hatt, C., Young, D. and Molner, N. (1995) The incidence and utility of the ACID, ACIDS and SCAD profiles in a referred population. *Psychology in the Schools*, 32(4), 267–276.

Watkins, C. (2004) AD/HD and enuresis (bedwetting) Retrieved 25 December 2014, www.baltimorepsych.com/adhd_and_bedwetting.htm.

WebMD (2014) Dyslexia – symptoms. Retrieved 25 December 2014, www.webmd.com/children/tc/dyslexia-symptoms.

Wertlieb, D., Weigel, C., Springer, T. and Feldstein, M. (1987) Temperament as a moderator of children's stressful experiences. *American Journal of Orthopsychiatry*, 57, 234–245.

West, T. (1991) *In the Mind's Eye: Visual Thinkers, Gifted People with Learning Difficulties, Computer Imaging, and the Ironies of Creativity.* Amherst, NY: Prometheus Books.

Whitbourne, S.K. (2010) The Essential Guide to Defense Mechanisms. Can you spot your favorite form of self-deception? *Psychology Today.* Retrieved 15th June 2015, www.psychologytoday.com/blog/fulfillment-any-age/201110/the-essential-guide-defense-mechanisms.

White, M. (2002) Magic Circle to enhance children's self-esteem. Retrieved 15 June 2015, www.murraywhite-selfesteem.co.uk/circtime.html.

White, R. (1974) Strategies of Adaptation: An Attempt at Systematic Description. In Coelho, G.V., Hamburg, D.A. and Adams, J. (eds) *Coping and Adaptation.* New York, NY: Basic Books.

Willcutt, E.G. and Pennington, B.F. (2000) Psychiatric comorbidity in children and adolescents with reading disability. *Journal of Child Psychology and Psychiatry*, 41, 1039–1048.

Winkley, L. (1996) *Emotional Problems in Childhood and Young People.* London: Cassell.

Winter, R. (1997) Action research, universities and theory (a revised and abridged version of a talk presented at the annual CARN conference 1997)

Wolf, M. (2007) *Proust and the Squid: The Story and Science of the Reading Brain.* New York, NY: HarperCollins.

Wolf, M. and Bowers, P. (1999) The 'Double-Deficit Hypothesis' for the developmental dyslexia. *Journal of Educational Psychology*, 91, 1–24.

Wolf, M., Bowers, P. and Biddle, K. (2000) Naming-speed processes, timing, and reading: A conceptual review. *Journal of Learning Disabilities*, 33, 387–407.

Wolff, U. and Lundberg, I. (2002) The prevalence of dyslexia among art students. *Dyslexia*, 8, 32–42.

Wolff, P.H. and Melngailis, I. (1994) Family patterns of developmental dyslexia: clinical findings. *Am J Med Genet*. 54 122–131.

Wright, L.W. (2015) 10 Tips for Keeping Your Relationship With Your Partner Strong. Understood.org. Retrieved 6th July 2015, www.understood.org/en/family/relationships/significant-other/10-tips-for-keeping-your-relationship-with-your-partner-strong.

Zetterqvist-Nelson, K. (2003) *Dyslexi – en diagnos på gott och ont.* Lund: Studentlitteratur.

Ziegler, J.C., Bertrand, D., Tóth, D., Csépe, V., Reis, A., Faísca, L. and Blomert, L. (2010) Orthographic depth and its impact on universal predictors of reading: A cross-language investigation. *Psychological Science*, 21, 551–559.

SUBJECT INDEX

AUTHOR INDEX

Printed in Great Britain
by Amazon